Lexical Pragmatics

Hituzi Linguistics in English

No. 4 *A Historical Study of Referent Honorifics in Japanese*   Takashi Nagata
No. 5 *Communicating Skills of Intention*   Tsutomu Sakamoto
No. 6 *A Pragmatic Approach to the Generation and Gender Gap in Japanese Politeness Strategies*   Toshihiko Suzuki
No. 7 *Japanese Women's Listening Behavior in Face-to-face Conversation*   Sachie Miyazaki
No. 8 *An Enterprise in the Cognitive Science of Language*   Tetsuya Sano et al.
No. 9 *Syntactic Structure and Silence*   Hisao Tokizaki
No. 10 *The Development of the Nominal Plural Forms in Early Middle English*   Ryuichi Hotta
No. 11 *Chunking and Instruction*   Takayuki Nakamori
No. 12 *Detecting and Sharing Perspectives Using Causals in Japanese*   Ryoko Uno
No. 13 *Discourse Representation of Temporal Relations in the So-Called Head-Internal Relatives*   Kuniyoshi Ishikawa
No. 14 *Features and Roles of Filled Pauses in Speech Communication*   Michiko Watanabe
No. 15 *Japanese Loanword Phonology*   Masahiko Mutsukawa
No. 16 *Derivational Linearization at the Syntax-Prosody Interface*   Kayono Shiobara
No. 17 *Polysemy and Compositionality*   Tatsuya Isono
No. 18 *fMRI Study of Japanese Phrasal Segmentation*   Hideki Oshima
No. 19 *Typological Studies on Languages in Thailand and Japan*   Tadao Miyamoto et al.
No. 20 *Repetition, Regularity, Redundancy*   Yasuyo Moriya
No. 21 *A Cognitive Pragmatic Analysis of Nominal Tautologies*   Naoko Yamamoto
No. 22 *A Contrastive Study of Responsibility for Understanding Utterances between Japanese and Korean*   Sumi Yoon
No. 23 *On Peripheries*   Anna Cardinaletti et al.
No. 24 *Metaphor of Emotions in English*   Ayako Omori
No. 25 *A Comparative Study of Compound Words*   Makiko Mukai
No. 26 *Grammatical Variation of Pronouns in Nineteenth-Century English Novels*   Masami Nakayama
No. 27 *I mean as a Marker of Intersubjective Adjustment*   Takashi Kobayashi
No. 28 *Lexical Pragmatics*   Akihiko Kawamura

Hituzi Linguistics in English

28

AKIHIKO KAWAMURA

Lexical Pragmatics

Teaching English Communication and Pragmatic Skills to Japanese Learners

HITUZI
SYOBO

Copyright © Akihiko Kawamura 2018
First published 2018

Author: AKIHIKO KAWAMURA

All rights reserved. Except for the quotation
of short passages for the purposes of criticism
and review, no part of this publication may be
reproduced, stored in a retrieval system,
or transmitted in any form or by any means,
electronic, mechanical, photocopying, recording
or otherwise, without the written prior
permission of the publisher.
In case of photocopying and electronic
copying and retrieval from network personally,
permission will be given on receipts of payment
and making inquiries. For details please
contact us through e-mail. Our e-mail address is
given below.

Hituzi Syobo Publishing

Yamato bldg. 2f, 2-1-2 Sengoku
    Bunkyo-ku Tokyo, Japan 112-0011
Telephone: +81-3-5319-4916
Facsimile: +81-3-5319-4917
e-mail: toiawase@hituzi.co.jp
http://www.hituzi.co.jp/
postal transfer: 00120-8-142852

ISBN978-4-89476-903-8
Printed in Japan

Acknowledgements

First and foremost, I would like to express my wholehearted gratitude to my supervisor, Dr Rosamund Moon at the University of Birmingham, for her patient and thorough supervision throughout the time I was working on the original thesis, on which this book is based. Without her help, I could not have pursued my study. Thanks are also due to Professor Helen Spencer-Oatey at the University of Warwick for her encouragement and enormously helpful suggestions on the original thesis, and two Examiners of the thesis who gave me invaluable comments and suggestions: Professor Norbert Schmitt at the University of Nottingham and Dr Suganthi John at the University of Birmingham.

I would also like to thank friends and colleagues who kindly took the time to read an earlier version of this work (either as a thesis or as a draft if this book), and gave me extremely useful suggestions: Professor Scott Gardner at Okayama University, Professor Melodie Cook at the University of Niigata Prefecture, Professor Masayuki Kai at Kyoto Women's University, Professor Kazuhito Yamato at Kobe University, and Professor Dennis Riches at Seijo University. Mr Michael Riches also took the time to proofread the pre-final version of the thesis, as well as this book, and gave me beneficial assistance.

I'm also greatly indebted to Obunsha Co Ltd, Word Works LLC, Professor Keizo Nomura at Tokyo Woman's Christian University, and Professor Satoru Uchida at Kyushu University for their help in conducting the research discussed in Part II. My additional thanks to Hituzi Shobo Co Ltd and two editors, Ms Azusa Kaneyama and Ms Eri Ebisawa, for their thorough assistance in publishing this work on a tight schedule.

This work was also supported by a publication subsidy from the Faculty of Social Innovation at Seijo University, and by JSPS KAKENHI Grant Numbers 25370729 and 16K02934.

Last but not least, I wish to give my thanks and love to my family, especially my wife, Miwako, our daughters, Ayami and Misato, and to the memories of my parents, Kazushi and Takako, and to the memory of my father-in-law, Mr Koji Kuribayashi.

Table of Contents

	Acknowledgements	v
	List of Figures, Graphs and Tables	xv
	List of Abbreviations and Acronyms	xvi

PART I
Pragmatic Information

	Abstract	2

CHAPTER I
Introduction

1.1	Lexical pragmatics	3
1.2	Outline	6

CHAPTER II
Defining Pragmatics

2.1	Overview	11
2.2	Key concepts	13
2.2.1	The function of language	13
2.2.2	The user of language	14
2.2.3	Context	14
2.2.4	Appropriateness	15
2.2.5	Compromise	15
2.3	Related fields and objects of investigation	16
2.3.1	Pragmatics and semantics	16
2.3.2	Hearer meaning	18
2.3.3	Pragmatics and sociolinguistics	19

2.4		Constituents of pragmatics and their relationships with other levels of language	21
2.4.1		Linguistic resources	21
2.4.2		A command of linguistic resources	21
2.4.3		Pragmatics, a definition	22

CHAPTER III
Defining Pragmatic Information for EFL Dictionaries

3.1	Types of meaning	23
3.1.1	Pragmatic meaning, a definition	23
3.1.2	Dictionary meaning, a definition	24
3.1.3	The difference between pragmatic meaning and dictionary meaning	24
3.2	Existing definition of pragmatic information for EFL dictionaries	25
3.2.1	Dictionaries and glossaries	25
3.2.2	Confusion over pragmatic information for EFL dictionaries	26
3.3	Restricting the coverage from a lexicographic perspective	28
3.3.1	Discourse and pragmatic functions	28
3.3.2	Pragmatic biases	29
3.3.3	Paralinguistic features	31
3.3.4	Criteria for deciding what pragmatic information to include	32
3.3.5	Issues for pragmatics in the EFL context	34
3.3.6	Descriptive versus prescriptive	35
3.3.7	Pragmatic information, a definition	36

PART II
Lexical Approach to Pragmatic Failures

Abstract   40

CHAPTER IV
Data Collection

4.1	Existing sources of pragmatic information for learners	42
4.1.1	Dictionaries	41
4.1.2	Corpora	44
4.1.3	Academic research	44
4.1.4	Non-academic literature	46
4.2	The research project	48
4.2.1	Overview	48
4.2.1.1	Questionnaires vs. spoken data	49
4.2.1.2	Selection of topics	50
4.2.1.3	Parallel questionnaires	51
4.2.1.4	Demographics of the informants	53
4.2.1.5	Question formats	55
4.2.1.6	Limitations	58
4.2.1.7	Selection of data	61

CHAPTER V
Causes of Pragmatic Failures and Case Studies

5.1	Classification and distribution of potential causes	63
5.2	Case studies	66
5.2.1	Identification	66
5.2.2	Direct expression	69
5.2.3	Wrong choice	70
5.2.4	Style and register	72
5.2.5	Pragmatic transfer	74
5.2.6	Teaching	77
5.2.7	Others	80
5.3	Summary	84

CHAPTER VI
Issues Arising from Analysing the Data

6.1	Risky topics	85
6.2	Differences between British and American Englishes	88
6.3	Quantitative and qualitative data	91

6.3.1	Case study 1: *Could you...?* as used when inviting others	92
6.3.2	Case study 2: *Will* as used to talk about others' future plan	93
6.3.3	Case study 3: Whether one needs permission to help	94
6.3.4	Case study 4: Order of different person subjects	96
6.4	Summary and implications for Part III	98

PART III
Compatibility Between Pragmatics and Lexicography with Particular Reference to Politeness

Abstract   104

CHAPTER VII
Politeness and EFL Lexicography

7.1	Pragmatic failures revisited in terms of politeness	106
7.2	The state of the art—how politeness is treated in latest EFL dictionaries	108
7.3	Units of description and foci	109
7.4	Contextual information	111

CHAPTER VIII
Compatibility Between Pragmatics and Lexicography

8.1	Overview	113
8.2	Dictionaries' claims concerning their treatments of pragmatics	114
8.2.1	The coverage	114
8.2.2	Overlapping categories	116
8.2.3	Inconsistencies	116
8.3	Traditional topics in pragmatics and their compatibilities with lexicography	118
8.3.1	Implicature	118
8.3.2	Deixis	119
8.3.3	Speech acts	121
8.3.4	Politeness	123
8.4	Approaches to language function	124

8.4.1	Lexical phrases	125
8.4.2	Text functions	126
8.5	Reaching a compromise between pragmatics and lexicography	127

CHAPTER IX
Politeness

9.1	Linguistic politeness	129
9.2	Theories of politeness	130
9.2.1	Overview	130
9.2.2	Brown and Levinson's face theory	134
9.2.2.1	Face theory	134
9.2.2.2	Limitations of face theory	135
9.2.3	Spencer-Oatey's rapport management	138
9.2.3.1	Rapport management	138
9.2.3.2	*I don't suppose* revisited in terms of rapport management	139
9.3	Theories on politeness and their implications for EFL lexicography	140
9.3.1	Identifying formulae, speech act markers and politeness markers as embedded in utterances	141
9.3.2	Speech events and activity types	143
9.3.3	Speech acts and other domains of politeness	145
9.3.4	Ethos and communication style	146
9.3.5	Pragmatic conventions	147
9.3.6	Sociological variables	148
9.3.7	Deference, register and absolute politeness	150
9.3.8	The influence of translation equivalents	151
9.4	Summary	152

CHAPTER X
Methodology

10.1	Procedures	155
10.1.1	Selection of dictionaries	155
10.1.2	Selection of research items	156
10.1.3	Classification of the 76 lexical items according to their functions	158

| 10.1.4 | Lemmatisation | 160 |
| 10.2 | Key issues when examining the treatment of politeness in lexicography | 161 |

CHAPTER XI
Politeness as Described in Monolingual Dictionaries

11.1	Explanations	164
11.1.1	*Polite* in monolingual dictionaries	164
11.1.2	The absence of a perspective on politeness and speech acts	166
11.1.3	Typical uses of a lexical item	169
11.1.4	Sense description from the perspective of speech act	170
11.1.5	Speech act as a series of actions	170
11.1.6	Summary of 11.1	172
11.2	Speech labels	172
11.2.1	List of labels	172
11.2.2	The use of labels	175
11.2.2.1	Absence of necessary labels	175
11.2.2.2	Confusions over the use of labels	177
11.2.2.3	Summary of 11.2	178
11.3	Illustrative examples	178
11.3.1	Lack of context	178
11.3.2	Mismatched examples	182
11.3.3	Difficult examples	184
11.3.4	Multi-lexical realisation of politeness	185
11.3.5	Register	186
11.3.6	Collocation and speech acts	187
11.3.7	Summary of 11.3	188
11.4	Other issues	188
11.4.1	Accompanying functions	188
11.4.2	Identification of distinct senses of lexical items	190
11.4.3	Confusions over speech acts	191
11.4.4	Usage notes	192
11.4.5	Summary of 11.4	194

CHAPTER XII

Politeness as Described in Bilingual Dictionaries

12.1	Issues common to monolingual and bilingual dictionaries	197
12.1.1	*Teinei* in bilingual dictionaries	201
12.2	Translation equivalents	203
12.2.1	Complements to translations	203
12.2.2	Attempts at reducing misunderstanding by translations	204
12.2.3	Inconsistencies caused by translations	205
12.2.4	Summary of 12.2	205
12.3	Usage notes	205
12.3.1	Monolingual versus bilingual dictionaries	206
12.3.2	Types of usage note	207
12.3.3	Criteria for utilising usage notes	211
12.3.4	Accessibility to usage notes	211
12.3.5	Reliability of usage notes	212
12.3.6	Summary of 12.3	213
12.4	Other issues	214
12.4.1	Request and getting permission	214
12.4.2	The necessity of explaining different politeness strategies in Japanese and English	215
12.4.3	Biases towards negative politeness	215
12.4.4	Summary of 12.4	216
12.5	Dictionaries as tools for learning pragmatics (Closing remarks to Chapters XI and XII)	216

CHAPTER XIII

Recommendations to Dictionary Makers

13.1	Approach pragmatics from the functional perspective	219
13.1.1	Speech acts and politeness	220
13.1.2	Accompanying functions	220
13.1.3	*Polite* and *teinei*	221
13.1.4	Explanations in Japanese	221
13.2	Review all the descriptions from the educational perspective	222
13.3	Cooperate with non-lexicographic resources	223
13.4	Make the best use of the latest technologies	224

13.5	Pay attention to differences between pragmatic conventions in learners' native language and English, with help from a team of Japanese and English-speaking lexicographers	225
13.6	Worked examples	226

CHAPTER XIV
Conclusion

14.1	Summary and overview	229
14.2	Compatibility between pragmatics and lexicography	230
14.2.1	Differences between pragmatics and lexicography, revisited	230
14.2.2	Making compromises	231
14.2.2.1	Narrowing the scope of pragmatics with the functional perspective	231
14.2.2.2	Filling the role of dictionaries as a learning material	233
14.3	Users with specific linguistic and/or cultural backgrounds	234
14.4	Closing remarks: Limitations of the study and implications for the future	235

Appendix I	Cover letter and instructions for EV	238
Appendix II	Questions and the summaries of the results excluding statistically insignificant ones	242
Appendix III	Text functions	276
Appendix IV	Research items	280

Bibliography	283
Index	295

List of Figures, Graphs and Tables

Figure 1: Comments/reasons sorted by sex (male), nationality (British) and choice (b)   53
Figure 2: Actual interface of MCYN.   56
Figure 3: Actual interface of MC   56
Figure 4: Part of GEJD4's entry for thank you   208

Table 1: Distribution of age and sex among the native informants   54
Table 2: Distribution of age and sex among the Japanese informants   54
Table 3: Labels used in the monolingual dictionaries   174
Table 4: Labels used in the bilingual dictionaries   199

Graph 1: Results of Questions 28. I and II (*Long time no see.*)   58
Graph 2: Results of Question 67 (*How do you do?*)   60
Graph 3: Distribution of the causes: all the questions   65
Graph 4: Distribution of the causes: questions with significant differences   65
Graph 5: Distribution of the causes: questions with highest difference values   65
Graph 6: Results of Question 14. (A) (*I know.*)   66
Graph 7: Results of Question 85 (*difficult*)   68
Graph 8: Results of Question 44. I (*I want*)   70
Graph 9: Results of Question 78. II: (A) (*short* person)   71
Graph 10: Results of Question 48. (A) (*gonna*)   73
Graph 11: Results of Question 31. II (negative questions)   75
Graph 12: Results of Question 72 (Permission versus request)   76
Graph 13: Results of Question 59 (*I will*)   77
Graph 14: Results of Question 70. II (declination)   78
Graph 15: Results of Question 65. I (*I like drinking.*)   81
Graph 16: Results of Question 65. II (*I'm drunk.*)   82
Graph 17: Results of Question 89. II: (A) (*lover*)   83
Graph 18: Results of Question 52. (A) (whether to say *You're a liar.*)   86
Graph 19: Results of Question 52. (B) (when someone calls another *a liar*)   87
Graph 20: Results of Question 15. I (*he* referring to a person nearby)   89
Graph 21: Results of Question 77. I: (A) (*thin* person)   90
Graph 22: Results of Question 11 (*Could you …?* used to invite others)   92
Graph 23: Results of Question 35 (*will* used to talk about other's future)   94
Graph 24: Results of Question 26. I (permission to help)   95
Graph 25: Results of Question 49. I (order of different person subjects)   97

List of Abbreviations and Acronyms

CALD3: *Cambridge Advanced Learner's Dictionary*, 3rd ed. (2008) Cambridge: Cambridge University Press

COBUILD2: *Collins COBUILD English Dictionary*, 2nd ed. (1995) London: HarperCollins

COBUILD3: *Collins COBUILD English Dictionary for Advanced Learners* (2001) Glasgow: HarperCollins

COBUILD4: *Collins COBUILD Advanced Learner's English Dictionary* (2003) Glasgow: HarperCollins

COBUILD6: *Collins COBUILD Advanced Dictionary of English*, 6th ed. (2009) Boston: Heinle Cengage Learning

COBUILD7: *Collins COBUILD Advanced Dictionary of English*, 7th ed. (2012) Boston: National Geographic Learning

CP: Cooperative Principle

EV: English version of the questionnaire used in Part II for native speakers

FTA: Face-threatening act

GEJD4: *Taishukan's Genius English-Japanese Dictionary*, 4th ed. (2006) Tokyo: Taishukan Shoten

H: Hearer, or a receiver, including a reader, as distinguished from a person who overhears an utterance or oversees a piece of writing (Part I only)

JV: Japanese version of the questionnaire used in Part II for Japanese learners

LDOCE2: *Longman Dictionary of Contemporary English*, 2nd ed. (1987/1991) Harlow: Longman

LDOCE4: *Longman Dictionary of Contemporary English*, 4th ed. (2003)

LDOCE5: *Longman Dictionary of Contemporary English*, 5th ed. (2009) Harlow: Pearson Education

LEJD2: *Luminous English-Japanese Dictionary*, 2nd ed. (2005) Tokyo: Kenkyusha

LOEJD: *Longman English-Japanese Dictionary* (2007) Harlow: Pearson Education

MC: Multiple choice with more than two alternatives in the questionnaire used in Part II

MCYN: Multiple choice questions with two alternatives, Yes or No in the questionnaire used in Part II

MED2: *Macmillan English Dictionary for Advanced Learners*, 2nd ed. (2007) Oxford: Macmillan Education

OALD8: *Oxford Advanced Learner's Dictionary of Current English*, 8th ed. (2010) Oxford: Oxford University Press

OLXEJ: *O-Lex English-Japanese Dictionary* (2008) Tokyo: Obunsha

PP: Politeness Principle

S: Speaker, or a producer of an utterance including a writer, as distinguished from a person who talks or writes to himself/herself (Part I only)

WEJD2: *Wisdom English-Japanese Dictionary, The*, 2nd ed. (2007) Tokyo: Sanseido

PART I

Pragmatic Information

Abstract (Part 1)

A promising way to tackle pragmatics in the EFL context is a lexical approach focusing on pragmatic behaviours of lexical items in particular contexts. This may suggest that dictionaries are good sources of pragmatic information for EFL learners; in fact, most EFL dictionaries today claim to include a wealth of information on pragmatics. However, it has been rarely discussed what this information comprises. Strangely, it has become an important part of EFL lexicography without there being an agreed-upon definition. This is at least partly because pragmatics in itself does not have a satisfactory definition. Considering its importance for foreign learners of English, it will be necessary to have a common basis on which the dictionaries' treatment of pragmatic information can be judged objectively enough. Without such a basis, it could not be hoped to improve the way that dictionaries treat such information. In this study, I will therefore seek to explore what pragmatics is, and then move on to defining pragmatic information for EFL dictionaries. As pragmatics and lexicography are distinct both in nature and scope, I will define pragmatic information, trying to reach a compromise between the two disciplines.

CHAPTER I

Introduction

The topic of this book is what may be termed lexical (or lexicographic) pragmatics; that is to say, those portions of pragmatics which can be dealt with in terms of words and phrases. While pragmatics plays a crucial role in our communication, it is still not clear how it should be treated in language teaching. In this book, I will explore the possibility of incorporating the subject of pragmatics into teachings of communicative skills from a lexical perspective, because, for that purpose, I believe it is most promising to focus on pragmatic behaviours of lexical items in particular contexts.

Because this book is based on my PhD thesis submitted to The University of Birmingham, UK, in 2013 and two other related pieces of work,[1] the book includes the following three parts: Part I in which I explored the subject mainly from a theoretical viewpoint; Part II which discusses an empirical study to collect data concerning pragmatic failures between Japanese learners and English speakers; and Part III, main body of the book with discussions of how politeness can be treated in language teaching with particular reference to EFL lexicography and Japanese learners of English. See 1.2 below for details of the structure and outline of the book. In the next section, I will explain the rationale of my lexical approach to pragmatics.

1.1 Lexical pragmatics

With the growing awareness of the importance of communication skills in today's globalising world, the acquisition of communicative competence in English is now regarded as the main goal of English teaching in Japan (Ministry of Education, Cultures, Sports, Science and Technology 2002), and in 2006, the National Center Test for University Admissions, administered in Japan, introduced listening comprehension sections in which applicants' communicative skills could be tested. There are also plans to introduce standardised tests of

English such as TOEFL and IELTS, which can measure their communication skills more objectively. Apart from university entrance examinations or formal education, communication skills in English have been gaining in importance with the growing impact of the global economy. Some leading companies in Japan such as UNIQLO and Nissan have already introduced English as an official language for not only international but internal communications. In addition to formal schools and colleges, there are many English conversation schools throughout Japan, and many non-academic books are on sale, with the goal of improving the English communication skills of those who utilise them. These facts prove that Japanese learners of English are very eager to acquire competence to communicate in English.

Pragmatics is known to play crucial roles in linguistic communication ranging from the choice of an expression to how one utters it (see Chapter II). Yet, it is still not certain how pragmatics should be taught. There are several reasons for this; for instance, pragmatics is concerned with delicate areas such as one's values and/or outlook on the world (see 3.3.5). It is also true that what we regard as communication or communication skills will vary from person to person and from context to context. In the context of language learning, however, we can safely say that a foreign learner has a sufficient command of a foreign language if he or she can successfully *do* whatever he or she wants to do in the target language, such as promising or requesting (see 7.3). Language learners need instructions in how they can perform an act they want to perform in a foreign language. Here it should be remembered that pragmatics was born with Austin's revelation concerning speech acts that people do not only convey information but do things with words in our daily lives (cf. 14.4). While the great majority of academic surveys in the field are often concerned with so-called pragmatic principles and/or strategies, their findings seem rather difficult to apply directly to classroom teaching because they are basically context-dependent (cf. 4.1.3). On the other hand, there are many formulae to perform various acts such as 'excuse me'. Their pragmatic behaviours are relatively fixed and thus easier to deal with in the context of language teaching. I would argue that the use of speech acts is one of the most important pragmatic phenomena with which learners need to be familiar, and that it is very likely that language instructors can offer sufficient help to learners, focusing on such pragmatic formulae.

Looking at our communication in terms of speech acts and pragmatic behaviours of lexical items can enlighten us in many ways. In May 2016 US President Barack Obama visited Japan and, after his meeting with Japanese Prime Minister Shinzo Abe, addressed a joint news conference about the murder of a young woman by U.S. military personnel in Okinawa, saying: 'I extended my sincerest condolences and deepest regrets'. It is interesting to note that many

Japanese people interpreted this statement as an apology, and the morning edition of *The Yomiuri Shimbun* cited comments by Professor Kaoru Ishikawa at Kawamura Gakuen Woman's University that the remark from Mr. Obama literally expressed the deepest regret from the highest representative of the country (27 May 2016). Professor Ishikawa, a specialist in international politics, pointed out that use of 'sincerest', the superlative of 'sincere', was normally not used in the context of diplomacy and that the use of 'regret' itself was a strong expression. Professor Ishikawa continued by saying that Mr. Obama's choice of 'deepest' rather than 'deeper' showed his good faith. CNN also reported that Mr. Obama had apologised (Kepnes 2016). However, it seems to me that it is at least questionable whether Mr. Obama actually apologised in its strict sense, or rather it can be questioned as to exactly which speech act involving 'expressing one's regret' he was using.

Mr. Obama was about to visit Hiroshima as the first incumbent US president to do so, acting against certain corners of public opinion in the US. What is more, we can easily imagine that in such situations anyone in his position as a representative of a country would be very hesitant to apologise because, depending on the definition of the act of apologising, making an apology may basically result in taking responsibility for what one is apologising for. This would be an essential condition (cf. Searle 1969) for the act of making an apology, and such conditions for particular speech acts cannot be dealt with only in terms of words and phrases. Moreover, it is to be noted that Mr. Obama used the past tense in his remark, which means he did not perform an act of apologising but reported what he said to Mr. Abe.

We can also consider his statement from a perspective of lexical pragmatics, focusing on the behaviour of *regret*. According to the results of the survey discussed in Part II of this book, in considering the acceptability of the use of the verb *regret* when making an apology, 95% of informants found its use inappropriate (see results of Question 29 in Appendix II for more details). With 100 English speakers and 114 Japanese learners of English taking part in the survey as informants, it is one of the largest-scale surveys in the field of cross-cultural or intercultural pragmatics (see 4.2 for details), and many English-speaking informants comment that with the use of *regret* the speaker would sound too formal, insincere and/or lacking responsibility. Even considering that the remark from the US president was a very formal one, we should not simply regard it as an official statement of apology. We may well wonder what his intent was (see 2.2.2 for my use of the term, intent; see 8.3.3 for a role one's intent plays in pragmatics); some informants in the survey even commented that the verb *regret* could be used to *avoid* responsibility. Its use as a noun by Mr. Obama might be slightly different from its use as a verb, however. Most importantly, in the survey, 25% of Japanese learners answered that the use of the verb when making an apology is appropriate. They would benefit from more awareness in how to use the verb when apologising.

The use of a particular lexical item does not always produce the same effect irrespective of contexts, but it would be most promising or at least easiest to approach pragmatics in terms of lexical items. Towards the end of this book I will show that pragmatics can be successfully dealt with lexically and also illustrate how this lexical approach to pragmatics would be of benefit to language learners in general.

Concerning language learning, especially vocabulary learning, dictionaries are still one of the main tools used for learning. Although the number of users of conventional paper dictionaries has been declining, more learners have come to refer to electronic dictionaries in various forms instead, including those available online with, say, an iPhone. Whichever forms dictionaries may come in, language learners need a 'dictionary' when learning about lexis. Moreover, it is worth mentioning in passing that findings from the research described in Part II fed directly into one book on pragmatic issues for Japanese learners of English (Kawamura 2006a) and four English-Japanese dictionaries for intermediate or advanced learners (*Core-Lex English-Japanese Dictionary* [2005]; *O-Lex English-Japanese Dictionary* [2008]; *Core-Lex English-Japanese Dictionary*, 2nd ed. [2011]; *O-Lex English-Japanese Dictionary*, 2nd ed. [2013]; see also 4.2.1). It has also been suggested by Spencer-Oatey and Žegarac (2010: 85) that the lexicographic approach to pragmatics has potential as a source for developing pragmatic proficiency. All this implies that lexicography can deal with pragmatics satisfactorily. In this book I will therefore explore how pragmatics should be treated in terms of words and phrases mainly from the viewpoint of lexicography.

1.2 Outline

It now seems customary for EFL dictionaries to claim to contain a great deal of information on pragmatics. In view of the fact that pragmatics is closely concerned with actual communication using language, the inclusion of pragmatic information is no doubt a welcome innovation. However, it would be too optimistic to believe that there is no more room for improvement in the dictionaries' treatment of this information since it is not even certain what either pragmatics or pragmatic information is in the context of EFL lexicography. While pragmatics has become an important part of EFL lexicography, strangely, there is no agreement on what it is. Dictionary critics only seem to discuss pragmatic information without specifying what they are talking about (Sharpe, 1989 and De Cock, 2002) as if the scope of their topic were already clearly defined somewhere or self-evident. This is also the case with dictionary makers (see 3.2.1 and 3.2.2 for details). It naturally follows from this that in order to examine or judge objectively the treatment by EFL dictionaries of pragmatic information, it is essential to have a basis for the discussion. Otherwise, it could not be hoped to improve their treatment of the information. Moreover, although many EFL dictionaries claim to include a sufficient amount of information on pragmatics, it is questionable whether they can satisfactorily incorporate pragmatics, since pragmatics and lexicography are distinct from each other both in scope and nature (see 3.1). In Part I, I will therefore begin my exploration of what pragmatic information is in the context of EFL lexicography by seeking to find out how EFL dictionaries can incorporate pragmatics.

Before moving on to the definition of pragmatic information, it is also necessary to have a satisfactory definition of what pragmatics is. I will thus begin this study by defining what pragmatics is in Chapter II with all the relevant factors in mind, particularly its borders with closely related fields such as semantics. Although pragmatics is sometimes classified very elaborately even within the field itself such as Leech's distinction between General pragmatics, Pragmalinguistics, Socio-pragmatics and Referential pragmatics, (1983: 10–3), such classification might blur the boundary between pragmatics and related fields. I will thus not deal with that issue in this book. Nor will I seek to discuss different approaches to the field such as Relevance Theory (Sperber and Wilson, 1986), as these are also outside the parameters of the current study.

On the basis of findings from Part I, I will then seek to discover how and which lexical items are likely to cause serious pragmatic failures between English speakers and Japanese learners. This will lead to Part II, which identifies many candidates and shows that there are striking differences in the ways English speakers and Japanese learners interpret particular words and phrases pragmatically. Part II begins with a literature review then provides a detailed account of the research project I carried out. In the chapters that follow, I discuss the results: potential causes of pragmatic failure (Chapter V), and other issues arising from analysing the data (Chapter VI).

Lastly, in Part III, I will raise the simple but fundamental question of whether pragmatics and lexicography can ever be made compatible at all since their goals, approaches and methods in dealing with distinct types of meaning are rather different. Politeness, for example, should be among the most difficult pragmatic phenomena to describe lexically as well as lexicographically, because it is more concerned with one's motivation behind his or her language use rather than language use itself. On the other hand, it is an indispensable umbrella function for many speech acts (see 8.3.4). In order for an act to be performed successfully, it should be performed appropriately in terms of politeness (cf. 9.3.1). It is imperative that information on politeness be provided in dictionaries for language learners; its value would be appreciated. It will be worth considering whether politeness can successfully be dealt with in terms of lexical items.

It is interesting to note here that there are not many books or articles which discuss politeness or its importance in the context of EFL lexicography. In fact, while they occasionally touch upon politeness, there are scarcely any discussions about how politeness can be dealt with effectively in a dictionary, with a few exceptions such as Otani (2006). Since 1983, there have been only seven papers read at conferences of the European Association for Lexicography (www.euralex.org/publications/) which deal with or mention politeness in some way (Svartvik 1992; De Cock 2002; Nesi 2002; Cacchiani 2004; Erjavec, Sangawa and Erjavec 2006; Rundell 2006; Russo 2008), and none of them have discussed in depth what it is or how it should be dealt with in lexicography. As they all have other main topics and do not focus on politeness, their failures to tackle it are not something I should criticise here. However, it needs pointing out that, to the best of my knowledge, politeness has almost never been thoroughly discussed in conjunction with lexicography. Even the *Dictionary of Lexicography* (Hartmann and James eds. 1998) does not include *politeness* as a headword. I will therefore discuss how politeness should/could be described lexically as well as lexicographically in the final part of the book.

Note

1 Part I (Chapters I to III) and Part II (Chapters IV to VI) are respectively based on the following two essays: 'An empirical study towards the better treatment of pragmatics in EFL lexicography: Comparing the appreciation of pragmatic failures in Japanese learners of English and English native speakers', submitted to The University of Birmingham as a coursework towards the degree of Doctor of Philosophy by advanced study in Applied Linguistics, October 2009; and 'How a compromise can be reached between theoretical pragmatics and practical lexicography', submitted to The University of Birmingham as a coursework towards the degree of Doctor of Philosophy by advanced study in Applied Linguistics, November 2003. Part III (Chapters VII to XIV) is based on the following thesis: 'Pragmatics and lexicography, with particular reference to politeness and Japanese learners of English' submitted to the University of Birmingham as a thesis towards the degree of Doctor of Philosophy by advanced study in Applied Linguistics, August 2013.

Parts of earlier versions of the thesis and the essays were published as follows: 'How a compromise can be reached between theoretical pragmatics and practical lexicography, a definition of pragmatic information' (2005) in: *Lexicon* 35, 254–67 (Chapter III); 'The speaker's command of linguistic resources to realise their intent, a definition of pragmatics' (2005) in: *Social Innovation Studies* 1/1, 79–94 (Chapter II); 'Problems in Incorporating Pragmatics into EFL Lexicography' (2006) in: *English Lexicography in Japan*. Tokyo: Taishukan Shoten, 168–81 (Chapter IV).

The following papers were also based on the original thesis and the essays: 'Goyouronteki eibeisa ni kannsuru oboegaki—she to homely o rei ni totte—' [A Note on Pragmatic Differences between British and American Englishses, cases of she and homely] (2007) in: *Social Innovation Studies* 2/2, 37–48; 'Issues in collecting data for better treatment of pragmatics in language teaching: a case study of the *Planet Board* project in lexical pragmatics' (2011) in: *Random* 33, 47–70; 'EFL Jisho to goyoron—poraitonesu o chushin ni' [EFL dictionaries and pragmatics with particular reference to politeness] (2016) in: K. Minamide, K. Akasu, N. Inoue, Y. Tono, and S. Yamada eds. *Eigo Jisho o Tsukuru: Henshu Chosa Kenkyu no Genba kara* [Making of English Dictionaries: From the Viewpoints of Editors and Researchers]. Tokyo: Taishukan Shoten, 118–34. See also 1.1 for a book and dictionaries based on the research discussed in Part II of the book.

CHAPTER II
Defining Pragmatics

In this chapter, I will define what pragmatics is, paying particular attention to its borders with its related fields: semantics and sociolinguistics. Before moving on to the discussion, I will present an overview of the term *pragmatics* in 2.1, and this will be followed by more specific examinations of the existing definitions based on its four key notions (2.2): the function of language; the user of language; context; appropriateness; and their combination. In 2.3, after discussing its border with semantics, I will briefly discuss the inference that an interpreter of language draws in response to an utterance, and then I will move on to the discussion about a boundary between pragmatics and sociolinguistics; the constituents of pragmatics and its priority over other levels of language. Lastly, in 2.4, I will be working towards the definition of pragmatics as being concerned with a command of linguistic resources in order to realise one's intent, or make it recognisable.

2.1 Overview

With such exceptions as introductory books or glossaries of technical terms in linguistics, there seem to be only a few researchers who have presented their definitions of pragmatics explicitly (Thomas, 1995: 22f; Vershueren, 1999: 7f). Some have even listed several definitions (Yule, 1996: 3). This shows how difficult it is to define pragmatics (see also Huang (2014)).

As Searle et al. observes (1980: viii), "Pragmatics' is one of those words ('societal' and 'cognitive' and others) that give the impression that something quite specific and technical is being talked about when often in fact it has no clear meaning'. While philosophers and linguists have defined pragmatics in various ways (Morris, 1938; Thomas, 1995; Verschueren, 1999), there is as yet no agreed definition. It has even been called a 'waste-basket of linguistics' among linguists (see, for example, Mey, 1993) because competence-oriented mainstream linguistics cannot treat those issues as its proper subjects. At the same time, as exemplified by numerous books and papers on the subject, it has come to occupy an important part of current linguistics, or rather it is attracting greater attention nowadays, especially in conjunction with language teaching (Rose and Kasper, 2000). Apparently, this does not mean that it is no longer necessary to attempt to define pragmatics, because both its topics and methodologies will be considerably affected by how it is defined. Without clearly defining its proper subject, it could not be possible to have common topics to investigate, or to have methodologies of analysing data. While, unlike the diversity of its definitions, there seems to be an agreement about the range of topics within the purview of pragmatics, it will be difficult to reach a satisfactory definition by simply listing such agreed topics. As Levinson points out, 'For in common with all extensional definitions, it provides no criteria for the inclusion or exclusion of further phenomena that may come to our attention' (1983: 27).

Among the most favoured definitions of pragmatics may be Morris' trichotomy of semiotics: Semantics is the study of 'the relations of signs to the objects to which the signs are applicable' (1938: 21). Pragmatics is the study of 'the relation of signs to interpreters' (*ibid.*). Syntax (syntactics) is the study of 'the formal relation of signs to one another' (1938: 22). Although Morris was not the first or the only scholar who divided semiotics in this way, it will be safe to say that he was the first who explained this trichotomy clearly and made this idea generally familiar (Lyons, 1977: 114). As Mey (1993: 35) states, many pragmatists have been supporting his definition either explicitly or implicitly ever since.

Still, there are at least three problems in the trichotomy. First, the trichotomy may not be applicable to natural language, because when analysing the meaning of natural language, it is necessary for semantics to refer to pragmatics (Lyons, 1977: 116f; Levinson; 1983: 3f; see also 2.2.3; 2.4.2). Second, Morris' use of the term pragmatics could be ambiguous in that it is applied not only to branches of inquiry but also to features of language under investigation and to those of the metalanguage (Levinson, 1983: 3). Third, it is questionable whether pragmatics should be restricted to interpreters, for in any use of signs there are usually two participants, the encoder and the decoder, that is, the speaker and the hearer in the case of natural language (see also 2.3.2). In Part I, I will use the terms speaker (S) and hearer (H) respectively, referring to a producer of an utterance including a writer, as distinguished from a person who talks or writes to himself/herself, and a receiver, including a reader, as distinguished from a person who overhears an utterance or oversees a piece of writing.

In addition to Morris' definition, there are two favoured ways of defining pragmatics, one in conjunction with the user of language and the other context:

... the study of LANGUAGE from the point of view of the users, especially of the choices they make, the CONSTRAINTS they encounter in using language in social interaction, and the effects their use of language has on the other participants in an act of communication (*A Dictionary of Linguistics and Phonetics*, 2003)

The branch of linguistics which studies how utterances communicate meaning in context (*Key Concepts in Language and Linguistics*, 1999)

While both of the above definitions capture an important aspect of the subject, they are not satisfactory because they cannot properly show where the boundary lies between pragmatics and its closely related fields (see 2.2.2 and 2.2.3 for details). Importantly, the two concepts, the language user and context, are closely connected with two other key concepts of pragmatics, the function of language and appropriateness. The idea of a 'user', for example, is duly associated with a 'tool with a particular function'. In the context of pragmatics, this should be language and its function, and it largely depends on the appropriateness of context whether the function is successfully fulfilled. If someone says, 'Nice to see you' to their family in the morning, the utterance will not be taken literally. Even greetings, one of the most basic functions of language, may fail to fulfil its function in an inappropriate context. This may be the reason several scholars attempt to explain pragmatics in terms of the function of language (Leech, 1983: 47ff; Verschueren, 1999: 11 and *passim*) or appropriateness (Van Dijk, 1976: 29; Allwoods et al., 1977: 153ff). In the following sections, I will therefore consider if it is possible to define pragmatics satisfactorily, using each of the above four key notions; or their combination: the function of language; the user of language; context; appropriateness; and their combination.

2.2 Key concepts

2.2.1 The function of language

The definition of pragmatics in conjunction with the function of language explains the subject, focusing on what humans do by using language and how it actually works. It is the advantage of this definition that those issues which are inexplicable from inside the formal structure of language become accessible, but Levinson points out that this approach does not make it possible to distinguish pragmatics from other levels of linguistics which also approach language from functional viewpoints, such as sociolinguistics (1983: 7).

2.2.2 The user of language

The notion of 'the user of language' was originally derived from Morris' trichotomy, and attracted attention, particularly within the movement in linguistics known as generative semantics. The definitions of pragmatics in terms of the language user explain the subject paying attention to the relation between S and H, and language. The advantage of this approach is to be able to deal with such important concepts as S's intent. Here I use the term intent rather than intention, which is often used in the study of pragmatics, because the term intention is ambiguous, referring to either its ordinary sense as 'one's determination to do something' or its technical use in pragmatics as force (one's will to do something by the use of language). In order to distinguish the former from the latter, I will use intent when referring to the former in this book.

Whereas the definitions in terms of the language user have the above advantage, two serious deficiencies are pointed out by Levinson (1983: 4f): the notion of the user of language is too broad, admitting such non-linguistic studies as Freud's on slips of tongue; at the same time, this approach is too narrow in that this excludes such issues as temporal or place deixis.

2.2.3 Context

Definitions of pragmatics in conjunction with context explain that semantics is restricted to a study on the meaning of a word, phrase or sentence out of context, while meaning in context should be dealt with under the heading of pragmatics. This approach is helpful in that it can take into consideration the actual use of languages rather than language as an abstract entity, though it requires a clearer idea of what context is (Levinson, 1983: 22f). Without clearly defining context, it would be difficult to delimit the scope of pragmatics. Even if it is restricted to the part of it which is encoded or grammaticalised in the formal structure of language, context is not always encoded in language (Mey, 1993: 40). More importantly, conversational implicature, one of the most popular topics in the field of pragmatics, will be outside of its domain, if context is limited to only those grammaticalised in language (Levinson, 1983: 9f).

Levinson, in this connection, suggests that semantics should be restricted to truth-conditional issues of meaning and that other issues relating to meaning should belong to pragmatics (1983: 14f and *passim*). However, Levinson also admits that to follow a common definition of utterance as the pairing of a sentence and a context (see also Gazdar, 1979: 131), it is not sentence but utterance which can be dealt with truth-conditionally; it is impossible to judge whether a sentence is true or not without referring to the actual context in which it is uttered (18–20 and *passim*). It follows from this that both semantics and pragmatics deal with meaning in context. Pragmatics cannot be defined properly in conjunction with context, particularly when considering a boundary between pragmatics and semantics.

2.2.4 Appropriateness

The definitions of pragmatics in terms of appropriateness investigate the use of language focusing on its appropriateness in a particular context. This approach makes it possible to take into account various important factors in actual communication. Levinson (1983: 25), however, points out that to follow Hymes' explanation of sociolinguistics as the study of communicative competence (1975: 24) means that pragmatics will be identical to sociolinguistics. Although Levinson continues by saying that this approach requires almost every speech community to have its own pragmatics, I would argue that this might not be so problematic in itself without such hypotheses as universality of politeness proposed by Brown and Levinson (1978; 1987; see also 9.2.2.2). It is also to be noted that S does not always speak in a way that is appropriate in a particular context (Grice, 1975: 48f; Levinson, 1983: 24–7). Moreover, pragmatics is generally believed to be concerned with the actual use of language, so it is contrary to expectations when it only focuses on the appropriate uses of language.

2.2.5 Compromise

Although each of the above four key notions of pragmatics is not entirely satisfactory in defining the subject, they capture an important feature of pragmatics. More importantly, they are not distinct from each other, or rather they are closely connected, as explained in 2.1. This may be why so many attempts have also been made to define pragmatics, which has resulted in the combination of the above four approaches. Thomas, for example, covering most of the above key notions, defines pragmatics as meaning in interaction, where she takes into account 'negotiation of meaning between speaker and hearer, the context of utterance (physical, social and linguistic) and the meaning of an utterance' (1995: 22). Still, it will be difficult to tell from this definition exactly where the boundary lies between pragmatics and sociolinguistics, particularly when considering phenomena generally known as politeness. What would be hoped for in the definition of pragmatics is first of all to show clearly the boundary between pragmatics and its closely related fields of linguistics.

Levinson states that 'the upper bound of pragmatics is provided by the border of semantics, and the lower bound by sociolinguistics' (1983: 27) using the strategy of a boundary-drawing exercise proposed by Katz and Fodor (1963: 483–91). In the next section, I will therefore seek to restrict the scope of pragmatics, especially focusing on its borders with semantics and sociolinguistics.

2.3 Related fields and objects of investigation

2.3.1 Pragmatics and semantics

It is generally agreed that both pragmatics and semantics are deeply concerned with meaning (Thomas, 1995; Cruse, 2004), and it is sometimes extremely difficult to distinguish them clearly; several linguists even insist that pragmatics is in fact a part or aspect of semantics (Wierzbicka, 1991: 5). It will naturally follow from this that it would be also important to have a clear understanding of what meaning is. Although not only linguists but philosophers have been attempting to define meaning in various ways, as Cruse suggests, 'Meaning makes little sense except in the context of communication' (2004: 5). In this book I will thus confine myself to meaning in the context of actual communication, and I will tentatively define meaning as something conveyed in actual communication via language.

Thomas (1995: 2–21) divides meaning into three levels: abstract meaning (dictionary meaning), utterance meaning (contextual meaning) and force. The abstract meaning is a range of meaning, or sense inherent in a particular word, phrase or sentence. The utterance meaning is a particular sense used in a particular utterance. The force is the speaker's intention (see 2.2.2) of an utterance in a particular context. According to Thomas, abstract meaning belongs to semantics, while speaker meaning, consisting of utterance meaning and force, belongs to pragmatics. This is clear enough as a starting point, but abstract meaning can sometimes become rather similar to force in the case of such expressions as *I guess*. Moreover, abstract meaning necessarily or logically generates another level of meaning, entailment. As entailment is basically derived from abstract meaning, I will include entailment under the domain of semantics. When considering pragmatics, however, there is another type of meaning, presupposition.

In the following sentence, 'Mary's brother bought three horses' (Yule, 1996: 25), in addition to the above three levels of meaning, presuppositions and entailments are observable. Yule explains that entailment is something logically derivable from what is asserted in the utterance, while presupposition is something S assumes to be true prior to making an utterance. The entailments in the above example include the following:

(A) 'Mary's brother bought something'
(B) 'he bought three animals'

On the other hand, the presuppositions are as follows:

(a) 'there is a person called Mary'
(b) 'she has a brother'
(c) 'she has only one brother'
(d) 'he has a lot of money'

As entailment is the result of logical reasoning based on abstract meaning, it is necessarily true as long as abstract meaning is true. On the other hand, presupposition is not always the case; it can in fact be wrong. It is thus cancellable without any contradiction. This cancellability of presuppositions is important because this can be a criterion for distinguishing semantic meaning from pragmatic meaning. For instance, the following statement, 'It's rather hot in here' can convey much more than its abstract meaning does. In a particular social situation, it may be taken as an indirect request to open the window in the place of the utterance. On another occasion, it can be taken as an excuse for opening the window suddenly without asking permission from others. These interpretations cannot be attained only through the abstract meaning of the statement or logical reasoning based on it. Moreover, they are cancellable, if S says, for instance, 'It's rather hot in here. Can I have something cold to drink?'. Yule explains the two types of meaning as follows: 'Speakers, not sentences, have presuppositions' and 'Sentences, not speakers, have entailments' (1996: 25). It will be apparent here that S's intent plays a crucial role in this phenomenon (see also Levinson, 1983: 16ff).

Whenever S uses language in actual communication, S employs it to realise or make recognisable S's particular intent with due exceptions such as an unintentional cry of pain, *ouch*. I use the verb *realise* here in order to cover a wider range of phenomena than another verb like *express* can. In the case of speech act, using language, S may even perform some action, as well as express how S feels by inducing in H's mind a particular belief reflecting S's intent (Grice, 1979: 219). In this connection, the phrase *achieve one's goal* is among the most favoured in the field of pragmatics. Leech, for instance, argues that the term *intended meaning* or S's *intention* in an utterance is less neutral than *goal* or *function* of an utterance, and therefore misleading (see also 2.3.2). However, as noted in 2.2.1, the term *function* is also misleading when discussing pragmatics. While Leech also argues that the intended meaning or S's intention confines itself to S's conscious or deliberate action (1983: 13–4), as I will argue in 2.3.3, whether S's decision is deliberate or not would be the only criterion available for drawing the boundary between pragmatics and its related fields. Thus I use the phrase to *realise one's intent* in this paper.

When S's intent can be realised sufficiently only through the abstract meaning of S's utterance or logical reasoning based on it, pragmatics and semantics overlap on the surface. Similarly, when S's intent cannot be realised through the abstract meaning or logical reasoning, S's intent must in some way go beyond the scope of abstract meaning and logic; in other words, S's intent becomes pragmatically marked. This is where the boundary lies between pragmatics and semantics. The above utterance, 'It's rather hot in here' is one such example.

I thus conclude that semantics is concerned with those kinds of meaning which can be gained from the abstract meaning of a word, phrase or utterance and/or logical reasoning based on it. Other levels of meaning beyond that scope should be regarded as belonging to the domain of pragmatics. Levinson (1983) also suggests that the most promising criterion which could be used to distinguish between pragmatics and semantics would be to restrict pragmatics to the rest of meaning that semantics treats, but his opinion is slightly different from mine in that he basically insists on confining semantics to those issues which can be dealt with truth-conditionally (see also 2.2.3).

2.3.2 Hearer meaning

In the context of actual communication, it may be also necessary to consider those kinds of inference that H draws in H's mind in reaction to S's utterance. In fact, one of the recent trends in the study of meaning is a consideration of the negotiation of meaning between S and H (see also 2.2.5). Cruse even includes H's inferred message in meaning (2004: 6 and *passim*), and the inferred message is usually referred to as hearer meaning.

Hearer meaning is usually identical to speaker meaning, for S normally makes every effort to realize S's intent, even considering H's mental state, such as whether H possesses the same reasoning pattern as S's. S will thus repeat an utterance several times more slowly or even paraphrase it with easier expressions, once S notices that H is a foreigner and does not have a good command of S's language. In this way it will become possible to take into account the process of how H recognizes S's intent, though it is crucial to decide to what extent hearer meaning should be treated in the domain of pragmatics.

Verschueren argues that it is problematic to define meaning in terms of S's intentionality because such a view cannot properly treat the case where hearer meaning has become completely different from S's intent (1999: 46–9). Verschueren gives the following example:

> Dan: Como is a giant silk worm.
> Debby: Yukh! What a disgusting idea! (1999: 48)

In this example, Dan simply intends to say that Como produces a large amount of silk, which apparently results in Debby's failure to recognise Dan's intent. Although when examining meaning it would be useful to consider H's mental state to some extent, I will strongly argue that it is not meaning but a mistake or failure if H cannot capture S's intent correctly. Miller states:

> Most of our misunderstandings of other people are not due to any inability to hear them, or to parse their sentences, or to understand their words. Such problems do occur, of course. But a far more important source of difficulty in communication is that we so often fail to understand a speaker's intentions. (Miller, 1974: 15)

Debby's incorrect inference above should be regarded as an example of pragmatic failure (Thomas, 1983: 91) rather than another level of meaning. Thus I do not include in meaning H's failure to recognise S's intent. Thomas (1983: 94), in this connection, points out that pragmatic misuse and/or misunderstanding of an expression cannot be judged according to prescriptive rules such as grammatical ones, and that it is not legitimate to refer to pragmatic misuse and/or misunderstanding of an expression as 'mistake' or 'error'. She therefore terms it pragmatic failure, and I will follow her terminology in this book.

2.3.3 Pragmatics and sociolinguistics

Pragmatics and sociolinguistics overlap, particularly when considering such phenomena as politeness. Thomas explains how politeness is different from deference and register in terms of whether S has a choice (1995: 150–5). In some languages such as Japanese, S is obliged to speak in a particular manner or use a particular expression to show S's respect for S's superior in a particular social situation. In this case S has no choice. On the other hand, S is not forced to speak in a particular manner in the case of politeness. S *intentionally* speaks or behaves as S wishes, either politely or rudely. Thomas continues by saying that it is only when S does not speak as people normally expect that deference and register become pragmatically interesting, and that as long as S follows the conventions of society, deference and register should be investigated under the heading of sociolinguistics. If there is in fact no choice as to S's way of speaking, however, S is not allowed to speak as S wishes, which means that S cannot speak in a pragmatically interesting manner. I should here like to point out the fact that it is also S's deliberate decision to follow the social conventions, though this kind of decision will usually be made almost unconsciously and instantly. I would argue that one of the most important features of pragmatics is to be concerned with S's intent, as I have shown in 2.3.1.

When S uses language according to S's sociolinguistic norms, S intends to follow the social conventions; that is to say, S's intent and sociolinguistic knowledge happen to agree on the surface. On the other hand, when S does not follow the socially desirable conventions, S's intent goes beyond the scope of sociolinguistic knowledge and therefore S's intent becomes pragmatically marked (see also 2.3.1). This can provide support for Thomas' explanation, which is that only when S does not speak in a sociolinguistically appropriate manner do deference and register become pragmatically interesting. This view, however, can include too wide a range of linguistic phenomena under pragmatics, and so it should be restricted to those cases where pragmatics and other levels of linguistics do not overlap, in other words, where S's intent is pragmatically marked.

Although Thomas insists that the use of intimate address should also belong to the domain of pragmatics (1995: 186), like deference and register, the use of intimate address depends on S's intent. S may or may not decide to use it bearing in mind the social conventions, and when S decides to use intimate address appropriately according to S's sociolinguistic knowledge, S's intent agrees with S's sociolinguistic knowledge. Only when S does not use intimate address as S's sociolinguistic knowledge normally requires, does its use become part of pragmatics.

My explanation will not suffice, unless this can provide S's motivations for not expressing S's intent explicitly such as 'Please open the window'. When S requests H to open the window, S first intends to realise S's intent. At this stage pragmatic principles work, such as Grice's famous Cooperative Principle (hereafter CP) and its four Conversational Maxims (1975: 45ff). The point is that the principle and the maxims alone cannot explain why S often does not express S's intent explicitly (Imai, 2001: 195). Leech therefore proposes a Politeness Principle (1983: 7–10 hereafter PP) which motivates S's way of speaking in terms of politeness. In the case of a face-threatening act (hereafter FTA), for instance, after S's intent has gone through the above pragmatic principles, or processes, S measures how demanding S's request sounds, exercising S's sociolinguistic knowledge and PP. Then S normally decides to realise S's intent using a less forceful and politer way of speaking.

Now that the borders between pragmatics and its related fields have been determined, in the next subsection I will consider the constituents of pragmatics and their relationships with other levels of language.

2.4 Constituents of pragmatics and their relationships with other levels of language

2.4.1 Linguistic resources

In actual communication, as we have seen in the previous discussions, S has a particular intent from the outset, and then, in order to realise it, employs almost every part of language which I will term linguistic resources. Verschueren uses a similar term, language resources, when distinguishing pragmatics from traditional component disciplines of linguistics. Language resources are different from my term, linguistic resources, in that the former can be identified with a particular unit of analysis, while the latter cannot. Sociolinguistic knowledge is thus not a part of language resources because it does not have any specific unit of analysis. Linguistic resources, on the other hand, include every constituent of language ranging from abstract meaning to sociolinguistic knowledge. I therefore do not use the term language resources when discussing pragmatics.

I also avoid the term competence in Chomsky's sense or Saussure's *langue* because it is doubtful if language can in fact be divided into two in that way. The two-way division may make competence and langue too abstract, even excluding the context of an utterance (see also Levinson, 1983: 33f). In actual communication, S may use sociolinguistic knowledge that is closely connected with such variables as context and cannot be part of abstract notion like competence. For the purpose of causing in H's mind a belief that S is really angry, S may even employ phonological resources such as intonation (see also 3.3.3).

Therefore, it can be concluded that pragmatics is concerned with linguistic resources.

2.4.2 A command of linguistic resources

Pragmatic phenomena are observable in almost every part of language. Verschueren therefore proposes a definition of pragmatics as a perspective (1999: 7 and *passim*). Levinson also points out that pragmatics can be 'a way of looking afresh at the data and methods of linguistics' (1983: 33). Nevertheless, what is missing in these opinions is that pragmatics is in fact prior to any other level of linguistic resources. While many linguists have been supporting the idea that pragmatics is prior to semantics in the sense that it necessarily refers to pragmatics (Gazdar, 1979: 164-8; Stankler, 1972: 383; also 2.1.4 for details), this priority of pragmatics is also applicable to other aspects of linguistic resources. As illustrated in 2.3.1, 2.3.2 and 2.3.3, only S's intent first exists and then moves on to other levels, not the other way around. It might be also true that S's thought is strongly influenced by S's native language and culture, as the

Sapir-Whorf hypothesis suggests, but as long as an utterance on a particular occasion is concerned, S's intent must have priority. I will therefore argue that S's intent, or pragmatic intent, possesses control over linguistic resources, which I will term a command of linguistic resources.

2.4.3 Pragmatics, a definition

While the definitions of pragmatics are diverse, S's intent can be the key to pragmatics. S's intent can go beyond the scope of abstract meaning or social conventions in order to realise itself. Without considering the role S's intent plays in actual communication, it could be almost impossible to draw a line between pragmatics and its related fields.

It is equally important to note that pragmatics precedes any other level of linguistic resources. Whenever S intends to realise S's intent via language, S exercises S's command of linguistic resources, including intonation or sociolinguistic knowledge. This may be why pragmatic phenomena can be seen in almost every aspect of language.

I therefore define pragmatics as being concerned with S's command of linguistic resources to realize S's intent, and I basically restrict its scope to those cases where S's intent is pragmatically marked.

In view of the fact that pragmatics is attracting considerable attention nowadays, especially in the context of language teaching and lexicography, it is necessary to reconsider the field in conjunction with these related disciplines. In the next chapter, I will thus attempt to explore the possibility of applying the above definition to EFL lexicography.

CHAPTER III
Defining Pragmatic Information for EFL Dictionaries

In this chapter I will seek to achieve a satisfactory definition of pragmatic information for EFL dictionaries based on my definition of pragmatics in Chapter II. In 3.1, I will define the kinds of meaning that each of pragmatics and dictionaries has traditionally dealt with, and then move on to the discussion about their differences. In 3.2, after reviewing an existing definition of the information, I will also briefly examine its treatment in EFL dictionaries in order to identify problems. In 3.3, I will attempt to determine how pragmatics should be incorporated into EFL lexicography, trying to reach a compromise between them. After discussing how the information should be dealt with, I will define pragmatic information for EFL dictionaries.

3.1 Types of meaning

3.1.1 Pragmatic meaning, a definition

In Chapter II, I have defined pragmatics as being concerned with S's command of linguistic resources to realise S's intent. As this definition can include too wide a range of topics under its heading, I restrict the scope of the subject to those cases where S's intent is pragmatically marked; that is, where it goes beyond other levels of linguistic resources. Still, this definition allows within its purview very diverse phenomena because they are the reflections of S's intent, which is basically boundless.

In the case of irony, depending on the context and S's intent, S's utterance may even convey exactly the opposite of its abstract meaning. S's utterance can also perform a certain act such as a request in the case of speech acts. It is also to be noted that some words, mainly function words, do not have meaning in a proper sense but only use (Moon, 1987: 99; Akmajian et al, 2001: 13), and, importantly, the use reflects S's intent pragmatically (see 3.3.1 for details). In this study I will refer to as pragmatic meaning the whole of these phenomena, which reflect S's intent in a pragmatically unmarked way.

3.1.2 Dictionary meaning, a definition

Thomas (1995) uses the term 'dictionary meaning' almost interchangeably with the term 'abstract meaning', a range of senses inherent in a particular word, phrase or sentence (see 2.3.1). While abstract meaning can range from the meaning of a word to that of a sentence, dictionaries have traditionally not been concerned with a sentence (see also Higashi, 1980: 52). In this sense, Thomas's use of the term 'dictionary meaning' should not be taken to cover the whole range of abstract meaning, or rather it should be regarded as the kind of meaning explained in a dictionary, which is usually abstract.

The abstract character of the kind of meaning that dictionaries present is pointed out by several scholars. Jackson, for instance, explains dictionary definitions 'as provisional, as representing the potential meaning of a word, waiting for actualisation in a context' (1988: 126). It is not to be overlooked here that the meaning that dictionaries treat is not only possible but typical of a headword defined (Hanks, 1979: 38), and it would be also interesting to note that there seems to be the tendency towards typicality rather than possibility due to the influence of corpora. Ikegami, for instance, points out that distinction between different senses of a word is basically fuzzy and that illustrative examples in dictionaries are aimed at incarnating typical uses of a sense (1996: 37). In this book I will use the term 'dictionary meaning' in a slightly different manner to Thomas', referring to the kind of decontextualised meaning that the dictionary has traditionally treated.

3.1.3 The difference between pragmatic meaning and dictionary meaning

One of the most striking differences between pragmatic meaning and dictionary meaning consists in the fact that while the former is almost infinite in scope, the latter is very limited. In fact, dictionary meaning treats an even narrower range of phenomena than abstract meaning. This may be at least partly because any dictionary is influenced by its physical constraints. The dictionary should be a manageable size, and, in countries like Japan, easy for students to carry to school, so this imposes a limitation on its size and space, especially in the case of a paper dictionary. The space restriction will also be affected by how the information is laid out, including the size of font. Considering the fact that any dictionary is usually designed for a specific group of users, the compilers must carefully select what information to present in a limited space. Dictionary meaning is thus continually monitored and controlled in scope, whilst there is basically no such restriction on pragmatic meaning.

The above disparity in scope leads to another level of difference between pragmatic meaning and dictionary meaning. Dictionaries must employ an economical method of presenting as much information as possible in a limited space. Dictionary meaning therefore gets condensed, purified and abstracted with its peripheral parts left out (see also Ikegami, 1996: 38). In contrast, pragmatic meaning is basically the description of those phenomena within its purview, and it sometimes even focuses on the peripheral parts of meaning that have traditionally been excluded in dictionaries. While pragmatic meaning is concrete in nature based on actual usages, dictionary meaning can be considered as a potentiality or as typicality abstracted from the actual uses (see also Higashi, 1980: 52). It might therefore be possible to compare the difference to that between token and type.

Pragmatic meaning and dictionary meaning are distinct both in scope and nature, and so in order for EFL dictionaries to include pragmatic information it will be necessary to reach some compromise between them. However, before moving on to the discussion about how to achieve the goal, it will be advisable to know what the pragmatic information is generally considered to be. I will thus examine an existing definition of the information in the next section, and then move on to EFL dictionaries' treatment of the information.

3.2 Existing definition of pragmatic information for EFL dictionaries

3.2.1 Dictionaries and glossaries

While the majority of dictionaries, or glossaries of linguistics or applied linguistics, do not list pragmatic information as a headword, the *Dictionary of Lexicography* (1998) and the *Kenkyusha's Oyo Gengogaku Jiten* [Kenkyusha's Dictionary of Applied Linguistics] (2003) do have it as an entry. However, the latter just discuss it without explaining what it is. Despite the importance of pragmatic information in EFL lexicography, there is surprisingly, as far as I know, only one attempt at defining the information. This might also show how ambiguously pragmatics has been treated in the EFL context.

The *Dictionary of Lexicography* defines pragmatic information as follows:

> Information on the sociocultural rules of speaking. Exponents include paralinguistic features such as tone and intonation, gesture, pitch etc., as well as choice of vocabulary in terms of politeness and formality

conventions, which can reinforce or contradict the speaker's intended meaning. In the past, dictionary compilers have paid little attention to this aspect of communication, merely giving unsystematic indication via USAGE LABELS such as 'informal', 'derogatory', 'sarcastic'.

This definition is perfectly satisfactory as a starting point, and it is important to note here that, according to this definition, pragmatic information can range from vocabulary to paralanguage, though it is doubtful or at least uncertain whether paralanguage can be satisfactorily included in a dictionary. As that will be discussed more thoroughly in 3.3.2, in this subsection I would like to examine this definition critically in order to identify problems when considering pragmatic information. The definition is arguably incorrect or too sketchy in three respects.

First, even allowing for the fact that EFL dictionaries today have come to pay more attention to spoken English, this definition should be amended concerning its exclusive reference to 'rules of speaking'. Although Moon points out that in conversation there is 'an enhanced range of pragmatic devices' (1998a: 352), she also states that conversation 'can be compared to other genres such as technical writing or literary writing' (*ibid.*). Pragmatic phenomena are observable in written English as well.

Second, it may be misleading to confine the subject to 'vocabulary', because that will give the reader a wrong impression that dictionaries only deal with words. Recent dictionaries, especially those for foreign learners, have come to treat longer phrases as a kind of basic unit conveying meaning. The fourth edition of the *Longman Dictionary of Contemporary English* (2003 hereafter LDOCE4), for instance, lists in the entry of the verb *like* several phrases such as: *would like* and *if you like*. Significantly, these phrases reflect S's intent pragmatically (see 3.3.2 below; Moon, 1998a: 352; Summers, 1999: 261f).

Third, the above definition should also be amended concerning its confusion of pragmatics with sociolinguistics. It confines the information to 'the sociocultural rules of speaking', and it will be also worth considering whether 'formality convention' should be part of pragmatics (see also 9.3.7). This confusion is also seen in the way that pragmatic information is treated in EFL dictionaries, as I will illustrate in the next subsection.

3.2.2 Confusion over pragmatic information for EFL dictionaries

The first systematic approach to pragmatics by EFL dictionaries started with two works published in 1987: the first edition of the *Collins COBUILD English Language Dictionary* (1987) and the second edition of the *Longman Dictionary of Contemporary English* (1987/1991 hereafter LDOCE2) (Akasu,

1989: 291; 297f n4; Moon, 1987: 70 and *passim* for the account of how the COBUILD lexicographers tried to capture pragmatic information in the work; Murata, 1997: 39), and pragmatics began to attract attention in the context of lexicography with the arrival of the second edition of the *Collins COBUILD English Dictionary* (1995 hereafter COBUILD2), which introduced the label PRAGMATICS. Following their first attempts, many EFL dictionaries today mention the importance of pragmatics in the EFL context (Channell, 2002: LA12–3 in the *Macmillan English Dictionary for Advanced Learners* [2001]; also in the *Macmillan English Dictionary for Advanced Learners of American English* [2002]; 'Pragmatics' in LDOCE4 [982–5]; Nomura, 2003 in the *Obunsha Lexis English-Japanese Dictionary* [2003 hereafter OLEJD: xx]).

Several EFL dictionaries list pragmatic information as one of their merits, but what they regard as information on pragmatics appears rather inconsistent. In the front matter of LDOCE2, Leech and Thomas claim to take into account as part of pragmatic information the degree of formality in the situation of an utterance, such as whether it is a business meeting (1987/1991: F12f). On the other hand, COBUILD2, the *Collins COBUILD English Dictionary for Advanced Learners* (2001 hereafter COBUILD3) and the *Collins COBUILD Advanced Learner's English Dictionary* (2003 hereafter COBUILD4) state that when 'some words or meanings are used mainly by particular groups of people, or in particular social contexts' they mark the words and the meanings with 'style and usage' labels (COBUILD2, xx; COBUILD3, xx; COBUILD4, xii). In this respect the COBUILD dictionaries have an advantage. If the use of a particular expression is normally required or expected in a particular social situation, it should belong to sociolinguistics rather than pragmatics (see 2.3.3), though style and usage may not always be part of sociolinguistics.

Kawamura (2002a: 5), however, points out that the following entry for *majesty* in COBUILD3 apparently confuses the pragmatic information with that on sociolinguistics:

> You use majesty in expressions such as **Your Majesty** or **Her Majesty** when you are addressing or referring to a King or Queen.

Although this definition is accompanied with the pragmatic politeness it should have a style and usage label if the above guidelines for the labels were followed. Unfortunately, this criticism also applies to COBUILD4, which might suggest that the COBUILD policy on pragmatic information was not sufficiently understood among the lexicographers. Unless lexicographers have a deeper understanding of pragmatic information it will be difficult to eliminate this kind of confusion.

I must also point out that the explanation of a pragmatic label, formulae, in

COBUILD3 and COBUILD4 below is quite misleading:

> There are many words and expressions in English which are fairly set, and are used in particular situations such as greeting and thanking people, or acknowledging something (COBUILD3: xxiii; COBUILD3: xiii).

At first sight, |formulae| would seem to cover too wide a range of expressions, if the above guidelines for the label were followed. More importantly, the use of the phrase 'in particular situations' blurs the difference between the pragmatic label and the style and usage labels. In the explanation of the style and usage labels cited above, the lexicographers use the phrase 'in particular social contexts'. Foreign users will naturally wonder what the difference is between 'in particular situations' and 'in particular social contexts'. As long as the lexicographers put the examples of |formulae| in the form of gerund, 'greeting and thanking people, or acknowledging something', they should have used another phrase, such as 'in performing a certain action', though pragmatics is not only concerned with speech act. Again, it appears to me, though without complete conviction, that the difference between pragmatics and sociolinguistics is not clear enough even to the lexicographers.

The point is that, as we have seen in 2.4.1, pragmatics is concerned with almost every aspect of language and sometimes, on the surface, completely overlaps with other levels of language (see also 2.3.1 and 2.3.3 for details). The confusion about pragmatic information in lexicography seems to have been directly transferred from that between theoretical pragmatics and its related fields, particularly sociolinguistics. I therefore believe that my definition of pragmatics in Chapter II can be a basis for clearing up these kinds of confusion. So long as the use of a particular expression is usually required in a particular social situation, it belongs not to pragmatics but to sociolinguistics. If the meaning of a word, phrase or utterance is correctly gained from the abstract meaning and/or its entailment, that is basically semantic. In the next section, I will define what pragmatic information is in the context of EFL lexicography.

3.3 Restricting the coverage from a lexicographic perspective

3.3.1 Discourse and pragmatic functions

It might be tentatively possible to define pragmatic information for EFL dictionaries as the part of pragmatic meaning that is accommodated in the dictionaries, but it will soon turn out that this definition does not provide any criterion for determining what the information is, or what portion of pragmatic meaning should be included in the dictionaries. So long as pragmatic meaning and dictionary meaning are distinct both in scope and nature, it is at least necessary to specify what portion of pragmatic meaning can and should be included in the dictionaries. While pragmatic meaning is diverse, the easiest part to capture in dictionaries may be pragmatic uses of words.

As mentioned in 3.1.1, some words, mostly function words, do not have meaning in its proper sense. They have uses instead which fulfil various discourse functions such as emphasisers, or pragmatic functions such as thanking (Moon, 1987: 100). The uses duly reflect S's intent, and they are, inherently, pragmatically marked in that as long as they do not have semantic meaning, they usually do not overlap with other levels of linguistic resources such as abstract meaning. In fact, what dictionaries have traditionally done concerning these words is nothing apart from explaining their pragmatic meaning (see also Moon, 1987: 99f).

The point is that there are also many words which have both a pragmatic function and semantic meaning (*ibid.*), and their semantic meanings can sometimes blur their counterpart pragmatic functions. It is thus more difficult for learners to recognise their functions and, importantly, learners' failure to recognise that function is likely to cause a misunderstanding. As Moon proposes (1987: 100), when a word has both semantic meaning and function, the function needs to be explained clearly as part of an entry in EFL dictionaries. In the next subsection I will discuss how the functions can be captured in EFL dictionaries.

3.3.2 Pragmatic biases

Although it is crucial for EFL dictionaries to provide their users with clues to discourse or pragmatic functions of a word, a word can have more than one such function. Moreover, its functions may considerably vary according to contexts. It is thus inevitable that lexicographers should restrict their coverage of the functions. It is worth noting here that many words have a tendency to be interpreted in a particular manner, and that if H and/or S do not recognise the tendency, it can result in a pragmatic failure. Leech and Thomas (1987/1991: F12) provide the following example, where a British teacher of English requested a foreign student to read a passage and the request was seemingly rejected quite rudely:

> Teacher: James, would you like to read this passage?
> James: No, thank you.

Leech and Thomas observe that the teacher may take James' reply 'as being very rude, or as a bad joke' (1987/1991: F12), but James apparently did not mean to be taken as such. He failed to capture the teacher's intent because the teacher's request was in the interrogative rather than the imperative; he probably did not know that the sentence pattern, *would you like to do something?* was typically interpreted as a request.

In this respect Thomas (1983: 101) points out that there is bias which lets H see one meaning first when interpreting pragmatic ambiguity, just as there is almost always such bias in other linguistic ambiguities such as grammatical ones (Kess and Hoppe, 1981: 95–100), and she attributes the above misunderstanding to James' failure to recognise the bias. In fact this kind of conventionalised interpretation, or bias, often realises S's intent beyond its surface structure, that is, in a way that is pragmatically unmarked. If the above exchange had taken place between native speakers of English, the teacher's intent would have been realised through the bias in spite of the interrogative construction on the surface. Since these biases are basically finite, more fixed and therefore far easier to capture in dictionaries, it will be effective for EFL dictionaries to focus on this kind of bias typically assigned to certain expressions.

In addition to the above speech act example, the pragmatic biases are observable in almost any pragmatic inferences or implicatures. The following utterance, 'Who cares?', for instance, can be interpreted as a question at least from its semantic meaning, but it is far more often taken as irony. S may utter it to realise S's intent such that S does not want to talk about the present topic any longer. If H fails to recognise that, it might result in a serious pragmatic failure; S might view H as importunate.

Considering the character of dictionary meaning, dictionaries can and should only deal with most fixed parts of pragmatic meaning. I thus determine the scope of pragmatic information as the part of pragmatic meaning which can be captured through the discourse or pragmatic functions and the pragmatic biases. Although Wang pointed out that pragmatic meaning restricted in this way might not be complete (2015: 208), as discussed above, no dictionary can afford to cover all the areas investigated under the heading of pragmatics (see also 8.2.1 and 8.3.1 for examples of pragmatic phenomena which dictionaries cannot thoroughly deal with). Any kind of pragmatic meaning which cannot be gained in this way is basically outside the scope of lexicography. In the next subsection, I will consider another important aspect of pragmatics, paralanguage.

3.3.3 Paralinguistic features

Paralanguage is no doubt closely related to pragmatics, and it must play a crucial role in the EFL context (see for example Hurley, 1992). Accordingly, as defined by the *Dictionary of Lexicography* (see 3.2.1 for its citation), there may be nothing wrong in the inclusion of paralanguage in EFL lexicography, or rather it should be ideally incorporated into the dictionaries. Nevertheless, since dictionaries have traditionally dealt with meaning in the form of lexical items, or alphabetical strings, it will be almost impossible for any dictionary to treat paralanguage properly without using many complements, including complicated codes and illustrations, which is obviously against the recent trend towards user-friendliness. More precisely, the use of the codes and illustrations will become rather undesirable, especially for the following three reasons:

(1) The codes will make entries and texts too complicated and easily discourage foreign learners from consulting their dictionaries, especially monolingual ones (see Yamada, 1996: 105f).

(2) The explanations of each code in the front matter will necessarily become longer and more thorough, but few users may tackle them (see, for example, Béjoint, 1981: 216; 219), which suggests that the majority of important pragmatic information will remain incomprehensible to the users.

(3) The illustrations will take up a significant amount of space and make it difficult for lexicographers to include the kind of information which, like that on pragmatics, is important for EFL learners but unpopular among teachers and students (see Kawamura, 2002b: 89f).

Even if a dictionary can afford to employ many complements, it is still doubtful whether paralinguistic information can be fully captured in the dictionaries (see Moon, 1998a: 354; see also 11.1.3).

It is also questionable how lexicographers can gain reliable data on such phonological features as intonation because even the latest spoken corpora are basically no more than a collection of a transcription of spoken English (Moon, 1998a: 348f), which also makes it difficult to treat intonation properly in pedagogical lexicography (1998: 353f). Still, the value of intonation cannot be denied when discussing pragmatics. Even the same word or phrase can realise S's different intents depending on intonation (Moon, 1987: 95). Moon in this connection suggests that it will become necessary to structure dictionaries completely differently if spoken English is to be treated fully in EFL dictionaries

(1998a: 354). Among her suggestions is the expansion of the number of speech labels, which are followed by recent EFL dictionaries. While COBUILD2 has only one pragmatic label, PRAGMATICS, its successor COBUILD3 has more finely classified it into the seven labels: approval, disapproval, emphasis, feelings, formulae, politeness, and vagueness, which are also found in COBUILD4. In addition to the seven pragmatic labels, moreover, COBUILD3 and COBUILD4 have the following nineteen style and usage labels: [COMPUTING], [DIALECT], [FORMAL], [HUMOROUS], [INFORMAL], [JOURNALISM], [LEGAL], [LITERARY], [MEDICAL], [MILITARY], [OFFENSIVE], [OLD-FASHONED], [RUDE], [SPOKEN], [TECHNICAL], [TRADEMARK], [VERY OFFENSIVE], [VERY RUDE], and [WRITTEN], whereas COBUILD2 has only eleven labels. It appears that the trend in EFL lexicography is towards spoken English, though this does not mean that EFL dictionaries can capture intonation fully.

As far as monolingual EFL dictionaries are concerned, they usually do not contain information on intonation, while many EFL dictionaries designed for Japanese users very occasionally indicate basic intonation patterns employed with particular lexical items (*The Grand Century English-Japanese Dictionary* [2000]; *Kenkyusha Luminous English-Japanese Dictionary* [2001]; OLEJD; *Taishukan's Genius English-Japanese Dictionary*, 3rd ed. [2001]; see 12.3.2 for an example). Although there may be much room for improvement in the bilingual dictionaries' treatment of intonation, some of their explanations are pragmatic, which suggests that it might be also possible for monolingual EFL dictionaries to treat intonation to a certain extent. At this stage it is uncertain whether phonological features can be captured fully in the dictionaries, and I will return to this issue in Part III, especially 13.4.

Facing the fact that any dictionary has a severe limitation of space, the discourse or pragmatic functions and the pragmatic biases may need further restriction. As EFL dictionaries are designed for foreign learners of English, it will be worth considering if it is possible to further limit their coverage from an educational viewpoint. In the next subsection, I will explore the possibility.

3.3.4 Criteria for deciding what pragmatic information to include

There is a considerable difference in the degree to which a learner's pragmatic failure could place that learner in difficult situations. While minor failures can only make S and H feel awkward, in the worst case, S and H will not only misunderstand each other's intent but their personality (see also Thomas, 1983: 96f and 110). In James' case in 3.3.2, he was taken as a rude student without his being aware of that. Thomas even suggests that pragmatic failures could potentially be a cause for every instance of what we call national or ethnic stereotypes (1983: 107). Pragmatic information in EFL dictionaries should ideally be confined to those discourse or pragmatic functions and pragmatic biases, a learner's ignorance of which could cause a serious problem, especially in those cases where S's utterances might sound rude or offensive.

Significantly, it is not always predictable which pragmatic failure could cause serious problems. The teacher misunderstood James due to his failure to recognise the teacher's intent to request, but H's failure to recognise S's intent to request will not necessarily result in a serious pragmatic failure. At the same time, any pragmatic failure can cause a serious problem.

In order to detect potential causes for a pragmatic failure, it is necessary to investigate the socio-cultural difference between English and other languages. For example, while Moon points out that in English 'to borrow a sheet of paper' is slightly different from 'to borrow a book' in that the former does not necessitate the borrower returning the sheet (1987: 101), things to return after borrowing may vary from culture to culture (see, for example, Thomas, 1995: 130). This kind of difference is basically sociolinguistic, but it can cause a pragmatic failure. Also, linguistic difference between English and a learner's native language can be a potential cause for failure. In the Japanese language, for instance, the translation equivalence of *borrow* and that of *hire (rent)* are usually not distinguished. A Japanese speaker uses the same word, *kariru*, which covers both of the English verbs. Accordingly a Japanese learner of English will often confuse the two English verbs. Although this difference is basically semantic, it might cause a pragmatic failure if a Japanese learner confuses the verbs and utters, 'I'd like to borrow a car' at an office of a car-hire company, while in fact meaning that he wants to hire (rent) a car.

As far as Japanese is concerned, relatively little reliable research has been carried out into these areas. The majority of the studies seem rather subjective, being confined to the authors' personal experiences when communicating with native speakers of English (Osugi, 1982), although there are several exceptions like Kashino (1996) who distributed questionnaires among twenty native speakers. His study only deals with four lexical phrases: 'Will you do something?', 'Can you do something?', 'Would you do something?' and 'Could you do something?'. In view of the fact that most EFL dictionaries today contain at least fifty or sixty thousand headwords, it would be hoped that a lot more research could be carried out in this area. Until then lexicographers' intuition will be the only major criterion for deciding which pragmatic uses and biases to include in their works.

In the next section, I will discuss two important characteristics of pragmatics in the EFL context, and then move on to the discussion about how lexicographers should present information on pragmatics.

3.3.5 Issues for pragmatics in the EFL context

As Thomas observes (1983: 97), pragmatics is a delicate area and, as is also the case with the way it is treated in EFL dictionaries, it is not sufficiently apparent how it should be taught. However, there are at least two aspects which should be kept in mind when giving instruction in pragmatic issues either in a classroom or a dictionary. First, while pragmatics is closely connected with S's intent, S's intent is not something that teachers or lexicographers can correct or impose their opinions on; the instruction in pragmatics should not be confused with that in S's intent. Thomas states:

> It is not the responsibility of the language teacher *qua* linguist to enforce Anglo-Saxon standards of behaviour, linguistic or otherwise. Rather, it is the teacher's job to equip the students to express himself/herself in exactly the way s/he chooses to do so—rudely, tactfully, or in an elaborately polite manner. What we want to prevent is her/his being *unintentionally* rude or subservient. (Thomas, 1983: 96)

It is essential that whenever a teacher notices a learner's pragmatically inappropriate use of English that teacher should at least seek to detect where the inappropriateness is derived from. Even though a learner's use of English can sound rather rude, there is a possibility that they are intentionally flouting pragmatic principles in the language. In that case, their rude utterances should not be corrected, at least in terms of language teaching. Otherwise, any careless correction of a learner's particular way of speaking could simply result in the teacher imposing their preference on their students. Teachers should correct their students' use of language only when it is caused by their unintentional errors or failures such as linguistic ones. Leech in this connection proposes a subfield of pragmatics, pragmalinguistics, which is mainly concerned with the linguistic side of pragmatics. Following the distinction Thomas divides pragmatic failures into pragmalinguistic and sociolinguistic failures (Thomas, 1983: 99 and *passim*), though it will not be easy to maintain the two-way distinction always between the linguistic aspects and the rest of the field. Thomas herself admits that any absolute distinction cannot be drawn between the two types of failures (1983: 109). I will therefore not go into details of the distinction here.

It is also reported that it is sometimes extremely difficult to recognise a pragmatic failure when it has occurred, because, when a learner fails to speak English in a pragmatically preferable manner, ordinary native speakers and even teachers could take it as the manifestation of the learner's true intent without sufficient knowledge about the pragmatic differences between English and the learner's native language (Thomas, 1983: 96f). As long as the importance of pragmatics is not fully appreciated in the EFL context (Kawamura, 2002b: 87), serious misunderstandings caused by pragmatic failures will not be cleared up. This may be why pragmatic failures sometimes can be a cause of more serious problems.

Second, unlike grammar or pronunciation, pragmatics often reflects one's values and/or outlook on the world (see also Thomas, 1983: 99). The danger of there being a pragmatic failure in a classroom will accordingly increase when teachers and students do not share a linguistic or cultural background, and, in the worst case, might result in a rather unhappy situation where 'Students who feel that their view of the world is being dismissed out of hand or who feel unable to express themselves as they wish, are scarcely likely to develop positive attitudes toward learning foreign language' (Thomas, 1983: 110). Since there are apparently different sets of pragmatic rules in almost every language and/or culture, when giving instruction in pragmatics, teachers only have to alert their students to cross-linguistic and/or cross-cultural pragmatic differences rather than intervene in their view of the world (see also House and Kasper, 1981: 184).

Just as teachers should be careful when teaching pragmatic issues to their students, so should lexicographers be careful when presenting pragmatic information in their works. Nevertheless, there are difficulties for lexicographers when deciding how to present information on pragmatics in their dictionaries. This will be discussed in the next subsection.

3.3.6 Descriptive versus prescriptive

In the last subsection, I have suggested that teachers and lexicographers should not impose their pragmatic preference on language learners, which would suggest that EFL dictionaries should present information on pragmatics in a descriptive manner rather than in a prescriptive way. However, while the description of languages is one of the basic aims of linguistics, the mere description of pragmatic phenomena will not be sufficient for teachers. Teachers should to a certain extent correct their students' mistakes and give them some guidance; they are basically expected to be prescriptive rather than descriptive.

Significantly, it is pointed out that foreign learners sometimes feel pressed to speak a 'superstandard English' (Thomas, 1983: 96; also Schmidt and McCreary, 1977: 429). Kawamura also points out that native speakers occasionally seem too hypercritical about foreign learners' use of English such as *they* referring to single antecedents, while the native speakers themselves often do use the word in that way (Kawamura, 2001: 64–5). It appears that foreign learners are often expected to speak and behave in the way that native speakers find most preferable. Tsuruta, Rossiter and Coulton (1988: 11) therefore advise

Japanese learners of English to let native speakers take the initiative when speaking in English, perhaps because they believe that by so doing the learners can avoid the native speakers' misunderstanding of them. To follow this advice, however, will discourage the learners from expressing themselves in the way that they want to. Such a dilemma may derive from the fact that even ordinary native speakers have strong authority over foreign learners. This will be even truer of teachers and dictionaries.

Even if the lexicographers claim to be descriptive, most users will not regard their dictionary as simply presenting a description of language, because the dictionary has very strong authority (Carter, 1989: 150f; Hanks, 1979: 38; Jackson, 1988: 42; Landau, 2001: 6; Moon, 1998a: 352). It is also the fact that what ordinary users might want in their dictionary is prescription rather than the accurate description of language (Jackson, 1988: 42; Landau, 2001: 254–61; Moon, 1998a: 353), whilst the trends are towards descriptiveness (see also Ikegami, 1996: 280f).

It seems that the real problem lies in the fact that whether dictionaries present the information descriptively or not, ordinary users will not believe that dictionary explanation is just a description of language, or rather they may to a certain extent prefer their dictionaries to be prescriptive. Thus this predicament cannot be resolved until the views of the dictionaries change, which may suggest that some instruction in dictionary use will become necessary in a classroom. Although this may be one of the real problems that needs to be addressed in the EFL context, this is apparently outside the parameter of this current study. I will come back to this problem in Part II and Part III.

3.3.7 Pragmatic information, a definition

While both pragmatics and dictionaries are concerned with meaning, the kinds of meaning that each of them treats and their coverage are different. Also, pragmatics is concerned with almost every aspect of language. I have accordingly tried to reach some compromise between them, and have determined its scope as discourse or pragmatic functions of a lexical item and pragmatic biases assigned to a certain expression.

As EFL dictionaries are designed for foreign learners, the dictionaries should only focus on those functions and biases learners' ignorance of which is more likely to cause serious pragmatic failures, though it is difficult to determine which functions and biases could cause the failures. I have also recommended that EFL dictionaries should present information on pragmatics in a descriptive manner. Allowing for the above discussions, I define pragmatic information for EFL dictionaries as the description of discourse or pragmatic functions and pragmatic biases that is presented in an EFL dictionary in order to help a user avoid a serious pragmatic failure that could potentially be caused by his/her ignorance of them.

However, I must admit that at least three problems remain to be solved. First, although intonation may be basically outside the scope of lexicography, it plays a crucial role in pragmatics. Even the same lexical item can realise S's different intents depending on intonation. As long as many EFL dictionaries for Japanese users occasionally indicate several basic intonation patterns in conjunction with pragmatics, it might be possible for both monolingual and bilingual EFL dictionaries to treat intonation in conjunction with pragmatics to a certain extent. Second, it is necessary for foreign learners to change their attitude towards the EFL dictionary and pragmatics. Even though EFL dictionaries present pragmatic information in a descriptive way, users will regard their dictionaries as prescriptive, which may affect learners' motivation to study. Also, the learners and even teachers are not fully aware of the importance of pragmatics in the EFL context, which makes it rather difficult for the lexicographers to include more pragmatic information systematically. As these issues are central to pragmatics in the EFL context, I will more thoroughly discuss them in Part II and Part III. Third, in order for lexicographers and teachers to know which functions and biases are necessary for foreign learners, it is essential to get reliable data on the pragmatic difference between English and learners' native language. I will thus consider this issue in Part II.

PART II
Lexical Approach to Pragmatic Failures

Abstract (Part II)

In Part II, I will seek to identify how and which lexical items are likely to cause serious pragmatic misunderstandings between Japanese learners and native speakers of English. For this purpose I carried out a large-scale questionnaire survey. Discussions of the data collected will follow the literature review and an account of the research project. Although I believe my initial aim—to determine the lexical items likely to cause pragmatic failures—was achieved satisfactorily, analysing the data made me more aware of the complicated nature of the processes and situations in which pragmatic failures occur.

CHAPTER IV
Data Collection

While EFL dictionaries today claim to contain plenty of information on pragmatics, it should be pointed out that it is extremely difficult for lexicographers to obtain reliable authentic data in order to analyse and describe the pragmatic behaviours of their target words and phrases. There are several problems in the existing source materials which they have traditionally used for the compilation of their works: other dictionaries and corpora. Concerning pragmatic information, academic and non-academic literature on pragmatics is also available to lexicographers, but it is not that satisfactory for a lexicographic analysis either.

In Part II, I will therefore seek to identify lexical items likely to cause serious pragmatic failures between Japanese learners and English speakers. For this purpose I carried out a large-scale research exercise under the sponsorship of a publisher in Tokyo (see 4.2 for details). At least in terms of the numbers of informants and research items, this would be one of the largest surveys conducted in the field of cross-cultural or interlanguage pragmatics. Moreover, as a pragmatic survey specially designed for lexicographic study, this would be the first research of this kind. Although existing dictionaries, corpora, and both academic and non-academic literature may be helpful in examining pragmatic failures, they are not always satisfactory in particular, in not providing appropriate and accurate data. My goal was to correct this situation, and my findings have been used in one non-academic book for Japanese learners and four published dictionaries (cf. 1.1).

Problems of existing literature, including dictionaries, will be discussed in 4.1, and a detailed account of my research project and the methodology employed will be provided in 4.2.

4.1 Existing sources of pragmatic information for learners

4.1.1 Dictionaries

It is a common practice followed by lexicographers to look at each others' works in order to ensure that the coverage in their dictionaries may match that in their competitors' (Landau 2001: 402). Apart from the coverage, lexicographers often examine their competitors' works for ideas on how to improve theirs. In the highly competitive EFL market, there are many dictionaries, both monolingual and bilingual, which claim to be based on the most up-to-date findings of linguistic research. There is thus a great deal of source material for lexicographers to refer to.

It is also to be remembered that while bilingual dictionaries of language pairs such as English and French are often compiled jointly by teams of English and French speakers, English-Japanese and Japanese-English dictionaries for Japanese learners are usually compiled by non native speakers of the target language; that is, by Japanese speakers. On the other hand, monolingual dictionaries are usually compiled by competent native speakers, and so good monolingual dictionaries could be satisfactory source material for the compilation of English-Japanese and Japanese-English dictionaries for Japanese learners. Yet, aside from a potential problem of plagiarism, there is another serious problem with the use of monolingual dictionaries as source material for compiling bilingual dictionaries.

Monolingual dictionaries are in principle expected to serve a broad readership. This is not problematic at all in itself, but clearly they cannot satisfy the specific needs of users with a particular linguistic background such as Japanese learners. According to Thomas (1983: 102), one of the major causes of a pragmatic failure is the interference of a learner's native language, and if this is the case, monolingual dictionaries may not provide sufficient help for the user in this respect. Higashi (1981: 108), for instance, points out that Japanese learners often learn English vocabulary through their translation equivalents from an early stage, and there is a possibility that Japanese translations may interfere severely with their understanding of English words. *Liar* and its Japanese translation, *usotuski*, may exemplify this point. *Liar* may cause an undesirable effect in such utterances as 'You're a liar' if used referring to a person, but *usotsuki* can be used as almost equivalent to 'You're joking' in a casual way. If a Japanese learner regards *liar* as an equivalent to *usotuki* due to their learning of the English word through the Japanese translation, it may lead to a serious pragmatic failure (see 6.1 for the results of a question as to this problem).

So far as I have found, *Cambridge Advanced Learner's Dictionary*, 3rd ed. (2008 hereafter CALD3), *Collins COBUILD Advanced Dictionary* (2009 hereafter COBUILD6), *Longman Dictionary of Contemporary English*, 5th ed. (2009 hereafter LDOCE5), *Macmillan English Dictionary for Advanced Learners*, 2nd ed. (2007 hereafter MED2), *Oxford Advanced Learner's Dictionary of Current English*, 7th ed. (2005 OALD7), and even the latest editions of major monolingual EFL dictionaries (as of 2010) do not alert the user to the above potential danger. On the other hand, all the major English-Japanese dictionaries I consulted (*Taishukan's Genius English-Japanese Dictionary*, 4th ed. [2006 hereafter GEJD4], *Kenkyusha Luminous English-Japanese Dictionary*, 2nd ed. [2005 hereafter LEJD2], *O-Lex English-Japanese Dictionary* [2008 hereafter OLXEJD], and *Wisdom English-Japanese Dictionary*, 2nd ed. [2007 hereafter WEJD2] include a usage note or assign a relevant label to the word *liar* so that the user can avoid using the word carelessly referring to a person. This clearly shows the disadvantage of the monolingual learners' dictionaries mentioned above. At the same time, as pointed out above, bilingual English dictionaries for Japanese learners are usually not compiled by native speakers of English; this may affect the reliability of their descriptions, especially those concerning minute subtleties or nuance of expressions such as related with pragmatics.

It is also to be noted that both monolingual and bilingual dictionaries sometimes lack a pragmatic viewpoint despite their claims to be pragmatic-conscious. Tsuruta, Rossiter and Coulton (1998: 103) point out that if a Japanese learner confuses *must* and *have to*, it is likely to cause a pragmatic failure in certain contexts. According to them, *must* expresses one's own judgement, and *have to*, obligation. For example, if A requests B to do something, and B declines by saying 'I *must* do something else instead' rather than 'I *have to* do something else instead', it might sound as though B judges that B's own business is more important than A's request. If this is the case, B's use of *must* may lead to a serious pragmatic failure, making B sound selfish and egocentric. If B actually believes B's own business is more important than A's request, B's use of *must* will be perfectly acceptable. What B surely needs to avoid here is B's unconscious misuse of the phrases (see Question 36 in Appendix II for details).

As mentioned, Japanese learners tend to learn English words through their translations, and, importantly, *must* and *have to* have traditionally been assigned the same Japanese translation, *shinakereba naranai*. I must also point out that in Japan they teach that the two phrases are interchangeable. Apart from these two unfavourable factors, "when advanced learners select the 'wrong' word it is usually because they have *some* information about it, but not as much as they need" (Maingay and Rundell 1987: 130), and any misuse of English by a foreign learner, either grammatical or pragmatic, could potentially cause a communicative failure. Concerning the two phrases, neither monolingual nor bilingual EFL dictionaries provide sufficient help for Japanese learners. To the best of my knowledge, most major EFL dictionaries (LDOCE5, MED2, OALD7, GEJD4, LEJD2, and WEJD2)[1] include detailed usage notes, grammatical descriptions, and/or semantic descriptions of the differences between the two phrases, though none mention nor alert to the above danger. Clearly, current dictionaries lack a pragmatic viewpoint in this respect.

4.1.2 Corpora

Large-scale electronic corpora are now an indispensable part of modern lexicography, and they have changed or affected almost every stage of dictionary compilation from the selection of headwords to their descriptions. However, they are not very satisfactory for pragmatic studies for the following four reasons: (1) even the latest spoken corpora used by lexicographers are basically no more than a collection of a transcription of spoken English, usually lacking such phonological features as intonation (Moon 1998a: 348f), and it should not be overlooked that depending on the situation, intonation can even change pragmatic meaning completely. Apart from phonological features, other paralinguistic features may naturally be lost in electronic corpora, though it is not really certain whether they could be successfully captured in dictionaries. (2) While pragmatic behaviours of lexical items can vary according to context, corpora usually do not contain sufficient contextual information such as the relationship between interactants. To the best of my knowledge, the only exception is the Cambridge and Nottingham Corpus of Discourse in English (CANCODE), which contains information on the relationship between the speakers such as whether they are intimates or not. Other spoken corpora are arguably still in the trial stage. (3) Corpora typically lack sufficient co-text to explore pragmatics as with KWIC formats. Even though lexicographers can gain fuller co-text whenever necessary, they usually cannot glance through the results of their search. This may greatly lessen the advantage of electronic corpora. (4) One's intent should be a key to pragmatics (cf. 2.3.1), but it is not something we can observe from their utterances recorded in an electronic format. In order to find out more about a speaker's intent, and, ideally how it is interpreted by a hearer, it would be necessary to use another source material.

Pragmatics is still relatively new to lexicography, and thus necessitates employing another methodology designed specifically so that lexicographers could describe more satisfactorily pragmatic behaviours of their headwords. I will return to this problem in 4.2.

4.1.3 Academic research

While existing source material for lexicography may not be really helpful with respect to pragmatics, many pragmatists have carried out various empirical surveys throughout the world, especially under the heading of cross-cultural or interlanguage pragmatics (e.g. Bergman and Kasper 1993; Nelson, Bakary and Batal 1996; Norris 2001; Pavlidou 2008). Even restricting the scope to those related with Japanese learners of English, there is a flood of academic research in this area (Ide, Hori, Kawasaki, Ikuta and Haga 1986; Usami 2002; Tanaka, Spencer-Oatey and Cray 2008; among others).

Because there is a vast amount of reliable data and findings gained from the research, it would be quite reasonable for lexicographers to use them as source material for analysing and describing pragmatic behaviours of lexical items. However the results of the academic studies cannot be easily applied to dictionary compilation since they are not originally targeted at lexicographic analysis and writing of dictionary entries. As far as I found, most of the research focus on pragmatic strategies or attitudes rather than the pragmatic behaviours of particular lexical items.

For example, in Tanaka, Spencer-Oatey and Cray (2008), they investigate when and how British, Canadian and Japanese informants apologise linguistically, and they successfully proved that the traditional stereotype of Japanese apologising unnecessarily often was not always correct. The problem for lexicographers would be that the *act* of apologising has no place in a dictionary. A more feasible and also more promising way to incorporate the result into lexicography may be to compose a usage or cultural note for a lexical item used in apology, but there are several candidates such as *(I'm) sorry* and *Excuse me*. Lexicographers need to determine which headword is the most suitable to the note, which means they need to decide which headword is most likely consulted by the learner wanting information about the act of apologising in English. However, it is very unlikely that the learner will consult their dictionary at all in order to find out about how to apologise properly. So long as dictionaries basically approach language in terms of words and phrases, lexicographers must tackle language accordingly. The majority of reliable academic findings cannot therefore be applied directly to the compilation of a dictionary.

There are also several studies which focused on the pragmatic behaviours of lexical items (e.g. Fraser 1978; Walters 1979; Kashino 1996). For example, Fraser (1978) sought to find out how deferential particular linguistic forms can be recognised without any context. In his experiment, he asked the informants to rate the degree of deference among various forms such as *Would you ...?* and *Can you ...?* As Thomas points out (1995: 156), however, even surface level linguistic forms which are considered deferential may not be perceived as deferential by the hearer. Even admitting that some forms such as *Could you do that* tend to convey more deference than others like *Do that, can't you* (Fraser 1978: 12), I would argue that the hearer's recognition of deference in the use of a particular phrase may entirely depend on such factors as how, when and who uses that form (see 6.3.1 for an example of *Could you ...?* as used to invite people). Even direct imperatives can sound polite or friendly if used with appropriate intonation.

Kashino (1996) took a step further providing the informants with context but not so specific as necessary. In his questionnaire, he asked 20 informants to select the best auxiliary verb from among *will, can, would* and *could* to complete a blank in four sentences. Although he instructed the informants that the request below was addressed to a friend, he did not specify the degree of closeness between the friends:

– do me a favour? (to a friend)

According to Kashino, the informants should choose *can* or *could* because this is a personal request between friends, but 13% of the informants chose *will* and 23%, *would*. He explained that *will* and *would* were chosen probably because the informants interpreted the above instruction 'to a friend' as to a close friend.

I believe that there are at least two serious flaws in the study. First, so long as the informant did not mention the reason why they chose *will* and *would*, Kashino should not have inserted his personal interpretation. Instead, he should have accepted the results as they were. Second, he should have specified the degree of closeness from the beginning; or he should have asked the informants for the reasons for their choices. Otherwise, we cannot really know how the informants judged the appropriateness of the four auxiliary verbs in given situations (see 4.2.1.5 for details).

There is another problem for lexicographers in common with the academic literature. Considering the number of headwords a dictionary contains, the coverage of lexical items in academic literature is rather narrow. Kashino, for instance, examined only four auxiliary verbs. Although some of the academic studies have a high potential as source material for lexicographic analysis, lexicographers may need further material to refer to.

4.1.4 Non-academic literature

Communication through a foreign language, especially English, has been attracting a lot of attention from Japanese people. The website of amazon.co.jp, for instance, has a special section for English learning, and in the section there are 18 subsections such as 'general English conversation' and 'English conversation for business'. In the former subsection, there are 3,522 books being sold (as of 12 September 2017). This demonstrates how keen Japanese learners are to improve their communication skills in English, though this does not always lead to actual improvements.

Most of the books on English conversation that are easily available to ordinary learners in Japan are non-academic books, and they often deal with pragmatic issues, especially in terms of politeness, such as how to make a polite request in English. As mentioned above, pragmatics is relatively new to lexicography, and this is, surprisingly, also the case with English teaching. Non-academic books are therefore a major source for Japanese learners to become familiar with pragmatic issues. In this subsection, I will thus briefly review a few in order to investigate their educational value, and whether they can provide adequate source material for the compilation of EFL dictionaries.

Non-academic books are usually not designed as formal textbooks but as reading material. They are thus easy to read, providing the reader with the authors' personal experiences, such as a trouble they themselves encountered as foreign speakers of English. I am willing to admit that such experiences may be important to share, but, at the same time, I must point out that the contents of the books are sometimes over-generalised without being based on objective data.

Wakiyama (1990: 29), for instance, mentioned a British colleague who often used the phrase *May (Could) I trouble you ...?* among colleagues. According to Wakiyama, the phrase was an overly polite British phrase and the British person was called an 'apple-polisher' among colleagues because of his/her habit of using the phrase and other deferential expressions like *sir*. Although the episode may be a true story, I would strongly doubt that the person was called as such simply due to his/her frequent uses of the phrases. Wakiyama commented that they felt uncomfortable when the British colleague used such polite phrases, and emphasised to the reader the importance of appropriate style as required in a particular situation. One may well wonder here whether *May (Could) I trouble you ...?* and *sir* should be avoided because they are inappropriate among colleagues. If the colleagues were on very close terms with each other, the polite phrases might be inappropriate especially in an informal setting. In that case, however, the British person may not have been called an apple-polisher behind his/her back. It seems to me that the British person might have been called an apple-polisher for other reasons. Moreover, if the person intentionally used the phrases to express the distance between them or to sound jocular, there was nothing wrong with his/her use of the phrases to the colleagues (see 3.3.5 for discussions of intentionality).

Although it is good for a book to be entertaining with funny or interesting episodes, people such as teachers and books such as dictionaries can hold strong authority over learners (cf. 3.3.6). It is very likely that a book on English conversation written by a supposedly competent Japanese speaker of English will have a similar impact on an ordinary learner who is willing to improve their speaking skill by reading such books. They should therefore be objective enough, and the authors should try and make every effort not to over-generalise their experiences. In this respect, Wakiyama is to be criticised, and this applies to other non-academic books as well (see also 4.2.1.2 for another example).

While the differences among variants of English, especially British and American Englishes, attract much attention in Japan, such differences and their potential impact on pragmatic issues do not seem to be considered sufficiently in the non-academic books I have examined for this study. For instance, Wakiyama (1990) cited above seems biased towards American English, and Tsuruta, Rossiter and Coulton (1998) seem to focus on British English. This is partly because the contents of the books are mainly restricted to the authors' knowledge and personal experiences, which Tsuruta, Rossiter and Coulton explicitly mention in the introduction (viff). So long as pragmatics may reflect one's values and/or outlook on the world (Thomas 1983: 99), pragmatic preferences among countries may sometimes vary considerably. I would argue that anyone working in the EFL industry, including teachers, text writers and lexicographers, should keep the diversities of pragmatics in mind and try to be as objective as possible when dealing with pragmatics.

In order to obtain reliable data for lexicographers to analyse pragmatic behaviours of lexical items, I therefore conducted a large-scale questionnaire survey in 2005, and I will discuss its relative advantages and disadvantages in 4.2.

4.2 The research project

In this section I will present a detailed account of my research, conducted in 2005. As I chose to carry out the survey using a questionnaire, after giving the outline of my research project in 4.2.1, I will begin with discussions of general characteristics of a questionnaire and its relative merits and demerits compared with other research methodologies favoured in the field of pragmatics in 4.2.1.1. I will then move on to more detailed explanations: the criteria for deciding the topics (4.2.1.2), the two versions of questionnaires employed (4.2.1.3), the demographics of the informants (4.2.1.4), the question formats (4.2.1.5), the problems and limitations of the methodology (4.2.1.6), and the selection of data (4.2.1.7).

4.2.1 Overview

Although the research project was initially planned as part of a dictionary project for Obunsha, a publisher in Tokyo, it was conducted in 2005 as a joint project of the dictionary project and my study at The University of Birmingham towards the degree of Doctor of Philosophy in Applied Linguistics (see 1.1 for the published outcomes). The questionnaire used consists of 90 main topics or questions, most of which were carefully selected from examples of pragmatic failures pointed out in related literature to be typical of Japanese learners (cf. 4.1.4). Examples I myself encountered as a learner and teacher of English were also included. Controlling necessary variables such as gender and age, a considerable number of sub-questions were incorporated into the main questions whenever necessary, each with slightly different settings such as conversations between peers versus those between a person and their superior. This led to 178 questions and sub-questions in total (see 4.2.1.5 for details). As for the informants, 100 native speakers and 114 Japanese learners took part in the project (see 4.2.1.4 for details). So far as I know, this is the first large-scale investigation of this kind.

4.2.1.1 Questionnaires vs. spoken data

There have been arguments over which is more reliable, the written questionnaire or spoken data. Beebe and Cummings (1996), for instance, compared the results gained through the two methods and concluded that it was impossible to decide either was actually better. On the other hand, as Kasper (2008: 279) has pointed out, in the field of interlanguage or cross-cultural pragmatics there has been a growing shift of data collection method from questionnaires to the analysis of situated interactions. However, the choice of methodology should depend on the purposes of the studies.

Considering the aim of my studies—to determine how and what lexical items are apt to cause misunderstandings between Japanese learners and native speakers of English—it will be extremely difficult to gain a sufficient amount of data from observing authentic interactions as well as role plays and elicited conversations. There is no guarantee that the lexical items which I need to examine are used in these interactions. More importantly, quite a few of EFL dictionaries today, especially those designed for advanced learners, claim to contain a large number of headwords. For example, OALD7 (2005) claims to contain '183,500 British and American words, phrases and meanings' (back cover) and LDOCE5 (2009), '230,000 words, phrases, and meanings' (back cover). Their ways of counting 'headwords' are not at all clear, and could appear misleading, in including undefined phrases and individual senses, but it would be safe to assume that even hundreds of hours of conversations may be far from enough to gain a sufficient amount of data to cover the dictionaries' contents.

There are also several other favoured data collection methods, such as interview, diary and verbal report, but they are also not very promising for dealing with the vast amount of information, nor for focusing on pragmatic behaviours of particular phrases. I therefore chose to use questionnaires for my study because they could more easily deal with the relatively large amount of data. Moreover, they are generally more suitable to find out about what informants believe, think, feel or know rather than to observe their actual behaviours (Kasper 2008: 291f). Thus with a questionnaire we could directly ask informants what they think about the use of particular lexical items as used in a certain context.

It is true that questionnaires may have their own advantages and disadvantages; therefore, I designed a special questionnaire for this study in such ways to overcome some of their known disadvantages and to meet the specific conditions of my study. The descriptions of my survey and the features of the questionnaire will be provided in the subsections which follow.

4.2.1.2 Selection of topics

One of major sources of the topics in the questionnaire is non-academic books, discussed in 4.1.4. As pointed out, non-academic books available in Japan are often not based on objective data, and I sometimes come across counterexamples in the books. For example, Osugi (1982: 44f) explains that such phrases as *I'm afraid you must be tired* and *I'm tired* should be avoided in English speaking countries. According to Osugi, English speaking people do not want to disclose their weakness to others. Accordingly, if a person uses the latter phrase, *I'm tired* at their office in front of their boss, it could be taken as a confession of their weakness, or a complaint against their being forced to work by their boss. I do not really see where these explanations came from, but if they are not based on objective data, they must be based on Osugi's experiences and/or those of people around him. I simply picked up these examples as candidates. In addition to non-academic books, I used academic literature, and examples of pragmatic misunderstandings I myself encountered as a foreign learner and teacher.

When selecting the topics from among the candidates, I took into consideration various factors, including the degree of seriousness and the likelihood of misunderstandings, and one of the most important criteria was educational value, e.g. whether a candidate is a frequently used expression in English, and/or whether it has wide coverage not restricted to a particular field or genre. Less-common words and phrases were not included in this study because I believed such phrases were less important for learners.

As was seen in Part I, however, it is sometimes extremely difficult to separate pragmatics from its related fields, semantics and sociolinguistics; even other levels of language may interfere with pragmatics. Moreover, pragmatics can often reflect one's values and/or outlook on the world (Thomas 1983: 99). This is also the case with pragmatic failures. Although my study is mainly concerned with lexical items that can cause pragmatic failures, these failures are not always caused by a single factor. Sometimes several factors or several items in an utterance combine to be the cause. Other factors such as cultural differences and teaching in school, or their combination, could also cause the failure.

In English speaking cultures, for instance, it would be generally polite to make sure whether or not a person is looking for help even when the person appears to be in need of help, because the person may not actually want assistance. In Japan, on the other hand, it could sound rather haughty if we explicitly ask a person whether they need help in that situation. Therefore, such utterances as 'Would you like me to help you?' or its Japanese translation equivalents may sound rather pompous to a Japanese speaker. These differences might well cause a pragmatic failure between Japanese learners and English speakers, but the point here is where in a dictionary lexicographers can put this kind of information (see 6.3.3 for the results of a question dealing with this matter). Even though some topics look outside the purview of lexicography, I included them in the questionnaire because of their educational value.

4.2.1.3 Parallel questionnaires

In 4.1.1, I pointed out that neither monolingual nor bilingual EFL dictionaries alert Japanese users to potential dangers caused by their ignorance of the differences between *must* and *have to*. However, it is also the fact that we do not really know how native speakers use and/or interpret particular phrases in a particular context; nor do we know how Japanese learners use and/or interpret it in the same context. So long as the majority of the non-academic books dealing with Japanese learners' pragmatic failures are not based on reliable data, we cannot tell anything definite about their pragmatic behaviours. I thus decided to use two parallel versions of a questionnaire: an English version for native speakers (hereafter EV) and a Japanese version for Japanese learners (hereafter JV) in order to compare objectively how native speakers and learners use and interpret particular expressions in a specified context.

The contents of the two versions were identical except that EV was written in English and JV Japanese, and in the process of translation every effort was made to ensure that their contents were identical by reviewing them several times among several competent Japanese speakers of English. As to the English words/phrases in question, they were not translated into Japanese. Apart from the contents, their designs were different in the following respects: (1) while in EV each topic began with an introduction to demonstrate the issue at hand, JV did not; (2) whenever native speakers found a particular expression inappropriate in a particular context, they were asked for an alternative expression to be used instead; (3) Japanese informants were able to leave a question unanswered when they did not know what the answer was or if they had never considered the issue; (4) Japanese informants were given instructions to answer on the assumption that they were in a situation where they needed to use English, e.g. studying or travelling abroad; (5) while EV was distributed through the Internet, JV was distributed as printed material.

The difference (1) reflects different policies I adopted for the two parallel questionnaires. Although the questionnaires could reveal the pragmatic behaviours of both native speakers and the learners, the emphasis should be given to native speakers' uses of English, since it is native speakers' uses of English which EFL dictionaries are supposed to describe. Japanese learners' answers are also of importance academically, but I decided to use them mainly to determine where native speakers and Japanese learners behave most pragmatically differently. Native speakers are therefore expected to answer the questions with full understanding of what the issues are (see 4.2.1.5 for details). On the other hand, Japanese learners do not have to know what the issues are; or rather they should not know that because their answers may be affected by them. It was most important to ensure that their answers correctly reflect how they use or interpret a particular expression in a particular context without any preconceived idea.

The difference (2) is concerned with educational value. As seen in Part I (3.3.6), educators cannot simply take a descriptive attitude towards language. They are expected to be prescriptive; more precisely, they are expected to give students instructions on how to use language properly. This is even truer of dictionaries, especially those for learners. I thus asked native speakers for an alternative expression whenever they found inappropriate a particular expression in a particular context.

The differences (3) and (4) reflect the fact that Japanese learners of English do not usually use English in their daily lives. If they had never thought of the acceptability of a phrase in a particular context or which expression they should use in a particular situation, it would be less likely that they would have a fixed way of behaving pragmatically. Thus it seemed appropriate for them to leave a question unanswered unless necessary. At the same time, they were required to explicitly state that this was the case, so that I could distinguish this from an inadvertent failure to answer. By so doing, the amount of work for Japanese informants could be decreased. In addition, I made it a condition that they answer the questions on the assumption that they have to use English, in order to avoid their leaving a question unanswered simply because they do not usually use English in their daily lives.

The difference (5) is mainly concerned with the profile of informants. I distributed EV via the Internet because I required responses from native informants living in English speaking countries (see Appendix I for the covering letter and instructions for EV). On the other hand, as for the Japanese informants, I only asked those living in Japan to participate in the project (see 4.2.1.4 for details), and the questionnaire was distributed fairly easily either in a classroom or by post. Another reason for the different distribution methods was the ease of data collection and analysis. The amount of information gained through EV was enormous, so it had to be stored and analysed in an electronic format. Distributing the questionnaire via the Internet enabled me to treat their answers electronically using computer software, so that I could easily sort out the answers I wanted by such factors as nationality, gender and age. See Figure 1 below for an exact interface of answers to Question 70. II sorted out by variables:

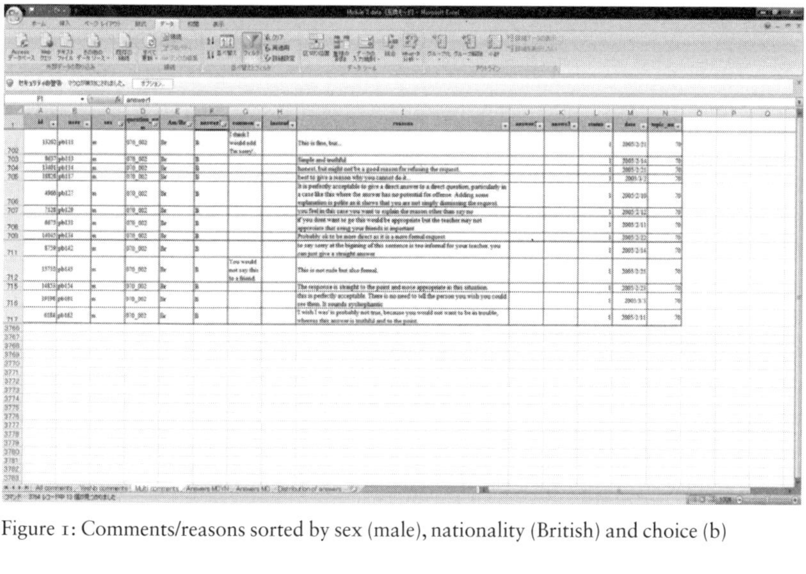

Figure 1: Comments/reasons sorted by sex (male), nationality (British) and choice (b)

4.2.1.4 Demographics of the informants

Fifty-three speakers of British English, 47 speakers of American English, and 114 Japanese learners completed the questionnaires (See Tables 1 and 2 below). However, it turned out later that three British minors as of January 2005 were inadvertently included in the project, and so their answers were excluded from this study. Thus the total number of the British informants is 53, and all appropriate protocols are observed[2]. See Table 1 below for details.

Age	UK (M/F)	US (M/F)	Total
18–19	9 (4/5)	2 (0/2)	11 (4/7)
20–29	23 (11/12)	21 (10/11)	44 (21/23)
30–39	14 (6/8)	13 (3/10)	27 (9/18)
40–49	7 (7/0)	8 (3/5)	15 (10/5)
50–59	0 (0/0)	3 (1/2)	3 (1/2)
Total	53 (28/25)	47 (17/30)	100 (45/55)

Table 1: Distribution of age and sex among the native informants

The number of native informants was controlled in such a way that there were about 50 speakers of British English and another 50 of American English; speakers of other varieties were excluded, because even though a relatively large number of native speakers took part in this project, the number would still be too small to represent all the varieties of so-called world Englishes.

The informants did not necessarily have higher educational backgrounds, because usages in language, especially those of pragmatics, should reflect how ordinary people use language in their daily lives. Moreover, only those living in English speaking countries were invited because if they lived in Japan, and/or were used to errors or failures typical of Japanese learners, their judgements might be affected in some way by their previous experiences (Sakamoto 2004: 71). In fact, four native speakers of English, two British, and two American who helped me with the pilot test were either living in Japan or had stayed in Japan for a significant time, and did not notice that I had used the swung dash throughout the preliminary version of the questionnaire as a sign of ellipsis: 'Can you ~?' or 'Let's ~'. This is a common Japanese writing convention, but did not really make sense to ordinary native speakers of English. Although they were very competent language teachers, they were too familiar with Japanese typographic conventions to foresee problems in communities elsewhere. This is one of the reasons I distributed the EV via the Internet only among those outside of Japan. If an informant is quite familiar with Japanese, it will naturally interfere with their pragmatic judgement as well.

Age is another crucial variable which may affect usages of language and need to be controlled carefully, so I mainly invited relatively young people, those in their twenties or thirties, because I was more concerned with their usages.

As for Japanese informants, they were all university students in Japan. See Table 2 below for details:

Age	Total (M/F)
18–22	114 (48/66)

Table 2: Distribution of age and sex among the Japanese informants

As the entrance examination of a university is a major goal in learning English in Japan, all of the Japanese participants could accordingly be considered as having reached this goal. Moreover, those who majored in English or related subjects, and/or those who had stayed in English-speaking countries for more than six months, were also excluded from this study, because the study is mostly concerned with standard Japanese learners of English. I believe that the Japanese informants selected in this way may be regarded as representatives of ordinary Japanese learners of English.

4.2.1.5 Question formats

The 178 (sub-)questions cover a wide range of topics from simply linguistic to cultural, or a mixture (see 4.2.1.2 for details), and two formats of question were used in the questionnaire: multiple choice with two alternatives, *Yes* or *No* (hereafter MCYN) and multiple choice with more than two alternatives (hereafter MC). Other popular formats often used in questionnaires are discourse completion tasks and rating scales, but they do not suit my study. The former cannot really control which lexical items are tested by the informants, and the latter may be rather difficult to apply to dictionaries. Below are examples of the two formats used in the questionnaire (for the actual interface see Figures 2 and 3 which follow).

Example MCYN[3]
35. Is it possible to use 'will' when talking of others' future plans?
We should usually not use 'will' when talking about others' future actions because it will sound as if we are in a position to decide their actions for them. We can use 'will' in this way only on such occasions as when we are representing an organization or we are talking about someone who is not able to decide their own actions, like children. Do you agree? Please answer the following question:

One of your friends William is having a barbecue party this weekend and is checking who is coming to the barbecue. William asks you whether you happen to know if another friend of yours, Geoffrey is coming. Although he is not with you at present, he told you last night that he was going to the barbecue. Would you say 'Geoffrey will come to the party'?

Example MC
86. Which is strongest among 'fairly', 'quite' and 'very?'
If we confuse such adverbs as 'very,' 'quite' and 'fairly,' it can cause a misunderstanding. For example, if we use 'fairly' while in fact meaning 'very,'

we could inadvertently convey the wrong meaning. Do you agree? Please answer the following question:

One of your friends Mary lent you a CD of her favorite singer. It was really good, and you enjoyed it a lot. When returning the CD which of the following would you find most suitable for praising it?
    a) 'It's very good!'
    b) 'It's fairly good!'
    c) 'It's quite good!'
    d) None of the above is acceptable

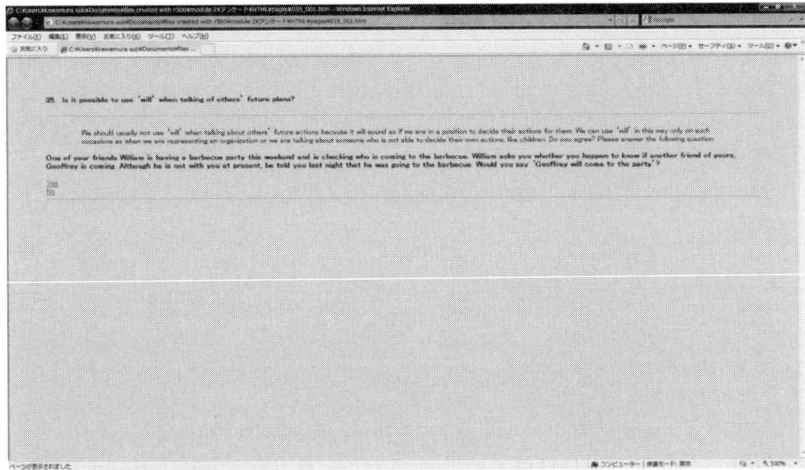

Figure 2: Actual interface of MCYN

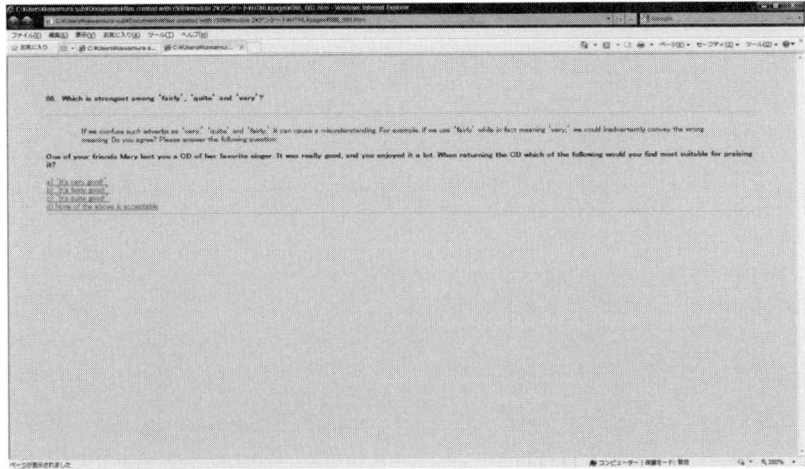

Figure 3: Actual interface of MC

One of the disadvantages of questionnaires is that each informant can answer a questionnaire with varying degrees of understanding (Belson 1981: 49–370), which necessitates a questionnaire to be designed carefully (Brown 2001: 46f). Especially with respect to pragmatic studies, it will be important to ensure that each informant answers in full understanding of the issue. Otherwise, some may answer 'no' only because they personally do not like a part of the utterance which has nothing to do with the issue concerned. Each question, both MCYN and MC, therefore begins with a title followed by an introduction to show what the issue is.

The description of the setting and the question follow the introduction. The informants are then directed to the next step according to their choice. Because it is virtually impossible to predict all the variables which might affect informants' judgement (cf. Kasper 2000: 331), the informants are always encouraged to leave their comments, whichever choice they may make. If they find an expression or all the alternatives inappropriate, they are required to state the reasons and are encouraged to provide their comments if any.

As mentioned in 4.2.1.1, questionnaires are known to be better at testing informants' knowledge rather than their actual behaviours (cf. Belson 1981: 389), since it is basically self-reporting (Kasper 2008: 291). Accordingly, the settings were carefully invented so that each setting would be familiar to the majority of informants and be relatively easy to generalise for dictionary descriptions. At the same time, it is often necessary that important variables should be controlled sufficiently. I thus posed many sub-questions with slightly different settings in order to control variables such as age and gender. Here is an example:

28. **Is it rude to say 'Long time no see?'** (deriving from Wakiyama 1990: 26)
It is advisable to avoid saying 'Long time no see' to our superiors like teachers because it sounds too informal. Do you agree? Please answer the following questions:

I: You see one of your best friends after a long time. Would you say 'Long time no see'?

II: You see one of your former teachers after a long time. Would you say 'Long time no see'?

See Graph 1 below for details of the results.

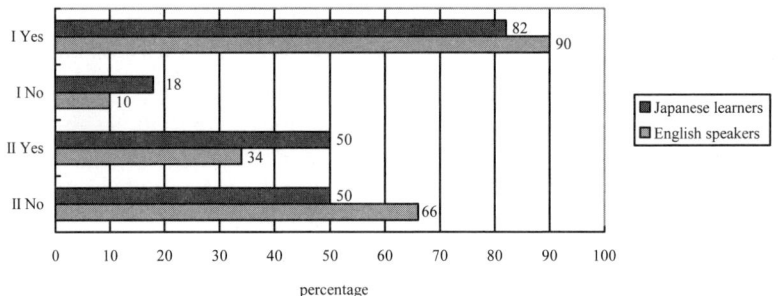

Graph 1: Results of Questions 28. I and II (*Long time no see.*)

This question has two sub-questions; I: *Long time no see* as used to our peers, and II: to a superior. Considering the research question for this topic—whether *Long time no see* is too informal to use to a superior, only asking sub-question II might have been theoretically sufficient. However, the two sub-questions showed the contrasting results, which clearly shows that the acceptability of the phrase considerably depends on the addressee. Accordingly, by comparing the results of the two sub-questions I could rule out other possibilities such that the phrase was not a commonly used expression in English or that it was a rude expression in any context.

4.2.1.6 Limitations

I must acknowledge that there are a few minor limitations in my research. First, even though my project is concerned with a relatively large number of lexical items, the number is still very small compared with the number of headwords in a recent EFL dictionary. Second, when storing the answers in an electronic format with computer software, inexplicable technical errors occurred for a few questions, and I was unable to read the comments nor count their choices, which made the number of the (sub-)questions available 162 in total (MCYN: 116 and MC: 46). Third, the informants were sometimes not satisfied with certain scenarios, especially those related with gender or feminism, and made comments. However, such reactions comprise important data on how people feel about various factors, which may have relevance to pragmatics.

Fourth, even though the questionnaire was piloted several times among English speakers, part of an utterance as used in a scenario occasionally did not sound right enough to some informants. However, an introduction preceding each question was helpful in these cases. When I was able to confirm from their comments that they answered such questions in full understanding of the issue presented, I used the data for my investigation. However, it will be necessary to pay more attention to the naturalness of examples since these may affect the results of the research.

Fifth, the amount of data was too large to deal with properly even with computer software. In addition to 178 questions, I asked the informants for comments whenever they found necessary, because pragmatics is concerned with almost every aspect of language and other unpredictable outer factor. The informants were also required to state the reason(s) whenever they found all the alternatives inappropriate in a particular context. These resulted in nearly 600 answer columns. I still believe they were necessary in order to provide a balance between quantitative and qualitative data, but since there were too many questions to answer at a single time, I made it possible for the informants to start with any of the 90 main questions. Although they were basically expected to answer all the questions in numerical order, some informants accidentally skipped several questions. I therefore excluded from this study the questions which were not answered by at least 90 native-speaking informants.

Sixth, before distributing EV and JV, I piloted both several times, and both British and American speakers took part in the pilot test for EV. However, in a few questions, differences between the two major variants interfered with the informants' judgements. Below is an example:

15. Should we use 'should' in our answers?
We ought to avoid using 'should' when answering even if the question contains 'should' (e.g. 'What should I do?') because the word 'should' is a very strong word and might sound too forceful. Do you agree? Please answer the following question:

You and Mike, a friend of yours are going for a drive tomorrow, and you want him to collect you at 9:00. Before he leaves he asks you 'What time should I collect you?' Would you answer 'You should collect me at 9:00'?

With this question, I tried to find out whether *should* is acceptable when replying to an offer in the form of an interrogative containing the auxiliary verb, because while we usually repeat an auxiliary verb to answer a question containing one, 'You should do ....' may sound haughty, especially when someone is offering help. Although the question was preceded by an introduction to provide context, several American informants still seemed hesitant to answer either *Yes* or *No* simply due to the fact they usually use *pick up* rather than *collect* in the US.

Seventh, as my analysis developed, I came across another important variable to be controlled which might affect pragmatic issues in relation to social class. Strictly, this is not a problem or deficiency of my methodology, but I will discuss this because this will have implications for future surveys of this kind. Here is an example:

> **67. How do you reply to 'How do you do?'** (deriving from Vardaman and Morimoto 1999: 24)
> One should not say 'How do you do?' in reply to another person's greeting 'How do you do?' because it will sound as if you are just repeating mechanically. Do you agree? Please answer the following question:
>
> At the house of your friend you are introduced to a person of almost the same age as you named Harry Sharpe, and the person says 'How do you do, X [Your name]?' to you. When replying, would you say 'How do you do, Harry?'

See Graph 2 below for details of the results.

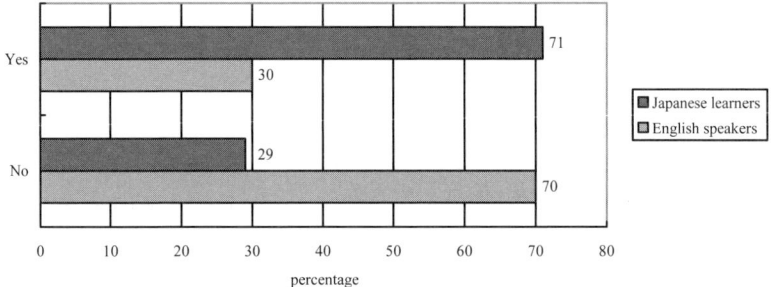

Graph 2: Results of Question 67 (*How do you do?*)

In Japan it is often taught that *How do you do?* is a phrase one says when meeting someone and that *How do you do?* is also used as a response (Kakehi 1998: 537; Matsumoto and Matsumoto 1987: 92f; Tsuruta, Rossiter, and Coulton 1998: 6). This may be a reason most Japanese learners answered *Yes*. On the other hand, most English speakers, both British and American, answered *No*. Their comments suggested that to repeat the same phrase sounded mechanical and unnatural; some also mentioned that this phrase was dated and/or formal. When using the results to write a dictionary article I thus concluded relatively easily that it was not now a normal English convention to repeat *How do you do?* as a response to *How do you do?*.

Nevertheless, I later learned that a British person was very unhappy with my conclusion. She was not an informant of this research but took part in the pilot test. She also played a role as an academic advisor to *Core-Lex English-Japanese Dictionary* (2005) based on the data from this survey for its pragmatic descriptions. According to her, my conclusion only reflected American usage and was therefore mistaken. I again checked all the comments from English speakers, both British and American, sorting them out by such variables as nationality, gender and age, but I could not find support for her reaction. Although some informants commented that the phrase was old-fashioned, there were some younger informants, even in their teens, who answered that they would repeat *How do you do?* as a reply. I also noted that more British informants (17) answered *Yes* than American (12), though this was statistically insignificant.

The only other possibility left is social class, and in fact it is pointed out that *How d'you do?* and *Pleased to meet you* are respectively used by the upper and middle classes (Gramely and Pätzold 2003: 59). At the present writing I still cannot explain whether this is the case or not, but if it were possible to sort the results by the informants' social backgrounds, it might be clarified.

While some surveys defined informants' educational backgrounds, as mentioned in 4.2.1.4, the informants for this study did not necessarily have higher educational backgrounds; I believe that usages in language should reflect how ordinary people use language in their daily lives. We therefore randomly invited informants to this research project without limiting their social backgrounds. By so doing, I obtained a sufficient number of informants, and I believe this was essential because what I tried to find out was neutral English usage not restricted to any particular social class. At the same time, I have come to think that it will become necessary to consider this matter more carefully in the future, which may enable us to review the results from a different viewpoint.

4.2.1.7 Selection of data

Before starting analysis of the results, the significance of each question was tested with a chi-square test for MCYN and Fisher's exact test for MC[4]. I have basically excluded from the analysis all the questions where the results from English speakers may not be statistically significant, because even though differences between the answers from Japanese learners and English speakers looked significant, there may be no typical pragmatic behaviours of English speakers if there are no statistically significant differences in their answers. The only exception is when there is a statistically significant difference between the answers from British and American informants. As that may affect the results of statistics, I included such cases in my study.

It is true that all the results, even statistically insignificant ones, are academically interesting, but the aim of this research is to determine how and what lexical items are likely to cause pragmatic failures for Japanese learners. Statistically insignificant answers should therefore not be over-emphasised, which reduces the number of the questions to 133 in total for this study (MCYN: 92 and MC: 41). See Appendix II for all the questions and the summaries of their results.

One of the major criteria for determining the topics for the questionnaire was the likelihood of misunderstandings between Japanese learners and English speakers. In fact, the majority of the questions, 124 out of 133, (MCYN: 84 and MC: 40), show statistically significant differences between the answers from Japanese learners and English speakers. In the next chapter, I will classify the questions, or topics, according to their major causes of pragmatic failures, and present their distribution in order to demonstrate the general tendency of the results. Case studies of each classified cause will follow.

Notes

1 Only OLXEJD out of the 9 dictionaries which I examined contains relevant information on the possible pragmatic difference between 'must' and 'have to'. As I was in charge of the pragmatic information in the dictionary, it is only natural that the dictionary contains the piece of information which I believe an EFL dictionary should have. I will thus not include the dictionary in the discussion here.
2 The questionnaire, both EV and JV, was distributed and collected through Obunsha, and the written consents from the informants were kept by them.
3 Hereafter the number preceding the introduction in a question cited is the question number originally assigned in the questionnaire. Sub-questions with only different context are basically distinguished with an alphabet letter in parentheses like '69. (A)', and those with different scenarios with Roman numerals like '47. II'.
4 A chi-square test is usually not suitable when expected values are low, and for this reason Fisher's exact test was used for MC, which contained more than two alternatives and therefore the informants' choices tended to disperse, and expected values were lower.

CHAPTER V
Causes of Pragmatic Failures and Case Studies

In this chapter, I will discuss the results of my investigation into the lexical items that are apt to cause serious pragmatic failures between Japanese learners and English speakers. As I cannot deal with each question individually, I will first present the overview of the results with the classification of the major possible causes of pragmatic failures. Case studies of each cause will be described in the subsections which follow.

5.1 Classification and distribution of potential causes

It is sometimes difficult to identify causes of pragmatic failures, especially when several different factors could combine to cause a failure. I therefore tried to identify major causes and grouped them into categories—with the seventh, *Others*, containing miscellaneous responses/pragmatic failures which did not fit into any particular category. The categories are as follows.

(I) *Identification*: This is where Japanese learners identify an English phrase with its Japanese translation equivalent, usually because they have learned a phrase via its translation. When a Japanese learner identifies an English word with its Japanese translation and uses the English word following Japanese pragmatic conventions, it might also be considered as an example of *Pragmatic transfer* (V) below. However, *Identification* only covers cases where there is a strong connection between an English word and its Japanese translation. See 5.2.1 for examples.

(II) *Direct expression*: Direct expression of one's intent, often caused by Japanese learners' unfamiliarity with a preferred English phrase and/or way to express their intent in a particular context, such as 'I want' when making a request. When there are several candidates that learners are likely to know and they still choose the wrong phrase or way, it is considered as an example of *Wrong Choice* below. Also, even when it seems less likely that a learner knows more than one candidate, if more than one candidate was presented in the questionnaire and the learners chose the wrong one, it was counted as an example of *Wrong Choice*, since the Japanese informants were allowed to use their dictionary. See 5.2.2 for examples.

(III) *Wrong choice*: Wrong choice of an English phrase often caused by Japanese learners' unfamiliarity with semantic differences between synonyms or synonymous expressions in English. This also includes those cases where English phrases are not really synonyms but their Japanese translations are. See 5.2.3 for examples.

(IV) *Style and register*: Japanese learners' unfamiliarity with proper use of English in terms of style and register. See 5.2.4 for examples.

(V) *Pragmatic transfer*: Background cultural or pragmatic differences between Japanese learners and English speakers. See 5.2.5 for examples.

(VI) *Teaching*: Incorrect, insufficient or misleading teaching of English in Japan, including teaching materials. I classified as *Teaching* such cases where the results of English speakers showed that they behaved pragmatically differently from what is taught in Japan, or where teaching in Japan is not sufficiently detailed. See 5.2.6 for examples.

(VII) *Others*: A few other causes which cannot be classified as one of the above, such as mixture of more than one cause listed above. See 5.2.7 for examples.

The distribution of the causes above is shown below. As some questions have more than one sub-question, only one from each major question is included in the graphs. The only exception is Question 81, which has both MCYN and MC sub-questions, and they are respectively counted as one.

CHAPTER V CAUSES OF PRAGMATIC FAILURES AND CASE STUDIES   65

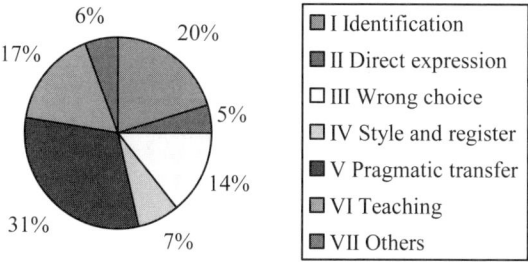

Graph 3: Distribution of the causes: all the questions

As can be seen from Graph 3, (V) *Pragmatic transfer* accounts for the largest proportion of the causes. This tendency remains the same if restricted to the questions with significant differences between Japanese learners and English speakers (Graph 4).

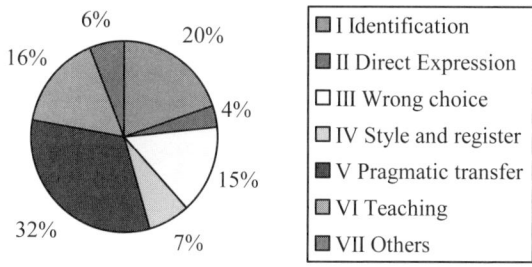

Graph 4: Distribution of the causes: questions with significant differences

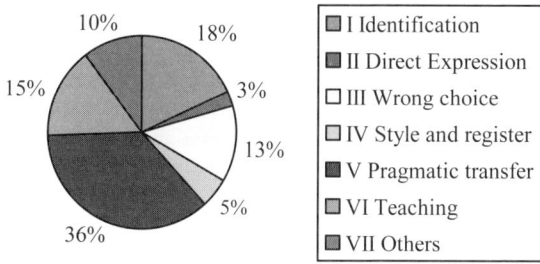

Graph 5: Distribution of the causes: questions with highest difference values

If further restricted to the questions with highest difference values between the learners and the native speakers[1] (Graph 5), *Pragmatic transfer* again increases. Clearly, it is by far the largest group of potential causes of pragmatic failures between Japanese learners and English speakers. In the next subsections I will present the case studies of each type; the examples are those with the highest difference value of the group. When both MCYN and MC questions in a group show a difference value higher than 30, I will give two examples. For other questions and their results, see Appendix II.

5.2 Case studies

5.2.1 Identification

Below is an example of *Identification* (MCYN).

> **14. Does it sound rude if we say 'I know (what you mean)'?** (related to Tsuruta, Rossiter, and Coulton 1998: 26; Wakiyama 1990: 91)
> 'I know' or 'I know what you mean' will sound offensive when it is uttered in response to someone expressing their opinion, because it implies that you mean they are saying something which is too obvious to mention. Do you agree? Please answer the following questions:
>
> You and your friend Carter are discussing opening a refreshment stand at the school festival. Carter says 'It's important to get a good place,' and you are indicating you agree with him.
> (A) Would you say 'I know'?

See Graph 6 below for the details of the results.

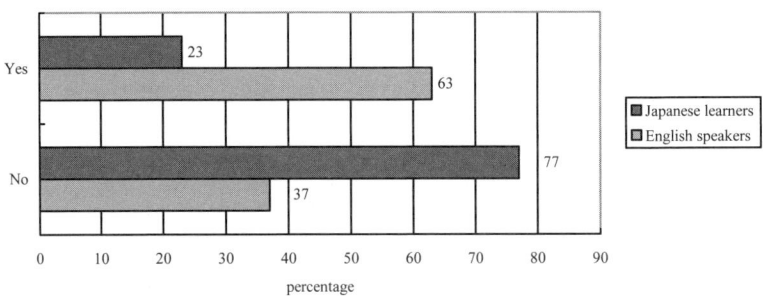

Graph 6: Results of Question 14. (A) (*I know.*)

In *Identification*, this question shows the highest difference value between the learners and the native speakers (40; See Note 1 in Chapter V to interpret this figure). *I* and *know* will be among the most familiar words even to a beginner, and the problem is that *know* is traditionally assigned a translation *shitteiru* or *shiru* in Japanese. The Japanese translation of the combination *I know*, *Watashi ha* (neutral form of *I* followed by a particle indicating a subject) *shitteiru*, and its informal form *Shitteru*[2] may imply the speaker is mentioning something already known or too obvious to mention. Accordingly, if a Japanese learner identifies *I know* with *Shitteru*, they would avoid the English phrase while listening to other's opinion as in this scenario. In fact, while 63% of English speakers answered *Yes*, 77% of Japanese learners answered *No*.

Comments from Japanese informants supported the above interpretation of *I know*, and one of the phrases they listed as more preferable in that situation was *I agree (with you)*, which suggested that they were unaware that *I know* could also be used to show their agreement with others. On the other hand, it is clear that both the British and the American informants use the phrase with their empathy or agreement for the speaker, as exemplified by the following comments: 'Yes, so long as you were saying it in agreement, rather than in a tone that implied you actually had already thought of that and he was stupid for saying it. But i think between friends, "i know" is a common response in agreement' (147 Br F 20s; sic.)[3] and 'using "I know" can truly be because of empathy. I do know because I've experienced the situation before. Here, saying "I know" can also mean just "I agree"' (11 Am F 30s; sic.).

It can be easily imagined that native speakers' use of *I know* may discourage Japanese learners from continuing to communicate. As mentioned in 3.3.6, moreover, native speakers have strong authority over foreign learners, and so learners may even feel as if they were pressed to speak and behave in the way native speakers find most preferable. Naturally, it is not necessary for native speakers to refrain from using this phrase. Or rather, learners should learn that this could express agreement, as this is part of natural English usage. This piece of information should be given to Japanese learners and will be easily incorporated under the entry for **(I) know** in an EFL dictionary, though it is questionable whether learners will seek to consult their dictionaries for a note or some explanation for this phrase (cf. 12.5); so long as they are unaware that this expression could convey a pragmatic intent which they do not know, they may not find it necessary to determine how it is used in a particular context.

It should be added in passing that quite a few English speakers mentioned the role of tone and intonation. Some American informants, even those who answered *No*, made comments that their answers to the question depend on the tone. Interestingly, no Japanese informants mentioned the importance of tone and intonation. This might be simply because their linguistic intuition may not work properly for a questionnaire about the usage in a foreign language, but I cannot and/or should not say anything more about this issue without any supportive comments from the informants.

In *Identification* Question 85 below, a MC question with the highest difference value, also shows the difference value higher than 30 (70).

85. How do you interpret 'difficult?'

In the Japanese language, the translation of 'difficult,' *muzukashii* can often be taken to mean 'impossible,' especially when you are refusing something politely. Is this the same for 'difficult' in English? Please answer the following question:

You are taking a very important examination which is starting in 10 minutes. As it would take about 15 minutes to walk there, you decide to take a taxi. However, when you tell the driver that you have to get there in 10 minutes, the driver says 'It's difficult to get there in 10 minutes.' How would you take the driver's utterance? Which is closest to your interpretation?

a) The driver thinks it impossible to get there in 10 minutes.
b) The driver thinks that it is not easy to arrive there in 10 minutes.
c) Neither of the above

See Graph 7 below for details of the results.

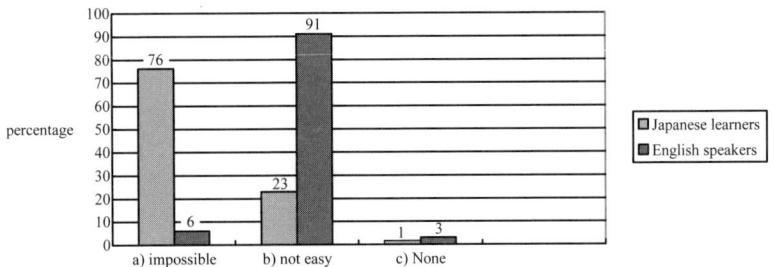

Graph 7: Results of Question 85 (*difficult*)

While 91% of English speakers accepted *difficult* at its face value, 76% of Japanese learners interpreted it as meaning 'impossible'. The Japanese translation equivalent of *difficult muzukashii* is often used to decline something indirectly. The above results clearly show that Japanese learners identify *difficult* with *muzukashii*. On the other hand, comments from native speakers suggested that *difficult* was usually not used to mean 'impossible'; some even commented that the driver wanted a larger tip by saying this.

The results of this question showed that Japanese learners evidently confused this word with *muzukashii*, and so if Japanese learners use *difficult* when declining something politely, it is highly likely that English speakers will misunderstand that. Especially in the context of business, the Japanese use might result in rather serious problems such as an English speaker's not recognising a Japanese customer's supposedly polite refusal of their business offer. This possible danger should be treated more thoroughly in the EFL context; for example, by a special comment in the entry of **difficult** in an EFL dictionary for Japanese learners.

The potential causes of pragmatic failures discussed in this subsection are mainly concerned with Japanese learners' identification of English phrases with their Japanese translation equivalents, and so this is classified as an example of *Identification*. From a lexical and/or lexicographic viewpoint, this group may be the easiest to deal with in an EFL dictionary. The following questions can be classified as *Identification*: 1; 9; 12; 13. I; 13. II; 14. (A); 14. (B); 19. I; 19. II; 20. I; 25; 32; 45; 47. II; 52. (A); 52. (B); 56; 74. I; 74. II; 84. I; 84. II; 85; 87 (See Appendix II for details of the questions).

5.2.2 Direct expression

Below is an example of *Direct expression* (Difference value: 44).

44. Does it sound arrogant if we say 'I want' when we express our wishes?
(deriving from Azuma 1994: 40; Wakiyama 1990: 55)
We should avoid 'I want + (pro)noun' or 'I want to do' a particular thing because it might sound as if we are rude or selfish. We should instead use other expressions depending on the situation. Do you agree? Please answer the following questions:

I: You are at the house of a friend of yours, when you become thirsty. You ask the friend to give you something to drink. Would you say to the friend 'I want something to drink'?

While 46% of Japanese learners answered *Yes*, almost all English speakers, 98%, answered *No*.

See Graph 8 below for details of the results.

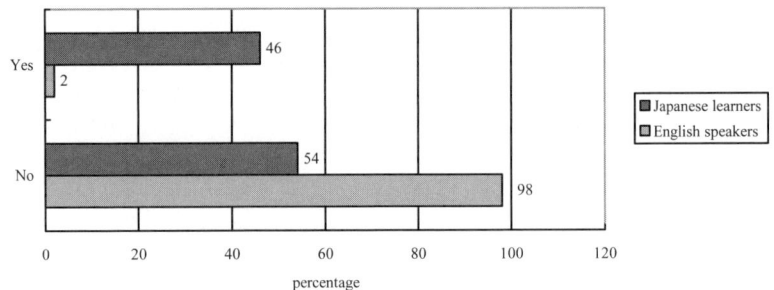

Graph 8: Results of Question 44. I (*I want*)

Most English speakers who chose *No* made comments that this phrase was too direct, rude and/or selfish. There are only two English speakers, one British and one American, who answered *Yes*, but the American informant commented, 'It's a little direct but if your close it could work. I would probably use "Could I have something...." its more polite' (57 Am M 20s; sic.). It will be safe to say that Japanese learners' careless use of *I want* in a similar situation makes them sound rather rude and/or selfish. Japanese learners should keep this in mind.

Interestingly, alternative expressions most favoured by English speakers were permission formulas such as *Can I ...?, Could I ...?* and *May I ...?*, whilst thirteen Japanese informants who answered *No* made comments that they should request to bring something to drink using request formulas like *Would (Will, Could, Can) you give me ...?*. English speakers and Japanese learners prefer to employ different strategies to achieve the same goal. I will return to this issue in 5.2.5 and 12.4.1.

Apart from Japanese learners, *I want* will be one of the most direct phrases to express one's desire for something; hence its classification as *Direct expression*, and in this sense, this type of problem is not limited to Japanese learners. However, it is often taught in Japan that when speaking English one should express our intent directly in order not to be misunderstood (cf. Azuma 1994: 3), which might affect this issue. The following questions can be categorised as *Direct expression*: 6; 27. I; 27. II; 30; 44. I; 44. II; 44. III.

5.2.3 Wrong choice

Below is an example of *Wrong choice* (Difference value: 44).

> 78. **Do you say someone is 'short?'** (related to Matsumoto and Matsumoto 1987: 46; Wakiyama 1990: 178)
> One should not use 'short' when talking about a person of below average

CHAPTER V CAUSES OF PRAGMATIC FAILURES AND CASE STUDIES

height, but in the case of a woman or a child we can use 'petite.' Do you agree? Please answer the following questions:

II: (A) When referring to a female person of below average height which of the following would you find most appropriate?
a) 'a short woman'
b) 'a small woman'
c) 'a petite woman'
d) 'a woman of below average height'
e) None of the above is acceptable

See Graph 9 below for details.

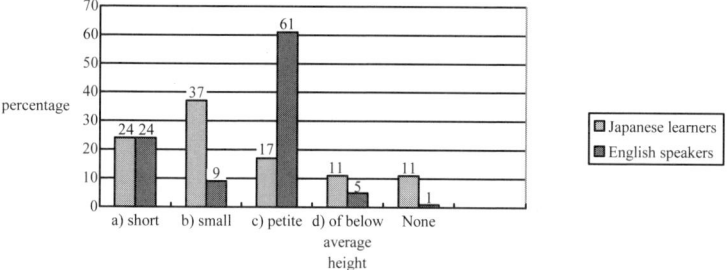

Graph 9: Results of Question 78. II: (A) (*short* person)

The most favoured term by Japanese learners was *small* (37%), and *petite* for English speakers (61%). It is also to be mentioned that the answers from Japanese informants were relatively widely dispersed and that even the least favoured choices d) and e) account for 22% (11% respectively). As for English speakers, this was not the case. Quite a few English speakers, both British and American, who chose *petite* mentioned that the term could be complimentary, especially for a female person. In fact, only 1% chose *petite* for another sub-question where a most-preferred term for a male person was asked (Question 78. I: [A]). For this question, 61% of them chose *short*, and only 13% of native speakers chose the so-called politically correct phrase *of below average in height*.

Some native speakers commented that all the options could be available depending on the woman referred to, so it would appear less likely that serious pragmatic failures would occur in this case. However, in another sub-question (Question 78. II: [B]), I also asked the informants which word should be avoided, and 20% of English speakers chose *small*, which was most favoured by Japanese learners in Question 78. II: (A). So long as pragmatics is concerned, moreover, quantitative data should not be given absolute priority. For Question

78. I: (A) there were comments as follows: 'However, whenever possible, try to describe the man by some of his other attributes rather than by his height' (40 Am F 30s) and 'Avoid talking about it unless you have to' (101 Br M 40s). These may sound quite reasonable even though there were not many who explicitly state this. There were also comments that *small* if used for a male person might sound as though the person referred to was small not only in terms of height but everything including his character. Interestingly, some informants pointed out that *short* implies being short and overweight, and *petite* implies being short and slim. Some usage notes on these facts would be useful if included in the entries for **short** and **small** in an EFL dictionary.

Although cultural differences and other issues such as people's attitude to political correctness may also be concerned with this topic, this is mainly concerned with the choice of a preferred term in a particular context. This question is thus classified as an example of *Wrong choice*. The following questions can be categorised as *Wrong Choice*: 17; 29; 34. I; 34. II; 37; 68; 75; 76; 77. I (A); 77. I: (B); 77. II: (A); 77. II: (B); 78. I: (A); 78. I: (B); 78. II: (A); 78. II: (B); 80. I: (A); 80. I: (B); 80. II: (A); 80. II: (B); 82. I; 82. II; 86.

5.2.4 Style and register

Below is an example of *Style and register* (Difference value: 39).

> 48. **Is it cool to say 'gonna' or 'wanna?'** (deriving from Wakiyama 1990: 28) Such expressions as 'gonna' or 'wanna' should be avoided when we are in formal situations. Do you agree? Please answer the following questions:
>
> You are having an interview for a university place, and wish to tell the interviewer that you are doing your best. Please answer the following questions:
> (A) Would you say 'I'm gonna do my best?'

See Graph 10 below for details of the results.

CHAPTER V CAUSES OF PRAGMATIC FAILURES AND CASE STUDIES 73

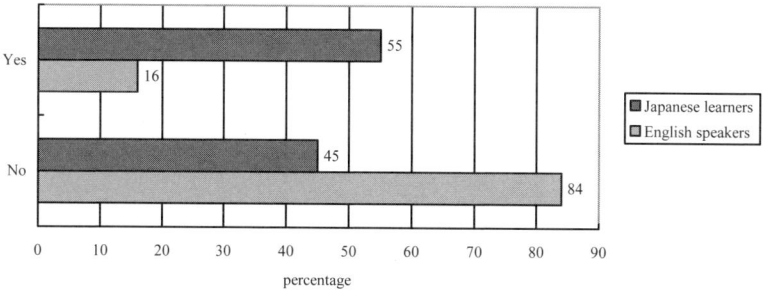

Graph 10: Results of Question 48. (A) (*gonna*)

While 84% of English speakers answered *No*, 55% of Japanese learners answered *Yes*. A Japanese informant who chose *Yes* even wrote that *gonna* could express the interviewee's willingness and determination. On the other hand, most comments from native speakers were strongly against the use of *gonna* in this situation, and advised learners not to contract *going to* in this way, especially in a formal context. Their comments suggested that the phrase sounded too informal or casual, and some, especially British informants, also wrote that it could even sound unintelligent, uneducated, vulgar, lazy and so on. It will be no doubt advisable to avoid this phrase, especially on a formal occasion.

Another important issue arose from informants' comments—how this phrase should be treated in the EFL context. An informant wrote as follows: 'Whilst it is important to encourage non-native speakers to use accurate everyday pronunciation, treating "gonna" and "wanna" as words in their own right is a dangerous practice. I understand that students see these words written, especially on the internet and in song lyrics, but they are not proper words. There is nothing worse than hearing a student "throw in" one of these shortened forms when the rest of the sentence does not contain the same intonation and other weak forms' (118 Br M 40s; sic.). The informant implied that *gonna* was part of everyday use of English, and he explicitly admitted that it was important to encourage foreign learners to learn accurate everyday pronunciation. However, he seemed reluctant to treat them as proper words. He also pointed out its awkwardness accommodated in an otherwise appropriate sentence. In 3.3.6, I mentioned the danger of 'superstandard English' which was taught to foreign learners but not used by native speakers. What is needed here would be not to keep this expression completely away from learners but to tell them how and when the phrase should or should not be used. Although EFL dictionaries have traditionally tackled these phrases by simply providing labels, it is questionable whether that practice is effective enough.

Incidentally, many British informants said that this phrase was American: 'It's horrbily American and vulgar' (101 Br M 40s; sic.), but there were also comments as follows: 'This is really a question of where you are from. As i don't speak with an RP accent, i am unlikely to say "I am going to...", as I am used to contracting the phrase into "im gonna". However, this isn't the case all of the time, it depends on how self-aware i am at the time. I wouldn't necessarily say it was "cool" to do this' (153 Br F 10s; sic.). It may be outside the purview of the current study whether this phrase is Briticism or Americanism, but one thing is clear: learners should be careful when using this contracted form, especially how and when the use of this is acceptable.

I noted that Japanese learners tended to use slang expressions once they had learned them because they often naively identified the use of slang expressions with a good command of English. English teachers in Japan may need to alert their students to this potential danger, and sufficient description of the nature of this phrase would be useful in an EFL dictionary.

As the possible cause of pragmatic failures discussed in this subsection is mainly concerned with register, this question is classified as *Style and register*. The following questions can be classified as *Style and register*: 16. I; 16. II; 16. III; 21. (A); 21. (B); 21. (C); 28. I; 28. II; 48. (A); 48. (B); 53. I; 53. II; 73. I; 73. II.

5.2.5 Pragmatic transfer

Below is an example of *Pragmatic transfer* of MCYN (Difference value: 57).

> **31. Do 'Couldn't you do ...?' and 'Don't you do ...?' sound threatening?**
> (deriving from Vardaman and Morimoto 1999: 69)
> Negative questions like 'Couldn't you do something?' and 'Don't you do something?' should not be used as a request or question because it might sound as if the speaker is blaming or threatening the hearer. Do you agree? Please answer the following questions:
>
> II: You are chairperson of the organizing committee of the school festival and are about to close a meeting. As you seem to have discussed all the items on the agenda, you want to propose ending the meeting if there are no more comments. Would you make sure there are no more comments by saying 'Don't you have any more comments?'

See Graph 11 below for details of the results.

CHAPTER V CAUSES OF PRAGMATIC FAILURES AND CASE STUDIES 75

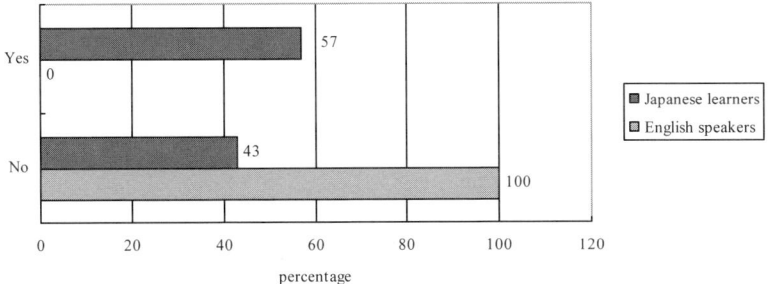

Graph 11: Results of Question 31. II (negative questions)

No English speakers answered *Yes*; however 57% of Japanese learners chose *Yes*. Negative questions are often used in Japanese to make sure or request something politely, and the results show that quite a few Japanese learners follow that convention even when speaking in English. Most comments from English speakers support the introduction above, and they advised learners to use positive questions instead. In another sub-question (Question 31. I), I asked whether *Couldn't you tell me what time it is?* was appropriate when asking a passing stranger the time. The results were comparable; while 99% of English speakers chose *No*, 45% of learners answered *Yes*. There was only one British informant who answered *Yes*, but he also admitted that it was not a good way to ask. Moreover, native speakers' comments suggested that negative questions in English could imply that the speaker was threatening and/or disappointed, contrary to Japanese learners' expectations to sound polite. It would be reasonable to assume that there are not many occasions when negative questions could be used properly.

So long as negative questions are not restricted to a particular word, dictionaries may not be able to deal with them properly. *Not* would be a candidate to accommodate this piece of information, but it will be questionable whether learners consult their dictionaries for some guidance on this. Practically, this might be outside the purview of lexicography.

In *pragmatic transfer*, an MC question with the highest difference, Question 72, also shows the value higher than 30 (60):

72. How should we use 'Could you ...?' and 'Could I ...?' (deriving from Tsuruta, Rossiter and Coulton 1998: 118–32)
When we can make the same request with either of the following patterns: 'Could you ...?' and 'Could I ...?', the former does not sound polite because it sounds as if the speaker is trying to force the listener to serve him/her. For example, 'Could I have a glass of water?' is more polite than 'Could you bring me a glass of water?' Do you agree? Please answer the following

question:

You work part-time at a watchmaker's. A customer seems interested in a watch displayed in the showcase. If the customer wanted to look at the watch, how would you prefer that they asked you?
a) 'Could you show me the watch displayed in the showcase please?'
b) 'Could I have a look at the watch displayed in the showcase please?'
c) Both a) and b) are equally appropriate
d) None of the above is acceptable

See Graph 12 below for details of the results.

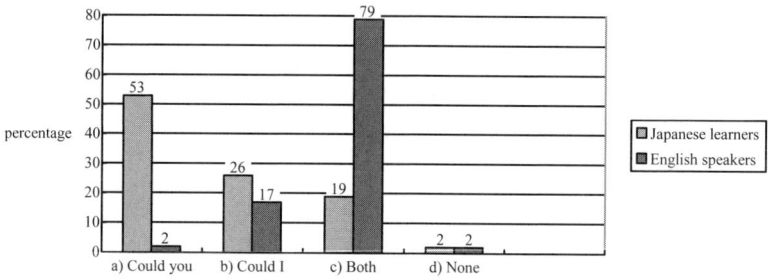

Graph 12: Results of Question 72 (Permission versus request)

As was seen in 5.2.2, when one feels like something to drink, permission formulas were preferred to request formulas by English speakers. In contrast, Japanese learners seemed more comfortable with requesting. The results of this question confirm that Japanese people find requesting more preferable in order to achieve a goal. As for English speakers, while 17% of them preferred the permission formula, *Could I...?*, only 2% chose the request formula, *Could you ...?*. However, the rest of them, almost 80% answered both were equally acceptable.

In Japanese, when one has a desire to do something, request formulas often sound politer because one often cannot attain their desire without the help of others. In other words, one often has to trouble others in order to achieve their goal, for which the act of requesting will become necessary. This is Japanese logic. Tsuruta, Rossiter and Coulton (1998: 127), for example, state that if in Japanese one asks others for permission to borrow some money rather than requesting them to lend it, it may sound arrogant. Japanese learners might therefore be offended by English speakers asking for permission when learners expect them to use a request form. Japanese learners must be aware of this difference, and this should be treated properly in the EFL context (see also 12.4.1).

The above two questions deal with Japanese learners (un)consciously

CHAPTER V CAUSES OF PRAGMATIC FAILURES AND CASE STUDIES   77

following their social, cultural and pragmatic norms in Japan, even when communicating in English, so they are classified as *Pragmatic transfer*. The following questions can be categorised as *Pragmatic transfer*: 2. I; 2. III; 3. I; 3. II; 3. III; 3. IV; 4. I; 4. II; 4. III; 4. IV; 7. II; 8. I; 8. II; 8. III; 8. IV; 10. I; 10. II; 11; 23; 24; 26. I; 26. II; 31. I; 31. II; 38. I; 38. II; 38. III; 41; 43. (A); 43. (B); 46. (A); 46. (B); 49. I; 49. II; 50. I; 50. II; 50. III; 54; 57; 63; 71. I; 71. II; 72; 81. I; 81. II; 83; 90. I; 90. II; 90. III.

5.2.6 Teaching

Below is an example of *Teaching* of MCYN (Difference value: 67).

59. Does it sound arrogant if we use 'will' when talking about our personal plans? (deriving from Tsuruta, Rossiter and Coulton 1998: 84–7)
'I will ...' (not 'I'll') in everyday conversation especially when talking about our schedules sounds arrogant because 'will' is usually used in public announcements. Do you agree? Please answer the following question:

You are going to see your cousin in Paris during the coming vacation. After school you are asked by a classmate about your plans for the vacation. Would you answer 'I will go to Paris to see my cousin'?

See Graph 13 below for details of the results.

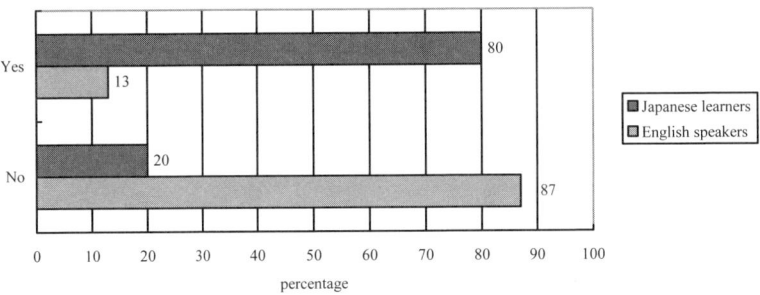

Graph 13: Results of Question 59 (*I will*)

While 87% of English speakers answered *No*, 80% of Japanese learners answered *Yes*. Most English speakers felt that the expression sounded too formal and/or unnatural; some even wrote that this was grammatically incorrect, arrogant and/or strange. There were also comments that the use of *I will* implied that the speaker had just decided their plan or was not really sure about the plan. No Japanese learners made such comments.

In Japan it is often taught that *will* has three major uses: (1) to talk about the future, (2) to state one's volition, and (3) to express probability or expectation. I personally feel that the use (1) is sometimes so emphasised in Japan that Japanese learners tend to use *will* extensively when talking about the future. Tsuruta, Rossiter and Coulton also mention this (1998: 74f). It is therefore likely that Japanese learners almost blindly use *will* when talking about the future irrespective of the environment. This may in turn cause some unexpected misunderstanding when speaking in English. I will return to this problem when discussing example (2) in 6.3.2.

In *Teaching* Question 70 below, an MC question with the highest difference value also shows the value higher than 30 (31).

> 70. **Should we say 'No' clearly when rejecting something?** (deriving from Wakiyama 1990: 18)
> When declining an invitation or when denying a request we should avoid saying 'no'. We should instead explain why we cannot accept the invitation or agree to the request. Do you agree? Please answer the following questions:
>
> II: Your teacher says to you 'I need to talk to you later. Are you free after school?' However, you are seeing your friends, and so you want to say that you are not free. Please choose the most appropriate reply from below:
> a) 'No, I'm not.'
> b) 'No, I'm not. I'm seeing my friends tonight.'
> c) 'I wish I was, but I'm seeing my friends tonight.'
> d) None of the above is acceptable

See Graph 14 below for the details of the results.

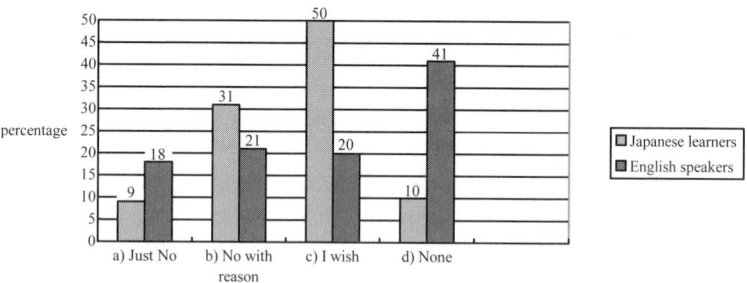

Graph 14: Results of Question 70. II (declination)

As mentioned in 5.2.2, in Japan it was often advised that when speaking English one needs to speak directly in order not to be misunderstood. However, non-academic books on English conversations in Japan often deal with

CHAPTER V CAUSES OF PRAGMATIC FAILURES AND CASE STUDIES   79

pragmatic issues (see 4.1.4 for details), and advised the reader to use polite expressions as required in a particular situation. Probably because of this, more learners found it more appropriate to add the reason than to simply say *no*, and most of them chose to use the preceding phrase *I wish I was*. As far as I found, most non-academic books on English conversation list this *I wish I could* pattern of declining as a preferable way of refusing something politely (e.g. Fukuda 2001: 33; Matsumoto and Matsumoto 1987: 67; Osugi 1998: 75; Vardaman and Morimoto 1999: 124; Wakiyama 1990: 112). As for English speakers, on the other hand, the percentage of a), b) and c) are about equal, and most informants found none of them particularly appropriate. Because there were only 10 percent of the learners who chose d), it seems likely that even when Japanese learners believe that they decline sufficiently politely, English speakers still find it insufficient. Comments from native speakers support this.

Interestingly, comments from English speakers suggested that this was not simply a matter of English usage; most informants who chose d) wrote that if the teacher wanted to see a student, the student has to cancel other plans. Quite a few of them added that seeing a friend was not a good enough excuse in this situation. This may be another example where pragmatics involves cultural issues as well as linguistic ones.

Whenever an informant answered that they did not use a particular phrase or found none of the alternatives acceptable, they were required to provide a phrase which could be used instead in the situation (see 4.2.1.3 for details). For this question, many English speakers who chose d) advised learners to offer an option or ask what the teacher wanted to talk about and/or whether it was urgent or not: 'Hmm, I told my friends that I would meet them this afternoon. Is there another time that would work for you? Maybe I can still see you before I go and meet my friends, if you don't expect it to take long' (34 Am F 40s; sic.) and 'Well, I am supposed to be seeing my friends... Is it urgent, or can we do it some other time?' (124 Br F 30s; sic.).

I should also point out that while half of the Japanese informants chose *I wish I was, but I'm seeing my friends tonight* as the best option, younger British informants were particularly not happy with the phrase *I wish*: 'Saying no would sound rude. Saying "I wish I was" may be interpreted as sarcasm as most people wouldn't "wish" they would talk to a teacher after school' (139 Br M 10s; sic.); 'None of them sound polite enough, and "I wish I was" sounds overly apologetic' (164 Br F 20s; sic.); 'Beginning with "no", especially in reply to a teacher, is quite rude. Also you don't want to say that you wish you were free after school as this might appear as though you are too eager to do what the teacher wants you to do' (163 Br F 20s; sic.); and 'You might use "I wish I was" when you are talking about something unpleasant that you have to do. E.g. "I wish I was, but I have to go to the dentist tonight"' (167 Br F 20s; sic.). These were comments which the informants put in the 'reason' sections, but the last person also filled in the comments section: '"No I'm not" is too direct. "I wish I was but I'm seeing my friends" is also strange as it seems as if you are saying, "I wish I was free tonight instead of seeing my friends"' (167 sic.). As mentioned above, most non-academic books on English conversation list this as a preferable way of declining something, but none of them provide the phrase with the detailed explanations like those the informants gave. They often simply list phrases available in a particular situation, but it is evident that learners need more information on the natural usage of English.

The above comments from English speakers may at least partly demonstrate that pragmatic studies need sufficient quantitative data as well as reliable qualitative data in order to determine how people use language in their daily lives. I will return to this issue in 6.3.

The possible causes of pragmatic failures discussed in this subsection are mainly concerned with misleading or insufficient English teaching, including teaching material, and so I classify these as *Teaching*. The following questions can be classified as *Teaching*: 15. I; 15. II; 33. II; 35; 39. I; 39. II; 40. I; 40. II; 59; 60; 62; 64; 67; 69. (A); 69. (B); 70. I; 70. II; 79, 88.

5.2.7 Others

Below is an example of *Others* of MCYN (Difference value: 55).

> **65. Do you say 'I like drinking' and/or 'I'm drunk?'** (deriving from Wakiyama 1990: 192f)
> One should not say 'I like drinking' or 'I'm drunk' because it might give the listener the impression that you are an alcoholic or that you are blind drunk. Do you agree? Please answer the following questions:
>
> I: You start a new part-time job, and your colleagues hold a welcoming party for you. One of them asks you if you are fond of alcoholic drinks, and in fact you are. Would you say 'I like drinking'?

Others consists of exceptional cases which are not comfortably accommodated in the six groups discussed so far. Question 65 above is a mixture of *Direct Expression* and *Pragmatic Transfer*. This was originally classified as *Direct Expression*, but comments from English speakers suggested that this was not simply a linguistic issue. See Graph 15 below for details of the results.

CHAPTER V CAUSES OF PRAGMATIC FAILURES AND CASE STUDIES 81

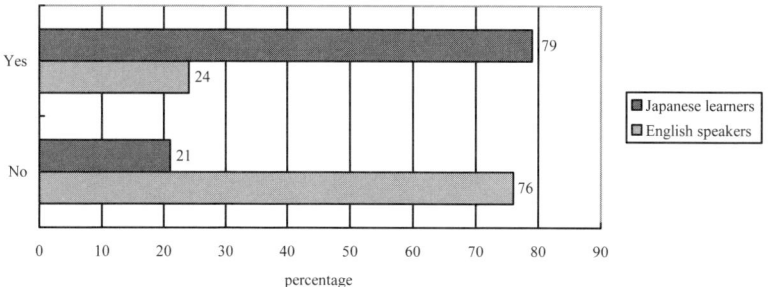

Graph 15: Results of Question 65. I (*I like drinking.*)

While 76% of English speakers answered *No*, 79% of Japanese learners answered *Yes*. Grammatically, there may be nothing wrong with this sentence; also, from a semantic viewpoint, the utterance may correctly convey a proposition that the speaker is fond of drinking something which typically refers to alcoholic drink. What English speakers were not happy with was not the utterance but the proposition itself: 'This is not culturally appropriate in most English-speaking cultures' (37 Am M 30s; sic.) and 'This varies a lot in different parts of British culture. There are groups in which the ability to consume large quantities of alcohol is considered an important attribute. I might answer differently if I thought I were in such a group' (127 Br M 40s; sic.). On the other hand, there are no comments from Japanese learners on this point. It will be simply because in Japanese culture it is acceptable to say one likes drinking (cf. Naotsuka 1998 241f). The contrasting results from English speakers and Japanese learners may reflect the differences between their cultures; more precisely, differences between their attitudes to drinking alcohol. This is why I changed my classification of this question as *Direct Expression*. In most of the cases I could identify a major cause of a problem, but there are questions which could not be easily classified under a single cause. When I could not identify a single major cause easily, I classified it in *Others*.

Because this problem is not a simple matter of usage, English speakers listed various phrases which could be properly used in this situation. Their advice could be summarised into the following: (1) change the object to something which may decrease the supposed frequency of drinking such as *a drink*; (2) limit the frequency of drinking by adding a phrase like *now and then*.

In order to find out more about English speakers' attitudes to drinking, it will be useful to see the results of another sub-question of Question 65:

> II: During the welcoming party one of your colleagues asks you if you are OK. In fact, you might have had a bit too much beer but are not sick. Perhaps you are just slightly drunk. Would you say 'I'm just drunk'?

See Graph 16 below for details of the results.

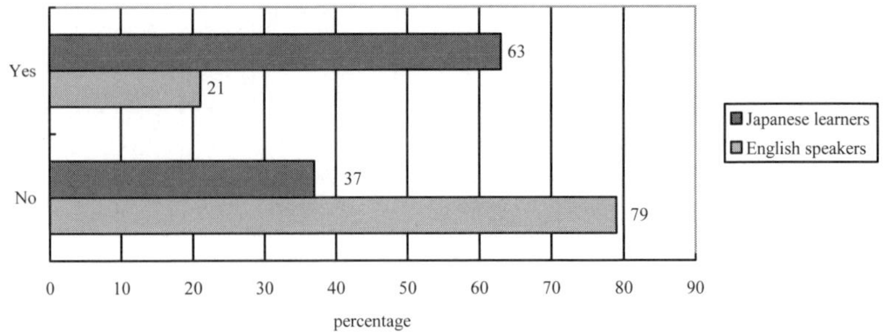

Graph 16: Results of Question 65. II (*I'm drunk.*)

	Yes	No
Japanese learners	63	37
English speakers	21	79

The results were almost the same as I; while 79% of English speakers answered *No*, 63% of Japanese learners *Yes*. However, English speakers' comments for this question may reveal another important aspect of this issue: 'Never admit you are drunk at a work event' (13 Am F 30s; sic.), 'It's a sign of weakness. Not a good idea in a business situation' (20 Am F 50s; sic.) and 'You don't know these people very well, so I wouldn't admit it' (116 Br F 30s; sic.). These comments may imply that informants' judgments considerably depend on the situation; again there were no comments from Japanese learners in this respect.

It is very likely that these differences will cause a serious misunderstanding between Japanese learners and English speakers. From a lexicographical viewpoint, clearly, some cultural note will be necessary for **drink** and/or **drunk** in an EFL dictionary. From a pedagogical viewpoint, on the other hand, it is questionable whether discussion of drunkenness should be included in a learners' dictionary.

In *Others*, a MC question with the highest difference value also shows the value higher than 30 (58). Below is an example.

89. Do you refer to your boyfriend or girlfriend as your 'lover?' (deriving from Vardaman and Morimoto 1999: 25)
We should avoid using 'lover' when referring to one's regular companion with whom we have a romantic relationship because it might imply that one has a sexual relationship with the person referred to.

II: (A) Which of the following would you find most appropriate when referring to one's regular female companion with whom they have a romantic relationship?
a) 'girlfriend'
b) 'steady'

c) 'lover'
d) None of the above is acceptable

See Graph 17 below for details of the results.

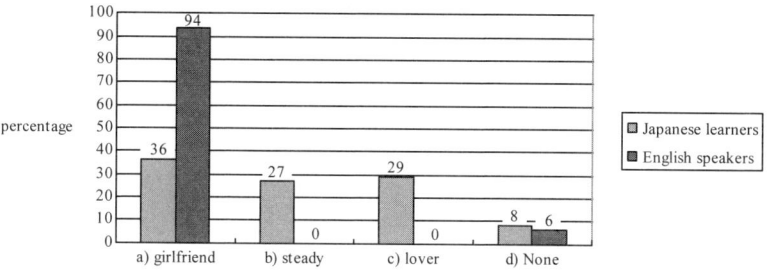

Graph 17: Results of Question 89. II: (A) (*lover*)

While the vast majority of English speakers chose a), the answers from Japanese learners were dispersed. Even though the most favoured choice by learners was also a), more than half of them chose b) or c). For this question, comments from English speakers can be summarised quite straightforwardly: (1) *girlfriend* is a default term; (2) *steady*, old-fashioned; (3) *lover* implies a sexual relationship, as suggested in the introduction. From an educational viewpoint it will be most crucial that learners should not use *lover* to mean a 'girlfriend'. The results of another sub-question about *boyfriend* support this.

Interestingly, many British informants wrote that *steady* was an Americanism; thirteen of them commented that they had never heard *steady* used in this way. If this is the case, the rest of the British informants might not have learned this term in their daily lives but from other sources, say, American TV dramas and/or movies. This is outside the purview of the current study, and I also lack sufficient evidence for this. However, it will be fair to say that the use of *steady* can cause some kind of misunderstanding, especially between British people and Japanese learners. Japanese learners should keep these facts in mind, and it will be desirable for an EFL dictionary to have a note or more detailed explanation at least for *lover*.

I classified this question as *Others* for two reasons. First, I reckon this to be an example of folk etymology on the side of the Japanese. I noticed that my students sometimes wrongly analysed word structures, and *girlfriend* and *boyfriend* were among such examples. They resolve the words into *girl* and *friend*; that is to say, *girlfriend* is almost equivalent to 'female friend', *boyfriend*, 'male friend'. Although *girlfriend* could in fact mean 'female friend', especially in the US, this usage may be less common. Japanese learners should therefore be careful about this. Second, in Japanese, both of the words can be used to refer to 'female friend' and 'male friend'; they could be regarded as so-called false friends. As stated, so long as I could not classify a cause into one of the six types, I classified them as *Others*. The following questions can be categorised as *Others*: 22; 36; 61; 65. I; 65. II; 89. I: (A); 89. I: (B); 89. II: (A); 89. II: (B).

5.3 Summary

Discussions in this chapter have revealed that quite a few lexical items are likely to cause pragmatic failures between Japanese learners and English speakers, and that pragmatic transfer is one of the major causes of such failure. This research focused on pragmatic failures from a lexical viewpoint, and I believe that the results can have important implications for future English teaching in general. As my analyses developed, however, several other important issues emerged from the results. In the next chapter, I will discuss them with more emphasis on qualitative data.

Notes
1 In order to compare the degree of the differences, the percentage of Japanese learners' answers were subtracted from those of English speakers'. For example, if 70% of English speakers answered Yes and 30% of learners answered Yes, I subtract 30 from 70 and get 40. The difference value in this case is 40. Similarly, if 30% of English speakers answered Yes and 70% of learners Yes, 70 subtracted from 30 equals minus 40. As I only use absolute values to obtain difference values, the difference value in this case is also 40. As to MC, I calculated the difference values using the alternatives, which showed the largest differences between native speakers of English and Japanese learners. The questions included here are those with difference values higher than 30.
2 Especially in informal Japanese, a subject of a sentence can often be omitted.
3 The information in the parentheses is arranged in the following order: informant's ID number, nationality (Br stands for British, Am for American), gender (M for male, F for female) and age (e.g. 10s stands for one in their teens).

CHAPTER VI
Issues Arising from Analysing the Data

In Chapter V, I discussed seven major potential causes of pragmatic failures between Japanese learners and English speakers, and presented their case studies. In this chapter I will deal with other important issues arising from the results of my research, particularly paying attention to qualitative data gained from my research.

I will start with topics inherently problematic in 6.1, and move on to pragmatic differences between British and American Englishes in 6.2. Finally, in 6.3 I will discuss the importance of qualitative data in pragmatic studies followed by their case studies.

6.1 Risky topics

In Chapter V, I only discussed examples with highest difference values from each of the seven types of cause. The difference value can be an index of the likeliness of pragmatic failures between learners and English speakers. The higher the value is, the more likely a failure will become. Considering pragmatic failures, however, likeliness cannot be the sole criterion for deciding what kind of pragmatic information should be provided for Japanese learners. Unlike a grammatical mistake and a mispronunciation, a pragmatic failure is sometimes difficult to recognise; it could be taken as a speaker's intentional utterance (Thomas 1983: 96f), and so it could even result in rather serious problems. Even though the difference value is not noticeably high, those which are concerned with delicate topics and therefore could cause serious failures should deserve sufficient treatment in the EFL context.

Some of the topics and questions in my research are inherently problematic in a sense that they deal with what is not favoured as a subject of conversation. For example, Question 52 below is concerned with one's unfavourable character or habit.

52. Do you call others 'liar?'

In English if you say 'You're a liar' to someone it might even sound as if you are trying to pick a fight. Do you agree? Please answer the following questions:

One of your classmates Henry often makes jokes and makes everybody laugh. One day when you are talking with Henry he very seriously says that he has seen a UFO.

(A) If you do not believe in UFOs, would you say to him '(You're a) liar'?

(B) (In the same situation) If another friend of yours were to call him a liar to his face, would you find this utterance appropriate?

There are two sub-questions for this topic. Their difference values are 20 and 18 respectively, so the figures themselves are not very high. See Graph 18 below for details of the results of (A).

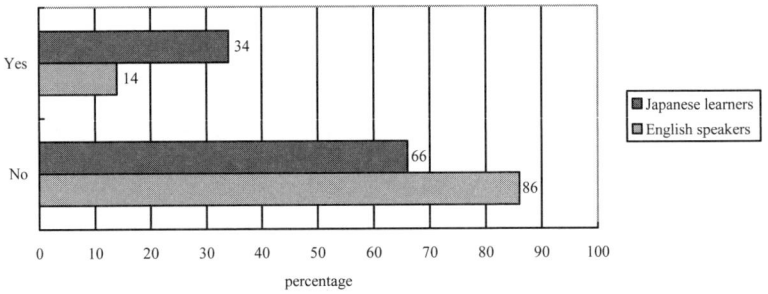

Graph 18: Results of Question 52. (A) (whether to say *You're a liar.*)

Nearly 90% of English speakers answered *No*, and all of them made negative comments on the use of the phrase in this situation; some even pointed out that this could start a fight. More importantly, 9 out of 14 informants who chose *Yes* also implied that this use could cause a problem: 'if he is a kidder it is appropriate to kid with him as well, but you need to say it with a smile' (56 Am M 20s; sic.) and 'but you can say it in a funny way to lessen the blow of the accusation' (148 Br M 20s; sic.). On the other hand, only 1 out of 39 Japanese learners who answered *Yes* mentioned the negative character of *liar* as used in this context.

I classified this question as *Identification* because in Japanese it is acceptable to use the translation of *liar usotsuki* in this context. If used in this context *usotsuki* may sound almost like 'You're joking?' in a light-hearted way. The results show that nearly 70% of the learners seem to identify *liar* with *usotsuki*. Question (A) was designed to investigate the use of the phrase in terms of encoding, and I also included another sub-question (B) to examine its

CHAPTER VI ISSUES ARISING FROM ANALYSING THE DATA   87

acceptability from a decoding viewpoint. See Graph 19 below for details of the results of question (B).

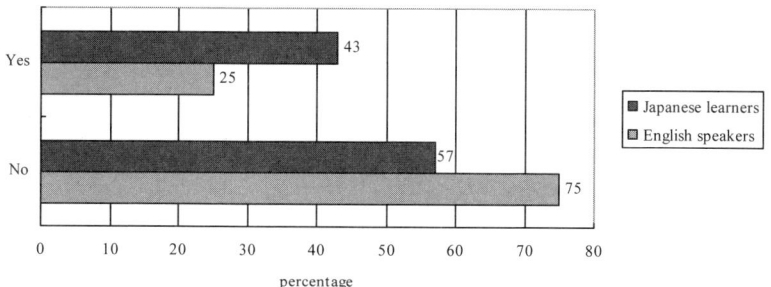

Graph 19: Results of Question 52. (B) (when someone calls another *a liar*)

Although the differences between the answers from English speakers and Japanese learners became smaller, the overall tendency was comparable. Comments from English speakers were again against the use of *liar* in this situation. Even those who answered this as appropriate commented as follows: 'Only if we all think Henry's joking, or if the person calling him a liar has a really good rapport with him' (2 Am F 30s) and 'I would find it very confrontational' (108 Br F 30s).

It would be fair to say that the use of *liar* is more likely to cause a serious pragmatic failure than simply expected from the comparisons of the numbers of *Yes* and *No*. Although informants suggested various phrases which should be used instead, the following phrases were given by many: *Really?; I don't believe you/that.; You're joking, (aren't you).; Are you kidding?*. Japanese learners should learn that *liar* and *usotsuki* are completely different in terms of the communicative effects they bring about in a particular situation. Naturally this should be dealt with more properly in the EFL context, and English dictionaries for Japanese learners may have to mention this potential danger under the entry for **liar**, and the above alternative expressions suggested by native speakers could be resources of useful expressions for learners to review from a pragmatic viewpoint.

It will be reasonable that questions dealing with potentially dangerous topics should deserve careful attention including close scrutiny of informants' comments. The same goes for the following questions: 19. I and II; 20. I; 47. II; 61; 77. I (A); 77. I (B); 77. II (A); 77. II (B) (Questions already discussed are excluded.).

6.2 Differences between British and American Englishes

40 out of the 133 questions (24 out of 92 MCYNs and 16 out of 41 MCs) showed that there were significant differences between answers from British and American informants: 6; 7. II; 8. IV; 9; 11; 13. I; 15. I; 15. II; 21. (A); 21. (B); 21. (C); 25; 26. II; 27. I; 34. I; 35; 38. I; 41; 43. (B); 50. I; 53. II; 61; 62; 65. II; 68; 71. I; 71. II; 74. II; 75; 76; 77. I (A); 77. II (A); 80. I (A); 80. II (A); 81. I; 82. I; 82. II; 83; 86; 88.

Considering that the two varieties are spoken in two distinct countries and that each of them has its own history, it is only natural that their speakers sometimes behave pragmatically differently. However, this means that a learner's careless use of English may sound especially offensive to a speaker of a particular variety, and vice versa. If pragmatics is successfully incorporated into English teaching, furthermore, such differences could create another cause of pragmatic failure in such countries as Japan where a particular variety of English, American English in the case of Japan, is almost exclusively taught. In this section I will therefore discuss problems deriving from the differences between the two varieties. For this purpose, I will use Question 15.I and 77.I: (A) as examples, since they show the highest British and American difference values in MCYN and MC respectively.

> 15. **Should we avoid 'he' and/or 'she'?** (deriving from Wakiyama 1990: 170) 'He' or 'she' should not be used to refer to a person when the person is in front of you or when the person is near you. Do you agree? Please answer the following questions:
>
> I: You are waiting for your friend Mary outside a shop, when a male passerby asks you where he can find the museum. However, you are a stranger yourself in that neighborhood, so when Mary comes out of the shop you ask her if she knows the way. Would you say 'Mary, he's looking for the museum. Do you know where it is?'

See Graph 20 below for details of the results.

CHAPTER VI ISSUES ARISING FROM ANALYSING THE DATA   89

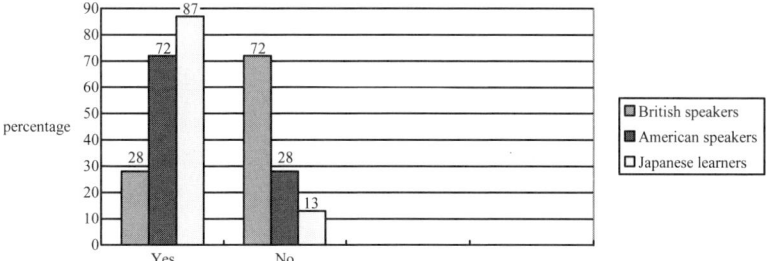

Graph 20: Results of Question 15. I (*he referring* to a person nearby)

The results of British and American informants were completely opposite; while 72% of American informants answered *Yes*, 72% of British informants answered *No*.

Most British informants who answered *No* commented that even though one does not know a person's name it would sound rude if one referred to the person using *he*. Some added that the use of *he* in this case would exclude the person referred to from the conversation. As for those who answered *Yes*, there were comments that one should avoid *he* depending on the age of the person referred to. However, some of them admitted in their comments that the use of *he* might sound rude. As almost 90% of Japanese learners answered *Yes*, their careless use of *he* in this situation would sound rude especially to British people. Most British informants listed *this gentleman* as a preferred term in this context.

As for American speakers, only a few who answered *No* made comments that this use of *he* might sound rude. In this connection, a British informant who answered *No* stated as follows: 'This is something that has been passed onto me from the older generations and I believe is not considered as bad manners as it used to be. It should still be avoided' (132 Br M 20s). Although this might suggest that future generation would not mind the use as much, as far as the British informants are concerned, some younger people still found this use of *he* inappropriate. On the other hand, American speakers have come to accept this use as time advanced.

The results from Japanese informants show a similar tendency to that of American informants, but this may not be the result of American English being taught in Japan. Because pragmatics is still relatively new to English teaching, it is less likely that pragmatic behaviours of Japanese learners will be affected by teaching of American English in Japan. Moreover, I strongly doubt that this difference between British and American attitudes to this pronoun was reflected in English teaching and teaching materials in Japan. The only plausible explanation for Japanese learners' preference for the pronoun is hypercorrection of the use of pronouns. In Japanese, pronouns are not as often used as in English, so, for example, when translating from English to Japanese, it is often advised to replace pronouns with nouns which the pronoun refers to because it is known to make the translation sound more natural (cf. Anzai 1982). This may interfere with the learners' answers to this question.

He and *she* are among the most basic vocabulary items in English, but such basic words can cause a pragmatic failure between British and American speakers. I believe more attention should be paid to this aspect of pragmatics, not only in the EFL context. As Japanese learners' careless use of *he* in this situation might sound particularly rude to British speakers, it would be desirable for learners to be alerted to this potential danger in a class room and/or by their dictionaries.

As for MC, Question 77. I: (A) below showed the highest difference value between British and American speakers.

77. Do you say 'a thin person'? (deriving from Wakiyama 1990: 177)
It is advisable to avoid 'thin' when talking about a thin person especially a woman. We should instead use 'slim' or 'slender.' Do you agree? Please answer the following questions:

I: (A) When praising the appearance of a male person for being thin which of the following would find you most appropriate?
a) 'a thin man'
b) 'a skinny man'
c) 'a slim man'
d) 'a slender man'
e) None of the above is acceptable

See Graph 21 below for details of the results.

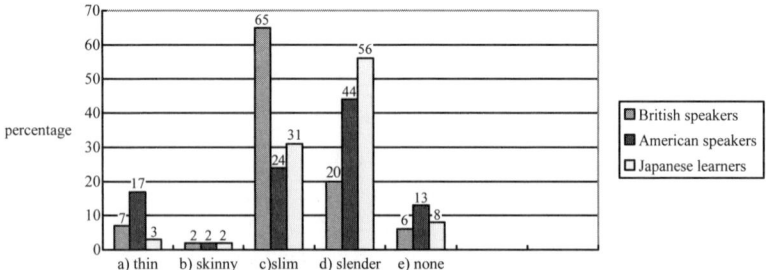

Graph 21: Results of Question 77. I: (A) (*thin* person)

British and American informants' answers presented great contrast with *slim* and *slender*. While 65% of British speakers chose *slim*, 56% of American speakers *slender*.

Many British speakers commented that *thin* and/or *skinny* had negative connotations such as being unhealthy, and some stated that *slender* was usually only applied to a female person. However, some American informants made similar comments, and the contrasting results from British and American informants could not really be explicable from their comments. Focusing on comments from American female informants, moreover, almost the same number of them chose *slim* or *slender*, nine informants for *slim* and 11 informants for *slender*. The distinction between *slim* and *slender* may seem less important from an EFL viewpoint. What should be provided for learners is that neither *thin* nor *skinny* would be preferred by English speakers, but in the case of Japanese learners, only 5% of them chose *thin* (3%) and *skinny* (2%). Even though the results of this question showed the striking difference between British and American speakers, they will not be very risky terms for Japanese learners.

I must again emphasise that when considering pragmatic issues, it is extremely important to view problems from different angles. For this purpose, one should keep a balance between quantitative and qualitative data, and I will discuss this in the next subsections.

6.3 Quantitative versus qualitative data

When conducting pragmatic research, as discussed in Chapter IV, it is crucial that all the important variables should be carefully controlled. I therefore designed the questionnaire in such ways to keep the variables well under control, for instance, by including many sub-questions with slightly different settings. I also sought to keep a balance between quantitative and qualitative data. While analysing the results, however, I became more aware of the importance of close scrutiny of the informants' comments. In 5.2.3, I discussed which word should be used when referring to a person who was not tall, and cited comments of an informant that whenever possible one should avoid describing a person by their height. Even though there was only one informant who explicitly stated this, I believe it is a fair observation.

In the subsections which follow I will present four case studies in order to demonstrate the importance of qualitative data: *Could you ...?* as used when inviting others (6.3.1); *Will* as used to talk about others' future plan (6.3.2); Whether one needs permission to help (6.3.3); Order of different person objects (6.3.4).

6.3.1 Case study 1: *Could you ...?* as used when inviting others

Here is a question directed to learn about the acceptance of *Could you ...?* as used for invitation.

> **11. Is it possible to invite others politely using 'Could you ...?'** (deriving from Tsuruta, Rossiter, and Coulton 1998: 180)
> You cannot properly invite a person to a party or similar event using 'Could you ...?' because it sounds like a request rather than an invitation. Do you agree? Please answer the following question:
>
> Mr. and Mrs. Jones have recently moved to your neighborhood, and you are thinking of inviting them to your house for dinner. Do you find the following invitation appropriate: 'Mr. and Mrs. Jones, could you come to our house for dinner next Sunday?'

See Graph 22 below for details of the results.

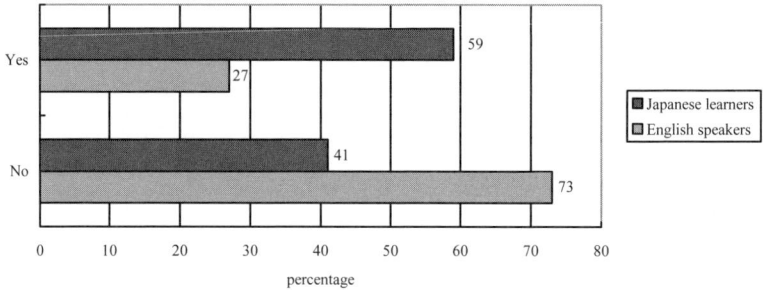

Graph 22: Results of Question 11 (*Could you ...?* used to invite others)

While over 70% of English speakers answered *No*, nearly 60% of Japanese learners answered *Yes*. These figures alone reveal that a pragmatic failure is likely to be caused by this difference, but comments from English speakers could tell what kind of failure it would be.

As mentioned in 4.2.1.5, an introduction preceding each question was intended to tell informants what the issue was, so that I could not only get their *Yes* or *No* answers but invite their comments on the topic. English speakers' comments for this question confirmed that *Could you ...?* actually sounded like a request rather than an invitation. Accordingly, even though a Japanese learner tries to invite others politely using *Could you ...?*, the invitee would take it as a request. This is a pragmatic failure in the sense that the learner's intent is not realised correctly. Yet, that is not all; many informants suggested that *Could you ...?* sounded too forceful: 'Sounds presumptuous, like a command' (164 Br F 20s; sic.), 'Sounds like a request - or a request with pressure - like it may be a surprise party, something else mysterious or that you have something unpleasant to discuss w/ them' (44 Am F30s; sic.) and 'It sounds like you are asking them if they would help you out by coming to dinner' (51 Am F 20s; sic.). Some even commented as follows: 'It sounds like it is necessary and needs to happen for a purpose' (157 Br F 20s) and 'sounds like one is prying into other people's business' (160 Br F 20s). There is a possibility that Japanese learner's careless use of *Could you ...?* with the intention of inviting others politely results in a rather serious failure making them sound as if they try to make others come to their site with some hidden purpose.

In Japanese culture, request formulas are often preferred even when one is doing a favour for others (cf. 5.2.2; 5.2.5; 12.4.1) in order to show that others' accepting a favour is also a great favour for them. The results of Question 11 clearly showed that many Japanese learners followed this Japanese politeness strategy, but the results also show that the Japanese strategy was likely to fail. In addition, comments from English speakers suggested that they might even take the Japanese invitation for some artifice. It would go without saying that the above potential danger could not be noticed simply from comparing the figures. This may well deserve more thorough treatment in the EFL context.

6.3.2 Case study 2: *Will* as used to talk about others' future plans

Here is a question posed to ascertain what effect *will* can cause when used for others' future plans.

> 35. Is it possible to use 'will' when talking of others' future plans? (deriving from Tsuruta, Rossiter and Coulton 1998: 78)
> We should usually not use 'will' when talking about others' future actions because it will sound as if we are in a position to decide their actions for them. We can use 'will' in this way only on such occasions as when we are representing an organization or we are talking about someone who is not able to decide their own actions, like children. Do you agree? Please answer the following question:
>
> One of your friends William is having a barbecue party this weekend and is checking who is coming to the barbecue. William asks you whether you happen to know if another friend of yours, Geoffrey is coming. Although he is not with you at present, he told you last night that he was going to the barbecue. Would you say 'Geoffrey will come to the party'?

See Graph 23 for details of the results.

	Japanese learners	English speakers
Yes	54	30
No	46	70

Graph 23: Results of Question 35 (*will* used to talk about other's future)

The results show a contrasting difference between Japanese learners and English speakers. Although some pointed out that the utterance was grammatically wrong, most comments from English speakers confirmed the introductory statement preceding the question. Most popular alternatives among native speakers were to use present progressive forms like *Geoffrey is coming to the party*. *He said he's coming.* and *I think he's coming.*

More importantly, quite a few informants also stated as follows: 'It sounds as if you are going to force Geoffrey to come to the party' (46 Am F 20s; sic.) and 'Sounds like you are going to force Geoffery to come to the party against his will' (149 Br M 20s; sic.). The utterance does not only make the speaker seem as though they are in a position to decide others' action, but as if the speaker forces Geoffrey to come to the party. This interpretation could not be known without examining informants' comments carefully, and again no Japanese learners mentioned this probably because they have never learned what effect the use of *will* would cause in this case (cf. 5.2.6). Although *will* is one of the basic auxiliary verbs in English, clearly, more detailed instruction should be given to Japanese learners. Ideally, an EFL dictionary must tell the user how to use *will* properly.

6.3.3 Case study 3: Whether one needs permission to help

Here is a question asked to find out whether it is polite to ask for permission to help others.

> 26. Is it polite to offer your help saying 'Would you like me to do …?'
> (deriving from Osugi 1982: 8; Vardaman and Morimoto 1999: 114)
> When you are not sure if others wish you to help them, you may politely offer your help by saying 'Would you like me to do …?' Do you agree? Please answer the following questions:

I: You are standing in front of your apartment building. One of your neighbors who lives in the same building and whom you do not know very well comes up the street towards you. The neighbor is carrying two small bags, one in each hand, and so might find it difficult to open the door to the building. Would you say 'Would you like me to open the door?'

See Graph 24 below for details of the results.

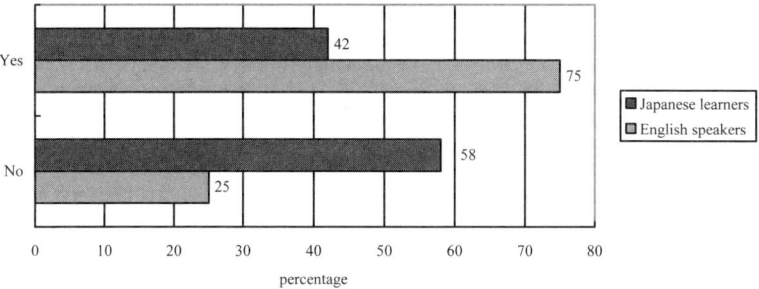

Graph 24: Results of Question 26. I (permission to help)

Nearly 60% of Japanese learners answered *No*, and many of them commented that asking the question sounded obtrusive. On the other hand, more than 70% of English speakers answered *Yes*. Although the results alone would be surprising enough, their comments revealed that there were larger differences between Japanese learners' and English speakers' attitudes to this situation.

Japanese society values more highly the intuiting of another's needs than asking directly (cf. Naotsuka 1980: 131–67). Moreover, in Japanese culture there is a social distinction between *uchi* (inside one's territory) and *soto* (outside of one's territory) (cf. Naotsuka 1998: 108), which divides people between *uchi*, those who are within one's own group, and *soto*, outsiders or strangers. This distinction sometimes makes it hard for Japanese people to interfere with others; even though one notices that a stranger appears to look for help, it will be considered some invasion of their territory to offer help without being asked for. Unless strangers are old or in need of special help, accordingly, Japanese people often hesitate to contact and offer help.

In fact, while there was only one Japanese informant who answered that she would not ask the question because she found it more polite just to open the door, the vast majority of British and American informants who answered *No* stated that they would open the door without asking the question. As for English speakers, moreover, even some of those who answered *Yes* made comments that they found it more polite to open the door without asking. Nevertheless, this does not mean that in a similar situation English speakers usually open the door without asking. Many English speakers admitted that asking the question was perfectly polite: 'It is polite to ask someone if they need something rather than just assuming, especially if you don't know that person to well' (3 Am M 40s; sic.) and 'some people don't like to be helped so asking is a good idea' (160 Br F 20s; sic.). Some even set a condition: 'I might also just open the door without saying anything first. But in this Case, I would be offended if the person did not thank me' (7 Am F 40s; sic.). Clearly, it is not a default option to open the door without asking in this situation.

It is evident that Japanese learners' and English speakers' attitudes to this situation are more different than expected from the simple comparisons of the figures. Simply comparing the figures would not reveal the above facts, and it will be these facts that are necessary in dealing with pragmatic issues. At the same time, it should be pointed out that this kind of information usually has no place in a dictionary. I will return to this question in Part III.

6.3.4 Case study 4: Order of different person subjects

Here is a question directed to find out about subject order and its pragmatic effect.

> **49. Is it selfish to put 'I' first when listing subjects?** (deriving from Matsumoto and Matsumoto 1987: 190f; Wakiyama 1990: 171f)
> When listing several subjects in a sentence, we usually list them like 'You, he and I are close friends.' putting 'I' at the end. If the order is changed, it may affect the impression given and make us sound arrogant. The only exception is when you are to blame. In such cases, you should put 'I' first. Do you agree? Please answer the following questions:
>
> I: Kevin's team won a soccer game; the score is 3 to 0. The scorers are Kevin, Tom and Richard. After the game Kevin says to Tom, 'I, you and Richard did a good job.' Would you find this utterance appropriate?
>
> See Graph 25 below for details of the results.

CHAPTER VI ISSUES ARISING FROM ANALYSING THE DATA 97

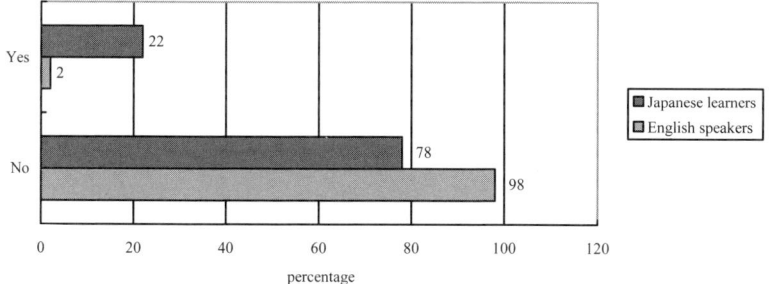

Graph 25: Results of Question 49. I (order of different person subjects)

Although Question 49 was originally designed to see whether it was preferred to put *I* first when one was to blame, I also included the above sub-question in order to investigate a case where one was to be praised. The vast majority of English speakers answered *No*.

While some of them simply commented that the order was wrong without providing any detailed reasons, 24 out of 98 who answered *No* explicitly stated that putting *I* first did bring about some pragmatic effects such as sounding arrogant or selfish. Apart from those 24 people, one informant pointed out that the order was both grammatically and pragmatically inappropriate; another made comments that this order sounded as though a person in very high rank like the Queen was talking.

It is generally considered that the order of different person subjects in English is more of a grammatical matter than a pragmatic issue; apart from non-academic books, Quirk, Greenbaum, Leech and Svartvik (1985: 155) and Swan (406) are the only two exceptions to the best of my knowledge. This may imply that the order would normally not interfere with one's pragmatic judgment. However, the above comments showed that the order of subjects was more than a grammatical problem.

There were also many who regarded this as a purely grammatical matter, and one of them stated as follows: 'Under correct English grammer should put "I" last but many young people today don't pay much attention to the rule' (134 Br M 20s; sic.). It is interesting that a young person in his twenties stated this, and it is equally interesting that 11, almost half of the 24 informants, were over 40. Obviously, this is not a matter of age but one's attitude to grammar or education.

In Japanese, there are no grammatical rules about the order of different person subjects, and this may be a reason why 22% of Japanese learners answered *Yes*. Yet there is a tendency to put a person first when the person is responsible for something, either good or bad, which often marks who is to be praised or to blame. Accordingly, if someone did something wrong, it would show a sense of responsibility to put him/herself first. Conversely, in the same situation, putting the person last may sound as though the person is trying to evade accepting the responsibility.

In this scenario where three people scored three goals, I expected that most Japanese informants would answer *No* because they would find it preferable to put Kevin last or not to mention himself. The results and their comments basically support my expectation. Interestingly, an informant who answered *Yes* stated that he found the above utterance appropriate because the order of the subjects agreed with the order of scorers; he thought that the order of the scorers in the scenario reflected the order of getting a goal, and that the first scorer Kevin should come first. In this case, it is clear that Japanese learners follow Japanese pragmatic conventions even when judging the appropriateness of an English sentence in a context.

As for alternatives which should be used instead, the English speakers' proposals can be summarised as follows: (1) usual order (e.g. *You, Richard and I*); (2) omission of *I*; (3) use of *we* instead of *I, you and Richard*; (4) putting *me* or *myself* instead of *I* after *you*, though there were also comments explicitly or implicitly against (1), (2) and (4). As there were only favourable comments towards (3), this item should be the best option for foreign learners: 'In a team sport, you would not single out the scorers as the only ones who did a good job. The scorers could not have scored without the help of the entire team. We have a saying: "There's no 'I' in TEAM"' (55 Am F 20s; sic.) and 'but a team game is a team game the whole team did well not just the three goal scorers' (117 Br M 30s; sic.).

Although the order of subjects has traditionally been considered as a purely linguistic matter, the results of this question have revealed that it could affect one's pragmatic judgement.

6.4 Summary and implications for Part III

In this chapter, I have discussed the findings of my research, paying particular attention to the nature of topics and comments from informants. As a result, some topics which at first appeared straightforward later turned out to be more nuanced or more complicated, which will show how important it is to keep a balance between qualitative and quantitative data for pragmatic studies.

While it is evident that pragmatics needs more thorough and careful treatment in the EFL context, there seem to have been few systematic approaches to it. For Part II, I therefore carried out a large-scale research questionnaire focusing on pragmatic behaviours of lexical items with particular reference to Japanese learners of English. As mentioned in 4.2.1.6, the methodology employed was not free from problems, but it was successful as a whole. My survey has revealed that, depending on the situation, some lexical items are very likely to cause serious pragmatic failures between Japanese learners of English and English speakers. As I could only discuss part of my research due to the limitation of space, I put the rest of the questions together with the summary of the results in Appendix II. They may show that there are more phrases which could cause serious pragmatic misunderstandings between Japanese learners and English speakers.

Although such examples of the latent pragmatic failures were relatively comfortably classified into the six groups according to their major causes, informants' comments have made me more aware that each of them involves quite complicated interactions between several factors, including topics being talked about and cultural preferences on how to express them. This means that even an apparently simple failure may not be so straightforwardly dealt with in the context of English teaching. This will be truer of lexicography because, as discussed in 3.3.6, dictionaries, especially EFL dictionaries, are very often considered purely prescriptive, even representing authority of language over language users. Once a particular way of pragmatic behaviour in a particular context is described in a dictionary, it might assume authority even to such an extent that it is considered the only proper pragmatic behaviour in a context specified.

With the findings of this study in mind, I will discuss how pragmatics can be properly incorporated into lexicography in Part III, and at least the following problems arising from Part II should be addressed:

(1) Context specific versus ubiquitous behaviours of headwords

As mentioned above, dictionaries' authoritativeness can sometimes make users believe that anything written in a dictionary applies to any context without exception. This is far from the case in pragmatics. Some compromise may need to be reached between lexicography and pragmatics, and learners may also need to change their views on dictionaries.

(2) Paralinguistic features

Depending on the situation, confrontational words like *liar*, if used to refer to a person, might even start a fight between the interactants. Yet, the impact could be lessened with appropriate tone and intonation (cf. 5.2.1 and 6.1 for details). Facial expressions could also make the undesirable effect less serious. From a lexicographic viewpoint, illustrations and special codes may help dictionaries to capture such paralinguistic features more properly, but such means will make the text less readable and occupy more printed space, which any dictionary tries so hard to save.

(3) Innovation to convey pragmatic information

It will follow from (2) above that dictionaries need to go beyond traditional ways of presenting conventional information categories such as semantic meaning and or grammar in order to accommodate pragmatics more satisfactorily. Although it is also a major question whether paralanguage should or could be incorporated into lexicography, there is no doubt but that they play important roles concerning pragmatics. They might even make the literal meaning of a phrase into the complete opposite. Any dictionary which ignores this aspect of language will be simply misleading in terms of pragmatics. Moreover, some types of pragmatic information have been traditionally and exclusively dealt with in the form of labels, but I do not think that they are effective enough always. So long as pragmatic meaning can vary from context to context, simply providing labels cannot be a good way to deal with pragmatics.

(4) Location of pragmatic information not restricted to a particular lexical items

The present study has also revealed that while my research focused on pragmatic behaviours of lexical items, some important information on pragmatics cannot be comfortably accommodated in an entry for a particular single headword (e.g. the necessity to ask permission to help others discussed in 6.3.3). This is a serious problem, for not only dictionaries but any reference work which cannot let its users easily locate what they are looking for in its contents may be a failure.

(5) Needs of users with particular linguistic backgrounds

Although this study focused on pragmatic failures between Japanese learners and English speakers, monolingual dictionaries have a very broad readership. Serving users with various linguistic backgrounds can be an advantage of monolingual dictionaries, but it can also be their disadvantage because they obviously cannot satisfy specific needs of all users with various backgrounds (see 4.1.1 for details). Concerning pragmatics, this would become particularly serious since, as seen in 5.1, pragmatic transfer is one of the most frequent causes of pragmatic failures. It would be almost impossible for dictionaries to cope with pragmatics satisfactorily without considering specific needs of users with particular linguistic and cultural backgrounds. Not only bilingual but monolingual dictionaries should pay more attention to this problem.

(6) Pedagogical care

Headwords such as those related to taboo in either a target or a source language community need to be treated carefully. For example, as was seen in 5.2.7, Japanese learners may need to know English speakers' attitudes to the drinking of alcohol and drunkenness, but it is questionable or at least uncertain how much discussion such words as *drunk* should deserve in a learners' dictionary. Lexicographers must decide the appropriate amount of information for their dictionaries from a pedagogical viewpoint.

Lastly, I should like to point out that even though this research deals with a wide range of lexical items, I must admit that this is far from enough to cover an EFL dictionary's headwords. Therefore I hope that more investigation of this kind will be carried out in the future. At the same time, I am confident that even the limited findings of my own investigation, as presented in Part II, have something to contribute as one of the first and largest (to date) surveys of this kind.

PART III

Compatibility Between Pragmatics and Lexicography with Particular Reference to Politeness

Abstract (Part III)

The book started with a literature review and theoretical explorations of pragmatic information for EFL dictionaries (Part I). Based on the findings from Part I, I approached pragmatics focusing on lexical items and their pragmatic behaviours in context, seeking to collect empirical data for describing pragmatics in EFL and lexicographical contexts (Part II). However, this is not enough; it is also important to raise the fundamental question of whether pragmatics and lexicography can ever be made compatible at all, since they have different goals, approaches and methods in dealing with different types of meaning. Their units of descriptions are also different; while dictionaries are in principle concerned with words and phrases, pragmatics deals with utterances and discourses. More importantly, dictionaries are basically concerned with decontextualised meanings, and are expected to set out relatively fixed meanings, perhaps prescriptively, in the form of a dictionary definition or explanation. In contrast, descriptive pragmatics treats meaning in context. In Part III, I will be working towards my conclusion that they are indeed compatible, with particular emphasis on politeness.

CHAPTER VII
Politeness and EFL Lexicography

Although Part I successfully established a definition of pragmatic information for EFL lexicography, it does not suffice. Further exploration is needed to pose the simple but fundamental question of whether pragmatics can actually be dealt with lexicographically; that is, in terms of words and phrases, because pragmatics and dictionaries have different goals, approaches, and methods in dealing with different types of meaning (see 3.1.1; 3.1.2; 3.1.3; 3.3.6). Their units of descriptions are also different; while dictionaries are in principle concerned with words and phrases, pragmatics deals with utterances and discourses. More importantly, dictionaries are basically concerned with decontextualised meanings, and are expected to set out relatively fixed meanings, perhaps prescriptively, in the form of a dictionary definition or explanation.[1] In contrast, descriptive pragmatics treats meaning in context and meanings which are situationally bound. An interesting point here is that, although the majority of current EFL dictionaries now claim to have a descriptive basis by utilising observations of corpus data, they are still expected to fulfil a prescriptive purpose by providing normative models for their target users as part of their pedagogical function.

I therefore decided to tackle the question of compatibility between pragmatics and lexicography in this final part, focusing on politeness, one of the most important and difficult phenomena to treat lexically as well as lexicographically. The six issues raised in the conclusion of Part II are all pertinent to the issue of the compatibility of pragmatics and lexicography, and they will be discussed thoroughly in the relevant chapters.

As stated, it is questionable whether pragmatics and lexicography are compatible or not, and their reluctance to tackle politeness may at least partly be attributed to the issue of compatibility between pragmatics and lexicography. Politeness is, for example, more concerned with one's motivation behind one's use of language than with language itself (cf. 8.3.4). Moreover, while dictionaries mainly deal with decontextualised meanings or uses of lexical items, there are no words, phrases or sentences which are inherently polite irrespective of context (cf. 4.1.3). In short, politeness is one of the most difficult of pragmatic phenomena for dictionaries to deal with. At the same time, one cannot deny the fact that politeness is a very important aspect of linguistic communication.

As part of my exploration of pragmatic information in EFL dictionaries, in Chapter VIII, I will explore the compatibility of pragmatics and lexicography mainly from a theoretical viewpoint. More detailed discussions of politeness and lexicography will be provided in Chapter IX, where I will consider the scope of pragmatic information in dictionaries. Using findings from these chapters, I will examine the latest editions of leading EFL dictionaries (as of 2010) for their treatment of pragmatic information: methodology in Chapter X; monolingual dictionaries in Chapter XI; and bilingual dictionaries in Chapter XII. On the basis of findings and discussions in these chapters, together with those from the previous chapters, I will offer five recommendations in Chapter XIII towards the better treatment of politeness in lexicography. In Chapter XIV, as the conclusion of the book, I will return to the question of the compatibility of pragmatics and lexicography.

7.1 Pragmatic failures revisited in terms of politeness

I will begin to consider politeness with my personal experience as a foreign learner of English. When I was an MA student at a university in the UK, my then-supervisor once said to me, 'I don't suppose you could come to the airport with me tomorrow to welcome a visiting professor from Japan'. My reaction at that time was that this sounded rather haughty, as it seemed to me that if he actually did not suppose that I could come with him, he should not suggest it. I later came across the phrase in a dictionary:

> You can say 'I don't suppose' as a way of introducing a polite request to someone when it might cause them some difficulty or inconvenience; used in spoken English (COBUILD2)

What I failed to interpret correctly was the supervisor's intention of politely making a request, and this was not only caused by my ignorance of the expression but by differences between Japanese and British cultures. In Japan, one usually makes a request explicitly in order to acknowledge the fact that they depend on others (see 9.2.2.2; 9.2.3.2), and so I felt at that time that I was expected to come voluntarily without being requested explicitly and properly. As pointed out in 3.3.5, pragmatic failures are often difficult to recognise, and, in the worst case, can even result in one's misunderstanding of the personalities of their interlocutors.

This experience may have grave implications for pedagogical lexicography and language teaching. I naively took the phrase simply as no more than a sum of the individual constituents: *I*, *do*, *not* and *suppose*, though I had several years teaching experience by that time, and always advised my students to consult a dictionary whenever they were not sure about a sense or usage of an expression they came across. From my experience, I believed I was well aware that unfamiliar senses or uses of familiar expressions and idiomatic expressions consisting of seemingly known words were particularly problematic. Still, I did not fully realise this until I came across the phrase in the dictionary. Also relevant is why I did not even try to consult a dictionary. Although one normally does not use a dictionary to decode language in real time as in the above case, one can at least consult one's dictionaries later (cf. 12.5). In short, I did not expect at all a dictionary to help me with a pragmatic function which the use of an expression can perform. There may be room for improvement in dictionaries' treatment of pragmatics, but learners must change their attitudes to dictionaries too.

I should also point out another important aspect of pragmatic failures. Probably because negative transfer is often cited as a main cause for pragmatic failures (cf. Thomas 1983: 102; Takahashi 2003: 316; see also 5.1), these studies seem to have been exclusively concerned with learners' pragmatically inappropriate uses of English and native speakers' misinterpretation of those uses, as if pragmatic failures could only occur when learners utter something pragmatically irrelevant to native speakers. However, the above experience suggests that even though a native speaker uses English in a pragmatically appropriate manner, learners may interpret it wrongly due to their insufficient command of English. That is to say, misunderstandings resulting from pragmatic failures could happen either on the side of native speakers or on the side of learners, which clearly shows that foreign learners need sufficient instruction in pragmatics both in terms of encoding and decoding. In the context of lexicography, this suggests that dictionaries designed for both encoding and decoding purposes must have sufficient information on pragmatics (cf. 10.1.1).

While one of the main aims of pragmatic information in a dictionary would be to help learners avoid serious pragmatic failures, these failures vary in terms of their degree of seriousness, from a simple and less harmful one of making a speaker sound odd, to a rather more important one of making them seem rude. Generally, failures concerning politeness are more serious than other kinds. This may explain why EFL dictionaries today usually provide some information on politeness, at least with such related labels as *offensive*, *rude* and even *(im)polite(ness)*.

In Part III, I will explore the ways in which dictionaries deal with pragmatic information and politeness in particular, looking at difficulties from the perspectives of both the dictionary user and dictionary compiler, with Japanese learners in mind. It is true that politeness could be realised through almost anything, and that dictionaries cannot fully capture it. These problems do not only apply to politeness but more or less apply to pragmatics in general. Whichever aspect of pragmatics lexicographers may seek to include in their dictionaries, they should restrict its scope; at the same time, dictionaries must go beyond their traditional units of descriptions, words and phrases.

7.2 The state of the art—how politeness is treated in EFL dictionaries

In order to have a clearer idea of how pragmatic information is presented in dictionaries, I examined nine leading EFL dictionaries (cf. 10.1.1): CALD3, COBUILD6, LDOCE5, MED2, *Oxford Advanced Learner's Dictionary of Current English*, 8th ed. (2010 hereafter OALD8), GEJD4, LEJD2, WEJD2, and *Longman English-Japanese Dictionary* (2007 hereafter LOEJD) for the following two uses of *kind*: *How kind of you to do* and *It's kind of you to do* (cf. 7.3). Surprisingly, no monolingual dictionaries explain that the two patterns are used to fulfil a function; that is, to express one's gratitude, though all of them contain the latter as an illustrative example, *It's kind of you to do*. On the other hand, all the English-Japanese dictionaries for learners explain that this pattern can be used to thank others.[2] The Japanese lexicographers must have identified this phrase as one of those expressions which Japanese learners may have some difficulty with.

Considering the fact that pragmatics reflects various parameters such as learners' native language and cultural backgrounds (cf. 3.3.4; 3.3.5; 5.2.5), it is clear that monolingual dictionaries cannot fully deal with every such parameter, as they need to serve a wider readership. More precisely, monolingual learners' dictionaries are aimed at a global market, and so cannot either cover specific crosslinguistic/crosscultural points, or anticipate what problems there might be with respect to all the languages, or all the likely languages, of their target users. At the same time, I need to point out that bilingual dictionaries, at least English-Japanese and Japanese-English for Japanese learners, are usually compiled by Japanese lexicographers. So long as pragmatics is deeply concerned with subtle nuances in the language use, there is a possibility that Japanese lexicographers may not be able to note every important pragmatic phenomenon when analysing pragmatic behaviours of words and phrases. Apart from differences between monolingual and bilingual dictionaries, there are other problems when incorporating pragmatics into lexicography. They will be discussed in the next sections.

7.3 Units of description and foci

Although recent EFL dictionaries occasionally contain longer examples of conversation where even several turns are taken by the interlocutors, dictionaries have traditionally been concerned with individual words and phrases. In contrast, pragmatics deals with larger units such as utterances.

Below is an example of how politeness is linguistically realised through the act of request:

> Do you mind if I ask you a big favour? I know you don't like lending your car, but I was wondering if I could possibly borrow it just for an hour or so on Tuesday afternoon, if you're not using it then. I need to take my mother to the hospital and it's difficult getting there by bus. (Spencer-Oatey 2008: 22)

If the requester only tells the requestee their intention, it would suffice to say, 'I was wondering if I could possibly borrow it just for an hour or so on Tuesday afternoon'. Or even this should be a bit too wordy for that purpose; it would be simpler to say, 'Lend me your car for an hour on Tuesday afternoon'. However, this is more likely to be declined; at least this is far less likely to be accepted willingly, as people usually expect a request to be made in a proper way depending on the situation, especially considering the size of imposition on the requestee. In fact, almost every part of the whole utterance is jointly used to lessen the size of the imposition: to borrow a car (cf. 9.3.1). Clearly, any dictionary cannot fully describe the mechanism of politeness working here because it needs to deal with the whole utterance.

From a lexicographic perspective, it is necessary to find out how much and/or what portion of politeness strategies can be taken from the utterance and restored in a dictionary; more precisely, lexicographers need to identify what part of the utterance, or how and what formulae and/or tokens should be included in a dictionary. Candidates should be sufficiently fixed or conventionally established expressions, and they should not be too dependent on particular contexts and/or co-texts for correct interpretation.

If it is possible to identify decontextualised basic forms common to a set of utterances fulfilling a particular function, then they may be targets for dictionary descriptions. Nattinger and DeCarrico in this respect pointed out that examples of forms of request and offer, given by Searle (1975: 75), such as 'could you pass the salt?' and 'will you quit making that awful racket?' could ultimately be parsed into one basic form: 'Modal + you + VP?' (1992: 50–2). Unfortunately, their model is too broad to specify forms of request or offer, because within this framework we cannot even distinguish properly request and offer from simple questions with a modal verb. It is interesting to note that they argued that this basic form could allow for versions with optional phrases like 'Modal + you (mind/kindly/be willing to) + VP?' and that the parenthesised options consisted of politeness markers. Then it would seem reasonable to assume that it is these politeness markers, rather than the basic form, that help make the form suitable for requesting and offering. Considering the fact that, in addition to politeness markers, almost any word could potentially deliver politeness depending on the context, lexicographers must also explore other lexical items. Moon points out that there are uses of words which seem striking in terms of their pragmatic behaviours (1987: 100–1) and provides several examples from the Bank of English, e.g. 'How kind of you to remember' and 'It's kind of you, Monty, but no thanks', whose sentence patterns are usually used to express thanking (cf. 7.2).

It is important to note here that such phrases as *I don't suppose* as well as the above two sentence patterns do not really have meaning in its strict sense; they have a function instead. This implies that learners need to know the matching of a linguistic form and its function whose use can fulfil, preferably together with information on what options are available in order to achieve that particular function; and when, where and how they are typically used.

Just as linguistic politeness cannot deal with whether a speaker is genuinely polite or not (see 9.1), dictionaries could never describe fully how politeness could be realised in people's lives. It is important to note that politeness could be regarded as a kind or part of speech act because it is an act of showing one's concerns for others, and that there are many formulae used to perform a particular act (im)politely. What lexicographers need to present in their dictionaries instead are those tokens, markers and/or formulae which are usually or at least often used to perform certain functions (im)politely, together with what their typical contexts of use are.

Lexicographers must carefully select words, phrases and other units of descriptions which conventionally deliver politeness. Although this is not an easy task, it could be taken as negligence if lexicographers, or indeed anyone in the field of language teaching, stop trying to help learners, and instead hope that they could acquire politeness strategies by themselves. As Wilkins points out, to know how to report something in a foreign language is different from knowing how to do something (1976: 41). The point is that foreign learners cannot always predict correctly such a function, or what act their interlocutor does, and this should be especially true of polite or deferential expressions because they are often rather indirect in form. Good dictionaries should offer better help to the user in this respect. Although preferred forms of showing politeness in a context may vary across languages, lexicographers can refer to findings from comparative and interlanguage pragmatics. Speech act analysis in particular can help lexicographers identify conventional forms used to perform specific actions (Yule 1996: 58; 3.3.1). Phraseology can also afford some insight into politeness in the lexicographic context. Cowie argues that native-like proficiency in a language depends on a stock of prefabs, or prefabricated units (1998: 1), and it would not be very difficult to imagine that there are many prefabs which could be used to deliver politeness in particular contexts (cf. De Cock: 2002). They should be able to help lexicographers capture those portions of politeness which can be squeezed out of the use of lexical items.

7.4 Contextual information

As Moon points out (1987: 100–1), it is very difficult for dictionaries to deal with existentially varying meaning systematically. This is especially true of politeness. Words, phrases and utterances could be taken as polite or not, depending on the context. Although there are expressions almost always occurring in FTAs (Moon 1998b: 263), Moon also points out '[t]he relationship between person and the selection of FEIs [Fixed Expressions and Idioms] is delicate and cannot be separated from other interactional patterns and processes' (1998b: 264). It is clear that lexicographers need to pay sufficient attention to the context of an utterance in order to capture politeness satisfactorily.

Although dictionaries cannot fully accommodate contextual information, it is possible to capture its most fixed part as part of dictionary descriptions. Various speech acts and discourse strategies are conventionalised by frequent use (Altenberg 1998: 121), and such language functions are realised in conventional ways according to the situation (Wilkins 1976: 63). These may mean that pragmatically established formulae have been/are frequently used in particular contexts, and so it should be possible to identify and include in a dictionary the matching or pair of a politeness formula and its typical context of use. Lexicographers should also identify such matchings of formulae with particular functions and contexts of use from a lexicographic viewpoint.

In the next chapter, I will start exploring the compatibility of pragmatics and lexicography mainly from a theoretical viewpoint.

Notes
1 In this book I will use the term *explanation* when referring to what is traditionally termed as *(dictionary) definition*, because one cannot really 'define' or delimit pragmatic usage formally; all they can do is 'explain' it (cf. Hanks 1987).
2 Even an unabridged English-Japanese dictionary, not designed for learners, lists the following

examples and uses a translation equivalent designating this is a phrase of thanking: 'It's very kind of [ˣ for] you to come. = You are very kind to come. = How kind of you to come!' (*Taishukan's Unabridged Genius English-Japanese Dictionary* (2006). The dictionary also provides a detailed usage note on these examples.

CHAPTER VIII
Compatibility Between Pragmatics and Lexicography

8.1 Overview

In this chapter, I will explore the compatibility between pragmatics and lexicography mainly from a theoretical viewpoint, and I will begin with the following citation from Bolinger (1985: 69):

> Lexicography is an unnatural occupation. It consists in tearing words from their mother context and setting them in rows—carrots and onions and beetroot and salsify next to one another—with roots shorn like those of celery to make them fit side by side, in an order determined not by nature but by some obscure Phoenician sailors who traded with Greeks in the long ago. Half of the lexicographer's labor is spent repairing this damage to an infinitude of natural connections that every word in any language contracts with every other word, in a complex neural web knit densely at the centre but ever more diffusely as it spreads outward. A bit of context, a synonym, a grammatical category, an etymology for remembrance's sake, and a cross-reference or two—these are the additives that accomplish the repair.

Lexicography, as Bolinger argues, is basically an attempt at restoring, in the form of dictionary explanations, true pictures of words as used in contexts, though their pictures will be distorted through the very process of restoring them. I must point out that this will be especially true of pragmatic information.

Dictionaries are in principle concerned with most fixed parts of language, decontextualised meaning of words and phrases. In contrast, pragmatics deals with how a speaker/writer uses a word, phrase, sentence, utterance and even discourse, seeking to realise their intent or achieve their goal depending on a particular context (see 2.4.3); similarly, how a hearer/reader interprets a

114 PART III COMPATIBILITY BETWEEN PRAGMATICS AND LEXICOGRAPHY

language use in a particular context is also a subject of pragmatics (cf. Imai 2009: iii). These discrepancies may suggest that pragmatics and lexicography are basically incompatible, yet dictionaries claim they contain a lot of information on pragmatics. In this chapter, I will therefore consider their (in)compatibilities mainly from a theoretical viewpoint, and I will begin with a brief examination of what dictionaries claim about their treatments of pragmatic information in 8.2. I will then consider their compatibility within the traditional framework of pragmatics in 8.3, functions of language in 8.4, and seek to find a way to reach some compromise between pragmatics and lexicography in 8.5.

8.2 Dictionaries' claims concerning their treatments of pragmatics

8.2.1 The coverage

Among the nine dictionaries I examined in 7.2, MED2 and COBUILD6 have independent sections or articles explaining their treatments of pragmatic information. To overview how they achieve compromise with pragmatics, I will look at their explanations of coverage in the articles.

It is clear that lexicography cannot properly deal with the whole range of pragmatics, and so it is inevitable that dictionaries restrict the scope of pragmatics in a way which can make them compatible (cf. 3.3.1; 3.3.4). In the articles, MED2 and COBUILD6 discuss the importance of pragmatics in the EFL context, and, as for the coverage, the following categories or functions of pragmatics are listed respectively:

> (1) Language functions or 'speech acts'; (2) Language and politeness; (3) Attitudes and feelings; (4) Vague language (MED2: LA10-1)[1]

> (1) APPROVAL; (2) DISAPPROVAL; (3) EMPHASIS; (4) FEELINGS; (5) FORMULAE; (6) POLITENESS; (7) VAGUENESS (COBUILD6: xiv-xv)

While MED2 lists only four categories, COBUILD6 lists as many as seven types of pragmatic information. This does not simply mean that COBUILD6 has the wider coverage, as the dictionary seems to classify the categories more finely than MED2. For example, MED2's Attitudes and feelings may well cover COBUILD6's APPROVAL, DISAPPROVAL and FEELINGS. It would also seem that EMPHASIS in COBUILD6 could be incorporated into another category in

COBUILD6, FORMULAE at least partially. According to COBUILD6, '[t]he label EMPHASIS indicates that you use the word or expression to show that you think something is particularly important or true, or to draw attention to it' (xv). If there are words or expressions, say, whose use indicates that the speaker thinks something is particularly important, they may be regarded as formulae to indicate the importance of something. Or this could even be entitled to APPROVAL in that it indicates the speaker's positive judgement.

MED2's Language functions or 'speech acts' should be equivalent to COBUILD6's FORMULAE in that both of these deal with expressions used for performing a particular action or act. MED2 and COBUILD6 respectively provide the following examples:

'In the end I said to him, "Look, forget it—I'm not paying you."'
'If you're just going to stand there and criticize, forget it'
'How much do I owe you?' 'Oh, forget it, it's nothing.' (MED2)

'Hi'; 'Thanks'; 'Congratulations!' (COBUILD6)

Incidentally, the terms MED2 and COBUILD6 use, 'speech act' and 'formulae', might be misleading. The former covers too wide a range of language use that lexicography cannot properly treat. So long as dictionaries can only deal with fixed expressions, COBUILD6's FORMULAE seems better at explaining what it refers to because dictionaries can only deal with fixed expressions like formulae. At the same time, it covers too limited a scope of speech act in that they usually do not allow variations. I will return to this issue in 8.3.3.

Other categories listed by MED2 and COBUILD6 also agree. They both have politeness, and MED2's Vague language and COBUILD6's VAGUENESS seem to cover the same portion of pragmatics such as indirectness. MED2 and COBUILD6 respectively provide such examples as follows: ...*or something (like that/of that sort)* and *presumably...* . Again, neither of the terms seems right when referring to those types of expression. Even if one uses vague language, people usually may attribute their use of vague expressions either to politeness or to other factors such as avoiding being too specific. A competent language user can usually interpret the speaker's intent correctly, and vague language may not be vague at all in such cases. Vague or indirect expressions will be more interesting in conjunction with politeness, and the relationship between indirect language use and politeness will be discussed in Chapter IX, esp. 9.3.4.

Comparing the articles in the two dictionaries, it appears that their coverage of pragmatic information is quite similar, dealing with speech acts, politeness, vague language, and expressing one's feelings and attitudes. There must be some reason that they chose these categories. Although both of the articles are written by the same author, Dr Joanna Channell, this may not be the only reason for their similar coverage. In the next section I will more closely look at the overlapping categories.

8.2.2 Overlapping categories

Looking at the articles in MED2 and COBUILD6 also shows how difficult it is to classify pragmatic phenomena. The relationship between vague language and politeness mentioned in the last section is one such example. The article in MED2 explains that the first two examples of *forget it* cited in the previous section are 'emotional and rather impolite' (LA10): 'In the end I said to him, "Look, forget it—I'm not paying you"', and 'If you're just going to stand there and criticize, forget it'. This means that these uses of *forget it* express one's emotion or feelings and also convey impoliteness. Although MED2 distinguishes *Attitudes and feelings* from *Language and politeness*, they clearly overlap here. Interestingly, these utterances also perform actions. The first example acts as preface to the speaker's declaration that they are not paying for something; the second, ordering someone to leave. This is also the case with the third example, 'Oh, forget it, it's nothing' uttered in response to someone asking, 'How much do I owe you?' It explains that this use is 'polite, and is often used for refusing an offer from someone else' (LA10). This use conveys politeness as well as performing the act of refusing. Again, politeness and speech acts overlap in this example. Although it will entirely depend on contexts whether a particular utterance sounds polite or not,[2] it should be noted here that all or at least the great majority of utterances can contain speech act and politeness elements (see 8.3.3 and 8.3.4 for details).

Apart from speech acts and politeness, pragmatic categories and functions often overlap, and I am not criticising their seeming inconsistencies in classifying the categories of pragmatic information, rather I am showing how difficult it is to classify them properly. Each of the pragmatic phenomena is often so closely connected with each other that they cannot always be separated from one another. This may suggest that exceedingly fine distinctions of pragmatic functions, especially in the lexicographic context, could be misleading. It will be clear that another approach to pragmatics is necessary which can satisfactorily deal with important pragmatic functions together in conjunction with lexicography.

8.2.3 Inconsistencies

MED2's treatment of the above three examples of *forget it* exemplifies another potential problem in dealing with pragmatics in lexicography. Although the article on pragmatics in MED2 mentions that the above examples are concerned with the speaker's feelings and politeness, explanations preceding the examples do not mention that explicitly. The last example cited, *'Oh, forget it, it's nothing'*, is presented as polite in the article, but the preceding explanation simply runs as follows: 'used for telling someone that they should not worry about something because it is not important'. Telling someone not to worry about something may usually sound polite. As Ikegami points out, moreover, distinction between different senses or uses of a word/phrase in a dictionary is basically fuzzy, and illustrative examples are aimed at incarnating typical uses of the sense or use (1996: 37). However, I still wonder whether ordinary learners would notice from the explanation and the example that the use is concerned with politeness because the explanation seems to lack sufficient contextual information, such as its typical context of use. The phrase will even sound rather ironic if it is uttered referring to something which the speaker seems to set a high value on; it will entirely depend on contexts whether a particular expression sounds polite or not. As far as pragmatics is concerned, therefore, lexicographers cannot be too careful about how and how much contextual information should be presented in dictionary explanations since they are basically expected to be prescriptive and authoritative (see 3.3.6).

It is also to be noted that while MED2 has a label, *impolite*, it does not assign the label to the first and second examples, which are presented as impolite: *In the end I said to him, 'Look, forget it—I'm not paying you'*, and *'If you're just going to stand there and criticize, forget it'*. As mentioned in 3.2.2, there is a possibility that their policies on pragmatic information were not sufficiently understood among every lexicographer involved.

Dictionaries' policies as explained in their outer matters are often not informative enough or even misleading (cf. Masuda et al. 2008: 82–4), and this is also the case with pragmatics. The article in COBUILD6 mentions that it adds special labels to entries with some pragmatic descriptions (xv), whilst that in MED2 does not. Yet, COBUILD6 is not the only dictionary using pragmatic labels. As mentioned in 7.1, most EFL dictionaries including MED2 use several labels designating entries containing pragmatic information, such as *OFFENSIVE* and *POLITE WORD/EXPRESSION* (CALD3). Moreover, only two out of the nine dictionaries explain their treatments of pragmatic information. I will continue to consider the compatibility between pragmatics and lexicography in the next section from the traditional framework of pragmatics.

8.3 Traditional topics in pragmatics and their compatibilities with lexicography

In the preceding sections, I have reviewed those categories of pragmatic information that the two articles in MED2 and COBUILD6 claim to contain. In this section, I will consider the compatibility of pragmatics and lexicography in terms of traditional topics in pragmatics. While every introductory book on pragmatics has slightly different coverage of topics reflecting the authors' attitudes and specialties, the following topics are usually covered as proper subjects of pragmatics (Koizumi: 2001; Leech 1983; Levinson: 1983; Mey: 2001; Thomas: 1995; Verschueren: 1999; Yule: 1996):[3]

deixis; implicature (conventional/conversational); speech acts; politeness

Both MED2 and COBUILD6 claim to cover speech acts and politeness, but neither of them mentions deixis or implicature as part of their pragmatic information, probably because they are totally context-dependent, except in the case of conventional implicature. In the following sections, I will consider each topic in turn, and will start with implicature in 8.3.1.

8.3.1 Implicature

Conventional implicatures, as its name suggests, are conventionalised and therefore relatively fixed (cf. Grice 1975/1991a: 26; 1975/1991b: 46). According to Thomas (1995: 57), *but* in 'She was cursed with a stammer, unmarried but far from stupid' could imply that a woman cursed with a stammer and unmarried is stupid. This unfavourable and mistaken representation of a woman is an example of conventional implicatures generated from *but* as used within this particular co-text, not context. While it is pragmatically interesting that *but* could generate such a problematic implicature, no dictionary can afford to describe fully this type of implicature since it can vary depending on the co-text and/or the context. From a pedagogical viewpoint, however, it would be of benefit for learners to become aware of the functions of *but*; the conjunction does not only mark a contrast between two propositions but also generates and thus signals some implicature. This may at least help learners to anticipate the existence of implicature when they come across *but* within a text or utterance, and then will prompt them to look for what can be implied. While this problematic implicature about a woman is pragmatic, the function of *but* should be more semantic because it is usually fixed irrespective of the context. I will therefore not deal with this type of function as part of pragmatics in this book.

As for conversational implicatures, it will be evident that any dictionary cannot treat them satisfactorily. Look at the following example from Levinson (1983: 97):

A: Can you tell me the time?
B: Well, the milkman has come.

In response to Speaker A asking Speaker B the time, B says something seemingly irrelevant, in fact attempting to provide A with as much information as possible and/or necessary; if the milkman always comes at a fixed time, and if both A and B know that, from B's remark that the milkman has already come, A must be able to deduce the approximate time or can at least conclude that it is already after the fixed time. Speaker A starts looking for what Speaker B implies assuming that B must follow CP (1975/1991a: 26–8), especially the maxim of relevance (*ibid.*). Speaker B may not reply to A's request in a more direct manner, probably because B is not sure exactly what time it is; that is to say, B follows the maxim of quality (*ibid.*). Similarly, B must provide as much information as necessary in order for A to infer what B implies correctly, following the maxim of quantity (*ibid.*). This is an example of conversational implicatures, and B's answer will make sense only if A does not simply take B's utterance at its face value but can correctly infer what B implies. This entirely depends on this particular context and on their shared knowledge that the milkman always comes at a fixed time. Clearly, it is very difficult for any dictionary to fully describe this type of implicature generated from B's utterance. This is undoubtedly the reason that neither MED2 nor COBUILD6 lists implicatures as part of their pragmatic information. Particular pieces of implicatures may become fixed expressions through frequent use (cf. 8.3.3), and, only in such cases, implicatures may become a target of dictionary descriptions. Otherwise, they are basically outside the purview of lexicography.

8.3.2 Deixis

Compared with conversational implicature, the proximal or distal distinction of deixis (Yule 1996: 9), i.e. near or away from the deictic centre, most typically the speaker in the case of person deixis, seems easier to describe in lexicography even though it is also context-dependent. OALD8 defines the determiners of *this* and *that* respectively as follows:[4]

used to refer to a particular person, thing or event that is close to you, especially compared with another (sense 1; *this*) used for referring to a person or thing that is not near the speaker or as near to the speaker as another (sense 1; *that*)

These two explanations seem fine at first glance, but they both fail to mention the shift of deictic centres. In actual communication, a speaker and a hearer normally take turns. The referents of *this* and *that* accordingly shift as a text, utterance or discourse develops, because they are referring to objects in the real world, not within the dictionary text. So long as it is not a lexical property of the two determiners, dictionaries do not have to mention that. Therefore, it is only natural that OALD8 does not mention the shift. However, this means that they cannot even help a learner to understand correctly the basic uses of one of the most basic words in English vocabulary. One may well wonder how far one should be away from the referent when using *that* rather than *this* referring to it. In this respect, one cannot too much emphasise the importance of context; that is to say, *this* and/or *that* can usually be understood correctly with ease if situated in the immediate context. Even though the shift of deictic centres is mentioned, the explanations must be complemented with sufficient contextual information. Otherwise, even the most basic deictic distinction of proximal/distal cannot be fully described in dictionary explanations. Considering the fact that dictionary explanations often lack sufficient context due to severe space limitations (cf. 3.3.3), it is likely to be very difficult for a dictionary to deal with deixis properly.

Deictic phenomena are also observable in the use of basic verbs like *come* and *go*. Tsuruta, Rossiter and Coulton (1988: 191–2) point out that the choice of verbs, *go* or *come*, is crucial in such pairs of the utterances as: 'I was wondering if you'd like to *go* to the cinema' and 'I was wondering if you'd like to *come* to the cinema' (Italics are mine). According to them, when either of the two utterances is used as an invitation, the choice of *come* could sound as though the inviter has already decided to go to the cinema irrespective of the invitee's response. They continue by saying that the use of *come* in this case could accordingly sound rather rude. Although they do not mention how the use of *come* will sound as such, the different effects could be produced by the different deictic centres that *come* and *go* have.

According to Levinson (1983: 83–4), *come* could be glossed as 'movement towards either the location of the speaker, or towards the location of the addressee, at CT [coding time]' (see also Verscheren 1999: 19 for the differences between *come* and *go* in terms of deixis). In the above invitation, neither of the interpretations seems logical because it is referring to a location where neither the inviter nor the invitee is present. What makes this invitation possible is another deictic phenomenon: deictic projection (cf. Yule 1996: 12–3); more precisely, the inviter can project themselves into another location, the cinema in this case, prior to being there. Thus, the invitation with *come* could read as follows: the inviter has decided to go to the cinema irrespective of the invitee's response, and then projects themselves into the cinema prior to going there. If the invitee notices this, the invitee might find the invitation rude, as that may sound as though the inviter would not really want or need the invitee's attendance. Levinson also argues that when one moves towards, say, the house of another person, *I'm coming* to the person's house may be preferred to *I'm going* to the house in terms of politeness, because the use of *come* shifts the deictic centre from the speaker to the person addressed, and therefore can show respect for the person (1983: 83). Again, it would be very difficult for any dictionary to fully describe this type of deictic phenomena. This is probably why neither MED2 nor COBUILD6 lists deixis as part of their pragmatic information.

8.3.3 Speech acts

Austin, usually credited as the first to propose the concept of speech acts, initially sought to distinguish constatives from performatives, but finally concluded that all utterances contained both constative and performative elements (Austin 1962: 147; see also Verschueren 1999: 22; Cruse 2006: 34). I entirely support this view; so long as one uses a language to realise their intent in a particular context (cf. 2.4.3), it should be naturally regarded as performing an act to realise that particular intent. Even a cry of pain could perform an act of expressing one's pain. As Grice argues, the meaning of an utterance is closely connected with the intent of a speaker (1969/1991: 87–8). In this sense, the description of pragmatic meanings can be equated with that of the intent of language users; that is to say, the act they seek to perform. I would argue that it is most promising or at least easiest for lexicographers to approach pragmatics through speech act.

Below is an example of speech acts given in Leech and Thomas (1987/1991: F12): 'Is that your car?' According to them, this utterance could mean various ideas depending on the context, such as (1) 'Your car is blocking my gateway—move it!'; (2) 'What a fantastic car—I didn't know you were so rich!'; (3) 'What a dreadful car—I wouldn't be seen dead in it!' Each of these interpretations is an example of conversational implicature, and Leech and Thomas continue by saying that '[t]he very same words can be used to complain, to express admiration, or to express disapproval' (*ibid.*). It is important to note that each interpretation can be identified as performing an act like complaining, and that this is also the case with almost any utterance. It is true that lexicography cannot fully describe the whole range of pragmatics, which necessitates lexicographers' restricting the scope of pragmatics in a way compatible with lexicography, but it is possible to restrict the scope through a group of fixed phrases with which speech acts can be realised.

Altenberg argues that there is a group of relatively fixed speech acts and discourse strategies conventionalised by frequent use (1998: 121), and their functions are also conventionalised according to the situation (Wilkins 1976: 63). This may mean that there are pragmatically established expressions which have been/are frequently used in particular contexts, which suggests that lexicographers should focus on the matching or pair of such an expression and its typical context of use. Let us look at again the example of conversational implicatures discussed in 8.3.1:

A: Can you tell me the time?
B: Well, the milkman has come.

Speaker B says something seemingly irrelevant in response to Speaker A's asking B the time, but B in fact seeks to provide A with as much information as possible. This is an example of conversational implicatures, and through the implicature B's utterance also performs the act of replying or answering. It is to be noted that Speaker A's utterance does not literally mean what is said. On the surface, Speaker A asks whether Speaker B is able to tell A what time it is, but A actually requests B to tell A the time. That request is realised through using a frequently used pattern of request, *Can you...?*

While speech acts cover too wide a range of pragmatic phenomena which any dictionary cannot properly treat (see 8.2.1), formulae deal with too limited a scope of speech acts (*ibid.*). It will be necessary to complement formulae with other fixed expressions with particular pragmatic functions. My suggestion is to complement formulae with another type of fixed expression such as question patterns like *Can you...?* above, which are similar in nature to formulae in that they are also used to perform a particular speech act in a particular context. As they are incomplete in a way and could relatively freely combine with other phrases, they can allow variations and perform various acts depending on the context. *Can you ...?*, for example, is often used to make a polite request and can be used with a range of relevant verbs. I will term them speech act markers. If formulae and speech act markers can be identified as pragmatically meaningful, they deserve dictionary descriptions, and I believe they should be major targets of pragmatic information in EFL lexicography together with politeness markers (see 8.3.4 below for my use of the term, *politeness marker*).

One of the major causes of pragmatic failures is a learner's inability to guess correctly which force the use of a particular linguistic expression can perform (Miller 1974: 15). If dictionaries improve their treatments of speech acts by focusing on formulae and speech act markers, even the restricted portion of speech acts must be of great benefit to foreign learners of English.

8.3.4 Politeness

Just like a speech act element is observable in almost any utterance-level language use, any utterance should in some way be related with politeness. In fact, every example I have cited so far could be analysed in terms of politeness including such as deictic differences as between the two basic verbs, *come* and *go* (see 8.3.2). This is at least partly because any human behaviour could be assessed in terms of politeness. While a mere smile can convey politeness, one's way of looking at others can even express one's hostility towards them. So long as one lives in a society, performing an act either verbally or nonverbally may naturally necessitate one's considering others' feelings and/or social conventions in terms of politeness.

Although linguistic politeness is not concerned with whether one is genuinely polite or not (cf. 9.1), it still covers too wide a range of linguistic phenomena which lexicography cannot properly treat. In 7.3, I have pointed out that politeness could be incorporated into a kind of speech act, because it is also an act of showing one's concern for others with the use of language. In this respect, I need to add that showing one's concern for others is usually performed through another act. Compared with an order, for example, a polite request can be glossed as an act of asking someone to do a particular thing while showing the requester's concern for the requestee. In a sense, it would be reasonable to regard politeness as another level of language in that it is more concerned with people's motivation behind their language use than with linguistic forms.

When performing an act with the use of language, there are usually various alternatives with varying degrees of politeness. Using a language in a community is a succession of choices from possible alternatives. For example, all the following utterances can be used to ask someone to answer the phone but they are different in the degree of politeness, or rather forcibility: 'Answer the phone', 'I want you to answer the phone', 'Will you answer the phone?', 'Can you answer the phone?', 'Would you mind answering the phone?' and 'Could you possibly answer the phone?' (Inoue 2001: 130). One must choose the appropriate expression depending on the context. I believe this is where lexicography can offer help to learners. At the same time, there may be no lexical item that is always polite or impolite irrespective of context or co-text, as mentioned at the outset of Chapter VII. It entirely depends on, say, how, when, where and to whom we use a particular expression. Dictionaries' roles should include showing learners what options are available in a context.

Now, it should be reasonable to deal with politeness as an umbrella function of speech acts, and there is a lexical category of items closely connected with politeness but not strictly performing a particular act independently. I term these items politeness markers, and they include enhancers like *please* and speech softeners such as *possibly*. They are used to make an utterance sound politer depending on the situation. The use of the former would make a request sound politer by showing additional politeness or respect to the requestee. Although the use of *please* is not always identified as particularly polite, one's failure to use it in a particular situation might sound rude (see 9.3). As for the latter, it would make a request sound politer, making less forceful a request which is inherently face and/or rapport threatening. Incidentally, both enhancers and softeners are concerned with a relatively wide range of acts differently. Dictionaries may need to specify how they can be used whenever necessary; e.g. while *by any chance* is basically used for questions and requests, *perhaps* is for requests and statements. In this book, I will pay particular attention to these politeness markers together with speech act markers and formulae.

8.4 Approaches to language function

Any utterance-level language use could be regarded as an act, and it necessarily contains some politeness element. It is important to note that (a) part(s) of an utterance often fulfil(s) (an)other function(s) simultaneously such as emphasis. In 8.2.1, I have pointed out that some of the expressions labelled as EMPHASIS in COBUILD6 could be part of FORMULAE, but emphasising something is not always an act itself but often a function accompanying another act. For instance, one can apologise by emphasising how sorry they are, and this applies to other functions such as expressing one's attitudes and feelings. The following example of conventional implicature discussed in 8.3.1 is one such example: 'She was cursed with a stammer, unmarried but far from stupid'. The speaker of the utterance used *but* rather than *and*, and, either consciously or unconsciously, conveyed their attitudes towards an unmarried woman with a stammer.[5]

Although quite a few scholars have sought to classify functions of language, it is extremely difficult to identify and classify functions of language properly. Searle (1969) was one of the first to tackle the classification of functions of language, or speech acts. He tried to establish rules for distinguishing speech acts, but his formal approach has several problems. For example, his rules or conditions are too complex and vague (Thomas 1995: 102); at the same time, they cannot even exclude totally anomalous examples (*ibid.*). Yule (1996) presented a simpler speech act classification: *declarations, representatives, expressive, directives* and *commissives*, but what is missing here is such common functions of language as greeting.

In 8.4.1 and 8.4.2, I will look at two lexical approaches to the classification of words and/or phrases in terms of their pragmatic functions: lexical phrases by Nattinger and DeCarrico (1992) and text functions by Moon (1998b).

8.4.1 Lexical phrases

Nattinger and DeCarrico are well known for their work on phraseology, and they also classified functions of lexical phrases. However, their classification is arguably too detailed to apply to lexicography, presenting three major categories with 43 subcategories. More importantly, their methods of classifying the phrases seem rather inconsistent, even including sentence patterns which dictionaries may not be able to treat properly, such as *once upon a time... and they lived happily ever after* (1992: 40), whilst ignoring such basic functions as emphasising.

Nattinger and DeCarrico argued that only when a phrase or chunk had a pragmatic function, it was classified as a lexical phrase (1992: 36). According to them, *it's raining cats and dogs* was an idiom, not a lexical phrase, because it had no particular function. However, it seems to me that it does carry out a function of emphasising the fact that it is raining hard. Moreover, I often cannot determine what is meant by their phrases like *the (other) thing X is Y* (64) and *after X then/the next is Y* (*ibid.*) due to their failure to specify the referents of the letters *X* and *Y*. Furthermore, they are employed to represent several different things rather inconsistently. For example, *X* may stand for a (pro)noun in *do you know/remember X?* (61), but probably a verb in *may I X?* (62). They even refer to more than one thing in a phrase: a prepositional complement or a noun in, *I've got to run/go/do X* (61).

The most problematic category may be *Fluency device* (73). Nattinger and DeCarrico explain that it is a bigger chunk than a similar phrase with a similar function; e.g. *It seems to me that*, and gives the speaker 'more time to plan for the next routine, and thus promotes fluency' (*ibid.*). As they also pointed out, examples listed in this group had other functions, and it is not a problem at all. However, other functions look far more important pragmatically. For example, *by and large* (64) may be more often used to indicate that the speaker is not really sure about something rather than to make their speech sound more fluent. *As a matter of fact* (*ibid.*) may be almost exclusively used to add more details or introduce something which contrasts with what was said just now, and arguably these functions are more important than making the speaker sound more fluent.

Given the problems with these models, it will be very difficult to apply the framework of lexical phrases to the dictionary items I am investigating; a simpler framework may be better, such as that proposed by Moon (1998b) for categorizing the text functions of fixed expressions, from a broadly lexicographical perspective. I will look at these in the next section.

8.4.2 Text functions

Moon identifies five categories of functions which English fixed expressions can fulfil: informational, evaluative, situational, modalizing and organizational (1998b: 215ff.). The only category which I believe is outside of pragmatic information is *informational* because it is more concerned with the content of semantic propositions and with conveying information rather than pragmatic functions. Conveying information by saying something is also an act, but it should not be given priority in conjunction with EFL lexicography because it is not pragmatically marked (see 2.3.3).

Below is the framework of text functions, excluding informational (see Appendix III for the examples):

I) Evaluative: expressing speaker's evaluation and attitude, such as negative and positive.
II) Situational: relating to extralinguistic content; or responding to situation such as greetings/thanking/apologies.
III) Modalizing:
    a) epistemic: representing the speaker/writer's commitment to the truth value.
    b) deontic.
    c) conative/volitive.
IV) Organizational
    a) controlling the continuity of text or propositional content.
    b) organising and signalling discourse structure.

Situational is concerned with utterance-level language use, and is equivalent to formulae and speech act markers. The other three categories cover functions accompanying a speech act. I believe that lexicographers treat them as part of dictionary descriptions whenever necessary because they play crucial roles in realising politeness (see 11.4.1).

Although Moon used these text function to classify fixed expressions in English, it is possible, as Moon states (1998b: 219), to apply them to language in general. Halliday (1978: 116ff.) also presented a similar framework, text components, but Moon's text functions are more suitable in the following three respects: (1) they are concerned with both decoding and encoding aspects of language; (2) they can monitor the immediate effects of the use of an expression within its co-text; and (3) they are originally designed to classify functions of lexical phrases from a lexicographical perspective (cf. Moon 1998b: 217–9). In the next section, I will therefore consider how pragmatics can be incorporated into lexicography using the framework of core functions, politeness and text functions.

8.5 Reaching a compromise between pragmatics and lexicography

Dictionaries need to restrict the scope of pragmatics in order to deal with it satisfactorily, and the most promising way is to approach pragmatics focusing on speech acts from a functional viewpoint (8.3.3).

Although it is very difficult to treat functions of language properly, Moon's text functions are comprehensive and easy to apply to lexicography. Considering the fact that they are not originally designed for pragmatic functions, however, it seems necessary to amend them in order to make them more suitable for the description of pragmatic functions. I will thus make the following two changes in the framework: (1) Moon treats each of the functions as one with the equal status, but situational should be given priority over the other four functions in the investigation described here because it is directly connected with speech acts, designating what particular act the use of a lexical item performs. I term this particular act as a core function, and the other functions as accompanying functions; and (2) as mentioned in 8.3.4, politeness is concerned with every utterance, and fulfils important interpersonal functions. I will thus include it as the umbrella function of speech acts, or the core function.

Below is the framework within which pragmatic aspects of an utterance should be dealt with in terms of EFL lexicography:

Core function (speech acts)
Politeness (roughly, polite/neutral/impolite)
Accompanying functions (evaluative; modalizing, organaizational)

Any utterance-level language use can be identified as the realisation of core function, interpersonal function of politeness, and (an)other accompanying function(s), as shown above.[6] Through focusing on these constituents of an utterance, it should be possible to describe pragmatics in the context of EFL lexicography satisfactorily. In other words, if these three constituents can be identified as fixed expressions, such as a speech act marker of *Can you...?*, they deserve dictionary descriptions. Within this framework *Can you...?*, for instance, can be analysed as follows:

Core function: request
Politeness: usually polite depending on the situation (see 9.3.7; 14.2.2.1)
Accompanying functions: epistemic

These features of *Can you...?* will naturally need to be fleshed out and rephrased as a dictionary description. It is clear that politeness is not something which can be marked simply as polite without referring to a particular context (cf. 13.1.3). It is also not really certain what 'polite' means; it could refer to various distinctive properties depending on the situation (see 11.1.1; 12.1.1). Moreover, epistemic is too compact and technical for learners, and one should not forget the fact that there are many deferential expressions which are considered to be polite because they are indirect through the accompanying function of epistemic.

Towards the end of this book, I will seek to determine whether pragmatics and lexicography can ever be made compatible at all. Even restricting the scope properly, however, pragmatic information is still concerned with a very wide range of linguistic phenomena. I will therefore focus on one of the most important, at the same time most difficult, aspects of pragmatics, politeness, in the subsequent chapters. Before I discuss how politeness is dealt with in lexicography, I will explore politeness and its relation to lexicography mainly from the theoretical perspective in the next chapter.

Notes

1 When it is necessary to specify where a particular piece of information in the dictionaries is cited from, I will show which part of a particular entry contains that information or provide the page number in book format, depending on what is cited.
2 The adjective polite can refer to various distinct phenomena, and I will return to this problem in 11.1.1.
3 Leech is the only scholar who does not discuss deixis in his book.
4 As for *this*, only one explanation is given, covering both the determiner and the pronoun.
5 A speech act usually reflects the speaker's intent correctly, except when the illocutionary force and the perlocutionary effect do not agree, as in pragmatic failures. In contrast, accompanying functions may not necessarily be intentional. In the case of the example of *but*, the speaker may or may not intentionally reveal their attitudes towards the type of a woman.
6 As mentioned at the outset of Chapter VII, there are no (im)polite lexical items irrespective of context. Therefore, 'polite' in this classification is for reference purpose only.

CHAPTER IX

Politeness

9.1 Linguistic politeness

In this chapter, I will explore major theories on politeness and their potential impacts on lexicography. The findings will form the basis of my examinations of the EFL dictionaries and recommendations towards better treatment of politeness in lexicography in the later chapters.

The term *politeness* can refer to either its folk notion related with being 'polite' or the technical counterpart of how people show their concern for others through using language. This may be a reason that studies of politeness are sometimes wrongly identified with those concerned with '[p]oliteness as a real-world goal' (Thomas 1995: 149); that is to say, such studies as concerned with whether a person is genuinely polite or not. They are outside the purview of linguistics, and in the subsequent sections I will use the term *politeness* to refer solely to linguistic politeness. As the term can still cover quite a wide range of phenomena, in this chapter I will delimit principally such phenomena as deference, register and absolute politeness, which are sometimes confused with politeness (cf Thomas 1995: 149ff.).[1] It is not my intention to offer an explanation of the term that can satisfactorily and comprehensively cover every (potential) topic and approach in the domain of linguistic politeness. What I seek to do instead is to identify important concepts and phenomena in politeness and restrict their scope in terms of EFL lexicography. I will also seek to establish how findings from theoretical studies can enlighten lexicographers.

In the next section I will begin with an overview of theories on politeness where several important aspects and approaches to politeness will be discussed. After examining problems with the most influential theory within politeness studies, face theory, in 9.2.2, I will review politeness from another viewpoint in 9.2.3. More practical discussions about the application of politeness studies to lexicography will be provided in 9.3.

9.2 Theories of politeness

9.2.1 Overview

Lakoff was the first to draw the attention of linguists to politeness; at least it is safe to say that she was among the first to conduct linguistic research on politeness. One of the Lakoff's great contributions is her attempt at complementing CP with her rules of politeness (1973: 296). People usually, or at least often, do not follow CP in its strict sense. They often refrain from providing sufficient amount of information, violating the maxim of quantity. Similarly, they do not always say things directly and clearly, neglecting the maxim of manner (Grice 1975/1991a: 28). According to Lakoff, people's failure to follow CP can be explained through such rules of politeness as: 'Make A feel good' (1973: 298). For instance, if one supposes that their utterance might hurt the hearer's feelings, they may naturally reduce the amount of information by omitting (a) potentially offensive part(s) of their utterance, and may deliver the rest of the utterance less clearly.

Lakoff was not the only scholar who attempted to complement CP in terms of politeness. As mentioned in Part I, Leech also proposed PP: 'Minimize (other things being equal) the expression of impolite beliefs' (1983: 81) together with its positive version: 'Maximize (other things being equal) the expression of polite beliefs' (*ibid.*) which motivate people's way of speaking in terms of politeness; to borrow his term, PP 'rescues' CP (1983: 80). CP did not only attract the attention of linguists to such pragmatic phenomena as implicatures, but compelled interest in politeness. This is at least partly because politeness is an indispensable part of people's lives; politeness is so closely connected with people's lives and their language uses that they cannot consider politeness and their language uses separately.

PP is comprised of its sub-maxims, and they include the following:

(I) TACT MAXIM (in impositives and commissives)
(a) Minimize cost to *other* [(b) Maximize benefit to *other*]
(II) GENEROSITY MAXIM (in impositives and commissives)
(a) Minimize benefit to *self* [(b) Maximize cost to *self*]
(III) APPROVATION MAXIM (in expressives and assertives)
(a) Minimize dispraise of *other* [(b) Maximise praise of *other*]
(IV) MODESTY MAXIM (in expressives and assertives)
(a) Minimize praise of *self* [(b) Maximize dispraise of *self*]
(V) AGREEMENT MAXIM (in assertives)
(a) Minimize disagreement between *self* and *other*
[(b) Maximize agreement between *self* and *other*]

(VI) SYMPATHY MAXIM (in assertives)
(a) Minimize antipathy between *self* and *other*
[(b) Maximize sympathy between *self* and *other*]

(Leech 1983: 132)

Each of these maxims seems to focus on an important aspect of communication; for instance, the Agreement Maxim shares with the so-called Communication Accommodation Theory the central insight that it is necessary or desirable for one to reduce linguistic or communicative differences between themselves and their interlocutors in order to be polite or to make their communication more effective. Nevertheless, it should be noted here that the maxims are not sufficiently comprehensive. Leech therefore had to invent other maxims to complement them, such as the 'Pollyanna Principle' (1983: 147), which can be explained as 'postulating that participants in a conversation will prefer pleasant topics of conversation to unpleasant ones' (Leech 1983: 147). Thomas points out that the principle is least generalisable of Leech's maxims (1995: 166–7), and it is in this respect where PP was most severely criticised. One of the most serious problems with PP is that there are no motivated ways to restrict the number of the maxims, and they are almost open-ended (Thomas 1995; Brown and Levinson 1987; Fraser 1990).

Thomas also criticises the use of the term 'maxim' as it can be misleading. She maintains that the maxims should be best viewed as social-psychological constraints rather than maxims, so that problems with Leech's approach could be overcome (1995: 167–8). Perhaps in view of this, in the updated version of Leech's model, he did not use the term 'maxims', but replaced it with 'constraints' in order to avoid making them sound as moral obligations (2005: 12).[2]

Despite all the criticisms, PP should prove helpful in comparing politeness strategies across cultures. They could be used at least as indices or scales when comparing different politeness norms in different societies (Thomas 1995: 167). When comparing politeness strategies in Japanese and English, for example, the Modesty Maxim and the Agreement Maxim can help explain why Japanese speakers and English speakers react quite differently to compliments:

> It appears that in Japanese society, and more particularly among Japanese women... the Modesty Maxim is more powerful than it is as a rule in English-speaking societies, where it would be customarily more polite to accept a compliment 'graciously' (*eg* by thanking the speaker for it) rather than to go on denying it. Here English-speakers would be inclined to find some compromise between violating the Modesty Maxim and violating the Agreement Maxim.
>
> (Leech 1983: 137)

The different reactions to compliments in Japanese and British societies can also be regarded as an example of different communication styles or ethoses (see 9.3.4).

When incorporating politeness into EFL lexicography, it is essential to consider whether rules and/or principles of politeness in English are consistent with those in the learners' native languages. If English principles differ markedly from those of the learners, it will greatly affect the learners' acquisition of appropriate politeness competencies. The question of whether politeness principles are universal or culture-specific has huge implications for EFL lexicography, especially with its practice of aiming a single dictionary at an international, multilingual, and multicultural readership in the case of monolingual dictionaries.

It should be noted that face theory, the most influential and most widely cited theory of politeness proposed by Brown and Levinson, claims that their theory is universally valid. Brown and Levinson place the notion of face at the centre of their theory. According to them, face 'consists of two specific kinds of desires ("face-wants") attributed by interactants to one another: the desire to be unimpeded in one's actions (negative face), and the desire (in some respects) to be approved of (positive face)' (1987: 13). Politeness in their view consists of linguistic actions to lessen or avoid threatening an interactant's face, whether speaker's face or hearer's. They argue that politeness as captured in this way should basically be valid across cultures, which may imply that politeness can be treated in language teaching fairly easily without great difficulty.

Concerning the universality of politeness, there are roughly two major camps: relativists and universalists. The former regards politeness conventions as varying across cultures (Ide 2006; Spencer-Oatey 2000; 2008); the latter claims that there should be the universal property of politeness (Brown and Levinson 1987; Leech 2005). While Brown and Levinson claim that there are some universal politeness features across cultures, politeness strategies as well as ideas of what people regard as 'polite' may considerably differ depending on the culture. Even though their claim is correct at a deeper level, at least surface-level language uses, such as how one can make a polite request in a language, may naturally vary across societies. It is important to note that it is these surface-level language uses that language teaching is mainly concerned with, because they will have more direct or immediate impacts. For example, it will be more important to tell a learner of English that a speech act marker, *Can you...?*, can be used when making a polite request in English, rather than telling them something such that in English negative politeness strategies are often preferred when making a request. I must add here that Brown and Levinson also admit that there are cultural elaborations or varieties (1987: 13) and that their claim of universality is more or less concerned with the core notions of face. Spencer-Oatey, who advocates another analytical framework of politeness, *rapport management*, also admits that face itself is a universal phenomenon (2008: 14), but it is clear that face cannot always account for politeness phenomena properly. This will be more thoroughly discussed in 9.2.2.2, and I will now move on to other important views of politeness.

CP's inability to account for people's motivations to flout and/or breach CP led to such models as Lakoff's and Leech's rules and principles of politeness. Brown and Levinson attribute polite language uses to people's concern for their own or their interlocutor's face. What they have in common is that politeness is an intentional action to lessen conflicts between the interactants. In contrast, Fraser offers another view of politeness: conversational contract (1990: 232ff.). According to him, participants of a conversation have conversational rights and obligations which need to be maintained and fulfilled; in this framework, being polite can be regarded as remaining within the contract. They claim that this is a reason why people usually do not notice polite language use when they are polite, namely when they remain within the contract. They argue that only when people are not polite, their interactants notice their impolite language uses.

While the majority of researchers seems to regard politeness as dynamic phenomena, Fraser seems to consider it something static. However, it is important to note that he also points out that people can be impolite; that is to say, people may either intentionally or unintentionally go outside of the contract. There are criticisms of Fraser's conversational contract view of politeness that his explanations are too sketchy and difficult to judge how it operates in practice (e.g. Thomas 1995: 177). Arguably, however, he is not actually attempting to provide an analytical framework for describing politeness; all he is doing is to say that being polite is the norm. Taken this way, this view of politeness can easily coexist with other theories of politeness.

Ide also offers a static view of politeness; she distinguishes between two aspects of Japanese politeness, hatarakikake and wakimae. The former deals with politeness as intentional acts intended to achieve a particular goal, and the latter, a static or fixed aspect of politeness (see also 9.2.2.2 and 9.3.7). From a lexicographic perspective, it would not really matter whether politeness strategies are fixed or not.

Politeness is a vast field of research, and I will not discuss its further ramifications now. In the next sections, I will more closely look at Brown and Levinson's face theory and their problems, since this is the most influential and widely cited analytical framework of politeness. As for the dynamic and static aspects of politeness, I will return to this issue in 9.3.7.

9.2.2 Brown and Levinson's face theory

9.2.2.1 Face theory

Central to the politeness model proposed by Brown and Levinson is the notion of face. In this model, certain speech acts are inherently face threatening, and in such cases politeness is realised in the form of linguistic strategies for avoiding or lessening the threat to the face. Since there are two aspects of face, negative and positive, their politeness strategies can accordingly be classified into two: one appealing to positive politeness (positive politeness strategy) and the other directed to negative politeness (negative politeness strategy). As there can in fact be another option that one avoids doing an FTA at all, politeness strategies as identified in their model can be roughly classified into the following options (Brown and Levinson 1987: 68–70):

I: Avoidance of FTA
II: Performance of FTA
    A: Off record (e.g. indirect hint)
    B: On record
        i: Without redress
        ii: With redress
            (a): Positive politeness
            (b): Negative politeness

Strategies I through IIBi may be self-explanatory. The distinction between I and II simply depends on whether one performs an FTA or not. IIA and IIB are distinguished by the manners in which one carries out an FTA; that is, whether they do it openly or not. Similarly, the distinction between IIBi and IIBii depends on whether or not one performs an FTA in a way which can mitigate the impact of the FTA. IIBii(a) and b refer to options to employ either positive or negative politeness strategies.

Positive and negative politeness strategies are, as their names suggest, strategies for showing one's concern for others, appealing to the addressee's positive or negative face respectively. Brown and Levinson list three major positive politeness mechanisms: (1) 'Claim common ground', (2) 'Convey that S and H are cooperators' and (3) 'Fulfil H's want for some X', and they are further classified into fifteen more concrete strategies. For example, there is a sub-strategy of (1): 'Notice, attend to H (his interests, wants, needs, goods)', and below is an example:

Goodness, you cut your hair! (...) By the way, I came to borrow some flour. (1987: 103)

The requester is mitigating the imposition of their request by commenting on the requestee's recent haircut, in that the very fact that the requester makes comments on the requestee's haircut can be taken as an act to 'notice and attend to H', thus appealing to the addressee's positive face.

As for negative politeness strategy, the following five mechanisms are listed: (1) 'Be direct', (2) 'Don't presume/assume', (3) 'Don't coerce H', (4) 'Communicate S's want to not impinge on H' and (5) 'Redress other wants of H's'. They are further divided into ten strategies such as the use of questions and/or hedges deriving from (2). (1) may not seem part of negative politeness strategies at first sight, and it appears to contradict (3). Brown and Levinson explained this as follows, admitting that they are at least to some extent contradicting each other: '...there is an element in informal politeness that sometimes directs one to minimize the imposition by coming to the point, avoiding the further imposition of prolixity and obscurity' (1987: 130). All these strategies are directed to the hearer's negative face, and are supposed to realise politeness.

According to Brown and Levinson, negative politeness strategy is 'the most elaborate and the most conventionalized set of linguistic strategies for FTA redress' (130) '[i]n our [their] culture' (*ibid.*). Although they did not explicitly mention which culture they are referring to, it will not be any of those in Eastern countries. More importantly, while Brown and Levinson claim that there is some universal property in politeness, this statement will suggest that in other cultures and/or societies other politeness strategies are more highly valued, and that there should be different politeness principles and/or rules. As discussed in 9.2.1, their claim about universality may be more concerned with the concept of face, but their theory has a problem in this respect.

Apart from the above problem, their theory has a critical flaw when considering politeness in Asian languages. One reason that Brown and Levinson's theory has become one of the most influential in the study of politeness is that face, central to their model, can quite effectively account for diverse politeness phenomena. At the same time, it should be pointed out that some politeness phenomena are not necessarily related to face, especially when considering languages in the East, including Japanese. In the next section, I will consider problems with face theory from the perspective of Asian researchers.

9.2.2.2 Limitations of face theory

There are particular criticisms of Brown and Levinson's face theory, especially from Asian researchers (cf. Ohashi 2013: 12). One of the most serious problems with the theory seems to come from their failure to take Asian cultures into account. While the notion of individuals and their rights has been considered to be an essential basis for Western cultures, it is not always regarded as such in Asia, especially Japan (Nakane 1967; Doi 1971; Sugiyama Lebra 1976). From a viewpoint of Japanese speakers, Matsumoto explains a problem of face theory as follows:

> What is most alien to Japanese culture in the notion of face, as attributed to the model person, is the concept of negative face wants as the desire to be unimpeded in one's action. Postulating as one of the two aspects of the Model Person's 'face', the desire to be unimpeded, presupposes that the basic unit of society is the individual. With such an assumption, however, it is almost impossible to understand behaviour in the Japanese culture. A Japanese generally must understand where s/he stands in relation to other members of the group or society, and must acknowledge his/her dependence on the others. Acknowledgement and maintenance of the relative position of others, rather than preservation of an individual's proper territory, governs all social interaction. (1988: 405)

As a Japanese learner of English, I completely support this view, and it is shared by many speakers of other languages who are familiar with Japanese society. Sakamoto, an American who lived in Japan for many years, also points out the same characteristics of Japanese culture, including the way in which Japanese tend to state explicitly that they depend on others (Sakamoto and Sakamoto 2004: 20–1).

It would be far from the truth, however, to claim that there are no concerns about autonomy and impositions in the East. The point is that these are not considered as face concerns (Gu 1990: 241–2). English expressions addressing to negative face, such as those used in indirect speech acts, must be reanalysed from a Japanese viewpoint, if they are to be taught to Japanese learners.

Thomas criticises Brown and Levinson's description of FTAs as they imply that FTAs only affect either S's or H's face, while in fact both of their face can be lost simultaneously depending on the situation. Thomas gives an example of apology; when apologising, S's face can be lost in an obvious way, and the very act can also embarrass H and threaten H's face (1995: 176).

Ide (2006: 72–3) points out two further defects in face theory. First, while Brown and Levinson list honorific as the fifth strategy of negative politeness, the ranking or the relative value does not agree with its relative importance in the Japanese language. Ide argues the honorific was one of the primary methods of realising politeness in the Japanese language and that it should be more highly valued. Second, Japanese speakers do not always use honorific intentionally as Brown and Levinson claim. She continues by saying that the use and choice of honorific expressions is prescribed by the society to such an extent that they are used almost automatically.

Ide's first point may not be as important as the second, since Brown and Levinson do not explicitly state that the order of the strategies listed reflects their relative values. In addition, the use of honorific belongs to another linguistic phenomenon, deference, rather than to politeness. Thomas distinguishes deference from politeness in the following two respects. First, while deference is the opposite of familiarity, referring to the respect people show to others by virtue of their higher status, and/or greater age and so on, politeness is a more general matter of showing consideration to others. Second, deference is part of the grammar of languages such as Japanese and Korean, so people do not usually have a real choice in terms of deference (1995: 150–3). Thomas argues 'it is only when there is a choice, or when a speaker attempts to bring about change by challenging the current norms, that the use of deferent or non-deferent forms becomes of interest to the pragmaticist' (1995: 152). In 2.4.3, I have also restricted the scope of pragmatics to those linguistic phenomena where people can intentionally realise their purpose through using language. Deference, including honorific, may be basically outside the purview of pragmatics. In this sense, Ide's wakimae, the static aspect of Japanese politeness (see 9.3.7), is a distinct phenomenon (see also Eelen 2001: 14 for discussions of conversational contract view of politeness and its relation with deference). Yet, this does not mean that Ide's criticisms are irrelevant to politeness. Even though deference and politeness are distinct from each other, it is also a fact that they are closely connected. I will return to this point in 9.3.7.

Apart from Japanese scholars, the notion of face is pointed out to be problematic when considering politeness in the Asian context. Gu, for instance, argues that face should be seen in terms of societal norms rather than in terms of psychological wants (1990: 242). Taking into account the serious problems with face theory, one may well query whether there are indeed some universal properties of politeness, as Brown and Levinson claimed.

Leech, even admitting that there were striking differences between politeness strategies across cultures, denies the existence of an Eastern and Western divide in politeness. He also admits that it is premature to talk of universals of politeness, but claims that there are very widespread scales of value in human societies, such as vertical distance between self and other person(s), and 'self-territory' and 'other-territory' (2005: 21–8). According to Leech, seeming differences in politeness across cultures are the reflections of differences in peoples' interpretations of such values. He then raises four questions, by way of concluding his discussions, which need to be answered in order to determine whether there is an Eastern and Western divide in politeness:

(i) Does vertical distance have a higher weighting in assessing politeness?
(ii) Is vertical distance also qualitatively different: more identified with status, role and seniority, rather than with individual power alone?
(iii) Do in-group/out-group distinctions have a clearer and more important role than in the west...?
(iv) Are socially defined rights and obligations associated more with group identity than with individual relationships?

(Leech 2005: 27)

Although Leech basically argues against the existence of the Western and Eastern divide of politeness theory, the very fact that he does not clearly deny its existence seems to leave unsolved the original question of whether there is an Eastern and Western divide.

As I cannot either support or deny his view at this stage, in this book I will consider politeness using another analytical framework in which both Eastern and Western politeness conventions can be dealt with satisfactorily: rapport management, proposed by Spencer-Oatey (2000). She has developed the social view of politeness, and has proposed a concept of the sociality rights and obligations to supplement face with. In the next section, I will review this framework of rapport management.

9.2.3 Spencer-Oatey's rapport management

9.2.3.1 Rapport management

Rapport management can be paraphrased as 'the management of harmony-disharmony among people' (Spencer-Oatey 2000: 13) and is comprised of the managements of face, sociality rights and obligations, and interactional goals. In this framework, face is concerned with personal/social value, such as people's sense of worth, dignity, honour, reputation and competence, and sociality rights are concerned with personal/social expectancies, including people's concerns over fairness, consideration and social inclusion. Both face and sociality rights have the following two interrelated aspects respectively:

Face
Quality face is equivalent to Brown and Levinson's positive face, and can be defined as one's fundamental desire for others to value oneself positively in terms of one's personal qualities, such as competence and appearance.

Identity face is one's fundamental desire for others, like close friends, to acknowledge and uphold one's social identities.

Sociality Rights
Equity rights are equivalent to Brown and Levinson's negative face, and can be defined as one's basic presumption that people should show personal consideration to one so that one should be treated fairly and should not be exploited.

Association rights are one's basic presumption that one is allowed to associate with others as one wishes.

According to Spencer-Oatey (2000: 15), this framework is different from Brown and Levinson's face theory in the following two respects. First, this makes it possible to consider social aspects of politeness. Second, this distinguishes the issues of personal and social value (face) from those of personal and social entitlements (sociality rights). People's evaluations of the above four components may differ across cultures, but this framework enables one to analyse politeness strategies in the East as well as the West.

As for the final component of the rapport management, interactional goals, its notion is quite straightforward. One usually has a specific goal while interacting with others; when they cooperate in achieving the goal, it is regarded as a state where the interactional goal is managed well. Conversely, if one of the interactants does not behave as the other(s) wish(es), they cannot interact in harmony; thus they cannot manage the rapport satisfactorily. In the next section I will consider how this framework can actually work with the example of *I don't suppose* discussed in 7.1.

9.2.3.2 *I don't suppose* revisited in terms of rapport management

In 7.1, I discussed an example of a misunderstanding on my part, mainly caused by my ignorance of the phrase *I don't suppose*. The phrase was used in an utterance addressed to me: 'I don't suppose you could come to the airport with me tomorrow to welcome a visiting professor from Japan'. If my requestor had used a more direct expression, I would have easily understood his intent and more willingly accepted his request. However, I did not only take his utterance as implicit but also rather inappropriate because, as pointed out in 9.2.2.2, Japanese tend to express their dependence on others verbally. As a Japanese, I therefore felt that I should deserve a more proper way of request. The point is that I did not feel that my face had been lost at all because this was not concerned with my face but my equity right (cf. 9.2.3.1).

The phrase *I don't suppose* should sound polite in English because this is addressed to the requester's negative face; more precisely, with this phrase the requester can explicitly pretend to declare that they do not suppose that the requestee will accept their request. As a result, this may leave some room for the requestee to decline the request, and could show respect for the requestee's negative face. Unfortunately, it would not work that way in the Japanese society because, as discussed in 9.2.2.2, the notion of negative politeness is alien to Asian cultures.[3] This exemplifies a problem with face theory by showing that politeness strategies vary across cultures, and has serious implications for lexicography. I will return to this problem in 9.3.5.

9.3. Theories on politeness and their implications for EFL lexicography

While knowledge about formulae, speech act markers and politeness markers can help learners perform an act using language either politely or impolitely as they wish, they should also learn such things as when to perform a particular act and/or what act to be performed in a particular context. Certain kinds of behaviours are usually taken for granted, and so they may pass unperceived when they are performed. Nevertheless, they can cause an undesirable effect when they are not performed (Goffman 1963: 7). Examples would include the exchange of casual greetings. Similarly, there are also types of behaviours which may pass unperceived when they are not performed but produce a positive effect when they are performed. Fraser's conversational contract view of politeness, and Thomas's criterion for distinguishing sociolinguistics from pragmatics, seem to share an important fact with this concept (cf. 2.3.3); one usually expects others to behave in a particular manner in a particular context, and it is when the expectations are upset that the unexpected actions cause either positive or negative communicative effects. The notion of free and non-free goods (Goffman 1967) also illustrates that there are some agreed norms in a society.

It is important to note that expected norms vary across cultures. As seen above, different politeness principles work in Japan and English-speaking countries. Even within English-speaking cultures there may be varieties, and clearly they affect the way people communicate. Moreover, because the notion of negative politeness is not relevant in Japanese culture, English expressions addressing to negative politeness should be reanalysed and presented in a dictionary from a different viewpoint. I thus propose introducing to lexicography a more comprehensive approach such as rapport management, so that neglected aspects of politeness can become part of dictionary descriptions. Of course, this does not mean that technical terminologies from the theoretical framework should be used in dictionary texts; it should be used as the theoretical basis on which politeness can be analysed and described.

It is also important how lexicographers present necessary pieces of information to learners. Learners may sometimes need theoretical explanations to some extent; even though a dictionary explains that a particular lexical phrase can be used to perform an act politely, a learner may not fully appreciate its importance and so may not acquire that knowledge properly if there is a wide gap in politeness strategies between their first language and English. *I don't suppose*, discussed in 7.1 and 9.2.3.2, is a case in point. Theoretical explanations will naturally increase the amount of information in an entry, and may make dictionary texts harder to read, but they are indispensable and should not be avoided simply because it can make an entry too informative (see 13.2).

Before moving on to the examination of the nine dictionaries in Chapters XI and XII, in the following sections I will consider how theories on politeness can enlighten lexicographers.

9.3.1 Identifying formulae, speech act markers and politeness markers as embedded in utterances

The framework of rapport management makes it possible to consider differences between Japanese and English politeness strategies, principles and conventions. However, I should now like to return to the argument that such differences in strategies across cultures basically have no place in lexicography. That is, while politeness theories are mainly concerned with principles or strategies according to which people realise politeness in their societies, lexicography deals with lexical items. As discussed in 7.3, the units of analysis they each deal with are also different: utterances for pragmatics; and words and phrases for lexicography. The principal tasks for lexicographers would then include identifying and extracting, from utterance-level language uses, formulae, speech act markers and politeness markers used to realise politeness as well as deciding how they should be dealt with in their dictionaries (cf. 11.1.5).

Below is an example, discussed in 7.3, of how politeness is linguistically realised through the act of request:

> Do you mind if I ask you a big favour? I know you don't like lending your car, but I was wondering if I could possibly borrow it just for an hour or so on Tuesday afternoon, if you're not using it then. I need to take my mother to the hospital and it's difficult getting there by bus.
> (Spencer-Oatey 2008: 22)

The requester chose the above rather lengthy utterance, and almost every part of this whole utterance jointly contributes to realise the requester's intent; to borrow a car. The process in which linguistic politeness is realised is dynamic and complex; it involves the whole context, and changes as an utterance develops. Spencer-Oatey introduces three parameters when analysing the above type of polite speech acts: (1) main semantic components, (2) (in)directness and (3) boosters and hedges. In terms of (1), she identifies the following five main semantic components (numbering is mine):

1a. Do you mind if I ask you a big favour?
    (mitigating supportive move [preparator])
1b. I know you don't like lending your car,
    (mitigating supportive move [disarmer])
1c. but I was wondering if I could possibly borrow it just for an hour or so on Tuesday afternoon, (head act)
1d. if you're not using it then.
    (mitigating supportive move [imposition downgrader])
1e. I need to take my mother to the hospital and it's difficult getting there by bus.
    (mitigating supportive move [grounder])

(Spencer-Oatey 2008: 22)

Spencer-Oatey's head act (1c) is equivalent to my core function, polite request in this case. Other parts can be regarded as accompanying functions if this whole utterance is regarded as performing one act of polite request (cf. 8.4.2; 8.5).

Only when a particular phrase is usually or at least often used to perform a particular act at a particular context, its pragmatic behaviour and the contextual information may deserve a dictionary description. In this sense, none of the five candidates, 1a through 1e, really meet the condition. At the same time it seems possible to parse them into more fixed pieces. What enables 1c to be the core function of the above utterance should be the use of the phrase, *I wonder*. So long as this phrase is often used to carry out functions such as making an indirect and thus polite request, this can be regarded as a speech act marker, equivalent to Moon's category of situational idioms and fixed expressions. As Moon discusses (1998b: 270), speech acts realised through situational are simplest in nature; they are easiest for lexicographers to recognise, or identify.

Apart from *I wonder*, the other four components, 1a, 1b, 1d and 1e, look more context-dependent and less conventionalised, as they could only perform the above functions in this particular utterance. As mentioned above, this does not mean that they are outside the scope of lexicography. It should also be noted that each constituent contributes to the whole utterance by performing a distinct act. 1e, for instance, provides the reason that the requester needs to borrow a car, thus mitigating the impact of the request as a supportive move, or grounder for 1c. While a longer utterance can be identified as performing a speech act as a whole, its components can also perform different acts individually. This means that any of such components can be a core function depending on the context. Take 1e for example; it can perform an act of requesting, or asking for a lift in such context as when the speaker knows a person in front of them is going to the hospital by car. Every communication is composed of (an) act(s), and a lexicographer's tasks should include identifying and extracting act(s) from utterances, formulae, speech act markers and politeness markers.

It is to be noted that Spencer-Oatey's three parameters for analysing polite speech acts are not mutually exclusive: they are fairly closely related and overlap to some extent, and so lexicographers can combine them in order to identify important lexical items and their usage. As seen above, the first parameter, 'main semantic components', provides a framework within which the mechanism of politeness realisation in the whole utterance can be analysed. The second and the third parameters, '(in)directness' and 'boosters and hedges', can offer support for this framework. For example, 1c in its entirety cannot be a headword for any dictionary, but lexicographers can extract the opening 'I was wondering' as a candidate for a dictionary description with the help of (2) and (3). According to (2), one of the conventionally indirect strategies for making a request is the use of an utterance containing reference to preparatory conditions (e.g. ability and willingness) as conventionalised in a language (Blum-Kulka et al. 1989: 18). This is how the canonical form *I wonder* can introduce an indirect request. In terms of (3), moreover, this canonical form can also be identified as a lexical and phrasal downgrader (subjectiviser) for making a request, and can be further modified with syntactic downgrader (tense and aspect).

The average learner may not need to know all these technical details of the use of 'I was wondering' as a way of making an indirect and thus polite request. From a viewpoint of pedagogical lexicography, however, it is important to note the following three points: (I) *I wonder* is a speech act marker to introduce a polite request; (II) it can be made indirect further in the past tense; (III) it can further be made indirect in the progressive aspect (Osugi 1982: 9–10; Matsumoto and Matsumoto 1987: 22; Tsuruta, Rossiter and Coulton 1988: 114; Wakiyama 1990: 42). Lexicographers can use (I) when deciding which headwords/phrases to include in their dictionary, and (II) and (III) may be bases of a usage note on this phrase, which will in turn influence the selection of an example sentence.

9.3.2 Speech events and activity types

It is most promising for lexicographers to approach politeness through speech acts focusing on formulae, speech act markers and politeness markers (cf. 8.5).

There are two major reasons. First, politeness could be regarded as a type of act; more precisely, the act of showing one's concern for others through using language. Second, there are types of speech acts which can be captured through relatively fixed linguistic forms; namely, speech act markers. Performing an act through language should necessitate an utterance being recognised as such by the hearer. Even though one says something as a way of thanking others, it could not achieve that goal if it is not recognised as an expression of thanks. One of the most basic types of speech act is that performed with the so-called performative (Austin 1962). It is also true that several conditions such as felicity conditions need to be met in order for particular types of speech acts to be performed appropriately. Yet, these are not always sufficient; one may sometimes need some contextual supports and/or information to recognise speech acts. In order to deal with such contextual factors effectively, two frameworks are often used in pragmatic explorations: speech events and activity types.

Yule defines speech events as follows:

> A speech event is an activity in which participants interact via language in some conventional way to arrive at some outcome. It may include an obvious central speech act, such as 'I don't really like this', as in a speech event of 'complaining', but it will also include other utterances leading up to and subsequently reacting to that central action. In most cases, a 'request' is not made by means of a single speech act suddenly uttered. (1996: 57)

Levinson explains activity types as follows:

> ...a fuzzy category whose focal members are goal-defined, socially constituted, bounded, events with constraints on participants, setting, and so on, but above all on the kinds of allowable contributions. Paradigm examples would be teaching, a job interview, a jural interrogation, a football game, a task in a workshop, a dinner party and so on. (1979: 368)

Speech events have many points in common with activity types, but, as Thomas points out (1995: 189), there is an important difference in emphasis. In the former, context is viewed as constraining the way the individual speaks; in the latter, the individual's use of language is considered to shape an event. I cannot say either is a better framework than the other: it is clear to me that context and participants affect each other, and meaning is generated through negotiation, and that one can analyse speech acts from a wider viewpoint using the frameworks of speech events and activity types.[4]

While lexicographers label on broader scales such usage as register, style and geographic region in which particular words/phrases are associated with, they have traditionally not dealt with speech events or activity type. When they are successfully identified with the use of particular lexical items as telephone conversations and the use of **hello,** they may deserve labels or other relevant descriptions.

9.3.3 Speech acts and other domains of politeness

According to Brown and Levinson, '[s]ome acts intrinsically threaten face' (1987: 60). While this implies that there are other acts which would not threaten face, Matsumoto argues that in the Japanese language, all language use has potential for resulting in an FTA:

> Since any Japanese utterance conveys information about the social context, there is always the possibility that the speaker may, by the choice of an inappropriate form, offend the audience and thus embarrass him/herself. In this sense, any utterance, even a simple declarative, could be face-threatening. (1989: 219)

In relation to these divergent views of politeness, Tsuruta points out that there are several different domains of politeness, and continues by saying that Brown and Levinson, and Matsumoto discuss different domains (1998: 72–5). Brown and Levinson mainly deal with speech acts, the illocutionary domain, whilst Matsumoto is concerned with honorific, the stylistic domain. My main concern in this book is speech acts, but other domains of politeness can also play an important role depending on the situation. Especially when considering politeness in Japanese, the stylistic domain is so closely connected with politeness that it is frequently equated with politeness (cf. Thomas 1995: 150). Ide's criticisms of face theory may at least partly exemplify this (cf. 9.2.2.2). Taking these facts into account, I will pay particular attention to deference. This will be more thoroughly discussed in 9.3.7. At the same time it should be evident that lexicography cannot deal with all the domains equally properly. It is therefore necessary to restrict the scope of politeness in terms of domains of politeness as well.

Spencer-Oatey identifies the following five domains of politeness: (1) illocutionary domain, (2) discourse domain, (3) participation domain, (4) stylistic domain, and (5) non-verbal domain (2008: 21). While illocutionary and stylistic domains can be dealt with relatively easily as part of dictionary descriptions, discourse and non-verbal domains are basically outside the purview of lexicography. Dictionaries are in principle concerned with words and phrases, and they cannot properly deal with discourse and its related domain except some basic descriptions of the so-called discourse markers. Similarly, so long as dictionaries seek to describe language through linguistic forms, the non-verbal domain has no place in lexicography.[5] Although the importance of the non-verbal domain is evident (see, for example, 6.1 for comments from the informants about this domain), it is very difficult for lexicographers to treat them properly. I will return to this issue in 13.4 and 14.4.

The participation domain concerns procedural aspects of communication, such as turn-taking and listeners' responses. These aspects are more closely related with discourse, and dictionaries cannot fully deal with them. At the same time, at least some of these aspects can be captured in the form of lexical items. There are various phrases that are used to respond to someone talking, and the use of even a basic vocabulary item like *we* can include or exclude people present. Yule, for instance, explains that the following two utterances are different in this respect: 'Let's go' as said to some friends and 'Let us go' as said to the hearer who has captured the speaker and others (1996: 11–2). The former use is an inclusive *we*, and the latter an exclusive *we*. Naturally, these different uses of *we* can produce different communicative effects depending on the situation. They could be dealt with properly, say, as part of usage notes.

As for the illocutionary domain, lexicographers should consider exceptional cases occasionally. Although Brown and Levinson designate orders and requests as inherently face threatening, they can in fact enhance one's face depending on the situation. Spencer-Oatey argues that if one asks a friend for help, the friend may feel that it shows trust in their ability and/or acceptance as a close friend. Moreover, when one is requested to do something, it is not necessarily concerned with their face. They may in fact simply feel inconvenienced or infringed upon (2008: 19). In short, they are rapport sensitive but not always face threatening (*ibid.*). While lexicographers are basically expected to describe most fixed portions of language, keeping these facts in mind should give lexicographers some useful insights on how speech act markers should be dealt with in their dictionaries. They must at least seek to fill in the gap between dictionary descriptions of formulae and speech act markers, and their behaviours in actual communication.

9.3.4 Ethos and communication style

Brown and Levinson state '...societies, or subcultures within societies, differ in terms of what might be called 'ethos', the affective quality of interaction characteristic of members of a society' (1987: 243). The point is that ethos is closely connected with communication styles.[6] Among various styles of communication, there are two communication-style dichotomies which are especially important in terms of politeness. The first one is equivalent to Brown and Levinson's negative/positive politeness, and this is labelled in various ways:

negative/positive politeness (Brown and Levinson 1987), involvement/independence (Scollon and Scollon 2001), expressiveness/distance (Andersen et al. 2002) and associative expressiveness/restraint (Spencer-Oatey 2008).

According to Scollon and Scollon, the use of given names and nicknames can show involvement: 'Bill, can you get that report to me by tomorrow?' (Scollon and Scollon 2001: 51). In contrast, the use of family names and titles reflects independence: 'Mr Lee, there's a phone call for you' (*ibid.*). While it is not usual to call each other by their first name in Japan, English-speakers usually use first names. If a Japanese learner keeps to their preferred communication style, independence, when speaking English with an English speaker, it may give the interlocutor an undesirable impression such that the Japanese person may not want to establish a friendly relationship with them. The same can be said of an English speaker talking to a Japanese speaker with their default communication style, involvement. These are examples of their association rights being lost in opposite ways (cf. 9.2.3.1).

The second communication-style dichotomy to be mentioned is directness/indirectness. Spencer-Oatey points out that this dichotomy closely relates to explicitness/implicitness, and this further relates to bluntness and communicative strength (2008: 28–31). To put this simply, direct utterances are usually explicit and blunt, and such utterances tend to convey the greater degree of communicative strength. More importantly, the communicative strength assigned to a linguistic form may be culture and/or language-specific; highly conventionalised linguistic forms associated with particular illocutionary forces will not be recognised as such in a foreign language (*ibid.*). *Would you like to...?* is a case in point (see 3.3.2 for an example from Leech and Thomas 1987/1991), and it is clear that the notion of communication styles enables lexicographers to compare Japanese and English ways of communication effectively in terms of politeness.

9.3.5 Pragmatic conventions

Leech (1983: 10–1) and Thomas (1983: 99) draw a distinction between sociopragmatics and pragmalinguistics. PP belongs to the former, and, as discussed in 9.2.1, it offers a useful framework for the comparison of different cultures in terms of politeness conventions, because it specifies scales on which people realise politeness in societies. While sociopragmatics and PP are concerned with social aspects of pragmatics, pragmalinguistics deals with the linguistic counterpart.

White reports an example of pragmalinguistic failure he encountered (1997). When he stayed at a hotel in Korea, a reception clerk used *had better* to advise him to wait in his room for the repair of a phone. White found this inappropriate and pointed out that this was caused from the differences between pragmalinguistic conventions in English and Korean. According to Thomas, a pragmalinguistic failure 'occurs when the pragmatic force mapped by S [speaker] onto a given utterance is systematically different from the force most frequently assigned to it by native speakers of the target language, or when speech act strategies are inappropriately transferred from L_1 [first language] to L_2 [second language]' (1983: 99). The matching of a particular force and a particular linguistic form is exactly what I recommend lexicographers to capture through formulae or speech act markers (cf. 8.3.3), and this will be another support to my belief that it is most promising to tackle pragmatics through speech act by focusing on formulae and speech act markers. As this example also seems to be related with another important issue, translation equivalents, I will discuss it in 9.3.8.

Pragmalinguistic failures can also occur at a deeper level. For example, Miller (2008: 230) points out that an utterance such as 'Let's think about it' in Japanese can function as a preface to a negative assessment, while this is not always the case in English. Japanese speakers and English speakers respectively assign different forces to this utterance, and this is not only restricted to this exact phrase (Matsumoto and Matsumoto 1987: 163–4). It will be because Japanese speakers sometimes seek to decline things such as suggestions and invitations very indirectly, even to such an extent that speakers of another language cannot really recognise.

As mentioned above, sociopragmatic principles like PP can offer a useful framework for cross-cultural comparisons in terms of politeness. For example, Japanese speakers and English speakers react to the compliments strikingly differently, reflecting the fact that Japanese speakers and English speakers respectively value the Modesty Maxim and the Agreement Maxim more highly in their societies (cf. 9.2.1). Lexicographers should be careful about where Japanese speakers and English speakers value a maxim more highly than another. Although this cannot be described properly in monolingual dictionaries, this can offer lexicographers working on bilingual dictionaries some useful insights when selecting headwords which need to be treated with care in terms of pragmatics, because frequency data from large-scale electronic corpora is not sufficient for that purpose (Kawamura 2006b: 168–9). It may well be useful to compare when and how Japanese speakers and English speakers find it necessary to apologise, for instance (cf. Tanaka, Spencer-Oatey and Cray 2008).

9.3.6 Sociological variables

Brown and Levinson identify the following three sociological variables as crucial in determining the level of politeness which a speaker needs to use to a hearer: power, social distance, and the ranking of the imposition involved in doing an FTA (1987: 15). If a speaker has a relatively stronger position over a hearer, as in a relationship between a president of a company and its employee, the president normally does not have to use a very deferential phrase to the employee. When there is such a considerable imbalance as this in their relative powers, the president and the employee are also often socially distant from each other. Nevertheless, this does not mean that the president can always use less deferential phrases to the employee, because it also depends on what the president is going to say to the employee. If the message content will threaten the face of the employee to a considerable degree, like the termination of employment, the president may use a very indirect and thus polite phrase according to the ranking of the imposition. Such a variable usually cannot be separated from (an)other variable(s).

Thomas adds to the three variables another important factor: rights and obligations, in her discussions of indirectness (1995: 131). Indirectness is a distinct phenomenon but closely connected with politeness (cf. Channell 1994: 190–1). A president of a company naturally has a right to make their employees follow their instructions concerning their work. Accordingly, a president does not have to use a very deferential expression to an employee so long as their instructions are related with running the company smoothly. On the other hand, if the president asks an employee for a personal favour, they may naturally use a deferential expression.

One's recognitions of power, distance, the ranking of the imposition, and rights and obligations often depend on cultures and societies. In Japan, for instance, fathers are not usually (or at least not often) as involved in running a household as fathers in the UK. Mothers in Japan may therefore feel that they need to use a relatively deferential expression when asking their husbands to wash the dishes. In contrast, mothers in the UK may use a neutral or at least not very deferential phrase in the same situation.

To make the matters more complicated, participants with different roles can have power over the participants in different ways. Customers and passengers usually have power over waiters and taxi drivers respectively in that it is they who can choose whether or not to use a particular restaurant or taxi again in the future. On the other hand, waiters and taxi drivers also have power over customers and passengers; they can give them instructions on how and where the customers or the passengers should be seated. They can also refuse to accept the customers or the passengers under special circumstances (Spencer-Oatey 2008: 35). This is at least partly because there are several distinct types of power: reward power, coercive power, expert power, legitimate power, and referent power (French and Raven 1959; Thomas 1995).

It is also worth noting that the number of participants influences the management of face. In many cultures it can be more embarrassing to be criticised or praised in front of other people than on a one-to-one basis (Spencer-Oatey 2008: 36). Here, I must add that power, distance, and rights and obligations are also closely connected with this. For example, it would be far more embarrassing and/or frustrating to be criticised publicly by one's subordinate, stranger or student. In contrast, it can be less embarrassing to be criticised by one's boss, parent or teacher. As almost everything can jointly affect the realisation of politeness in a particular context (cf. 7.3), lexicographers need to keep them in mind either when analysing or describing the use of lexical items in terms of politeness. Since these variables are often not connected with individual lexical items, they may be better treated in outer matters than in each entry.

9.3.7 Deference, register and absolute politeness

In 9.2.2.2 I mentioned three phenomena which are sometimes confused with politeness: deference, register and absolute politeness. In the discussions so far, I have occasionally touched on them in passing, and I will discuss them together here in order to clarify their relationships with politeness in conjunction with lexicography. While deference and register can more easily be distinguished from politeness, absolute politeness is confused with politeness even by specialists (see 4.1.3; see also Note 1 in Chapter IX).

Deference is respect one pays to others for such things as their higher rank or older age, and is static or fixed in nature. It is even built into the grammar of several languages such as honorifics in Japanese (cf. 9.2.2.2; 9.3.3). In this sense, Ide's wakimae can be regarded as part of deference. While in terms of pragmatics one can choose the way they use language to achieve their goal, depending on context or situation, they in principle have no real choice in terms of deference. In the Japanese context, especially, deference is closely connected with politeness even to such an extent that they are almost indispensable.

As for register, Lyons explains that it is a systematic variation in relation to social context (1977: 584), and in terms of register one cannot have any real choice, just as with deference. While register is also static or fixed in nature, dichotomies such as formal/informal will be especially important when considering its relationship with politeness, since one's failure to use a lexical item appropriate for the type of situation will naturally produce some pragmatic effect, either positive or negative. One's choices of expressions can thus affect the hearer's perception of politeness in a particular context. Without knowledge of deference and register, one cannot pragmatically choose an expression which may effect the best result in context. In Part I, I defined pragmatics as being concerned with one's command of linguistic resources in order to realise one's intent, and deference and register are indispensable parts of linguistic resources (cf. 2.4.1). Accordingly, it is necessary to pay close attention to deference and register when considering politeness.

As pointed out in Part II (cf. 4.1.3), one cannot really consider pragmatics out of context. Even the same expression uttered by the same person may mean completely different things depending on the situation. In this sense, absolute politeness, which is surface level of politeness squeezed out of context, is no more pragmatic than deference and register are. However, one should also have knowledge concerning absolute politeness, such as how 'polite' a particular expression can potentially sound. This is also an indispensable part of linguistic resources, and lexicographers must provide learners with information on absolute politeness as well. In fact, dictionaries have already incorporated at least partly deference and register, and assigned labels to them such as FORMAL and HUMOROUS (COBUILD6: xiv). Absolute politeness may also have been included in lexicography partly; for instance, lexicographers sometimes designate particular lexical items as polite or rude with labels (e.g. APPROVAL and POLITENESS in COBUILD6: xv).

It should be learners themselves who decide to use a particular lexical item in a particular context, and a dictionary's role is to provide those learners with sufficient information on pragmatic behaviours of individual lexical items together with pragmatic principles or conventions. While the former could be relatively comfortably accommodated in each entry, the latter cannot. Lexicographers should present information on the latter somewhere else in dictionaries, say, in the outer matter (see 13.3).

9.3.8 The influence of translation equivalents

In 9.3.5, I discussed a pragmatic failure caused by differences between pragmatic conventions in English and Korean, where the use of the speech act marker, *You had better* do something, was reported to be a main cause. It is to be noted here that Japanese learners are also likely to misuse the speech act marker in the same way (see Appendix II Question 87 for details). Their typical mistake is to use the phrase when giving advice to others, and there are two reasons: (1) its component *better* can sound to them as if the speaker advises the hearer to do a particular thing because it is considered to be a 'better' option. They might therefore believe that the use of *had better* is polite and does not sound too forcible; and (2) its Japanese translation equivalent, *shitahougaii*, often provided in English-Japanese dictionaries and/or wordbooks, can be used to less forcibly advise others to do a particular thing (e.g. Azuma 1994: 25–8). These relatively simple pragmatic failures are very often caused by surface-level negative transfer, i.e. at a vocabulary level (see also 5.2.1), and so it will be possible and useful for lexicographers to look at pragmatic differences between English expressions and their typical translation equivalents.

9.4 Summary

Findings from this chapter, especially 9.2.2.2, suggest that there are striking differences in politeness conventions across cultures, at least at the surface level. Brown and Levinson, and Leech claim that there are some universal properties of politeness, and I would not completely disagree with them as long as deeper levels of politeness are concerned. However, I will emphasise again that it is the surface-level language use with which language teaching, including lexicography, should mainly be concerned (cf. 9.2.1). This would logically imply that monolingual dictionaries, which are in principle expected to serve a wider readership, cannot deal with culture-specific variables satisfactorily. A vitally important question also arises here: whether bilingual dictionaries make the best use of this advantage over monolingual dictionaries.

In Chapters XI and XII, I will therefore discuss the results of my examination of the nine EFL dictionaries as to their treatment of information on politeness by comparing monolingual and bilingual works carefully, keeping in mind findings from the previous chapters. On the basis of the results of my examination, I will then consider how it can become possible to improve EFL dictionaries' treatment of politeness for Japanese learners of English in Chapter XIII.

Notes

1 Absolute politeness is defined as the type of politeness which is not relative to context or situation (Leech 1983: 102 Note 3). It could be regarded as equivalent to such phenomena termed variously as surface level politeness (cf. Thomas 1995: 155ff.) in that they all deal with politeness out of context; e.g. particular lexical phrases and their realisation of politeness squeezed out of context.

2 Spencer-Oatey points out that even 'constraint' still sounds prescriptive or rather evaluative (2008: 41), especially with respect to the Tact Maxim/Constraint and the Generosity Maxim/Constraint. She continues by saying that one's failure to follow such constraints may have serious consequences (*ibid.*), and she renames them Sociopragmatic Interactional Principles in order to emphasise their importance.

Leech later proposed the Grand Strategy of Politeness, which comprises all the maxims or constraints of his earlier PP: 'In order to be polite, S expresses or implies meanings which place a high value on what pertains to O or place a low value on what pertains to S' (2005: 15; 'S' stands for self or speaker; 'O', other people).

3 Scollon and Scollon list as one of the polite linguistic strategies 'Be pessimistic' (2001: 51), and gives the example of *I don't suppose*. I personally believe that the phrase 'Be pessimistic' is mistaken or at least misleading in that the requester would not be pessimistic at all when mak-

CHAPTER IX POLITENESS   153

ing a request with this phrase.
4 Hymes, the advocate of speech events, identifies the following seven factors for describing the speech event: a Sender (Addresser), a Receiver (Addressee), a Message Form, a Channel, a Code, a Topic, and Setting (Scene, Situation) (1962: 25). Thomas also lists the following key elements of activity types: goals of the participants, allowable contributions, degree to which Gricean maxims are adhered to or are suspended, degree to which interpersonal maxims are adhered to or are suspended, turn-taking and topic control, and manipulation of pragmatic parameters (1995: 190–1). These should also be kept in mind.
5 English-Japanese dictionaries for Japanese learners occasionally treat such phonological aspects as intonation, but it is clear that dictionaries in their present form cannot fully describe them (see 3.3.3; see also 12.3.2 for an example).
6 Spencer-Oatey (2008: 28) argues that one's choices of communication style influence ethos, but I personally feel that ethos influences communication style more. At least, they influence each other and cannot be considered separately.

CHAPTER X
Methodology

In this chapter, I will account for the methodology I adopted for my examination of how politeness is described and treated in EFL dictionaries, both monolingual and bilingual. The results of the examination will be discussed in the next chapters: monolingual dictionaries (Chapter XI) and bilingual dictionaries (Chapter XII).

In my examination, I approached politeness with a focus on the following categories of lexical items: formulae, speech act markers, and politeness markers. In order to collect sufficient data for my examination, I selected nine EFL dictionaries and 76 lexical items. They were selected and analysed in a way which made it possible to make fair and objective comparisons. Details will be given in the subsequent sections. In 2010, when I began this study, conventional paper dictionaries and fairly conventional electronic dictionaries were the norm. Therefore, most of the discussions in this book are based on the conventional dictionaries as they appeared at that time. However, online dictionaries and other new forms of dictionaries have also become popular since then, and I will return to this in 14.4.

10.1 Procedures

10.1.1 Selection of dictionaries

For my examination, I chose five reputable monolingual EFL dictionaries (the latest editions of the so-called BIG FIVE (as of [2010]) for advanced learners: CALD3, COBUILD6, LDOCE5, MED2, and OALD8, considering their impact on EFL lexicography (cf. 7.2). With respect to bilingual dictionaries, the latest editions of bestselling English-Japanese dictionaries for advanced learners (as of 2010), LEJD2, GEJD4 and WWJD2, were chosen for the same reason.[1] In addition to the three bilingual dictionaries, I included LOEJD because it is a fairly new type of bilingual dictionary compiled by a team of Japanese and English-speaking lexicographers. As a result, nine EFL dictionaries were selected, and they in fact form an almost comprehensive collection of the best EFL dictionaries for advanced learners available now.

When examining bilingual dictionaries, it would be desirable to analyse Japanese-English dictionaries as well; yet they are not as commonly used as English-Japanese works in Japanese school context. Japanese students are often advised by their teachers not to use Japanese-English dictionaries (Iwasaki 2002: 118), probably because teachers believe that the use of them will deprive students of opportunities to make the best use of vocabulary items which they already know. Moreover, they are more dedicated to encoding tasks. As mentioned in 7.1, it is important for dictionaries to consider both encoding and decoding needs when incorporating pragmatics; at the same time, as general-purpose dictionaries, English-Japanese dictionaries are more suited to my study. It is also true that it is too ambitious to deal with them both thoroughly enough, and so I will not investigate and analyse Japanese-English works in this book.

10.1.2 Selection of research items

For my examination, I selected 76 senses or uses of words and phrases which are likely to be related with politeness, such as *please* and *not at all*. They were as carefully and objectively selected as possible with the help of a recent technological advance in lexicography: the advanced search function in CD-ROM versions of dictionaries.

Nowadays, most monolingual EFL dictionaries are available both in a book format and a CD-ROM format. The five monolingual dictionaries which I selected for my examination are also available in both formats, and the CD version of CALD3 can generate a list of headwords whose explanations contain a particular word form. Although the other four dictionaries can also locate a headword whose explanation contains a certain expression, they cannot generate a list of such explanations. I thus used the CD-ROM version of CALD3 and made a list of headwords whose explanations contain the following lexical items which are likely to be related with politeness: *polite, politeness, politely, impolite, impoliteness, impolitely, rude, rudeness, rudely, insult, insulting, insultingly, approve, approving, approvingly, disapprove, disapproving, disapprovingly, direct, directly, indirect, indirectly, angry, anger* and *angrily*.

As some explanations contained more than one keyword, I manually deleted such overlapping explanations. This resulted in a substantially long list of 169 explanations, and so I read through the explanations of all the items on the list and examined how the keywords were used. From this it became clear that, even though a keyword was used in an explanation, the use of the headword was not necessarily connected with politeness.

While working on the initial list, I identified several groups of explanations, and it is worth commenting on these in relation to the following three groups. Consider, for example, the following explanations from the three groups:

Group 1: a polite and often slightly humorous remark, usually made to help other people feel relaxed (CALD3 **pleasantry**)

Group 2: having a pleasant and polite way of speaking which is considered socially acceptable (CALD3 **well-mannered**)

Group 3: said when you are answering a polite question or remark (CALD3 **thank** sense 2 as *thank you*)

In the explanation of **pleasantry** (Group 1), one of the keywords *polite* is used, but what it modifies is not the use of the headword but the referent of the headword, **pleasantry**. This often happens, especially with nouns. To use a word which refers to a polite thing is one matter, and to achieve polite effects with the use of a word is quite another. When considering politeness in the EFL context, it is the latter use of language that educators, including lexicographers, need to be careful about. Therefore, those items in Group 1 are basically outside the purview of this study. The same goes for Group 2; the keyword *polite* is used in the explanation of **well-mannered**, but this only modifies a part of the referent of the headword. As for Group 3, the use of *polite* in the explanation strictly has nothing to do with the headword. It is not even concerned with its referent nor its use. Yet some items in this group turned out to be well connected with politeness. Although 'a polite question or remark' in the above explanations of **thank** is rather vague, it is important to examine and analyse the whole entry, including examples and usage notes when considering dictionaries' treatment of a headword. Below are the two examples following the explanation:

"*How are you?*" "*I'm fine, thank you.*"
"*You look very nice in that dress.*" "*Thank you **very much**.*"

The above two examples illustrate what a polite question and a polite remark can respectively refer to, and they also confirm that the use of **thank you** is closely connected with politeness in that even though to answer a question or remark is usually not particularly polite, to answer them with **thank you** in these particular cases should play an important role in the realisation of politeness. As pointed out in 9.3, some acts usually pass unnoticed when performed, but one's failure to perform the acts in a particular situation might cause an undesirable effect. This may well apply to the above use of **thank you**.

I selected items to investigate from the initial list, taking into account the various factors which may affect the realisation of politeness. The basic criterion is whether the use of a lexical item might contribute to the realisation of politeness. Items in Groups 1 or 2 above were basically excluded, but they were included in my final list when there were sufficient reasons to believe that an item could play a crucial role in terms of politeness. For example, lexical items in the two groups describe their referents and can convey the speaker's attitude to them. If lexical items in Groups 1 and 2 are used to directly refer to the hearer, the use of them can naturally affect the realisation of politeness. When discussing such speech acts as praise and dispraise, it is advisable to take into consideration not only the addressees themselves but anything which belongs to them or what they believe is important (Leech 1983: 131–2; Thomas 1995: 162–3). However, this could potentially be the case with almost any lexical item. Given that such uses can be important, I only included items in the two groups where they were usually or, at least, often used as address forms (e.g. **ma'am**), in order to eliminate those which are not closely connected with politeness.

Eighty-four lexical items were selected in the way stated above, and then I confirmed whether they were contained in all the five monolingual dictionaries, since dictionaries' coverage varies and I had to collect sufficient data evenly from among the nine dictionaries. Eight items turned out not to be in all the nine dictionaries, and I excluded them from my final list. I finally selected 76 lexical items for my examination, and they were arranged according to their core functions, accompanying functions, and their politeness value so that I could easily compare the dictionaries' treatment of words/phrases with similar pragmatic functions (see 11.1.2). See Appendix IV for the comprehensive list.

10.1.3 Classification of the 76 lexical items according to their functions

Politeness can best be viewed as an umbrella function of speech acts. One can politely or rudely make a request; similarly, one can politely or rudely express their disagreement with others. More importantly, in order for a particular utterance to perform an act, the utterance must first of all be recognised as such. Factors making this possible include a direct statement of one's intent (cf. 5.2.2), and the use of formulae and speech act markers; they can roughly be classified either as neutral, polite or impolite in terms of politeness. For example, when expressing one's disagreement with others, one can say something like 'I disagree' or 'I beg to differ.' The former is a direct statement, and its wording is neutral. However, this may sound slightly rude; although the expression itself is not particularly rude, expressing a disagreement overtly can be taken as rather impolite because it violates a principle of politeness such as the Agreement Maxim of Leech's PP (cf. 9.2.1). On the other hand, the latter also performs the act of disagreeing but may be interpreted as politer because it is generally perceived as a polite formula. Even though the speaker is not very polite at heart, it is a fact that they chose the polite formula, which could be taken as a token of politeness.

The 76 lexical items for my examination are arranged in a way which makes it possible to compare the dictionaries' treatment of words/phrases with similar functions (cf. 11.2.2.1). Politeness markers are classified as either enhancer or softener (see 8.3.4), and formulae and speech act markers are classified according to their core functions, accompanying functions, and politeness values. Core functions refer to a speech act which the use of a phrase/word performs, and politeness values are concerned with general recognition concerning an expression in terms of politeness, roughly: polite, neutral and impolite (cf. 8.5). As to accompanying functions, they can be defined as other functions which the use of lexical items can fulfil, such as evaluatives (see 8.4.2). For example, *I beg to differ* is used to indicate disagreement with something, and thus shows the speaker's evaluation. In this case, I classify the accompanying function of the phrase as evaluative. Evaluative can further be classified either as positive or negative, and the phrase is more likely to express the speaker's negative evaluation. Accordingly, the accompanying function of *I beg to differ* is classified as evaluative (negative). Another example is *in God's name*, classified as having epistemic and evaluative (negative) as its accompanying functions. As the use of *God* in this way may sound offensive to some people, its politeness value will be designated as impolite.

As Moon points out (1998b: 219; 239–40), more than one function can often be fulfilled simultaneously. Take *if you please* for instance; CALD3 gives the following example to this phrase: '*Take your seats, ladies and gentlemen, if you please*'. Although a request is basically not committed to the truth value, *if you please* can be used when the requester is not sure if the requestee will accept their request. In this sense, the use of the phrase can express the requester's uncertainty. Moreover, this could also be classified as having the following accompanying functions: (1) conative, the requester literally suggests a possibility that the requestee can take a seat; (2) evaluative, the requester must intentionally choose this phrase, feeling that it is necessary to use an expression less demanding according to the situation; and (3) volitive, a request is usually identified as expressing the requester's desire for the requestee to do a particular thing for them. In such cases, I only list for each item one or more functions which can be felt to be the most conspicuous in some way; in this case, epistemic. While it would be important to classify the functions more finely when describing them in dictionaries, I did not attempt this at this stage.

There are two other cases where some commentary is required. First, almost every language use can express one's intent, and so I only classify a phrase as volitive when there is not another accompanying function noted, such as *Excuse me* as used to tell the hearer that the speaker is leaving. Second, some phrases are almost always used to preface a statement. For example, *I don't suppose* is used for prefacing or introducing a request politely, but this is different from organisational in that it does not organise utterances within a discourse. A request immediately follows the phrase within an utterance. Accordingly, I label them with a relevant accompanying function noted.

Lastly, I should also briefly mention the relationship between one's intent and the use of language. Usually, one's intent is closely connected with their choice of an expression. Therefore, they may naturally use different expressions when they intend to achieve different purposes. However, this is not always the case. For example, phrases that are used to emphasise a statement usually convey the speaker's certainty as well, but people can emphasise their utterance either when they are aware that their utterance is true or false. In case the speaker is telling the truth with emphasis, they normally emphasise what they believe is true. Thus, they usually commit to the truth value of their statement. On the other hand, when they are telling a lie, they are stating something which they are aware is not true. Thus, they do not commit to the truth value at heart. Yet this does not necessarily mean that they use the same expression in different ways; that is to say, the use of an emphasiser delivers the same amount of certainty either when telling a lie or a truth. In either case, the hearer basically assumes that the speaker is telling the truth, unless there is some evidence that they are not telling the truth. When telling a lie, the speaker is making a false claim for both the content and their certainty about the truth value about the statement. In this study, I will therefore not make a distinction between one's language uses for either telling the truth or making a false claim.

10.1.4 Lemmatisation

While arranging lexical items on the final list, I made a few changes as to CALD3's sense distinction and identification of particular forms. For example, CALD3's explanation of a sense of **would**, as used in polite requests and offers, runs as follows: 'used as a more polite form of *will* in requests and offers' (sense 6). This explanation seems rather vague, but it is not the only problem. This explanation is followed by the following three examples: *Would you mind sharing a room?*', *Would you like me to come with you?*' and *Would you like some cake?* The second one is not a request, but an offer or rather a request for a confirmation of the hearer's preference before actually making an offer, and the third one is an offer. The first one is the only example of request, but it is arguably *mind*, not *would*, that makes that utterance function as a request. Moreover, the second and the third examples are more like examples of *would like*, not of **would**. I therefore split the sense accordingly, and then arranged them respectively as Would you mind doing sth?', Would you like me to do sth? and Would you like sth? Incidentally, CALD3 uses 'polite' in this explanation of **would**, and this must be the key when considering its function as discussed above. However, CALD3 does not explain exactly what 'polite' designates in the explanation; it should be more properly paraphrased as 'less direct' (see 13.1.3; 13.2). As noted, the above explanation is vague, and it is because the lexicographers fail to mention this function of making the statement less direct. I will return to this in 11.1.1.

10.2 Key issues when examining the treatment of politeness in lexicography

In Chapters VII, VIII and IX, I discussed how and what portion of pragmatics should be dealt with in dictionaries mainly from theoretical viewpoints. Before moving on to my investigation of the nine EFL dictionaries in the next two chapters, I will summarise the key issues to be kept in mind when examining the dictionaries: (1) politeness is an indispensable part of pragmatics, and it should be dealt with as an umbrella function of speech acts (cf. 7.1; 8.3.4); (2) it is most promising to approach pragmatics through language functions, especially speech act by focusing on formulae, speech act markers and politeness markers (cf. 8.3.1; 8.3.3; 8.3.4; 8.5; 9.3.2); (3) it is important to pay attention to different pragmatic styles/conventions in English and learners' native languages (cf. 9.3.4; 9.3.5); and (4) because context and sociological variables play crucial roles in realising politeness, dictionaries should provide learners with information on them in some way (cf. 9.3.6; 9.3.7).

In addition to the above findings from the previous chapters, discussions in Parts I and II also suggest the following: (5) while it is necessary to describe contextual information sufficiently, it will take much space and can be detrimental in commercial dictionaries (cf. 3.1.3); (6) paralinguistic features are crucial in realising politeness, but dictionaries in the present format cannot treat them properly (cf. 3.3.3); (7) negative transfer from learners' native languages, including the influence of translation equivalents, can be a major obstacle to their acquiring proper politeness knowledge and skills (see 5.1); and (8) while dictionaries are expected to be prescriptive with strong authority over learners, pragmatics should be dealt with descriptively. It is even pointed out that it can affect learners' motivation to study (see 3.3.7).

In the next chapters, I will seek to examine the nine dictionaries' treatment of politeness with all the above important issues in mind. For the sake of convenience, I will discuss monolingual dictionaries in Chapter XI and bilingual dictionaries in Chapter XII.

Note

1 In Kawamura (2016), I examined the latest editions of CALD3, COBUILD6, LDOCE5, OALD8, LEJD2, GEJD4, and WWJD2 (as of 2014) and found that all the problems I highlighted in the original thesis were left as they were.

CHAPTER XI
Politeness as Described in Monolingual Dictionaries

In this chapter, I will report and discuss findings from my examination of the five monolingual dictionaries. The purpose of my examination is not to decide which dictionary is the strongest or rank them in terms of their treatment of politeness, but to ascertain (1) what dictionaries (can potentially) do to capture politeness; (2) how effectively they (can potentially) deal with politeness; and (3) what problems are presented in their treatment of politeness. For these purposes I kept all the key issues from the previous chapters in mind while examining the dictionaries.

One of the most serious problems I have found is that the five monolingual dictionaries seem to have no clear and consistent idea of what politeness is. They often designate the use of a lexical item simply or casually as polite, but the meaning of 'polite' varies from description to description. There are of course many properties which can be recognised as 'polite', and this will be discussed in 11.1.1. Another serious problem is that they often lack a clear and consistent perspective on politeness and speech acts in general. This affects almost every aspect of lexicography, ranging from these dictionaries' selections of headwords to their formulation and construction of entries. As this problem affects a range of information categories, I will discuss them separately within the traditional dictionary framework: explanations (11.1); speech labels (11.2); illustrative examples (11.3); and other issues (11.4). As for those categories where there are not many differences between the monolingual and the bilingual dictionaries, to avoid duplication I will discuss them either in this chapter or in the next, depending on whether they are more closely related with monolingual or bilingual dictionaries. Accordingly, speech labels and illustrative examples are mainly discussed in this chapter, and usage notes in the next chapter.

11.1 Explanations

Explanations in monolingual dictionaries are their main device for describing senses or uses of lexical items. Unlike translations in bilingual dictionaries, explanations can directly describe pragmatics, or pragmatic functions of a headword. However, the five monolingual works do not make the best use of this advantage. In this section, I will discuss their problems in turn: the use of *polite* in explanations (11.1.1); the absence of a perspective of politeness and speech acts (11.1.2); their failures to specify typical uses of headwords (11.1.3); sense descriptions from the perspective of speech act (11.1.4); and speech act as a series of action (11.1.5).

11.1.1 *Polite* in monolingual dictionaries

As discussed in 9.1, the concept of linguistic politeness is sometimes misunderstood even among specialists, which may make one wonder whether *polite* can mean the same thing in our daily lives and in the context of lexicography. This may then lead to a question of whether it is acceptable and/or sufficient to explain a use of a word simply as 'polite'. Consider, for example, explanations and examples from CALD3 and MED2 below:

> (**Don't mention it.** CALD3)
> said to be politer after someone has thanked you
> *"Thanks for your help." "Don't mention it."*

> **with all (due) respect** or **with the greatest respect** in the entry for **respect** MED2[1]
> used for showing that you are about to disagree with someone or criticise them in a polite way
> *With all due respect, I think you're missing the point.*

In this respect, CALD3's explanation of **Don't mention it** may not satisfactorily explain what the speaker's intent is. Moreover, 'to be politer' does not really make sense without sufficiently specifying what *polite* means in this explanation. As for MED2, it clearly explains that the speaker is showing that they are going to disagree with the hearer, but one may well wonder how it can be done. MED2 simply describes it as 'in a polite way'. There is a possibility that the lexicographers intentionally avoid being too specific in order not to make their explanations too informative or over-restrictive. However, when considering such unrelated language pairs as Japanese and English, the concepts of being polite may so greatly vary (see Chapter IX) that it is desirable to specify what they mean (see 13.2). Even though monolingual dictionaries need to serve a broad readership, loose explanations in the above style cannot be acceptable.

On the other hand, there are cases where the five monolingual dictionaries successfully explain properties which can in some way be felt to be polite without using *polite*. Here are explanations of **pleasure** from COBUILD6 and LDOCE5:

(Sense 5 **pleasure** COBUILD6)
You can say '**It's a pleasure**' or '**My pleasure**' as a polite way of replying to someone who has just thanked you for doing something.

(Sense 3 of **pleasure** as **(It's) my pleasure** LDOCE5)
used when someone has thanked you for doing something and you want to say that you were glad to do it

While both of the dictionaries describe the same 'polite' use of **pleasure**, LDOCE5 does not use the word *polite*. It instead explains that the speaker uses this phrase in order to say that they were glad to do something for the hearer. The hearer in this case may feel that they are indebted to the speaker in a way, so the speaker's act of saying that they were actually 'glad' or happy will make the hearer feel better, appealing to the hearer's positive face (see 9.2.1 for Lakoff's rules of politeness). Concerning COBUILD6, learners may again wonder what 'a polite way of replying' means exactly.

There are also instances where *polite* is complemented with a more concrete explanation:

(1st of 2 examples for sense 12 **would** CALD3)[2]
used to express an opinion in a polite way without being forceful
I would imagine we need to speak to the headteacher about this first.

In this explanation, 'in a polite way' is followed by 'without being forceful'; this additional phrase satisfactorily explains this use of **would** as a politeness marker, which clearly makes the explanation easier to comprehend.

It is also to be noted that their modes of explaining vary, even within the sub-entries or senses of a single headword:

(Sense 2 of **perhaps** OALD8)
used when you want to make a statement or opinion less definite
This is perhaps his best novel to date.

(1st of 4 examples for sense 5 **perhaps** OALD8)

used when making a polite request, offer or suggestion
Perhaps it would be better if you came back tomorrow.

While the explanation of sense 2 successfully captures the speaker's intent as well as the function of the politeness marker as a speech softener, that of sense 5 seems rather vague. What is necessary here would be a functional perspective on politeness and speech act, and this will be more thoroughly discussed in the next section.

11.1.2 The absence of a perspective on politeness and speech acts

One of the most serious problems which the five monolingual dictionaries have in common is that they lack a clear and consistent perspective on politeness and speech acts in general. Compare explanations of **pardon** from the five dictionaries. To illustrate the sense which I am discussing, I will also cite an example from CALD3. LDOCE5 has two related explanations, senses 5 and 6. Although the latter is strictly different from the use which I discuss, in that it is followed by a noun rather than a gerund, I cite both of them for the following two reasons: (1) they are used to perform the same act; and (2) COBUILD6 and MED2 treat them together:

(2nd of 2 examples for sense 1 CALD3)
Pardon me interrupting, but there's a client to see you.

(Sense 1 CALD3)
to forgive someone for something they have said or done. This word is often used in polite expressions

(Sense 5 COBUILD6)
You can say things like '**Pardon me for asking**' or '**Pardon my frankness**' as a way of showing you understand that what you are going to say may sound rude

(Sense 5 **pardon me for interrupting/asking/ saying** LDOCE5)
used to politely ask if you can interrupt someone, ask them a question, or tell them something

(Sense 6 **pardon my ignorance/rudeness etc** LDOCE5)
used when you want to say something which you think may make you seem not to know enough or not to be polite enough

CHAPTER XI POLITENESS AS DESCRIBED IN MONOLINGUAL DICTIONARIES 167

(pardon me for (doing) something MED2)
used for saying 'sorry' for doing or saying something that you think might offend people

(Sense 2 of pardon OALD8)
to forgive sb for sth they have said or done (used in many expressions when you want to be polite)

Only MED2 successfully describes the above use of **pardon**; that is to say, to apologise or express one's regret in advance for one's saying or doing something because they are aware that it might offend the hearer or make the speaker sound silly.

Let us look at each of the explanations in turn. CALD3 and OALD8 are almost identical in their ways of explaining the use, and they are the weakest among the five monolingual dictionaries cited. While their explanations show that the verb is used to forgive someone, this use of **pardon** ought to apply to the speaker him/herself, not to someone else. Their explanations are rather misleading in this respect. Moreover, they do not mention anything about what act the speaker is performing. Furthermore, according to their explanations, **pardon** is used to apologise or express one's regret for something which happened in the past, which is clearly wrong in this case.

As to COBUILD6 and LDOCE5 (sense 6), if their explanations are correct, the use of the verb may be far from polite; it is a kind of declaration that the speaker is saying or doing something offensive even though they are aware that it might offend the hearer. The other explanation from LDOCE5 (sense 5) does not say that the use is a declaration, but it could be interpreted as an attempt at saying or doing something offensive intentionally. If one truly wonders whether what they are going to do might offend the hearer, they may give up doing that at all (see 9.2.2.1 I for Brown and Levinson's first options for doing FTAs). The fact that they ask whether they may say something potentially offensive would suggest that they are planning or have decided to say that in any case, as some kind of preemptive. Although it is usually taken as politer to get permission before they do or say something, it would not be the case with this use of **pardon**. Incidentally, LDOCE5's distinction of sense 5 treats several distinct acts together, and this is particularly confusing in terms of speech act. I will return to this in 11.3.2; 11.4.3 and 12.4.1. Only MED2 successfully explains the use of **pardon** both in terms of speech act and politeness.

Now, it should be noted that MED2 is not always successful; nor do the other four dictionaries always fail. Below are the explanations of the corresponding use of **forgive** from the five monolingual dictionaries. The verb is not one of the 76 lexical items for my examination but one of the 84 initially selected items (see 10.1.2); however, all the five monolingual dictionaries include this speech act marker, and it is a near synonym for the parallel use of **pardon**. Accordingly, the comparison of their explanations of **pardon** and **forgive** will show how (in)consistently they explain the uses of headwords. Again, I will cite an example from CALD3 to illustrate the sense of **forgive** which I am discussing:

(Sense 2 CALD3)
used before you ask or say something that might seem rude
Forgive me for asking, but how much did you pay for your bag?

(Sense 3 COBUILD6)
Forgive is used in polite expressions and apologies like '**forgive me**' and '**forgive my ignorance**' when you are saying or doing something that might seem rude, silly or complicated

(Sense 2 LDOCE5)
used when you are going to say or doing something that might seem rude or offensive and you want it to seem more polite

(**forgive me (for doing something)/forgive my doing something** MED2)
used when you want to say or do something that may offend the person you are talking to

(Sense 2 OALD8)
used to say in a polite way that you are sorry if what you are doing or saying seems rude or silly

CALD3 and MED2 simply explain that **forgive** is used in this way when the speaker is doing something which may offend the hearer. If this explanation is correct, the use of the verb can be a kind of declaration that the speaker is doing something offensive intentionally. This is exactly the same problem which COBUILD6 and LDOCE5 (sense 6) have with **pardon**.

COBUILD6 is only partially successful in that it mentions the act of apologising, but its description seems blurred to some extent. It explains the use as 'used in polite expressions and apologies like "**forgive me**" and "**forgive my ignorance**"', which suggests that an apology is no more than an example of acts which one can perform by using **forgive** this way. The latter part of the explanation is also rather vague as it treats together several distinct acts: 'when you are saying or doing something that might seem rude, silly or complicated' (see 11.4.3).

LDOCE5 mentions the speaker's intent when using **forgive** this way, and gives three examples including '*Forgive me, but I don't think that is relevant*'. According to the dictionary, one says this when they 'are going to say or doing something that might seem rude or offensive' but 'want it to seem more polite'. One may well wonder whether this is polite, or exactly what 'polite' means in this case (see 11.1.1). As discussed in 9.1, linguistic politeness is not concerned with whether one is genuinely polite or not, but *polite* used in this explanation simply does not sound right.

This time only OALD8 is successful, though it is the weakest concerning **pardon**. This suggests that their success in this case does not mean that their defining policies are better or that they have analysed the behaviours of the headwords more closely. If their success is due to better lexicographic technique, they would be more successful in describing both **pardon** and **forgive**. This clearly shows that the lexicographers lack a complete perspective on politeness and speech acts.

11.1.3 Typical uses of a lexical item

Lexicographers' lack of a speech act perspective also affects their explanations in another way. Compare the following two explanations from CALD3:

(**bugger off** CALD3)
to leave or go away, used especially as a rude way of telling someone to go away

(**clear off** *ibid.*)
used to tell someone to go away in a rude way

Both of the explanations mention that the two phrases are used to rudely direct the hearer to leave the place, but the latter is arguably easier to comprehend because it focuses on an act which the verb is typically used to perform. The explanation of **bugger off** begins with a paraphrase probably because the phrase is not always used as an imperative, but this somewhat blurs the basic function of the phrase. It is to be noted that this is also the case with similar phrases as **clear off**. It would be advisable to split uses of a lexical item and explain them properly in terms of speech act, if they deserve dictionary descriptions at all (cf.11.1.4). It should be mentioned in passing that not only the five monolingual but all the four bilingual dictionaries fail to show adequately that **piss off** and **bugger off** are normally perceived as more offensive unless said humorously and/or informally as, say, between close friends; at the same time, any dictionary should not bear the risks of appearing to sanction the use of the phrases. This is where dictionaries need to clarify the generality of their offensiveness in their mid- or end-matters. It is also very interesting to note here that the role of such paralinguistic features as facial expressions is seldom mentioned in the nine dictionaries except occasional references to intonation in bilingual dictionaries (cf. [I] d) and [III] in 12.3.2). This underlines the point that it is very difficult for dictionaries to deal with paralinguistic features in terms of pragmatics; intonation, for instance, varies according to context. It will be near-impossible for traditional paper dictionaries to describe them properly. In the future, online multimedia dictionaries could deal with them more effectively; for instance, video clips showing particular intonation and gesture patterns could be hyperlinked. I will return to this in 13.4 and 14.4.

11.1.4 Sense description from the perspective of speech act

A speech act perspective is also important in distinguishing senses of a word. For instance, the basic function of *perhaps* is to show the speaker's uncertainty about the truth condition of a statement and thus make it less definite, and almost all the uses are derived from this. Therefore, it is difficult to clearly distinguish its senses only in terms of semantic properties or basic functions. It is here that speech act perspectives become particularly important.

LDOCE5 arranges senses of **perhaps** according to acts which one is performing with the adverb: 'used to say that something may be true, but you are not sure' (sense 1); 'used to give your opinion, when you do not want to be too definite' (sense 2); 'used to say that a number is only a guess' (sense 3); 'used to politely ask or suggest something, or say what you are going to do' (sense 4). This is where translations alone cannot sufficiently help users grasp differences between such distinct but related senses. These four explanations also give support to my claim that it is most useful for dictionaries to deal with pragmatics in terms of speech act. In fact, the four bilingual dictionaries utilise notes and specify what act one performs with the adverb when it seems necessary.

It is easy to find out what particular linguistic forms are frequent with the help of large-scale electronic corpora, but, when dealing with pragmatic information, it is not adequate nor sufficient only to identify frequent linguistic forms. What is necessary is to analyse the behaviours of linguistic forms from the pragmatic perspective, or the functional perspective focusing on speech acts as well as its umbrella function of politeness. It is only when particular word forms are meaningfully identified with particular functions or speech acts that they should be clearly explained as part of dictionary descriptions.

11.1.5 Speech act as a series of actions

The investigation of the dictionaries underlines the important fact that speech

CHAPTER XI POLITENESS AS DESCRIBED IN MONOLINGUAL DICTIONARIES 171

acts do not always consist of a single act (cf. 7.3; 9.3.1). Compare the following two explanations of **excuse me**: 'You say "Excuse me" when you want to politely get someone's attention, especially when you are about to ask them a question' (sense 6 excuse COBUILD6) and 'used to politely get sb's attention, especially sb you do not know' (sense 1 **excuse me** OALD8). It should be noted that the two explanations contain different types of information. While the former specifies a typical purpose of using this phrase, the latter mentions a typical addressee of the phrase. From the perspective of speech acts, the former ought to be better because it covers the whole act which the speaker is performing. More precisely, although both of the explanations make clear that the phrase is used to attract the attention of others, getting the attention is usually not a purpose itself. Someone gets someone else's attention in order to perform another, often more important, act. In this sense, COBUILD6 explains the phrase far better than OALD8. This would suggest that, whenever necessary, lexicographers need to describe behaviours of headwords from a broader perspective. Among the five monolingual dictionaries, CALD3 and MED2 also fail to mention the subsequent action; this is also the case with the four bilinguals.

It should be added that people do not always ask a question after getting another's attention. If lexicographers specify functions of headwords too narrowly, the resulting explanations can sound too prescriptive. As argued in 3.3.6, especially when dealing with pragmatics, dictionaries should not approach headwords too prescriptively. Therefore, it may be preferable not to specify it too precisely. For instance, LDOCE5's explanation runs as follows: 'used when you want to get someone's attention politely, especially when you want to ask a question' (sense 1 **excuse me** LDOCE5). The use of 'especially' works well in this case, but casual learners might overlook this. The more sophisticated that dictionary descriptions become, the more important that instructions in dictionary use, including how to interpret explanations, should become. It will be also important to ascertain the appropriateness of a description from an educational perspective (cf. 13.3).

At the outset of this chapter, I list, as one of the purposes of my examination, to find out what dictionaries (can potentially) do to capture politeness, and the above explanation from LDOCE5 will give a support for the policy. Even though four out of the five dictionaries fail to successfully describe an important property of a headword, their failures do not mean that the property cannot be captured lexicographically. Or rather, if even only one dictionary is successful, that feature of the lexical item is in fact well in the realm of lexicography.

11.1.6 Summary of 11.1

Explanations are the main device for describing senses and pragmatic functions of headwords, but lexicographers' lack of a perspective on politeness and speech act is clearly observable in almost every aspect of the entries, such as in their careless uses of *polite* and failures to specify what act the use of a word can perform. As a result, while explanations in monolingual dictionaries have the potential to deal with politeness and speech acts successfully, their descriptions are often unsatisfactory.

11.2 Speech labels

In this section, I will discuss findings from my examination of speech labels in the five monolingual dictionaries, starting by looking at the lists of labels (11.2.1). So far as the 76 senses/words/phrases are concerned, there are two major problems with their use of labels: (1) relevant labels are often not given, even when they seem necessary; and (2) there is confusion in their choice of labels, and criteria for using a label vary from dictionary to dictionary. Although it is only natural that each dictionary will use a label in a different way, each must at least explain the label's use, unless it is self-explanatory or at least easily inferred. (1) will be discussed in 11.2.2.1, and (2) in 11.2.2.2.

11.2.1 List of labels

Labels are also among commonly used devices for describing those aspects of language closely connected with politeness, such as register. When examining the relationship between pragmatics and labels, particular mention should be made of the introduction of a special label by COBUILD2, arguably the first dictionary which tackled pragmatics systematically. LDOCE2 was also known to be a pragmatics-conscious dictionary, with its inclusion of an article on the importance of pragmatics in the context of EFL lexicography by Leech and Thomas (1987/1991), but COBUILD2 went a step further. It introduced a special label of PRAGMATICS and used the label to mark entries that contained some pragmatic information. Its successor, COBUILD3, classified the category of pragmatic information more finely and introduced, as one of the pragmatics labels, POLITENESS, which has been employed in all the subsequent editions including COBUILD6. Although this innovation should basically be a welcome feature, the introduction of the pragmatics labels has also made it easier to observe some confusion in their use of labels. In 3.2.2, I criticised such problems with their labels, and, unfortunately, my criticisms still apply to

CHAPTER XI POLITENESS AS DESCRIBED IN MONOLINGUAL DICTIONARIES   173

COBUILD6. Equally unfortunate, this is also the case with the other four monolingual dictionaries as well as the four bilingual works (see 12.1).

All the five monolingual dictionaries have labels related with politeness. Table 3 on the next page shows the labels employed by each, and a close examination of them can tell us their selections of these labels are rather confusing. For ease of comparison, the table also contains those labels that any of the four bilingual dictionaries use. See Table 4 in 12.1 for the use of labels in the bilingual dictionaries.

Theoretically, almost anything could potentially be related with politeness, and my criteria for selecting the above labels are whether they are directly related with politeness. It is interesting to note that all the dictionaries have **Formal** and **Informal**, and that most of them have **Humorous**. Clearly, there is a close consensus here, and there may be at least two reasons for this. First, these three properties are relatively easily recognised. Second, they are relatively long established concepts in lexicography. As for **Humorous**, a brief note would be in order. Humorous language use may not seem directly related with politeness, especially in the Japanese context, but jokes and humour are among the most frequent ways to relieve tension in English (Sakamoto and Sakamoto 2004: 17–8). This may be a reason that it is listed as one of the basic positive politeness strategies by Brown and Levinson (1987: 124–5). Incidentally, it is to be mentioned that jokes and humour are attracting more attention nowadays in language teaching (cf. Gardner 2016), and that it is also promising for tackling politeness in terms of jokes and humour.

The five dictionaries sometimes use different labels to refer to the same properties of headwords. Even when they use different labels, however, it is usually possible to infer what they each refer to, because they often use similar wording. For example, they use the following labels conveying one's approval towards the referents of headwords: *APPROVING* (CALD3), APPROVAL (COBUILD6), *showing approval* (MED2), and **approving** (OALD8); this is also the case with the bilingual dictionaries. They are thus grouped as **Approving** in both Tables 3 and 4 in order to make it easy to compare the coverage of labels in the five monolingual together with the four bilingual dictionaries. On the other hand, **Euphemistic** and **Vague**, which sound similar in referring to indirect expressions, are strictly different; the former only applies to words and phrases which tend to be associated with less acceptable counterparts such as *god* and *goodness* in **God/goodness/Heaven knows** (OALD8). I therefore distinguished between them accordingly.

It should be mentioned that even when their wordings for labels are the same, dictionaries sometimes refer to different properties. Clearly, there is no consensus concerning their choice of the labels. CALD3 identifies **Offensive** with **Rude**, explaining that *OFFENSIVE* words are 'very rude and likely to offend

	CALD3	COBUILD6	LDOCE5	MED2	OALD8
Approving	Y	Y		Y	Y
Criticising					
Derogatory					
Disapproving	Y	Y		Y	Y
Discriminatory					
Euphemistic					
Exaggerative					
Feelings		Y			
Formal	Y	Y	Y	Y	Y
Very formal				Y	
Humorous	Y	Y	Y	Y	Y
Impolite				Y	
Informal	Y	Y	Y	Y	Y
Very informal				Y	
Ironic					Y
Nicknames					
Negative nuance					
Offensive	Y	Y		Y	Y
Very offensive		Y			
Politically correct					
Polite	Y	Y			
Positive nuance					
Rude		Y			
Very rude		Y			
Satisfied					
Sexual					
Slang	Y				Y
Taboo			Y		Y
Vague		Y			

Table 3: Labels used in the monolingual dictionaries

Note. Some dictionaries list labels with modifiers such as *very*, but others also use labels with modifiers. LEJD2, for instance, mentions in the front matter that it sometimes uses modifiers for its labels (19). Yet, considering the fact that some do list the modified labels, I list them in Tables 3 and 4 when such modified labels are included in the lists. As there are no variations in their wording of **Impolite, Offensive, Very offensive, Rude, Very rude** and **Taboo,** I put them in the table as they were, except making them in bold and capitalising the initial letters.

people' (1). COBUILD6 basically treats **Rude, Very rude** and **Taboo** together. This may be the reason that CALD3 only has OFFENSIVE and does not have an equivalent to **Rude**. According to COBUILD6, RUDE words are 'used mainly to describe words which could be considered taboo by some people' (xiv) and VERY RUDE applies to words which are 'used mainly to describe words which most people consider taboo' (xiv). This explains why COBUILD6 has RUDE and VERY RUDE but not an equivalent to **Taboo**. While COBUILD6 does not have **Taboo**, interestingly, COBUILD6 has OFFENSIVE in addition to RUDE and VERY RUDE. COBUILD6 explains that OFFENSIVE words are 'likely to offend people, or to insult them' (xiv). As for the other dictionaries, OALD8 has **Offensive** and **Taboo**. Only MED2 has **Impolite**, whose use is 'not taboo but will certainly offend some people' (inside the back cover). Although this note may suggest that MED2 regards the label as similar to **Offensive**, the dictionary also has *offensive*. According to MED2, *offensive* words are 'extremely rude and likely to cause offence' (*ibid.*). These notes are rather confusing, and learners may well wonder what the differences are between 'to offend some people' and 'to cause offence'. As many as seven labels which convey the speaker's negative attitude are used in at least one of the five monolingual dictionaries (**Disapproving, Impolite, Offensive, Very offensive, Rude, Very rude** and **Taboo**); their general confusions are most clearly observable in these negative labels.

11.2.2 The use of labels

11.2.2.1 Absence of necessary labels

There is little consensus between the five monolingual dictionaries' coverage and selection of labels (see 12.1 for the bilinguals), and another serious problem is that they do not satisfactorily explain what each label designates; users can only guess what each label refers to. As their lists of labels and explanations in their front matter do not provide us with more information on how the labels are used, I also examined their use of the labels. The results will be discussed in this section and the next.

I will begin with their frequent failures to use relevant labels when they seem necessary. For instance, CALD3 and COBUILD6 have labels to mark polite expressions, *POLITE WORD/EXPRESSION* and POLITENESS respectively, but they are often absent. Compare two explanations below, which seem to deserve the labels:

(Sense 2 **so-and-so** CALD3)
a polite way of referring to an unpleasant person

(Sense 1 **lady** COBUILD6)
You can use **lady** when you are referring to a woman, especially when you are showing politeness or respect

While the two senses are clearly related to politeness, they are not given any such label. According to CALD3, *POLITE WORD/EXPRESSION* is used for 'a polite way of referring to something that has other ruder names' (I). It is to be noted here that, puzzlingly, the wording of this explanation is almost identical to the above explanation of **so-and-so**. The only plausible explanation is that CALD3 uses the label only for inanimate things because it specifies the target of the label as 'something'. However, this problem still applies to such nouns as **powder room**. Although this use of **so-and-so** may not be particularly polite, CALD3 ought to use the label since it explains the use as polite. The same goes for COBUILD6's explanation of **lady**. COBUILD6 clearly explains 'The label POLITENESS indicates that you use the word or expression in order to show good manners...' (xv) and to show that politeness or respect may well be regarded as showing good manners.

Apart from polite lexical items, there are several other cases where relevant labels are not given. Take **clear off** for example. CALD3 explains the phrase as 'used to tell someone to go away in a rude way', and this is not given any label. While COBUILD6 uses DISAPPROVAL for this phrase, the other four dictionaries do not provide any related label. At the same time, most of them mention either explicitly or implicitly in their explanations the unfavourable property of this phrase. This is also the case with the four bilinguals.

For my examination, I arranged the 76 lexical items according to their core functions, accompanying functions, and politeness values so that I can compare the dictionaries' treatments of similar expressions (cf. 10.1.3). I thus compared the dictionaries' use of labels concerning other similar phrases listed together with **clear off**: **bugger off**, **fuck off** and **piss off**. The results are again rather confusing. All the five monolingual dictionaries provide related labels for **bugger off**. As for **fuck off**, only COBUILD6 and MED2 label the phrase as such, though all of them but OALD8 mention the unfavourable character; OALD8 only specifies it as usually used in orders. Similarly, only CALD3, COBUILD6, LDOCE5 and MED2 use related labels for **piss off**, but OALD8 does not.

With respect to their frequent failures to use the relevant labels, there is a possibility that lexicographers intentionally avoid using a related label when the explanation or translations convey the properties of the headwords concerned, in order to reduce some redundancy. However, if this is the case, it would simply deny the rationale of labels: 'to mark a word or phrase as being associated with a particular USAGE or LANGUAGE VARIETY' (Hartmann and James 1998: 80). While not only labels but almost everything could potentially be incorporated into explanations or usage notes, it no doubt makes entries far harder to read and too condensed for users to locate necessary pieces of information (see 12.3.4). Labels should be used to mark such important pieces of information. More importantly, they often mark headwords with relevant labels, even when their explanations also mention the same qualities as indicated by the label; cf. **half-caste** (LDOCE5) and **effing** (OALD8). There is therefore much room for improvement in their assignment of labels.

11.2.2.2 Confusions over the use of labels

The monolingual dictionaries often use different labels for an expression; some confusion is clearly observable here (see 12.1 for the bilinguals). Take the four phrases discussed in the previous sections for example: **clear off**, **bugger off**, **fuck off** and **piss off**. LDOCE5 uses *not polite* for **bugger off** and **piss off**, but *taboo* for **fuck off**. MED2 uses *impolite* for **bugger off**, *offensive* for **fuck off**, and *impolite* and *offensive* for **piss off**. It is interesting to note that MED2 uses *impolite* for the whole entry for the phrase, and adds *offensive* only for sense 3. Although this may suggest that the dictionary distinguishes between them according to some hidden policies, it does not explicitly mention how they are different. Even considering the fact that these four headwords are distinct and independent lexical items on their own, they have similar properties. It is not obvious why their choices and assignments of labels are so different.

It is also important to note that their descriptions sometimes contradict even within an entry. Here is an explanation of **Jesus Christ** (interjection) from MED2:

> used for expressing surprise or anger. This use of the name Jesus Christ is offensive to many Christians.

The second sentence, or note, in the above explanation states that the use of the headword is offensive to many Christian people, but MED2 uses *impolite* at the beginning of this entry (cf. 11.4.4). MED2 has both *impolite* and *offensive*. If the lexicographers have coherent policies for their use of labels, they need to clearly explain what differences there are between *impolite* as a label and 'offensive' as used in the note. Because both 'impolite' and 'offensive' are included in MED2's defining vocabulary, it does not affect lexicographers' choice of the labels. Similar confusions are seen in all five dictionaries, and again, there is much room for improvement in their choices and use of labels.

11.2.2.3 Summary of 11.2

Although speech labels are another commonly used device for describing politeness-related properties of lexical items, lexicographers' uses of them are rather inconsistent. Moreover, it is often not really clear what property each of the labels designates. These prevent their use of labels from being successful in describing politeness.

11.3 Illustrative examples

When considering pragmatic information in EFL dictionaries, the importance of illustrative examples cannot be emphasised too much, and this is especially the case with speech act and politeness. However, as is the case with explanations, there are several problems in their use of illustrative examples. First, they tend to lack sufficient context due to the severe limitation of space (see 11.3.1). Second, while they are expected to flesh out abstract descriptions of headwords, they sometimes do not match what they are to illustrate (see 11.3.2). Third, a straightforward point: some seem difficult for learners to understand (see 11.3.3). Fourth, as seen in 9.3.6, politeness is a complex phenomenon realised through several factors and/or variables. Even restricting the scope to the use of lexical items, there can be more than one item in an example which jointly contributes to the realisation of politeness. This makes it difficult to deal with them properly (see 11.3.4). Fifth, examples are also expected to illustrate such stylistic properties as register, but they often fail to successfully designate them (see 11.3.5). Sixth, while recent electronic corpora enable lexicographers to determine frequent patterns of language use, the findings are not necessarily utilised to illustrate speech act through examples (see 11.3.6). In the next sections, I will discuss these issues in turn.

11.3.1 Lack of context

Mainly for commercial reasons, dictionaries must deal with as many headwords as possible in a limited space (see 3.1.3). Even though electronic dictionaries have the potential to make the space problem less severe, they must in principle offer simpler descriptions, economising on space for describing their headwords. This often leads to a lack of sufficient context in their descriptions (Jackson 1988: 133). In relation to pragmatics, this is especially problematic because pragmatic meaning is generated through interaction between interlocutors in a particular context (cf. Thomas 1995).

There are many cases where one cannot really understand what particular

CHAPTER XI POLITENESS AS DESCRIBED IN MONOLINGUAL DICTIONARIES   179

examples illustrate due to the lack of contextual information: 'Excuse me, could I just say something?' (2nd of 2 for sense 1 of **could** CALD3). This example is preceded by the following explanation: 'used as a more polite form of 'can' when asking for permission'. It is unclear whether this example illustrates the speaker politely asking for permission, and almost impossible to interpret fully and properly without understanding what 'something' refers to. In any case, the speaker has already said something before they get permission to 'say something'. The fact that the speaker asks for such permission may imply that it could be 'something' special such as something surprising, rude, embarrassing or the like. For example, the speaker might be prefacing what they are going to say because they are aware that it could hurt the hearer's feelings; or they may be planning to say 'congratulations' because the speaker has learned some good news about the hearer before them. How one can interpret this utterance depends entirely on what 'something' refers to. It would also be helpful to provide some information on the relationship between the interlocutors. In order to understand this example correctly, learners would need more contextual information. This would suggest that one sentence example often would not suffice.

It is also true that longer examples consisting of a dialogue can lack sufficient context. Compare the following examples of (**No,**) **thank you** from CALD3 and LDOCE5:[3]

(Sense 3 **thank you** CALD3)
"Would you like some more cake?" "Yes, I will have a small piece, thank you."

"Do you need any help?" "No, thank you."

(Sense 4 **thank you** LDOCE5)
'*Would you like some more coffee?*' '*No, thank you, I'm fine.*'

While CALD3's first example illustrates the use of **thank you** as used to accept an offer, LDOCE5's shows its use as declining an offer. CALD3's second example uses the phrase on its own, but LDOCE5's is followed by another phrase. This does not mean that CALD3's second example is less comprehensible, as this seems to satisfactorily depict the possible context; the speaker simply declines the offer, though the use of the phrase as presented here is not particularly polite.

It is important to note that the possible situational contexts in LDOCE5's could be relatively easily inferred from what is given in the example. On the other hand, CALD3's first example may need more information. It also has an additional phrase, 'I will have a small piece', but it does not really add sufficient information, or rather it makes the example need some extra information because the guest does not simply accept the offer but moderate their acceptance with 'a small piece'. Such a restricted acceptance as this is not a typical way to accept an offer, and thus they need more contextual information so that the users can correctly infer the situations (see also 11.3.2 for discussions of mismatched examples). Although 'more' in the offer may imply that the guest has some already, it is not explicit enough to explain this particular situation. In contrast to the monolinguals, LEJD2 gives the following examples: "Won't you have another piece of cake?" "*No, thank you. I've had enough.*" (**No, thank you**), and the additional phrase 'I've had enough' works well, though it inevitably leads to a longer example by that.

Again, the above examples would suggest that lexicographers need to select examples considering what they are illustrating; namely, what act the speaker is performing. In view of the fact that it is not very polite to limit one's acceptance of an offer like the above, the speaker may need to provide some excuse or clarification in order to make the refusal sound politer. This may have grave implications for establishing the criteria for selecting example sentences. Although Miller and Swift (1979: 76) point out that examples selected by lexicographers are in some way revealing of their cultural expectations, if there are some typical or universally imaginable situations for particular speech acts, examples explicitly representing such situations would be ideal for EFL learners. Such notions as schema (cf. Yule 1996: 85ff.) and speech events and activity types (see 9.3.2) may be useful in this respect. At least it is safe to say that the first example from CALD3 appears a bit too much situation-based for a dictionary to deal with in a canonical way as required in lexicography.

I must also point out that, when dealing with pragmatics, lexicographers need to take into consideration extralinguistic factors. Here are examples of **I wonder** from MED2 and OALD8:

(2nd of 3 examples of **I wonder if/whether** MED2)
I was wondering whether you would like to come to the theatre with me?

(2nd of 2 examples for sense 2 of **wonder** OALD8)
I was wondering whether you'd like to come to a party.

Both of the above examples are supposed to illustrate the use of **wonder** as making a polite request, but if the requester knows that the requestee is willing to accept the request for some reason (for instance, if the requestee has long wanted to visit the theatre or to go somewhere with the requester), the act illustrated in the above examples would not be a request but an invitation. It is important to note that this is not an extension but quite a natural interpretation in our daily lives, and that in the examples there are no clues in this respect. Although it is very difficult to decide to what extent dictionaries should deal with such extralinguistic factors as part of their descriptions, lexicographers occasionally need to go beyond its tradition when dealing with pragmatics in the context of EFL lexicography.

There are also cases where learners may find it hard even to identify the referents of headwords as used in examples:

(effing LDOCE5)
She's gone to effing bingo again.

(effing MED2)
He was calling her an effing this, an effing that.

Both of the examples are preceded by the explanation of the headword, and most learners may be familiar with all the other lexical items in the above examples. However, they may experience at least some difficulty in interpreting them due to the lack of sufficient context; the second one in particular is almost incomprehensible because it is not at all clear what either 'effing this' or 'effing that' refers to. People usually reach the pragmatic force of others' utterances after they have identified utterance meanings, including referents of each lexical item, and then the utterance meaning of the whole utterance (Thomas 1995: 2–21). Unless learners can correctly identify the utterance meanings of each expression used in an example, they are very likely to fail to understand its force, or how and what act the speaker is performing.

As Béjoint argues (1994: 135), the choice of semantic content of examples is relatively free because they are mainly concerned with syntax and semantics alone. Yet, when selecting illustrative examples for pragmatic behaviours of headwords, lexicographers must take into consideration various other factors which can influence users' recognition of plausible contexts where an example sentence could be uttered. Since this is closely connected with the highly complex procedures of how human beings can interpret a particular language use in a particular context, it will be difficult to draw up any simple guidelines or the like. Moreover, as it is almost impossible for any dictionary to fully describe every feature in a context, one should not be too critical about dictionaries' treatment of contextual information or expect too much out of them. I would argue that the most important thing should be to ensure that learners can relatively easily and correctly understand the situation or context in which a particular phrase is typically used (Jackson 1988: 188). It has been pointed out that lexicographers need to select examples considering such factors as:

typicality (Fox 1987: 138–9; Jackson 1988:155) and naturalness (Sinclair 1984; Fox 1987: 139–40; Jackson 1988: 188–9). Concerning pragmatic information, I would add to them the functional perspective of speech act and politeness; more precisely, how, when and where people perform a particular act, trying to maintain rapport with others. These variables have been neglected in the context of EFL lexicography, but they should be the keys when selecting examples illustrating pragmatic behaviours of headwords.

It is also to be mentioned that lexicographers should not be too much concerned about the length of examples. MED2 has the following relatively longer example and it seems to work quite well: 'I can't finish this meal.' 'Please yourself, but don't complain to me when you're hungry later on' (MED2 **please yourself**). Even though such examples as this occupy more space, the increasing availability of dictionaries in electronic formats means that the space problem has become less serious. In fact, some dictionaries, including MED2, will soon only be available in electronic formats (Rundell 2012; 7.5). We need to keep in mind that dictionaries should basically and/or ideally offer simpler descriptions (cf. 13.4), and that new technology could solve some lexicographic problems in the future. For the time being, it is important to keep a balance between being simple and being informative enough.

11.3.2 Mismatched examples

Illustrative examples in a dictionary are intended to present typical contextualisation of headwords (e.g. Ikegami 1996: 37). Due to lexicographers' lack of politeness and speech act perspectives, however, there are often cases where mismatches are overlooked between explanations and other descriptions in a dictionary. Although this is not a problem peculiar to politeness, I will discuss this in this section because it can greatly affect the success of dictionaries' treatment of politeness. Here are examples of a frequent pattern of the mismatches:

(Sense 2b **excuse** CALD3)
Excuse me, can I just get past?
used to politely ask someone to move so that you can walk past them

(Sense 1c **excuse** LDOCE5)
Excuse me, could I just squeeze past?
used to ask someone politely to move so that you can walk past

Both dictionaries explain that **excuse me** in these examples is used to ask the hearer to move so that the speaker can walk past. However, in both cases it is not the formula but the latter parts of the examples which function as such;

namely '*can I just get past?*' and '*could I just squeeze past?*" respectively. Clearly, **excuse me** in the examples functions as attracting attention of the hearer rather than requesting them to move, though there may be a slight possibility that it is used here in a very subtle way between requesting to move and attracting attention such as a polite clarification of a request. The same goes for CALD3's example of **thank** discussed in the previous section.

There are less-frequent patterns of the mismatch:

(3rd of 3 examples for sense 2 of verb **mind** COBUILD6)
'*Would you like me to read that for you?*'– '*If you wouldn't mind, please.*'

This is preceded by the following explanation:

You use **mind** in the expressions '**do you mind?**' and '**would you mind?**' as a polite way of asking permission or asking someone to do something.

While the explanation designates this use of **mind** in polite requests or requests for permission, the above example literally works as a hedge before accepting the offer or answering the question. Moreover, while the explanation lists only two patterns in which **mind** is used to request or ask permission, **do you mind?** and **would you mind?**, the above examples are not used in the particular forms specified. These may be reasons why the above example is listed as the last of the three examples. From an educational viewpoint, it would be useful to offer a variety of examples so that learners can make themselves more familiar with the real language use. However, at least some notes would be in order for such cases as this.

There are also cases where over-compact explanations without sufficient context can cause pseudo-mismatches, or such situations as learners not being able to identify what an example illustrates. CALD3's explanation of sense 3 of **my** runs as follows: 'used in front of a noun as a way of expressing love or as a polite or humorous form of address', and two short examples follow: '*My darling!*" and '*Do you want any help, my dear?*" It is difficult to see which uses the two examples illustrate respectively for the following two reasons: (1) the above explanation treats together two distinct acts, expressing affection, and addressing a person politely or humorously; and (2) the explanation has not provided sufficient context either. They will be more properly dealt with, if explained separately; preferably with more contextual information (cf. 11.3.1).

Here is another example. OALD8 includes **I don't suppose** as one of five examples for sense 3 of **suppose**: '*I don't suppose (that) I could have a look at your newspaper, could I?*" This is preceded by the following explanation: 'used to make a statement, request or suggestion less direct or less strong'. The explanation only mentions that the use of the phrase can lessen the impact of the act which the speaker is performing, but there is no indication that this example is one for making or introducing a polite request (see 7.1; 9.2.3.2).

The worst problem which the above examples of pseudo-mismatches have in common is again they lack the perspective of speech act and politeness, and such explanations and examples as these are legion. They need to be carefully reviewed in terms of speech acts and politeness.

As stated at the beginning of this section, the problem of mismatched examples is not only concerned with politeness, but explanations and examples are basically expected to complement each other in helping learners grasp the use of a headword more easily and correctly. Therefore, lexicographers need to reduce any type of mismatch. It should also be mentioned that mismatches between examples and other descriptions are closely connected with how lexicographers deal with the typicality of language use. Explanations in particular are basically expected to describe typical and frequent uses of lexical items out of context, and so those examples illustrating some pragmatic phenomenon that is often less frequent, non-typical and context-dependent are potentially liable to mismatches. Whenever necessary, therefore, lexicographers must at least provide examples with some note to fill in the gaps in order to deal with pragmatics more efficiently.

11.3.3 Difficult examples

EFL learners have far smaller vocabularies than native speakers, and their understanding of vocabulary items is also different from those of native speakers. This would be the main reason that the so-called defining vocabulary was introduced into EFL lexicography (Kawamura 2001: 336). Here, it is to be noted that dictionaries do not only provide explanations; and, ideally, every piece of information should be well accessible to foreign learners. So far as the 76 senses and uses of the headwords are concerned, there are sometimes quite difficult examples found:

(effing OALD8)
I'll smash your effing face if you don't eff off.

The problem of this example is straightforward; 'effing' and 'eff off' seem unlikely to be part of ordinary learners' working vocabulary. Although the former is the very word which this example illustrates with its own explanation just before this, the latter is not.

It is not always lexical items that make examples harder to understand:

(2nd of 3 example for sense 6 if CALD3)
Would you mind if I open/opened (=Can I open) the window?

(1st and 2nd of 3 examples for sense 8a **mind** LDOCE5)
Would you mind if I opened the window?
Would you mind if I came with you?

The Japanese language does not have the subjunctive mood, and so it is one of the most difficult grammar phenomena for Japanese learners. They might simply take 'opened' and 'came' as referring to past actions in the above examples. If this is the case with Japanese learners, the parenthesised note provided in CALD3's example would sound rather confusing to these learners. In terms of politeness, moreover, they cannot be the same (see 9.3.1 for explanations for syntactic downgraders); the use of the subjunctive mood is basically expected to make an utterance sound politer. At least some note would be in order.

Apart from politeness, lexicographers' presentations of examples can also make examples harder to comprehend.[4] Every effort must be made to ensure that learners can comprehend examples correctly.

11.3.4 Multi-lexical realisation of politeness

Politeness is a complex phenomenon involving many factors. Accordingly, a polite speech act is usually not performed successfully through the use of a single polite lexical item alone; the speaker needs to take into account such factors or variables as abstract meaning of lexical items, paralanguage, and context. Even restricting its scope to the use of lexical items, however, more than one item is often used to realise politeness. Although this is strictly not a problem in itself, an example is basically expected to illustrate or focus on a single lexical item or its behaviour; at least, it should not be too complicated for learners to understand (Fox 1987: 142–3). Concerning politeness in particular, it is simply wrong if dictionaries fail to mention the relationship between related items working together.

Here is an example from CALD3:

(Sense 2 **could** CALD3)
Could you possibly turn that music down a little, please?

The requester's intent behind the above utterance can be analysed as follows: since a request is an act inherently face/rapport threatening, the requester judges that the imperative is not appropriate. Therefore, the requester performs it less directly, and decides to make the request through the speech act marker,

Could you...? because this can make the request less direct in two ways. First, with the use of the question form, the requester can literally pretend that they are simply wondering whether the requestee can turn down the music, which leaves room for declining and thus sounds less forceful.[5] Second, the use of the past form can also make an utterance less direct because it can shift the tense from the present to the past; in other words, one can make an utterance sound as if they are uttering something they *were* thinking before (Wakiyama 1990: 42). The use of the past tense can also be analysed as the use of the subjunctive mood, but either way it will make an utterance less forceful.

It is important to note that other items than **could** also contribute to the realisation of politeness. The success of this request also depends on the following three politeness markers: *possibly, a little* and *please*. While *possibly* and *a little* are used to lessen the impact of this face/rapport threatening act, *please* is used to enhance the degree of politeness. Incidentally, they do not as equally contribute to the success of this request as the speech act marker, *Could you...?* Since the above request cannot be made without the speech act marker, it should be the key item in making the above utterance work as a polite request, because one can make a polite request even excluding from this utterance the three politeness markers. This could be a reason why CALD3 provides this example in the entry of **could**. Even though they can identify a single main item in terms of politeness like this, however, it would be simply wrong if they do not mention the relationships between related items which cooperate to perform a polite speech act.

Although it is questionable whether it is the role of dictionaries to teach learners how politeness can be realised through several lexical items in an utterance, some notes would be desirable; at least this should be explained somewhere such as in the mid-/end matter. COBUILD6, MED2 and LDOCE5 contain essays on pragmatics as part of their mid-/end matters, but they do not mention this. If these dictionaries are really serious about incorporating pragmatics into lexicography, they need to explain this clearly because this is one of the places where pragmatics and lexicography contrast most strikingly. Preferably, this should be cross-referred from entries whenever necessary (see 13.3).

11.3.5 Register

So far as the 76 lexical items are concerned, I have not found many examples which satisfactorily illustrate register, probably because it is necessary to provide sufficient context in order to illustrate register (cf. 11.3.1). Compare the following two examples for sense 2 of **gentleman** and the note containing alternative examples:

(2nd and 3rd of 3 examples for sense 2 of **gentleman** OALD8)
Can I help you, gentleman?
There's a gentleman to see you.

In more informal speech, you could say *'Can I help you?'* and *'There's someone to see you.'*⁶)

From this note, one can assume that its two examples are 'more' informal than the first two examples, but there are no clues to how informal they are in the examples. The following example is one of the few which illustrate register relatively well: *'With all due respect, Minister, I cannot agree with your last statement'* (CALD3 **with (all due) respect**). Here, the use of an address form, 'Minister', seems to work well in illustrating the formal character of **with respect**.

Even considering the difficulty in making illustrative examples compact and sufficiently informative, lexicographers would need to include more contextual information so that learners can more easily and correctly infer the degree of formality of the example (Minamide 2003: 48). As discussed in 11.3.1, the amount of contextual information is deeply concerned with how lexicographers treat illustrative examples. There is much room for improvement in their treatment of register in illustrative examples.

11.3.6 Collocation and speech acts

Mainly due to the development of large-scale electronic corpora, there is general agreement among the dictionaries in their treatment of collocation in illustrative examples. When analysing typical uses of lexical items in terms of pragmatics, it would be helpful to pay more attention to the relationship between particular collocation patterns and speech acts. CALD3 has two examples for sense 4 of **might**, both of which come with *like* as: *'You might like to try a little more basil in the sauce next time'* and *'I thought you might like to join me for dinner'* (sense 4 **might** CALD3). Three out of the five dictionaries (CALD3, LDOCE5 and MED2) have *might like* as a way to make a polite suggestion; all the four bilinguals also demonstrate this use. The same goes for *I thought we might do*. At the same time, it is true that not all the dictionaries completely agree in their treatment of collocation in examples, though all of them claim to be corpus-based. This may suggest that they are not simply corpus-based but that lexicographers' judgement of corpus data plays a considerable role.

If lexicographers are more aware of the importance of speech act and politeness, the quality of illustrative examples will be improved by making the best

188 PART III COMPATIBILITY BETWEEN PRAGMATICS AND LEXICOGRAPHY

use of corpus data from the pragmatics perspective. However, it should be emphasised again that even the latest spoken corpora are not really designed for detailed pragmatic analysis (cf. 4.1.2). They should at least take into account such variables as intonation and exact situational context. Otherwise, they cannot satisfactorily help lexicographers describe pragmatics. Both lexicographers and corpus designers should become more pragmatics-conscious in order to achieve better treatment of pragmatics, including politeness.

11.3.7 Summary of 11.3

Illustrative examples are especially important when describing speech acts and politeness because such pragmatic meaning needs to be fleshed out in an example with sufficient contextual information. However, mainly due to commercial restrictions, they often lack enough contextual information, and there are other problems in illustrative examples, such as difficult words being used in an example. Moreover, while an example is supposed to illustrate one lexical item, there is often more than one lexical item working together to realise politeness, which makes it harder for lexicographers to illustrate the pragmatic behaviours of a particular headword. Strictly, this need not be a problem, but it does require very careful treatment from an educational perspective. More importantly, it should be pointed out that lexicographers' lack of a perspective on politeness and speech act is again observable in many examples so that they do not really help learners grasp how and what act the use of a particular expression can perform in context. As a result, there are many cases where illustrative examples fail to illustrate pragmatics successfully.

11.4 Other issues

In this section, I will report and discuss four issues which have not been dealt with in the previous sections: accompanying functions (11.4.1); identification of distinct senses of lexical items (11.4.2); confusion over speech acts (11.4.3); and usage notes (11.4.4). Again, the absence of politeness and speech act perspective is clearly observable in them.

11.4.1 Accompanying functions

When performing an act with the use of language, one can simultaneously fulfil several other, often less important, functions. They are often accompanying functions, and often play crucial roles in realising politeness (see 8.5):

(Sense 10 **god**)
If someone uses such expressions as **what in God's name, why in God's name** or **how in God's name**, they are emphasizing how angry, annoyed or surprised they are. [IMFORMAL, EMPHASIS]

COBUILD6 explains that '[t]he label EMPHASIS indicates that you use the word or expression to show that you think something is particularly important or true, or to draw attention to it' (xv). This is clear enough and COBUILD6 uses the labels for **what in God's name**, so, according to this explanation, the speaker uses the phrase to show that they find something important or draw attention to how angry, annoyed or surprised they are. In order for them to show that the fact is important, however, they may also need to show that they are angry, annoyed or surprised. Accordingly, it is only natural to believe that the use of the phrase should convey the speaker's feelings too. My question here is why the lexicographers do not put FEELINGS together with EMPHASIS for this phrase. COBUILD6 explains that '[t]he label FEELINGS indicates that you use the word or expression to show how you feel about a situation, a person, or a thing' (xv). Which is the more important function of this phrase: to show that you think something is important, or to show how you feel about it? Moreover, both when the speaker shows how they feel and when they draw attention to their feelings, the use of the phrase can also show their attitude to the topic. For example, if the speaker shows that they are angry or annoyed using this phrase, it also deserves DISAPPROVAL: 'The label DISAPPROVAL indicates that you use the word or expression to show that you dislike the person or thing you are talking about' (xv). They are accompanying functions, and the use of the phrase either intentionally or unintentionally conveys the speaker's negative feeling, which is very likely to affect the realisation of politeness.

As discussed in 7.3, almost every part in a longer utterance can jointly contribute to the realisation of politeness. I would argue that the same can be said of many shorter utterances, and that accompanying functions play crucial roles there. For example, the speech act marker *I (woul)'d be obliged if S + V* can make a request through expressing one's appreciation. More precisely, with the use of this speech act marker, the requester can hint that they want the requestee to do a particular thing by thanking the requestee in advance for their future or potential action, so that the requestee can interpret the utterance as requesting them to do what the requester has already thanked them for. That is to say, the indirect request is made through the accompanying function of volitive. It is also to be noted here that the accompanying function of epistemic makes the request more indirect; the requester expresses the core function of the request in the form of the conditional clause, and shows that they are not perfectly sure whether the requestee will accommodate the request. The use of **would** also

190 PART III COMPATIBILITY BETWEEN PRAGMATICS AND LEXICOGRAPHY

works in the same way. Through showing one's uncertainty through the use of the conditional clause and the auxiliary verb, the requester can make the request indirect and thus 'politer'. The requester's use of the speech act marker fulfils more than one function simultaneously.

As far as the nine dictionaries are concerned, none of them explain this. The above view of speech acts and politeness is mine and completely new to lexicography, and so I have no intention of criticising the dictionaries for their failures to successfully describe them. However, I also need to point out that they need to be dealt with sufficiently as part of dictionary descriptions because it is sometimes far from sufficient to clearly explain a core function of an expression (see 13.1.2).

11.4.2 Identification of distinct senses of lexical items

It is most useful to approach pragmatics with a focus on politeness and speech act (cf. 8.5). This means that it is important for lexicographers to identify speech act markers and formula which play crucial roles in performing speech acts and treat them properly. In this section, I will report how they identify and deal with speech act markers, formula and distinct senses or uses of headwords. I will begin with a problematic case. While COBUILD6 lists *Pardon me for asking* and *Pardon my frankness* as examples of a sense of the verb, LDOCE5 treats them as separate senses, probably because it attaches greater importance to their forms rather than their functions; more precisely, it divides the sense according to what follows the verb: *me* + *for* + gerund for sense 5, and *my* + abstract noun for sense 6. Dictionaries must not only describe the behaviours of words correctly but also must offer easy access to the information necessary for users. This may be the reason that LDOCE5 treats the senses separately; it even includes the following 'signposts' to senses 5 and 6 respectively: '**pardon me for interrupting/asking/saying**' and '**pardon my ignorance/rudeness etc**' in order to help users locate the senses more easily. In this particular case, therefore, LDOCE5's sense description is understandable. Compare this with the entry for a speech act marker of **pardon** from OALD8:

> |pardon me for |doing sth
> used to show that you are upset or offended by the way that sb has spoken to you
> '*Oh, just shut up!*' '*Well, pardon me for breathing!*'

Although this is another sense of the verb, OALD8's short cut,[7] '**|pardon me for |doing sth**' is rather vague and does not indicate how this is different from the one LDOCE5 explains. This is closely connected with how they recognise the relationship between forms and functions. Because the above use of **pardon** is restricted to a few collocating verbs such as *breathe* and *live*, it should be relatively easy to identify basic forms of this speech act marker as *Pardon me for breathing/living/existing!* CALD3 treats these formulae as fixed phrases, and LDOCE5 as independent senses of the verb. Apart from the monolinguals, all the four bilinguals include them either as fixed phrases or as a sense of **pardon me**. Unfortunately, neither COBUILD6 nor MED2 contains these forms, and, as seen above, OALD8 only has **pardon me for breathing** as an example.[8]

On the other hand, successful cases would include *would* and *excuse me*: LDOCE5's treatment of a sense of **would** as used to make a reserved statement (sense 10) is straightforward and easy to locate. It identifies the following collocations as meaningfully frequent and uses them as a signpost: *I would think/ imagine/say*. Although this particular use of the auxiliary verb is not strictly restricted to these collocates, this can help learners to locate this sense more easily. As for *excuse me*, it can be used in various ways, and it is usually followed by *but* when used to politely preface a disagreement. In fact, not only the five monolingual but the four bilingual dictionaries have examples of this use followed by *but*, and COBUILD6 and LEJD2 even include *but* as part of the formula. COBUILD6 prints the formula and *but* in bold in its explanation of sense 9, and LEJD2 lists it as a fixed phrase with *but* in parentheses showing the parenthesised part as optional: 'excuse me but' (sense 9 COBUILD6) and 'Excuse me, (but) ...' (LEJD2). Although some inconsistency can be noted in the way the dictionaries identify distinct senses of headwords, they could identify and treat them more appropriately with the perspective of politeness and speech act. It is also to be noted here that almost all the examples of *Pardon me for interrupting* in both the five monolingual and the four bilingual dictionaries are followed by *but* and a contrasting statement. LEJD2 even includes *but* as part of the phrase: '**Pardon me, but ...**'. Since this does not only show that *but* often follows this particular use of the formula but also reflects the fact that this is often used to preface one's disagreement, LEJD2's treatment of this formula should be welcome and will greatly help learners locate this more easily (Iwasaki 2002: 35–6).

11.4.3 Confusions over speech acts

As pointed out in 11.1.2 and 11.3.2, the five dictionaries often treat together, as a single use or sense, distinct speech acts performed with the use of a lexical item: 'said to politely accept or refuse something that has been offered to you' (sense 3 **thank** CALD3). In this explanation, two distinct acts are explained together: acceptance and refusal. This may be reasonable only in terms of saving space, but such condensed explanations are rather confusing. It will be far more user-friendly to distinguish each distinct act and treat them accordingly, and this is a basis for my claim that it is most promising to approach politeness in terms of speech act.

It is also true that the dictionaries sometimes distinguish related acts too finely. Take **wonder** for example:

(Sense 7 of **wonder** COBUILD6)
You can say 'I wonder' if you want to be very polite when you are asking someone to do something, or when you are asking them for their opinion or for information.

(**I wonder if/whether** MED2)
a polite way of asking someone for something such as information or their opinion, or asking them to do something

COBUILD6 and MED2 distinguish the act of asking a person to do a particular thing from the act of asking a person for their opinion or information. However, what they have in common is that they try to get something: the former asks for the other's action; the latter, information. Even though they could strictly be distinct acts, at least from the Japanese learner's perspective, they are not meaningfully different (see also 12.3.1 for discussions of LDOCE5's treatment of **I wonder if/whether** and **I was wondering if/whether**.). The only example I find problematic as to their confusions over distinct speech acts is between making a request and getting permission. This is closely connected with differences between politeness strategies in Japanese and English, and I will return to this in 12.4.1.

11.4.4 Usage notes

While bilingual dictionaries basically distinguish usage notes from translations, monolingual works often accommodate them within an explanation. For example, LDOCE5's explanation of sense 2 of **dyke** runs as follows: 'an offensive word for a LESBIAN (=woman who is sexually attracted to women). Do not use this word'. While the first sentence explains the basic property of the headword and its referent, the second sentence metalinguistically advises the user not to use this word. Here is another example, CALD3's explanation of sense 1 of **faggot**: 'a homosexual man. This word is considered offensive when it is used by people who are not homosexual'. Again, the second sentence in this explanation is concerned with the use of the headword, and can be considered to be a note rather than an explanation. This does not mean that any gloss on the use of a lexical item should be treated as a note, because explanations of types of headwords such as function words must in principle be concerned with how a particular word is used. Apart from function words, explanations focusing on the use of headwords basically deal with how they are used: 'used when speaking or writing to a woman especially in a formal or business situation' (madam sense 1 OALD8). It is here that the distinction between explanations and notes has become rather blurred, but dictionaries sometimes treat these types of additional information as a note rather than part of an explanation (e.g. **God knows** in 11.4.4). When an explanation contains, together with a basic description of the headword and its referent, some additional information such as metalinguistic or encyclopaedic explanations, or advice on how a particular expression should be used at a particular context, such additional information seems better dealt with as notes (see also 11.2.2.1 for the rationale of labels). In this book, I will therefore treat as notes such additional information accommodated in explanations.

Concerning usage notes, the five monolingual dictionaries have far fewer varieties than the bilinguals (see 12.3.1 for details), and the vast majority of notes in the monolinguals are concerned with collocation, synonymous expressions, and grammar. Below are two of the examples related with politeness in some way. (1) In the entry for **lady** as used to address a female person, LDOCE5 employs a boxed note of register, and explains that the noun is old-fashioned for a young lady; (2) After an example for **Jesus** (interjection),[9] LDOCE5 includes the following note: 'Be careful about using **Jesus** in this way, because Christians find it offensive'.

A serious problem with usage notes in the monolingual dictionaries is that their criteria for utilising notes are rather inconsistent. Compare the following explanations and notes from CALD3 and OALD8:

(Goodness/God/Heaven/Christ knows CALD3)
used to mean 'I don't know' or to emphasise a statement. Some people may find this offensive

(Sense 1 **God/goodness/Heaven knows** OALD8)
used to emphasize that you do not know sth
HELP Some people may find the use of God knows offensive.

(Sense 2 **God/goodness/Heaven knows** OALD8)
used to emphasize the truth of what you are saying

As OALD8 has two separate explanations for this formula, I cite both above. Because CALD3 does not make a distinction between the two uses, its note for this phrase should apply to both: 'Some people may find this offensive'. While sense 1 from OALD8 is followed by a similar note, no notes are given to sense 2. It is not obvious what their criteria are for utilising the note for sense 1 alone and not for sense 2. There are religious taboos on using the names of God and saints (see [I] e) in 12.3.2), and this must be the reason that the phrase can sound offensive. Then, both senses 1 and 2 from OALD8 should sound equally offensive, and its failure to include a note for sense 2 cannot be accepted. It is also to be noted that OALD8's note for sense 1 is not accommodated in the explanations. It is preceded by a blue box in which 'HELP' is printed in white letters, and the box and the note are placed after illustrative examples as an independent usage note. However, the other monolingual dictionaries often provide similar notes within an explanation; there are arguably no essential differences between the above independent note from OALD8 and CALD3's note within the explanation: 'Some people may find the use of God knows offensive' (OALD8) and 'Some people may find this offensive' (CALD3) because both of them simply state that the uses of the expressions sound offensive. In fact, in the following explanation of **effing**, OALD8 incorporates such information into the explanation: 'a swear word that many people find offensive that is used to emphasize a comment or an angry statement; used instead of "fucking."' This is another reason that I treat together some notes accommodated in explanations and similar independent ones. I will return to problems of usage notes in 12.3.

After I have discussed the four bilingual dictionaries in the next chapter, I will conclude my discussions of all the nine dictionaries in 12.5.

11.4.5 Summary of 11.4

Those issues which have not been dealt with in the previous sections are discussed in 11.4. They include the importance of accompanying functions, and lexicographers' confusions over speech acts. Through discussions of them it becomes clearer that a perspective on politeness and speech acts is essential for lexicographers when describing pragmatics.

Notes
1 MED2 also lists the phrase in the entry for **due**, and gives another example there. While examples are printed in italic in the book format, they are not in the CD-ROM version probably because they are shown in blue and are set out with more space around them.
2 Unless necessary, I will cite only one example for an explanation which I believe is best illustrating the sense or use concerned. When there is more than one example given for an explanation, I will specify which example I cite as '1st of 2' indicating the first of two examples.

3 The two dictionaries use quotation marks in different ways; while CALD3 adopts the American style, LDOCE5 is in the British style; namely, the use of double quotes for the former, and the use of single quotes for the latter. This is the case with the four bilingual dictionaries. It is also to be noted here that their use of italic in examples varies. Other dictionaries also adopt other styles. Although these differences will not directly be related with the realisation of politeness, they may well confuse learners. Even though learners usually use one dictionary and do not have to be familiar with conventions in other dictionaries, some guidance on these diversities may be necessary in a classroom.

4 Here is an example from Sense 2 **suppose** CALD3: '*I don't suppose (that) you could/I suppose you couldn't lend me £5 till tomorrow, could you?*'. Even considering the problem of saving space, CALD3's use of '/' alone in the above example would arguably be too sketchy because it is not really clear what can be listed as alternatives. Learners may wonder whether one can say, for example, 'I don't suppose that you could lend me £5 till tomorrow, could you?' because in this case the negative auxiliary verb in the main clause is 'don't' but the tag is 'could' which may contradict learners' basic knowledge about typical tag questions. Thus, whenever it is likely that learners will get confused, lexicographers must present information in accessible ways.

5 Although asking about one's intention or preference with the auxiliary verb *will* can also make a polite request, asking about the requestee's ability with *can* or *could* is less forceful in that it is easier to decline a request by saying that one 'cannot' help the requester rather than saying one 'will not' help them. This may be the reason why *Can you...?* is preferred to *Will you...?* except when the requester is asking the requestee to do something which they have the duty to do, as with their job (Tsuruta, Rossiter and Coulton 1988: 92f).

6 In the actual entry this note is marked with a special icon and symbol.

7 OALD8 employs equivalents to LDOCE5's signposts and names them 'short cuts.'

8 While CALD3 lists the use of **pardon** followed by gerund without *for* as 'Pardon me interrupting, but there's a client to see you (**pardon** 1 CALD3)', the other dictionaries use *for* to this construction. Apart from the monolingual dictionaries, LEJD2 mentions that *pardon* in this construction can be used either with or without *for*. It is possible that the other eight dictionaries do not mention this because they find it too obvious to mention, but that is not really acceptable.

9 In the actual dictionary text, LDOCE5 uses the superscript number of 2 for the spelling of the interjection use of Jesus as in **Jesus**^{2}, but it can be taken as designating Note 2 in the book. I thus left out the number.

CHAPTER XII
Politeness as Described in Bilingual Dictionaries

In this chapter, I will mainly discuss findings from my examination of the four bilingual dictionaries. Since monolingual dictionaries need to serve a broad readership, they cannot always meet the specific needs of users with particular linguistic backgrounds. I will therefore focus on issues peculiar to Japanese learners. After I have discussed problems common to monolingual and bilingual dictionaries in 12.1 and 12.1.1, I will move on to other issues: translation equivalents (12.2); usage notes (12.3); and other issues (12.4). As for usage notes, I will mainly discuss them in this chapter because the bilingual dictionaries have more notes than the monolinguals both in variety and quantity. In 12.5, I will conclude my discussions of all the nine dictionaries, both monolingual and bilingual.

12.1 Issues common to monolingual and bilingual dictionaries

Before I begin the discussion of the bilingual dictionaries, I will briefly look at how problems found in the monolingual dictionaries are dealt with in bilingual dictionaries. As can be readily expected, virtually all of the problems are also observable in the four bilingual dictionaries.

In 11.1.2, for instance, I have discussed the absence of a perspective on politeness and speech acts in the monolingual dictionaries by comparing their explanations of **pardon** as used to interrupt or preface an unfavourable statement like *Pardon me for interrupting*. The four bilingual dictionaries are also not very satisfactory in their descriptions of this use of **pardon**. LEJD2 does not have the use of **pardon** as an independent sense or a fixed phrase; GEJD4 does not even mention this. LOEJD and WEJD2 have the use as a fixed phrase, but LOEJD only provides the Japanese translations (cf. Note 6 in Chapter XII; [I] d) in 12.3.2). WEJD2 includes a short note together with the translation, but the note has nothing to do with politeness, simply stating that *Pardon me for interrupting* is used to attract another's attention.

The five monolingual dictionaries often fail to reflect the typical uses of a headword (see 11.1.3) too. This is also the case with translations. For example, the four bilingual dictionaries provide the following translations to **piss off** which, is classified into the same group as **bugger off** and **clear off**: *useru* and *jamaoshinai* (LEJD2), *usero* and *kiero* (LOEJD), *usero* (GEJD4) and *usero*, *kiero* and *jamada* (WEJD2). All these translations are rather rude in style, so the unfavourable property of the phrase must be successfully conveyed. Nevertheless, LEJD2 fails to put the translation in imperative, though it includes a note that the phrase is used in imperative. This is rather confusing and can be considered to be another example where lexicographers lack a speech act perspective.

Problems in the monolingual dictionaries in sense distinction can be seen in the bilingual as well. The nine dictionaries except OALD8 and WEJD2 include **well done** as an independent sense or a fixed phrase; OALD8 and WEJD2 list it as one of the examples under the entry for a sense of the adverb. For instance, WEJD2 has the following example: '*Well done* [played]! You did a great job!' (sense 3 **well** WEJD2). It is interesting that **well done** is printed in bold and italic here, which may show that the lexicographers are aware that this phrase is fixed. However, this is embedded as an example in a sub-entry of the adverb, and users likely have difficulty in locating this formula.

Problems which the monolingual dictionaries have with labels also apply to the bilingual works. See Table 4 on the next page. Like the five monolingual dictionaries, there is little consensus as to their choice of labels (see 11.2.1), and they often fail to use relevant labels. Take **fuck off** and **piss off**, for example. While GEJD4 does not have relevant label for the former, the other three dictionaries label the word properly. As for **piss off**, only LOEJD and WEJD2 label it.

The bilingual dictionaries' worst label-related problem is again concerning those labels expressing negative connotations. WEJD2, for instance, has the largest number of labels of the nine dictionaries, and employs as many as five such negative labels: **Criticising, Disapproving, Negative nuance, Offensive, and Rude**.[1] Like the other dictionaries, WEJD2 does not specify their differences, and it is almost impossible to learn from them exactly what property each of the labels covers (cf. 11.1.2). Apart from those conveying the negative attitudes, their confusions of labels are observable. For example, WEJD2 has a label of **Satisfied**, and I list the label in the tables because it is supposed to be related with one's feeling. Still, it is nearly impossible to identify exactly what language use it covers. It is true that labels are not a principal device for describing senses or uses of lexical items, and that dictionary users only seldom read

	LEJD2	LOEJD	GEJD4	WEJD2
Approving	Y	Y		Y
Criticising				Y
Derogatory	Y	Y	Y	
Disapproving	Y	Y		Y
Discriminatory	Y			
Euphemistic	Y			Y
Exaggerative	Y			Y
Feelings				
Formal	Y	Y	Y	Y
Very formal				
Humorous	Y	Y		Y
Impolite				
Informal	Y	Y	Y	Y
Very informal				
Ironic	Y			Y
Nicknames			Y	Y
Negative nuance				Y
Offensive				
Very offensive				
Politically correct			Y	
Polite	Y			Y
Positive nuance				Y
Rude	Y	Y		Y
Very rude				
Satisfied				Y
Sexual			Y	
Slang	Y		Y	Y
Taboo	Y	Y		Y
Vague				

Table 4: Labels used in the bilingual dictionaries
(See Note to Table 3 in 11.2.1.)

through all the important information in the outside matter, including keys to labels. However, lexicographers should provide more information on how they use each label, not only for users but for themselves to ensure that each label is used consistently.

There are also many cases where illustrative examples lack sufficient context in the four bilingual dictionaries, but they sometimes present contextual information successfully in relatively short examples:

(1st of 3 examples for sense 8 **might** WEJD2)
He just showed up. *You might want [like] to* see him right away.

(1st of 2 examples for sense 2 **might** WEJD2)
You might show a little gratitude.

According to WEJD2, the first example shows the use of **might** in making a moderate proposal, and the second illustrates the expression of the speaker's anger or surprise at the fact that the hearer has not yet done something which must have been done. Both of them are not very long, but they seem to work relatively well in that the possible situations or contexts are relatively easily inferred from them.

The first example begins with a statement addressed to the hearer, 'He just showed up', which may imply that the hearer has some business with him. 'He' and 'him' must refer to the same male person, and so the hearer may naturally want to see the person as soon as possible, if he 'just showed up' and has just become available. Without the first statement, one cannot think of such a situation where the second phrase might be used on its own, but, in this context and/or co-text, an utterance like '*You might want [like] to* see him right away' may well function as a kind of proposal. The adverb 'right away' in particular seems to support that particular function of this phrase, and makes explicit the hearer's wish to see him as soon as possible. On the other hand, the second example is rather short, consisting of only one sentence. Considering the fact that it is not a normal convention either in Japanese or in English-speaking cultures to explicitly demand others' gratitude to oneself, it would not be very difficult to imagine that the utterance may convey the speaker's special feeling, such as anger. This also explains why CALD3's example of **could** discussed in 11.3.1 ('Excuse me, could I just say something?') sounds anomalous; it is not a normal convention to verbally ask for permission to 'say something' because the speaker has already said something. Unless examples are set in easily inferable contexts, more information should be provided so that learners can grasp the context more easily and correctly, and understand how the speaker feels and what speech act they are performing.

Lexicographers' failures to describe register through examples can also be noted in the bilinguals and can be more clearly observed when examined in terms of speech act. The nine dictionaries often treat distinct speech acts together (see 11.1.2; 11.3.2; 11.4.3), and this is also the case with register. GEJD4 designates sense 4 of **might** as (polite) suggestion and (casual) request, and explains that the following example is very informal: 'You *might* post these letters for me' (sense 4 **might** GEJD4), and the accompanying Japanese translation, '*Konotegami o dashitekureru*' sounds rather casual. There are four other examples, which are formal and reserved, such as 'I thought we *might* go for a stroll along the beach' (*ibid.*). What these formal examples have in common is that they are suggestions. The two acts are distinct not only in terms of speech act but in terms of formality. It is quite possible that learners can become confused with this unsystematic treatment of speech act and register. If these uses are different in both the act they perform and how (in)formal they are, they should be treated separately.

On the other hand, due to the use of the address form 'sir', the following example from LEJD2 seems quite successful in illustrating the formal character of **with respect:** and 'With ~, sir, I must disagree'[2] **with (the greatest [(all) due])** **respect** LEJD2).

Mismatches between examples and explanations in the monolingual dictionaries are also found in the bilingual dictionaries (see 11.3.2):

(2nd of 2 examples for **be obliged** LEJD2)
We should *be greatly obliged* if you would come with us.[3]
No notes given

(1st of 2 examples for **obliged** WEJD2)
I'd *be obliged* if you'd hurry it up.
No notes given

LEJD2 and WEJD2 give them the following translation equivalents respectively:

kanshashiteiru [be grateful], *arigatakuomou* [appreciate][4]

The translations given in the two dictionaries simply suggest that **be obliged** is used to express one's appreciation, but the above two examples clearly function as making a polite request. Again, these would clearly show that the bilingual lexicographers also lack the perspectives of speech act as well as politeness.

12.1.1 *Teinei* in bilingual dictionaries

Since bilingual dictionaries do not provide explanations, the monolingual dictionaries' problem with the use of *polite* does not directly apply to the bilingual dictionaries. However, they also use *teinei*, the Japanese translation equivalent for *polite*, as a label or in their usage notes without specifying its meaning sufficiently. I therefore deal with this issue here as part of problems common to the monolinguals. In the entry for **if you please**, for instance, LEJD2 uses *teinei* as a label, and GEJD4 and WEJD2 use the adjective and its adverbial form in their notes without any disambiguation. Only LOEJD does not use *teinei*, but it often gives translations alone without any supporting labels and notes (cf. Note 6 in Chapter XII; 12.2.2; and (I) d) and f) in 12.3.2).

As far as the 76 lexical items are concerned, the four bilingual dictionaries do not use many alternatives to refer to 'polite' properties of the lexical items. The few examples are *hikaeme, kansetsuteki, enryo, enryogachi* and *oshitsukegamashisaganai*. Whilst *teinei* is used in 59 out of the 76 items, the number of items used as an alternative by any of the four bilingual dictionaries is no more than 12 in total.[5] It is important to note here that, except *kansetsuteki*, which is a literal translation of *indirect*, the other four terms are near synonyms, all describing almost the same attitude of being reserved, and that all the five terms can be used almost interchangeably with *teinei* (cf. Miyake 2011: 85; 252). This means that, even though lexicographers use one of them to avoid *teinei*, it would not make much difference. More concrete or more explicit and unambiguous expressions should be used depending on what types of polite phenomena are described.

Japanese learners have a tendency to learn English words through their translations. As a result, they often identify an English word with its Japanese translation (see 4.1.1). If this is the case with *polite* and *teinei*, this may cause another serious misunderstanding. *Teinei* is often associated with *teineigo*, a category in *keigo* (honorific forms of Japanese language) (cf. *Kojien* [Kojien unabridged Japanese Dictionary] 6th ed.: 2008), which belongs to deference rather than politeness (see also Thomas 1995: 150–1). Deference and politeness may become closer in the context of EFL lexicography because dictionaries can and should only deal with the most fixed part of language (cf. 8.1). In this sense, Japanese learners' misidentification of *teinei* and *polite* may not interfere so much with their acquisition of important politeness strategies and knowledge about important formulae, speech act markers, and politeness markers. Yet another difference in the two concepts may be crucial. Deference is respect paid to others due to their older age, higher rank, and so forth. Accordingly, it marks distance between interlocutors rather than deepens ties. If Japanese learners identify the concept of *teinei* with deference, it will exclude that portion of politeness which is generally recognised as positive politeness (cf. Takiura 2008: 50). It is also important to note that, while English is biased towards negative politeness (see 9.2.2.1), negative politeness is pointed out to be alien to Asian cultures, including Japanese (see 9.2.2.2). The use of *teinei* and its synonyms throughout an English-Japanese dictionary will thus rob Japanese learners of opportunities to learn about politeness properly.

In what follows, I will mainly discuss other issues peculiar to bilingual dictionaries.

12.2 Translation equivalents

While Yamada states that foreign learners are easily discouraged by the overwhelming amount of English in monolingual dictionaries (1996: 105–6), English-Japanese dictionaries can offer almost all the information in Japanese. This is a clear advantage of bilingual dictionaries, but translations are not always such an easy solution. In this section, I will discuss the important issues in turn: complements to translations (12.2.1); attempts at reducing misunderstanding by translations (12.2.2); and inconsistencies caused by translations (12.2.3).

12.2.1 Complements to translations

Since pragmatics is concerned with the way one can realise one's intent using linguistic resources (see 2.4.3), it should be easier to directly explain what the speaker's intent is; in other words, how and what act they are performing with the use of a lexical item. This is exactly what monolingual dictionaries do with explanations, though, as discussed in the previous chapter, the lexicographers' lack of pragmatic perspective often prevents this from being successful. On the other hand, bilingual dictionaries are in principle required to do this through translation equivalents. However, especially with such distant language pairs as Japanese and English, translations are often not really sufficient. Even when their semantic meanings correspond to a considerable extent, their pragmatic behaviours may not always. This is a reason that a pragmatic failure is often caused by differences between an L1 expression and its L2 translation (cf. Thomas 1983: 101ff.). This suggests that it is very difficult to help learners satisfactorily with translations alone. Therefore, the bilingual dictionaries very often include short notes for translations in order to disambiguate and/or supplement them. Usually this works well. Take *thank you* for example; *arigato* is its most common translation and is interchangeable with almost all the uses of *thank you*. This means that it is very difficult to distinguish senses of **thank you** properly only with the translation given. WEJD2 therefore includes a short parenthesised note to its translation:

(Sense 2 **Thank you** WEJD2)
Arigato (Moushide nitaisuru henji toshite)
[Thank you (As a reply to an offer)]

There are also cases where translations can cause some misunderstanding even though complemented with a label:

(Sense 2 of **so-and-so** LEJD2)
[*Enkyoku*] *iyanayatsu*
[*Euphemism*] horrible guy

Even though **so-and-so** is not a particularly polite word, by using this word one can avoid directly mentioning the unfavourable referent, which is a basic function of the headword (See 5.2.3 for comments from the informants on the use of 'small' to describe a male person). One of the first options that Brown and Levinson offer for a person doing an FTA is to completely give up doing it (1987: 69), as it is normally politer not to mention such an unpleasant person. However, the translation, *iyanayatsu* literally refers to the referent of the headword without any redress; in other words, *iyanayatsu* is not equivalent to the original English word in terms of pragmatics. Moreover, while the above parenthesised note and the translation of **thank you** play complementary roles in explaining the use of the formula, the label to *iyanayatsu* does not really complement the translation because the relationship between the label and the translation does not seem clear enough. The label can potentially be taken as designating the Japanese translation, not the original English headword. Ideally, translations given in a dictionary should be equal in status with the original expression in terms of pragmatics as well as other properties, though, as seen above, it is very difficult to find such translations.[6]

12.2.2 Attempts at reducing misunderstanding by translations

In view of the fact that Japanese learners tend to identify an English word with its Japanese translation (see 4.1.1), it is interesting to note that LOEJD occasionally avoids over-precise specifications of the meanings of translations. Under the entry for **what/who in the name of God/Christ...?**, for instance, it gives two translations with similar meanings: *ittai* and *somosomo* [what etc on earth] in '「 」' followed by *nado* [and so forth]. '「 」' is usually used in Japanese writing convention to refer to a particular expression itself, not to its referent or semantic content. As a result, LOEJD's presentation of the two translations provides users with a basic idea of what the original English phrase can mean without over-restricting the range of possible meanings/uses of the original English phrase. Although it is not really certain how much this can in fact help learners avoid careless identification of English words with their Japanese translations, this might be considered to be an attempt at lessening unnecessary confusions among learners. Considering this and the fact that

LOEJD often does not include usage notes and labels, which the other three bilingual dictionaries use in order to complement translations, LOEJD might have sought to describe or explain the meaning of an English phrase only through translations. In fact, Mr Motoyuki Shibata, one of its advisors, mentions the naturalness of translations in the dictionary as one of its merits (v) (cf. 12.1.1).

12.2.3 Inconsistencies caused by translations

There is also a case where some inconsistencies are observable among translations of cross-referred entries. *Don't mention it!*, *Not at all!*, and *You're welcome!* are usually translated as *Doitashimashite*, which can only be used as a reply to another's expression of appreciation. Probably because of this, LOEJD lists *Don't mention it!* and *You're welcome!* as synonyms for **not at all** in its entry without any note to the two phrases. While *Don't mention it!* can be used either as a reply to another's thanks or to an apology, the other two phrases can only be responses to another's expression of appreciation. LOEJD points out this fact in the entries for the two phrases, but not in the entry for **not at all**. Ordinary users would not double check the use of a phrase once they have found some information on the headword they look for. When a headword is explained in more than one place, all the descriptions should be checked. In this particular case, lexicographers themselves do seem to be misled by the translations of the three formulae.

12.2.4 Summary of 12.2

While it is a clear advantage of monolingual dictionaries that they can provide almost all descriptions in Japanese, translation equivalents are sometimes quite misleading in spite of their attempts at reducing misunderstandings. There are even cases where lexicographers themselves seem to have been misled by translations. It is questionable whether pragmatics can be properly described through translation equivalents.

12.3 Usage notes

In this section, I will mainly discuss usage notes from the four bilingual dictionaries. As mentioned at the outset of Chapter XI, the four bilinguals have far more varieties of usage notes than the five monolinguals. Before I discuss usage notes in the bilingual dictionaries, I will briefly compare the five monolingual and the four bilingual dictionaries in 12.3.1. I will then move on to types of usage notes in bilingual dictionaries (12.3.2) and problems peculiar to them: criteria for utilising usage notes (12.3.3); their accessibility (12.3.4); and reliability (12.3.5).

12.3.1 Monolingual versus bilingual dictionaries

While monolingual dictionaries are expected to serve a broad readership, bilingual works are in principle designed for speakers of a particular language. Accordingly, they can take into greater account a user's specific needs, such as their linguistic and/or cultural backgrounds. Considering the fact that pragmatic transfer accounts for the largest proportion of the possible causes of pragmatic failures between Japanese learners and English speakers (see 5.1), this is a clear advantage of bilingual works; in fact, the four bilingual dictionaries often provide users with more usage notes on potential pragmatic failures caused by gaps between English expressions and their Japanese translations (see [I] f) in 12.3.2). On the other hand, the five monolingual dictionaries employ far fewer notes, and they are often embedded within explanations.

Take a polite request made through **I wonder**, for example. It can be made less direct in various manners depending on the context; e.g. through the use of such politeness markers as *just* and/or *possibly* in the following subordinate clause (see also 9.3.1). It can further be made less direct if used in the past tense and/or the progressive form either or both in the main and the subordinate clauses.[7] Although CALD3 has two examples of **I wonder**, both of them use the present tense for the main clause without using any politeness marker. Considering the space restriction which any dictionary faces, it is questionable whether dictionaries should present more than one similar example: '*I wonder whether you could pass me the butter?*' and '*I wonder if you could give me some information about places to visit in the area?*' (2nd and 3rd of 3 examples for sense 2 of **wonder** CALD3). CALD3 has two similar examples alone without any notes. As for the other four monolingual dictionaries, they have at least one example of **I wonder**, which includes (a) politeness marker(s) and is in the past tense and/or in the progressive form. However, they do not mention at all how the phrase can be modified with the use of politeness markers and the different tenses and aspects. LDOCE5 in particular seems rather problematic because it divides the entry of **I wonder** into two, according to the tense and aspect, without explaining how they are different in terms of politeness: **I wonder if/whether** as sense 2 and **I was wondering if/whether** as sense 3.[8]

As for the four bilingual dictionaries, all of them mention how **I wonder** can be used less directly or politely by providing relevant usage notes. The bilingual dictionaries tend to have more usage notes than monolingual works both in variety and number, though some of their notes appear problematic in some way. After looking at the varieties of usage notes briefly in the next section, their problems will be discussed in 12.3.3, 12.3.4 and 12.3.5.[9]

12.3.2 Types of usage note

As discussed in 2.4.1 and 2.4.2, pragmatics is concerned with almost every aspect of language, so usage notes on politeness also cover quite a wide range of phenomena. So far as the 76 words/phrases/senses are concerned, those related with politeness can roughly be classified as follows:

(I) Notes given to particular senses/uses or their examples
a) Syntactic
   Sense 2 of **wonder** in WEJD2 is an indirect request as in 'I was *wondering if* you could help me' (sense 2a of **wonder** WEJD2), and this is split into senses **2a**, **b** and **c**. Each of them cross-refers to the following notes at the end of the whole entry for sense 2:

> Although each of senses **2a, b** and **c** is in fact used to ask about the present state of things, the use of the past tense indicates one's modest attitude like 'not now, or has already given up' and the use of the progressive aspect suggests that the speaker has not yet made up their mind. These jointly contribute to the realisation of politeness, giving the hearer options. The following phrases are listed in the order of politeness, from politer to less polite: I was wondering if ... > I'm wondering if ...> I wonder if ....

> As the above notes are mainly concerned with how syntactic phenomena, tense and aspect can enhance the realisation of politeness, this is classified as Syntactic (see also 11.3.4 for multi-lexical realisation of politeness).

b) Sociolinguistic:
   At the end of the entry for half-caste, LOEJD includes the following notes:

> half-caste is a discriminative expression. When referring to 'konketuji' [a child of mixed parentage], 'a person of mixed race' should be used; and 'of mixed-race' should be used for 'konketsu(ji) no' [of (a child of) 'mixed parentage].

> These notes are concerned with political correctness and register respectively, and I classify them as sociolinguistic.

c) Pragmatic

Under the entry for sense 1 of **at all** in GEJD4, there are two sets of examples consisting of short dialogues, and one of them is concerned with the formula as used to reply to one's expression of gratitude: 'Thank you.' 'Not at all.'[10] The following notes are given to this example of **not at all**:

(1) In the US *You're welcome* is usually used; (2) **Not at all** is a formal expression; the use of this phrase alone sounds distant, and so this is often followed by another utterance like 'I'm glad I could help you'.

While (1) and the former part of (2) are concerned with sociolinguistic properties of the headword, regional variety and register respectively, the latter part of (2) deals with a pragmatic preference, and advises users to supplement this phrase with another expression.

As this last note is directly concerned with the speaker's realisation of their intent (see 2.4.3), this is classified as pragmatic.

d) Paralinguistic:
Immediately after the spelling of **thank you**, GEJD4 applies a sign to indicate that it is usually used with a falling intonation (see **Figure** 4 below).

*__Thánk you.__ (↘) (1) 〔…を〕ありがとう, どうも〔*for*〕(→ ㊧ ❶)《◆(1) 感謝を表す幅の広い言葉で, 多くの場面で気軽に用いる；「すみません」と訳せることも多い；軽い意味のときは (↗) となる；(↘) の方が本気の感謝；(略式)では通例, 高いピッチで /hǽnkju, ŋkju, k̬kju/ と発音される. (2) I ~ you. は (正式)》‖ T~ *you* anyway [just the same, all the same]. ともかく, ありがとう《◆ 自分の意図通りにならなくて

Figure 4: Part of GEJD4's entry for **thank you**

In addition, after the translations of sense 1, six short notes are listed, punctuated with semicolons. The following two are concerned with paralinguistic features and politeness:

When **thank you** is used casually, it is used with rising intonation.

When the speaker sincerely shows their appreciation, **thank you** is used with falling intonation.

While the five monolingual dictionaries and LOEJD do not include notes on paralinguistic features, the other three bilingual dictionaries have many. See also Note 6 in Chapter XII.

e) Encyclopaedic:

As mentioned in 11.4.4, the offensive character of *Jesus* (interjection) is annotated in LDOCE5. Although the note does not mention the reason, its offensive nature must derive from doctrines of Christianity. For instance, WEJD2 explains that it was a violation of commandments to recklessly use the names of God and/or saints, and thus they are now used as words of abuse (sense 1 **swear**).

As the offensive character of *Jesus* is closely connected with doctrines of Christianity, this may be classified as encyclopaedic.

f) L1 and L2 differences

It is understood that Japanese learners often identify English words with their Japanese translations (see 9.3.8); such pairs of English words and their Japanese translations, whose semantic meanings overlap but their pragmatic functions do not, may cause serious problems. For example, while the Japanese translation for **sorry**, *sumimasen* is very often used to thank others, **sorry** cannot be used that way (Ide 1998; Otani 2006). LEJD2, GEJD4 and WEJD2 mention this difference in their entries for **sorry** as used to apologise. Considering the fact that one of the most frequent causes of pragmatic failures is L1 interference (Thomas 1983: 102; see also 5.1), this kind of note should be highly evaluated. None of the five monolingual dictionaries mention this potential danger at all; nor does LOEJD. In this sense, the three bilingual dictionaries make the best of their advantage as a bilingual work designed for Japanese learners.

(II) Notes given to the referents of headwords

LEJD2 has detailed notes for the entry of **politeness**, which is not concerned with the use of the headword but with the referent, politeness as a concept. In the notes, LEJD2 lists, according to their degrees of politeness, seven phrases which can be used to ask others to do a particular thing: 1. Open this window; 2. **Will [Can] you** open this window?; 3.**Would [Could] you** open this window?; 4. **Do you think you could** open this window?; 5. **I wonder if you could** open this window; 6. **Would you mind** opening this window?; 7. **I'd be grateful [appreciate it] if you would** (be good [kind] enough to) open this window. LEJD2 also mentions that 1, 2 and 3 above could be made politer if they are used with *please*.

The notes are sometimes cross-referred to from other entries when it seems necessary, such as the speech act marker, *Could you...?* In terms of saving space, this may be a good way to deal with such matters as this, but obviously more information and more examples would be necessary so that politeness can be explained satisfactorily. There will be far more ways to perform it politely. Making a request is not the only act which is concerned with politeness. It is also to be noted that LEJD2's notes on politeness are only concerned with negative politeness, neglecting its counterpart, positive politeness (see 12.4.3). More importantly, as noted repeatedly, it is simply wrong or at least misleading, unless the phrases are considered in a particular context.

(III) Featured notes

At least partly for commercial reasons, the bilingual dictionaries have a wider variety of notes, including featured or boxed ones. So long as the 76 senses/uses of lexical items are concerned, the following series of notes are found to be concerned with politeness: Dokukai no pointo [Reading tips] (WEJD2), Hyougen [Expressions] (WEJD2), Bunka [Cultural differences] (LOEJD) and Era noto [Error notes] (LOEJD).

A Hyougen column in WEJD2 for sense 4 of **could** lists five ways to make a request politer, such as addressing the hearer by their given name (cf. Brown and Levinson 1987: 107ff.). It is important to note that this is the only positive politeness strategy listed, and that the other four are concerned with negative politeness such as the use of the subjunctive mood. Similarly, as seen in (II) above, LEJD2's note on 'politeness' is also devoted to negative politeness (cf. 12.4.3).

Apart from notes contained at entries, LEJD2 has a collection of tips for Japanese learners as part of its back matter, 'Tsuzuriji to hatsuon kaisetsu' [Spellings and pronunciations], consisting of 98 main topics or articles and their sub-articles, and they are often cross-referred to from dictionary entries. For example, the entry for **excuse me**, as used to ask the hearer to repeat something that they have just said, cross-refers to the 94th article, where functions and effects of the use of rising intonation are explained in terms of politeness, probably because this use of the phrase is typically used with rising intonation.

While these notes are basically welcome, there are three major problems. First, their criteria for utilising notes are not clear. Second, notes on politeness or the related phenomena are often buried or embedded in other notes rather randomly so that it would be very difficult for users to locate them; or rather it is likely that learners do not even try to find notes necessary for them (cf. 7.1). Third, notes in the bilingual dictionaries sometimes do not seem accurate enough or based on reliable data. These problems will be discussed in the next sections, where lexicographers' lack of politeness and speech act perspective is clearly observable in their treatment of notes as well.

12.3.3 Criteria for utilising usage notes

Like the five monolingual dictionaries (see 11.4.4), the four bilingual dictionaries often use notes rather inconsistently. Apart from lexical items with some clearly distinctive properties, they have no consensus on what items to annotate. For instance, **want** could sound rather rude or impolite if compared with such phrases as *would like*, but it is not a verb which is usually considered as particularly rude. However, GEJD4 and WEJD2 include notes for **want** in terms of politeness.[11] In order for users to find the notes successfully, they must have some prior knowledge that the verb has some potentially impolite properties and that the dictionary explains such dangers somewhere in its volume. This is contradictory to what one expects of ordinary dictionary users' knowledge. Especially considering the fact that **want** is usually not recognised as particularly rude, it is very unlikely that learners even seek to find such notes. Moreover, if notes should be necessary for such lexical items as **want**, almost every word/phrase needs one because they may sound ruder, compared with their politer counterparts. Even neutral pronouns like *he* could sound ruder than *gentleman* depending on the context (see 6.2), and it would simply be wrong for a dictionary to designate *he* as a rude pronoun which needs to be avoided. Their confusion as to what items to annotate may suggest that lexicographers do not fully understand how pragmatics should be dealt with in the EFL context.

12.3.4 Accessibility to usage notes

Bilingual dictionaries are in principle expected to provide more notes than monolingual ones because they need to supplement translations in some way. In fact, their translations are often followed by parenthesised short notes to disambiguate them (cf. 12.2.1). Even excluding these notes, bilingual dictionaries have more and wider varieties of notes. This often makes it harder for users to locate particular parts of notes.

Taishukan's Genius English-Japanese Dictionary, 1st ed. (1988) became one of the best-selling English-Japanese dictionaries for its detailed usage notes, and GEJD4 follows this tradition as the latest successor (as of 2010). This tendency is more or less the case with other English-Japanese dictionaries (cf. Yagi 2006: 5–6). While detailed usage notes are basically welcome, they often give too much information in an entry in a random and thus less accessible way. For example, GEJD4 does not treat **I wonder** as an independent sense or a phrase, but as one of the examples for a sense of **wonder** which expresses one's desire to know something or feel curious. The example runs as follows: 'I ~ if I could use the telephone'.[12] However, it adds three detailed notes to that example, two numbered notes and one note marked with a special icon, and even uses further examples for two of the notes. The two numbered notes begin by explaining that the verb can be used to make a polite request, and move on to how the degrees of politeness can be changed with a different tense and aspect, related expressions, and finally end with a note on punctuation. Immediately after these notes follows a further note: 'in informal speech, the word order in a subordinate clause of **wonder** can be arranged as in a question like "I wonder if is he OK?" However, this is considered to be incorrect in written English'. Just this one note only is marked with a Gohou [usage] icon, and one may naturally wonder whether this is so important compared with the unmarked notes. Ordinary users might not need this much information; at least, most of them may have difficulty in finding what they are looking for from among these notes because they are at least seemingly randomly embedded in an entry for a use of the headword.

Lexicographers need to select and/or arrange necessary pieces of information from the user perspective. At least, they should not put together notes on politeness and those on punctuation; pragmatic failures can cause serious misunderstandings because they are often not recognised as 'linguistic' errors or mistakes (cf. 3.3.5). Furthermore, considering the fact that GEJD4 identifies the function of **I wonder** as a speech act marker by mentioning that the verb can be used to make a request, they must have treated the speech act marker as an independent sense or as a fixed phrase. This would again suggest that they lack the speech act perspective. This tendency is especially the case with GEJD4 and WEJD2 (e.g. **not at all**; **Do you mind** doing?; and **please** (sense 1 WEJD2).

12.3.5 Reliability of usage notes

I will close my discussion of usage notes by citing GEJD4's notes for the use of **ma'am** as used to address a female stranger. To say the least, they are not reliable enough:

> (Sense 1 ma'am GEJD4)
> This word is usually used for a woman over 25; this is politer[13] than Miss but more casual than madam; basically, it is preferable to use Miss for a woman younger than yourself and Ma'am for an older woman than yourself respectively.

It is not clear whether the above notes reflect universal or objective uses of the headword and are based on reliable data at all. They seem rather subjective or restricted to the personal experiences of lexicographers and/or people around them. This is exactly what I have criticised in 4.1.4. At the very least, the age of a woman who deserves to be addressed as **ma'am** may greatly vary depending on such variables as the relationship between the interlocutors, context or cultural preferences. Even between British and American speakers, there are likely to be different attitudes regarding such matters as this. Moreover, it is questionable whether it is a dictionary's role to specify the use of *miss* and *ma'am* according to the ages of the addresser and the addressee. Dictionaries are expected to deal with abstract properties of lexical items (see 3.1.2). So long as pragmatics is concerned, dictionaries may need to go beyond that restriction to some extent. Still, the above notes from GEJD4 are arguably outside the purview of lexicography. Dictionaries have authority, and thus lexicographers should try not to sound too prescriptive, especially considering such matters as this. Even when lexicographers do not intend a note to be prescriptive, users might take them as such irrespective of dictionaries' claims (see 3.3.6). The same goes for **gentleman** (sense 2a GEJD4), and, probably, this is also the case with notes on intonation in the four bilingual dictionaries ([I] d) in 12.3.2) because there are no reliable data on them, even in the latest spoken corpora concerning such paralinguistic features (see 4.1.2). Moreover, intonation can play different roles depending on such variables as context and the relationship between interlocutors.

Usage notes in bilingual dictionaries in particular cover quite a wide range of phenomena concerning language use, and so lexicographers need to carefully think about how they should deal with them, and select what headwords and which use and/or aspect of them to annotate (see 12.3.3). For that difficult task, again, the functional perspective of politeness and speech act should be helpful (see 13.1). It will also be important to review all the descriptions in terms of language teaching, so that they could avoid sounding too prescriptive (see 13.2).

12.3.6 Summary of 12.3

Compared with monolingual dictionaries, bilingual dictionaries have far more usage notes both in terms of number and variety. However, lexicographers' lack of a pragmatic perspective causes three problems: (1) their criteria for utilising usage notes are rather inconsistent; (2) notes on important pragmatic phenomena are embedded with other notes on such issues as punctuation, which makes it very difficult for users to locate them; (3) usage notes in bilingual dictionaries are sometimes not accurate enough. There is much room for improvement in the treatment of usage notes in bilingual dictionaries.

12.4 Other issues

In this section, I will deal with other issues which do not belong with those in the previous sections: request and getting permission (12.4.1); face and rapport as the framework for analysis (12.4.2); and biases towards negative politeness (12.4.3).

12.4.1 Request and getting permission

In 11.1.2, I have pointed out that the monolingual dictionaries sometimes treat more than one distinct act as one use of a headword, and this is also the case with the bilinguals. Sometimes they even confuse related but distinct acts as one sense. Such confusions or mixing of related speech acts do not necessarily result in a serious problem. In the case of request and getting permission, however, this can be a cause of a serious pragmatic failure between Japanese and English-speaking people. Consider, for example, the following explanation and its example:

> (Sense 6 if CALD3)
> 'used when you want to make a polite request or remark'
>
> (2nd of 3 example *ibid.*)
> Would you mind if I open/opened (=Can I open) *the window?*

While the explanation designates the use as making a polite request or remark, its example illustrates a use of getting permission to open a window. Tsuruta, Rossiter and Coulton point out that when it is grammatically possible to express one's wish either as a request or as getting permission, Japanese speakers prefer the former and English speakers the latter (1988: 124–30). According to them, for instance, when a Japanese student in a classroom wants to listen to a part of audio material again, they tend to say 'Could you play it again?' whilst an English native speaker would say 'Could I listen to it again?' They argue that this reflects differences between politeness strategies in Japanese and English. In this context, Japanese speakers find important the fact that they cannot achieve their goal without troubling the teacher. Accordingly, they make a request in order to explicitly acknowledge that (see 9.2.2.2 for discussions of negative politeness in Japanese). On the other hand, English speakers prefer to get permission because they wonder whether their listening to the material again might affect the teacher's lesson plan. Tsuruta, Rossiter, and Coulton continue by saying that if students do not behave as teachers expect in the context, it may cause an undesirable effect. More precisely, if a British student says to a Japanese teacher 'Could I listen to it again?' and actually wants the teacher to play it again, the teacher may at first think that the student will play the audio material by themselves, and when the teacher has realised that the student actually wants them to play that part for them, the teacher may think that the student's way of asking the teacher to play the part is rather haughty. Unfortunately, their confusions between making a request and getting permission are found in all the nine dictionaries under such phrases as *Might I...?*, *Would you mind if I...?* and *Could you...?* While monolingual dictionaries basically cannot deal with such matters as this (see 12.3.1), bilingual dictionaries must offer users more help.

12.4.2 The necessity of explaining different politeness strategies in Japanese and English

I don't suppose discussed in 7.1 and 9.2.3.2 is another example where Japanese and English politeness strategies are so different that a translation and a short note do not suffice. All the bilingual dictionaries but LOEJD include some notes stating that the speech act marker can be used to make a request, but, as pointed out in 9.2.3.2, the use of the phrase when making a request does not sound polite at all in the Japanese context; or rather, it sounds rude or haughty. Even though a dictionary explains its core function clearly, Japanese learners may not be able to understand the mechanism. Whenever necessary, bilingual dictionaries should not only mention the function but clearly explain how the use of the phrase can make a request polite in the English context. Otherwise, learners cannot fully understand the use of the speech act marker. This should be where bilingual dictionaries offer more help than monolinguals (cf. 13.2).

It is also to be mentioned that the success of a request made with *I don't suppose* depends on English-speaking people's preference on negative politeness; on the other hand, from a Japanese perspective, the use of the phrase is not a matter of negative politeness or face at all but one of equality rights (cf. 9.2.3.2).

12.4.3 Biases towards negative politeness

Lastly, it is to be mentioned that all the nine dictionaries, both monolingual and bilingual, are clearly biased towards negative politeness, or sociality rights (see 9.2.3.1), though it is noted that the concept of negative politeness is alien to the Japanese culture (see 9.2.2.2). Out of the 76 items, **well done** is the only lexical item which is addressed to positive politeness, or quality face. LEJD2's note on *politeness* is also concerned with negative politeness alone ([II] in 12.3.2). While Brown and Levinson point out that politeness strategies in English are more elaborated on in terms of negative politeness (1983: 130; see also 9.2.2.1), it is clearly necessary for lexicographers to consider politeness from a broader perspective. As pointed out in 9.2.3, the framework of rapport management would be most suitable at the present writing.

12.4.4 Summary of 12.4

In this section the following three issues which have not been dealt with in the previous sections are discussed: (1) different attitudes Japanese learners and English speakers adopt to make requests and obtain permission; (2) necessity of explaining mechanisms by which politeness is realised differently in Japanese and English; (3) lexicographers' biases towards negative politeness. All these are likely to affect Japanese learners' proper understanding of different politeness strategies in Japanese and English, and should be treated more carefully. For this purpose the rapport management theory should be most promising as the framework for analysis because different politeness strategies in Japanese and English can be considered appropriately with the theory.

12.5 Dictionaries as tools for learning pragmatics (Closing remarks to Chapters XI and XII)

In Chapters XI and XII, I have discussed findings from my examination of the treatment of pragmatics, especially politeness, in the nine EFL dictionaries. The results show that their descriptions are not always very satisfactory and seem to do a disservice to Japanese learners. In this respect, there are three fundamental questions I need to address. First, is it really possible for dictionaries to treat politeness properly? Second, if the answer to the first question is yes, why is the treatment of politeness in the nine dictionaries not satisfactory? Third, will learners use their dictionaries to learn politeness if there is a good dictionary available which treats politeness properly?

As for the first question, one may well wonder whether the results of my examination simply suggest that dictionaries cannot deal with politeness properly. However, I would argue that they can greatly improve their treatment of politeness if only they demonstrate more awareness of the importance of politeness in the EFL context and convey a deepened understanding of politeness. As stated in 11.1.5, even though eight out of the nine dictionaries fail to capture an important aspect of politeness, that aspect should be well within the realm of lexicography, if even one dictionary is successful (see also 11.1.2). Many of the unsuccessful cases can in fact be incorporated into lexicography.

My answer to the first question may inevitably lead to the second question of why the nine dictionaries fail to treat politeness satisfactorily. One can assume that ordinary learners would not use their dictionaries in order to learn politeness, and thus lexicographers did not pay sufficient attention to politeness. Yet, it is a fact that many of the dictionaries do claim to offer substantial pragmatic information, and that politeness is one of the most important aspects of pragmatics. Some of the dictionaries even contain essays on the importance of politeness in the EFL context. Probably, they tried but failed. As discussed above, one of their most serious problems is that they lack the pragmatics perspective, and this will explain why they are not always successful or unsuccessful. If only they approach pragmatics with clear and consistent perspectives of politeness and speech act in general, their descriptions will be greatly improved. This will then lead to the final question of whether dictionaries can help learners if the dictionaries improve their treatment of politeness.

As for the third question, I need to point out two basic facts on learners' use of dictionaries. First, few Japanese learners use their dictionaries while talking with others in English; or rather, it is nearly impossible to use dictionaries in an ongoing conversation. Second, most learners do not seem to expect their dictionaries to have information on such things as politeness. These two facts may suggest that even though a very good dictionary is available, learners would not use it to learn politeness.

It is only natural that they do not consult a dictionary when communicating with others in a foreign language; dictionaries are reference works, not interpreters. Learners no more use their dictionaries to sustain a conversation than they do for memorising vocabulary items. They consult a dictionary when they are not sure of a sense or use of lexical items. If learners know their dictionaries can offer them help concerning a question about politeness, they may well consult theirs after a conversation. As mentioned in 7.1, I accidentally found a relevant description of **I don't suppose** in COBUILD2, and realised that I had misinterpreted the intent of my then-supervisor pragmatically. While it is very unlikely that people consult their dictionaries when talking with others in a foreign language, anyone may occasionally feel that they are not perfectly sure about what their interlocutor means by the use of a word/phrase in that context. It is after such occasions when they can refer to their dictionaries.

Although this is outside the purview of the current study, teachers and all those involved in language teaching must change their views of dictionaries, and encourage learners to consult their dictionaries when they have a question about pragmatic issues. More importantly, lexicographers need to improve their treatment of pragmatics in order not to disappoint them. Otherwise, their dictionaries will only disappoint most motivated learners.

Many problems of dictionaries' treatment of politeness are now identified through discussions in Chapters XI and XII. In the next chapter, I will conclude the results of my examination of the nine dictionaries in the form of five recommendations for dictionary makers, and also for anyone in the EFL industry including teachers and text writers.

Notes

1 The actual labels used are *hinanshite, kenashite, hiteitekini, zonzaini* and *hi* respectively.
2 '~' refers to either 'the greatest respect', 'all due respect' or 'due respect'. While LEJD2 shows these three options, it does not specify which is replaced with '~' here. I thus leave '~' in the example as it is.
3 **Obliged** is printed as '~' in the original text.
4 WEJD2 also shows a particle often used with these Japanese translations.
5 There are two ways to type *teinei*; that is, in kana [Simplified Japanese letters] and kanji [Chinese characters], and both are counted here.
6 It is to be mentioned that LOEJD is the only dictionary which does not mention the basic function of **so-and-so** in any way (cf. 11.4.4; 12.3.2). LOEJD is a unique dictionary compiled by a team of Japanese and English-speaking lexicographers, and, unlike the other bilingual works, it often provides translations alone without any notes or labels.
7 The use of the past tense can also be considered to be the use of the subjunctive mood (see also 11.3.4), but I do not make a distinction here because they are identical in terms of form.
8 Sense 3 is further divided into two: a) politely asking the hearer for help and b) politely asking whether the hearer wants to do a particular thing.
9 Apart from pragmatics, probably under the influence of highly competitive entrance examinations to universities in Japan, bilingual dictionaries tend to offer more help to learners, considering the interferences of their native languages. While most of them list words with the same pronunciation as the headword and help learners to be aware of the fact, LEJD2 takes a further step and even lists words with similar sounds such as *hay* and *hate* listed at the beginning of the entry for **hey**. The former was designated as having the same sound, and the latter as the similar sound to the headword.
10 In the original text 'all' is printed as '~' which is a Japanese writing convention to mark an omission.
11 As to the monolinguals, CALD3 is the only dictionary which includes a similar note to the verb.
12 In the original text **wonder** is printed as '~', and this is also the case with other examples in GEJD4.
13 The original word used is *teinei*.

CHAPTER XIII
Recommendations to Dictionary Makers

In this chapter, on the basis of findings from the previous chapters, I will offer five recommendations towards a better treatment of politeness in EFL lexicography, with particular emphasis on Japanese learners.

1) Approach pragmatics from the functional perspective.
2) Review all the descriptions from an educational perspective.
3) Cooperate with non-lexicographic resources.
4) Make the best use of the latest technologies.
5) Pay attention to differences between pragmatic conventions in learners' native language and English, with help from a team of Japanese and English-speaking lexicographers.

As discussed in 11.3.1, pragmatics is closely connected with highly complex procedures in human communication, and so they should not be regarded as strictly specifying how pragmatics should be dealt with in the EFL context. They are general guidelines which lexicographers need to keep in mind when dealing with pragmatics.

In the following sections I will discuss the above recommendations in turn: Approach pragmatics from the functional perspective (13.1); Review all the descriptions from an educational perspective (13.2); Cooperate with non-lexicographic resources (13.3); Make the best use of the latest technologies (13.4); Pay attention to differences between pragmatic conventions in the learners' native language and English (13.5), and Sample entries (13.6).

13.1 Approach pragmatics from the functional perspective

In this section, I will discuss the first recommendation: Approach pragmatics from the functional perspective. My discussions so far have mostly been dedicated to politeness because it is an indispensable part or function of pragmatics. It is important to note that it should become possible to deal with most, though not all, pragmatic phenomena from the functional perspective, paying attention to not only politeness but to such important pragmatic functions as speech acts (see 8.5). Considering these, it would be safe to at least roughly equate pragmatic functions with pragmatics. This is the reason that I use 'pragmatics' not 'politeness' in this recommendation. As the pragmatic functions or perspective cover several related but distinct issues, I will discuss them separately: speech acts and politeness (13.1.1); accompanying functions (13.1.2); *polite* and *teinei* (13.1.3); and explanations in Japanese (13.1.4).

13.1.1 Speech acts and politeness

Speech act and politeness are the most important functions of pragmatics, but my examination of the nine dictionaries has revealed that their treatment of speech act and politeness is rather inconsistent; they often fail to specify, through their explanations or translations, what act the use of a lexical item can perform or how a particular use of a headword is related with politeness. However, if a particular pragmatic function in the use of a lexical item is outside the purview of lexicography, no dictionary can deal with it. In actual fact, their degrees of success vary from headword to headword, also from dictionary to dictionary. A dictionary is not always successful; nor does it always fail (see 11.1.2). This would suggest that they clearly lack the perspective of pragmatics, and that, if only they keep the politeness and speech act perspective in mind, their treatment of pragmatics will be greatly improved.

Problems derived from the absence of the pragmatic perspective are concerned with almost every aspect of lexicography, ranging from the selection of headwords to their descriptions. Accordingly, such problems as the following should also be solved or eliminated with the perspective of speech act and politeness: failures to specify typical uses of a headword (cf. 11.1.3), blurred sense distinctions (cf. 11.1.4), limited description of a speech act (cf. 11.1.5), mismatches between illustrative examples and other descriptions (cf. 11.3.2), failures to add a relevant usage note (cf. 11.4.4; 12.3.3), hidden or embedded usage notes (cf. 12.3.4), and failures to use necessary labels (cf. 11.2.2.1; 12.1). The pragmatic perspective will also give lexicographers useful insights into typical situations for a particular speech act to be performed, which then tells them what contextual information should be provided in an example (cf. 11.3.1).

13.1.2 Accompanying functions

While some accompanying functions like evaluative are easily described with a label alone, this is not always the case. However, considering the fact that they often play a crucial role in realising politeness as well as performing a speech act (see 8.5), whenever necessary their functions should be sufficiently described as part of dictionary entries.

As discussed in 11.4.1, the core function of *I'd be obliged* is a polite or indirect request, and it is fulfilled through the accompanying functions of volitive and epistemic. Here, I must point out that it is far from sufficient for a dictionary only to explain clearly the core function of the speech act marker, because it is not a normal convention in Japan to make a request by thanking the requestee for their future action in advance, as this speech act marker literally expresses (or rather, this is likely to produce) an undesirable effect such as making the requester sound arrogant, exactly as with *I don't suppose* discussed in 7.1 and 9.2.3.2. The mechanism in which polite speech acts are performed should be clearly explained to learners. I will return to this in 13.2.

13.1.3 *Polite* and *teinei*

Politeness is an umbrella function of speech acts to maintain one's rapport with others. As discussed in 11.1.1 and 12.1.1, while the concepts as well as functions of polite and teinei vary depending on context, in dictionary descriptions they are often referred to vaguely as *polite* or *teinei* without disambiguating them properly. Although it is not always easy to describe correctly all the phenomena which can be felt to be polite or teinei, the functional approach should be useful for this purpose too. Lexicographers must at least explain how a particular use of a lexical item is considered to be polite; more precisely, what interpersonal function it performs (cf. 8.5). So far as the 76 lexical items are concerned, there are successful cases where their polite uses are explained properly even without using *polite* or *teinei* (cf. 11.1.1; 12.1.1). The two words should basically be avoided unless supplemented successfully with descriptions of more concrete functions. This can also help lexicographers deepen their understanding of politeness. I will also return to this in 13.2.

13.1.4 Explanations in Japanese

Compared with explanations, translation equivalents have two major disadvantages: (1) they cannot directly describe functions which the use of lexical items can fulfil[1] and (2) there are not many good Japanese translation equivalents which satisfactorily agree with their English counterparts both in terms of semantics and pragmatics (cf. 12.2.1). The few successful exceptions would include technical terms in science. It will follow from this that explanations in monolingual dictionaries are better in dealing with pragmatics; at the same time, it is known that Japanese learners are easily discouraged by the dictionaries' overwhelming amount of information provided in English (cf. 12.2).

In view of the fact that monolingual dictionaries cannot sufficiently treat problems peculiar to Japanese, I recommend that bilingual dictionaries should provide explanations in Japanese, and directly describe pragmatic functions.[2] As seen in 12.2.3, there are even cases where lexicographers themselves seem to have been misguided by translations. Unless an English word and its Japanese translations agree completely both in semantics and pragmatics, translations should basically not be given. Translations can be provided for learners only when it is clear that they will not mislead learners, and this policy should be clearly explained in outer matters in order not to confuse users in any way (see 13.3).

13.2 Review all the descriptions from the educational perspective

In this section, I will discuss the second recommendation: Review all the descriptions from an educational perspective. Dictionaries are among the most important tools for learning a language, and all the descriptions should be reviewed from the educational perspective so that they can offer more helpful guidance to the user. As pointed out in 13.1.2, different pragmatic conventions in Japanese and English sometimes make it difficult for Japanese learners to understand the way politeness is realised (see also 11.1.1). This implies that even though a dictionary clearly explains what act one can perform using a particular expression, a learner may not fully appreciate its importance or acquire that knowledge. It is in such cases that dictionaries must offer detailed accounts for the mechanism in which politeness is realised so that learners can make the best use of all the important information in their dictionary. *Polite* and *teinei*, discussed in 13.1.3, are another case in point because they are not only vague but quite misleading. Although this may naturally result in longer entries, inevitably taking more space, the criteria for deciding the length of entries should be whether sufficient amounts of information are provided in a clear and easily understandable way.

My examination of the nine dictionaries has also revealed that they use too many labels rather inconsistently, especially those designating negative properties of headwords, and that their explanations for the use of labels are too concise and sometimes contradicting to their actual use. There are also cases where they do not explain their use of particular labels at all (cf. 11.2.2.1). If they cannot explain their use of each label properly, it is equally likely that users will not distinguish them sufficiently. They also need to be reviewed from the educational perspective, and it would be useful to reduce the number of negative labels at least. If some subtle nuance needs to be explained, it should be described clearly in individual explanations. This will maintain the basic role of labels: to mark words with some special feature (see 11.2.2.1)

Considering the basic role of a dictionary, it is also important for it to offer users easy access to what they are looking for. For example, formulae, speech act markers and politeness markers that are identified with fulfilling particular functions, and/or the use in particular contexts or situations, should be arranged and listed accordingly in special indices so that users can easily locate them according to their functions and/or their use in situations.

Apart from the above suggestions, while dictionaries are basically expected to be prescriptive (see 3.3.6), pragmatic information should not be dealt with too prescriptively, especially when dealing with such delicate issues as the age of a woman and the address forms (see 12.3.5). It will surely be of benefit for lexicographers to review all the descriptions from the educational perspective. I will return to this in the next section.

13.3 Cooperate with non-lexicographic resources

In this section, I will discuss the third recommendation: Cooperate with non-lexicographic resources. There are important issues which are closely connected with learners' acquisition of politeness knowledge and skills but not always based on individual lexical items such as pragmatic principles, the way that more than one lexical item in an utterance can collaborate in realising politeness, and differences between general characters of pragmatics and lexicography. They need to be clearly explained to learners so that they can make the best use of their dictionaries, and they should be contained somewhere in a dictionary in a similar way as outer matter. Otherwise, users cannot easily refer to them when necessary. Outer matter is arguably part of a dictionary, but it is not part of the main dictionary text. I therefore treat it as non-dictionary resources here.

The inclusion of pragmatic information must inevitably change the way dictionaries exist today, and the importance of guidance on dictionary skills may be increasing in order to use pragmatic information in their dictionaries more effectively (cf. 11.1.5; 11.3.4; Note 4 in Chapter XI). As mentioned in 7.1, I did not expect a dictionary to help me with such pragmatic functions such as *I don't suppose*. Teaching of dictionary skills may start by general guidance on how and in what respect dictionaries can help learners. If lexicographers are serious about pragmatics and its importance in the EFL context, it is clear that they must work or cooperate with non-dictionary resources.

13.4 Make the best use of the latest technologies

In this section, I will discuss the fourth recommendation: Make the best use of the latest technologies. The development of technology has made possible a lot of things that one only hoped for in the past. In the context of lexicography, the birth of electronic dictionaries is a major example. These have great potential to deal with politeness effectively,[3] but they do not make the best use of the advantage except that some portable IC-type electronic dictionaries in Japan offer more examples than their paper counterparts. After examining the nine dictionaries, I have come to conclude that electronic dictionaries have been developed mainly in terms of ease of search alone. This is at least partly because their contents are basically identical to those of paper dictionaries. So far as the 76 items are concerned, their descriptions in the CD and paper versions of the five monolingual dictionaries are completely the same. However, some recent dictionaries took a further step, taking into account both formats as they were designed and compiled.[4]

One obvious advantage that electronic dictionaries have over paper dictionaries is their larger space availability; space limitations being a primary reason for the lack of context in examples as well as their failures to illustrate register (see 11.3.1; 11.3.5). However, even with space restrictions being eliminated, it is still the role of lexicographers to provide simpler entries (cf. 11.3.1). I would argue that it is necessary to make the best use of electronic formats because they offer more than larger space; they also enable users to search for necessary information in a variety of ways. For example, some IC-type electronic dictionaries need to present information with a small display, but they can store every piece of information hierarchically or link them via hypertext. More precisely, they can show a summary of the whole entry first, and then users can retrieve more specific information whenever necessary, depending on their needs. Moreover, they can make it possible for learners to search for particular items in various ways (cf. 13.2). Furthermore, all the words used in an entry can be linked to their own entries so that, for instance, learners can know the meaning of their unknown word if there is one, or learn the relationship between words in an example, which can facilitate the realising of politeness (cf. 11.3.4).

As mentioned in 11.1.3, the development of technology can also make it possible to show typical examples of such paralinguistic features as intonation and facial expressions through video clips stored as electronic data in a dictionary or downloaded through the internet. Apart from electronic dictionaries, current technologies can affect the way resources for lexicography are developed; they also enable corpus designers to incorporate pragmatics into their future corpora more easily and more effectively. The size of the audio visual data can be extremely large, but it is also true that it has become far easier to store and process such large amounts of data with the latest computers. If objective data on people's pragmatic behaviours become available to lexicographers, it will no doubt make a major contribution towards better descriptions of pragmatics in lexicography. It is clear that, with help from the latest technologies, lexicographers can greatly improve dictionaries' treatment of pragmatics.

13.5 Pay attention to differences between pragmatic conventions in learners' native language and English, with help from a team of Japanese and English-speaking lexicographers

In this section, I will discuss the final recommendation: Pay attention to differences between pragmatic conventions in learners' native language and English, with help from a team of Japanese and English-speaking lexicographers. As this is more concerned with bilingual lexicography, I discuss this after the other four. However, it is an especially important recommendation, and at least partly relevant to monolingual dictionaries as well. Moreover, it is also necessary for lexicographers to consider difficulties which users with particular cultural and linguistic backgrounds may have at least to some extent. A dictionary is an important learning tool, but at the same time it is a commercial product. Users in large markets like Japan should be considered accordingly. Such expressions as *I'd be obliged* (see 11.4.1) and *I don't suppose* (see 9.2.3.2) are especially difficult for Japanese learners to interpret correctly. In addition, such differences as one's preference of making a request and getting permission at a particular context (see 12.4.1) is not something learners are usually aware of. They need to be treated with care in dictionaries for Japanese learners.

It is also to be noted that the four bilingual dictionaries occasionally deal with issues that are delicate, such as the age of a woman who deserves to be addressed as *Miss* (cf. 12.3.5); such notes are arguably outside the purview of lexicography. However, this is not the only problem concerning this type of usage note. It is also questionable whether they are accurate or not. It would be a useful idea to form a team of Japanese and English-speaking lexicographers and let native speakers become more involved in the compilation of a dictionary, because even the latest spoken corpora are not sufficient in terms of pragmatics. This was one of the reasons I conducted the research discussed in Part II, which also showed how difficult it is to obtain reliable data on pragmatics. We should not overlook the fact that Japanese lexicographers were unable to filter out some unnecessary and unreliable notes in the four bilingual dictionaries. This may be because, even though some native speakers of English took part in their compilations, they are only expected to check the grammatical correctness of examples and answer questions from Japanese lexicographers when they happen to have one. My suggestion is that they should play more active roles in every process. So long as there is no reliable data which Japanese lexicographers can refer to, native speakers' intuition is one of the few good sources available now. Japanese and English-speaking lexicographers must collaborate in improving their dictionaries by all means. I believe, by so doing, many unreliable descriptions can be filtered out or corrected.[5]

In the next section, before moving on to the conclusion of the book in Chapter XIV, I will discuss two sample entries based on some of my recommendations.

13.6 Worked examples

While the third, the fourth and the fifth recommendations are difficult to demonstrate in a sample, the first and the second are relatively easy to illustrate. Below are sample entries of a speech act marker, **I don't suppose**, and a formula, **Good question!**, reflecting the first two recommendations:

> Sample 1: Speech act marker (*I don't suppose*)
> I don't suppose (that) S + V INDIRECT   REQUEST

I don't suppose indirectly signals that the speaker is asking the hearer to do what is mentioned after this phrase, usually something difficult and/or tiresome.

'*I don't suppose you could lend me 500 pounds*'. (to someone whom the speaker does not know well or when the speaker thinks their request is relatively demanding)

 POLITENESS   **I don't suppose** literally expresses that the speaker is not expecting the hearer to do what the speaker mentions, so using this phrase the speaker could pretend that they do not really expect their request to be met, which leaves more room for the hearer's declination. In this way, this phrase makes the request easier to decline and sound less forceful. In many English speaking cultures, it is more important that one does not invade others' territory, and people usually try not to force others to do something or exploit them. Therefore, it is usually a good idea to make a request indirectly. See NEGATIVE POLITENESS ; also INDIRECTNESS .
 GRAMMAR The subjunctive mood is usually used in the clause following this phrase.

[NOTE] The phrase can also be used in a positive form when making an offer, but it often signals the speaker does not really want to help the hearer. '*I could give you a lift to the hospital, I suppose*'. See also **suppose** (sense 3).

Sample 2: Formula (*Good question!*)
Good question! [INDIRECT] [HUMOROUS] [DENIAL]

Good question! indirectly or humorously signals that the speaker does not know the answer to a question, often when the speaker is supposed to/ should know the answer.

Student: '*Professor Austin, what is pragmatics?*'
Professor: '*Good question!*' (hinting the fact he does not know the answer)

[PRAGMATICS] **Good question!** literally expresses the speaker's approval or praise for a question the hearer just asked, but in fact indirectly and/or humorously implies that the question is too good, or difficult to answer. See [HUMOUR].

[NOTE] The speaker usually does not completely try to hide the fact they do not know the answer. '*Good question! I don't know. You should call this number.*' (to a customer)

Both **Samples 1** and **2** are clearly marked with relevant labels specifying their core and accompanying functions, and their explanations, illustrative examples and usage notes follow. Different types of usage notes are distinguished, and, whenever necessary, they cross-refer to other notes or articles in outer matters on more general topics such as [INDIRECTNESS] and [HUMOUR]. Notes on [POLITENESS] and [PRAGMATICS] respectively explain the mechanisms in which politeness or another pragmatic function is realised or carried out so that learners can deepen their understanding of the expressions. Other types of additional information are given as [NOTE], and they are also cross-referred to another entry when necessary (see [NOTE] in Sample 2). Vague/misleading/ technical terms such as *polite* and *volitive* are avoided in any of the descriptions above. Although only monolingual samples are given, I recommend that bilingual dictionaries provide explanations in Japanese rather than translations. Therefore, the two samples can also be regarded as samples for bilingual dictionaries.

For a real dictionary entry, it would be necessary to make the structures and descriptions more sophisticated; it should also be pointed out that speech act markers, formulae and politeness markers, as well as their functions, cannot always be so clearly classified and described as the above. However, they are basic designs based on my recommendations, and they are not only arranged alphabetically but according to their core/accompanying functions or their combination. It should be clear that dictionaries' treatment of politeness will be greatly improved by carrying out the five recommendations that I have made.

In the next chapter, as the conclusion of this book, I will answer the question of whether pragmatics and lexicography can ever be made compatible at all on the basis of my discussions in the previous chapters.

Notes

1 Apart from politeness, some types of pragmatic meaning like procedural meaning cannot be treated satisfactorily with translations alone.
2 There have been attempts at compiling semi-bilingual dictionaries in Japan (e.g. *Cambridge Learner's Dictionary* 2004), and they offered explanations in English. Nevertheless, they have never been popular among dictionary users, probably because they were in some way half-finished or incomplete with English explanations together with Japanese translations. As Atkins puts it, 'there can be little surprise at the reluctance of most students to reach for the monolingual if there is a bilingual at hand' (1985: 22). Moreover, considering the space restrictions, it is simply redundant for a dictionary to offer both always.
3 Apart from pragmatic information, electronic dictionaries have several features which paper dictionaries could not even hope to have; for example, when I started the CD version of LDOCE5 on 5 November 2011, it automatically showed the entry of **Guy Fawkes Night** and played its pronunciation. This example is only relevant to a British English context, but this kind of function may appeal to learners' interest.
4 From the initial stage of compiling *Shogakukan Progressive English-Japanese Dictionary* (5th ed. 2012), the lexicographers chose examples for its electronic version and those for the paper version separately on different criteria, because there were many examples which seemed very useful but they could not afford to include in the paper version due to the space restriction (personal communication with Prof. Yasutake Ishii, Seijo University).
5 In this respect, I must mention in passing that LOEJD did not make the best use of its advantage. It claims to be compiled by a team of Japanese and English-speaking lexicographers, but they seem only concerned with the appropriateness of translations. As pointed out several times so far (e.g. Note 6 in Chapter XII), it is basically more like monolingual dictionaries; e.g. not providing many usage notes.

CHAPTER XIV
Conclusion

14.1 Summary and overview

This book began with theoretical explorations into the scopes of pragmatics and lexicography in Part I, which resulted in my definition of pragmatic information for EFL dictionaries. Using this definition and other findings from Part I as theoretical bases, I then conducted the large-scale questionnaire research in order to collect empirical data as to how and what particular lexical items are likely to cause serious pragmatic failures between Japanese learners and English speakers. The findings were discussed in Part II, and showed that there were striking differences between Japanese learners' and English speakers' uses and interpretations of expressions in terms of pragmatics. Japanese learners must be aware of the fact, and dictionaries need to help them with pragmatics. This led to Part III.

Although politeness is an indispensable part of pragmatics, it has been seldom discussed thoroughly in conjunction with EFL lexicography. I therefore started by discussing it in the EFL context (Chapter VII), and then raised the question of whether pragmatics in general and lexicography can be made compatible at all (Chapter VIII). There were several problems which made it difficult to reach a compromise between them. At the same time, there were also some promising ways to restrict their scopes in a way that enabled them to reach an acceptable compromise. In order to find more clues to answer the big question, I reviewed major theories as to politeness (Chapter IX), and used the findings while examining the nine EFL dictionaries for their treatment of politeness (Chapters X, XI and XII). This resulted in the five recommendations towards better treatment of politeness in lexicography (Chapter XIII). Although current dictionaries did not deal well with politeness, my examination confirmed that they had a great potential to satisfactorily describe it if they had followed the five recommendations.

In this final chapter, I will answer the question of the compatibility between pragmatics and lexicography, on the basis of my discussions in the previous chapters. After briefly revisiting differences between pragmatics and lexicography, I will be working towards my conclusion that they are indeed compatible in 14.2. Findings from Chapters IX and XII in particular suggest that cultural and linguistic differences between Japanese and English could be major obstacles to Japanese learners' acquisition of sufficient pragmatic knowledge and skills, unless treated properly. I will therefore reconsider the advantages as well as the disadvantages that either monolingual or bilingual dictionaries have in terms of pragmatics in 14.3. Finally, in 14.4, I will identify and discuss several remaining issues for the future lexicography as well as language teaching in general.

14.2 Compatibility between pragmatics and lexicography

14.2.1 Differences between pragmatics and lexicography, revisited

There are fundamental differences between pragmatics and lexicography. They have different units of descriptions, for one thing: utterances and discourses for pragmatics, and words and phrases for lexicography. Although current dictionaries contain more glossed sentence-level phrases, this does not guarantee that dictionaries can treat utterances. Apart from this, pragmatics and lexicography have different goals, approaches and methods in dealing with different types of meaning (e.g. 3.1.1; 3.1.2; 3.1.3; 3.3.5). More importantly, ordinary learners are usually not familiar with dictionaries sufficiently (Kanazashi 2001: 9), and often do not even know what help they can gain from their dictionaries. Therefore, for instance, even though dictionaries try to describe pragmatics of words and phrases as descriptively as possible, users may expect them to be prescriptive, which might negatively affect their motivation to learn (cf. 3.3.7). Unfortunately, these are not problems which can be solved only from lexicographers' efforts.

Among the differences, the most difficult for dictionaries to treat should be existentially varying meaning, because it becomes necessary for dictionaries to treat contextual information in order to satisfactorily deal with meaning that varies depending on context. It may go without saying that context also varies and develops as an interaction goes. Clearly, it is nearly impossible for any dictionary to fully describe pragmatics in a canonical way, as required in traditional lexicography. However, as discussed in 8.5, it is at least possible to restrict the scope of pragmatics by focusing on its important pragmatic functions, especially speech act and politeness. The five recommendations in Chapter XIII can also help lexicographers to reach some compromise in an acceptable way. In the next sections, I will discuss how lexicographers can make pragmatics and lexicography compatible.

14.2.2 Making compromises

14.2.2.1 Narrowing the scope of pragmatics with the functional perspective

As discussed in Chapter VIII, there are those pragmatic phenomena which dictionaries cannot describe properly such as conversational implicature. In this respect, dictionaries cannot fully cover all the phenomena under the heading of pragmatics. However, this does not mean that pragmatics and lexicography cannot be made compatible. What is necessary would include grasping the scope of pragmatics which can be compatible with lexicography by identifying types of information necessary for learners to avoid serious pragmatic failures, and explaining it to learners clearly. In this section, I will consider the compatibility of pragmatics and lexicography from the functional perspective. When discussing their compatibility, it is also necessary to touch upon paralinguistic features, and they will be discussed in the next section and 14.4.

Generally, those pragmatic failures in terms of politeness are more serious than other types of failures. It may be safe to say that politeness is among the most important pragmatic phenomena, and that it is crucial for EFL dictionaries to offer information on politeness. The point is that politeness is a pragmatic function or act of showing respect for others through using language, and that it is usually fulfilled through another function, or act (cf. 8.3.4). As I have repeatedly emphasised throughout the book, it is most promising to approach pragmatics from the functional viewpoint, and that politeness should be treated as an umbrella function of speech act. This is the basis of my first recommendation: Approach pragmatics from the functional perspective.

To follow the first recommendation, lexicographers can reanalyse language use focusing on its functions. My examination of the nine dictionaries showed that they often failed to specify what act the use of a lexical item could perform or how it was related with politeness, but this problem can be solved with this recommendation. As Miller points out, one of the most important sources of difficulty in communication is that we often fail to understand others' intent (1974: 15; see also 2.3.2), and that to explain the core function of a phrase is exactly to explain the intent of the speaker who uses the phrase. If dictionaries consistently describe the core function of formulae and speech act markers, and describe properly the function of politeness markers, it surely will be of great benefit to learners.

The recommendation will also help lexicographers identify which phrases deserve dictionary descriptions (cf. 9.3.1), and this will then lead to the extraction of typical and fixed parts of contextual information from the actual context. Certain tokens of utterances come to assume a particular function of performing an act after they have been frequently used in a certain context (cf. 7.3). Once they have become associated with a particular act, they well deserve dictionary descriptions. More importantly, it is through the frequent use in a particular context that a phrase assumes a function. If lexicographers identify the matching of a function and its typical context, the identified typical context can be included as part of dictionary descriptions relatively easily. Following a common definition of utterance as the pairing of a sentence and a context (cf. Levinson 1983: 14f and passim; see also Gazdar, 1979: 131), utterances can in this way also become one of the targets of dictionary descriptions. Dictionaries can and should only deal with most fixed parts of language, so other types of existentially varying meaning which cannot be dealt with in this way are basically outside the purview of lexicography.

Unlike absolute politeness, deference and register, politeness is also context dependent, and the recommendation also advises lexicographers to avoid using the two vague and misleading terms *polite* and *teinei*. If lexicographers approach politeness through the functional perspective, they should be able to identify more specific politeness-related functions of lexical items such as making an utterance indirect. The identified functions are important parts of linguistic resources (see 2.4.1) and should be clearly explained in a dictionary. Pragmatics is concerned with one's command of linguistic resources (see 2.4.2), and learners must also learn such things as how and when to make a request indirect together with what phrases are available for that purpose in order to realise politeness. It is a dictionary's role to tell them what options are available from the lexicon of the target language (see 8.3.4), but it is again outside the purview of lexicography to explain pragmatic conventions, such as when to make an indirect request, unless it is closely connected with an individual lexical item. I will return to this in the next section.

The functional perspective makes it possible to satisfactorily restrict the scope of pragmatics, and even that limited portion of pragmatics should be helpful to learners of English if treated properly. As pointed out in 13.1.1, the recommendation will also solve or eliminate many other problems the nine dictionaries had, such as those in their illustrative examples. For instance, the identification of the core function of a formula/speech act marker will give lexicographers some useful insight into the setting for illustrative examples so that, when selecting illustrative examples, lexicographers can invent or look for appropriate ones, keeping in mind typical situations for a particular utterance to be made. These will also make a considerable contribution toward the better treatment of pragmatics in lexicography.

14.2.2.2 Filling the role of dictionaries as a learning material

It is possible to satisfactorily restrict the scope of pragmatics from the functional perspective, but I may also need to point out that, considering the role of a dictionary as a learning material, it is necessary for dictionaries not only to be compatible with pragmatics but also to offer sufficient help to learners in an easily accessible way. This is the basis of the second and third recommendations: Review all the descriptions from an educational perspective; Cooperate with non-lexicographic resources.

As mentioned in 14.2.1, the prescriptive character of dictionaries, or their authority, can negatively affect learners' motivation to learn. Moreover, dictionaries' presentations of information, such as marking register through speech labels, is often too complicated or rather confusing (cf. 11.2.2; 12.1). All the necessary information should be reviewed from an educational perspective to ensure that it is offered in an easily accessible way to users (cf. 13.2; 13.4). Otherwise, dictionaries cannot meet the users' needs as an important learning material, though this cannot be done only from lexicographers' efforts.

In order to make the best use of pragmatic information in a dictionary, users will need sufficient guidance on dictionary skills. They should also learn such things as the different characters of pragmatics and lexicography, and pragmatic conventions, including when to make a request indirect. The point is that they cannot be properly dealt with in entries for individual lexical items. Accordingly, I recommended putting them in outer matter. Moreover, lexicographers' attempts at incorporating pragmatics into lexicography may inevitably change the ways dictionaries exist now; for instance, the abolition of translation equivalents and the introduction of Japanese explanations in an English-Japanese dictionary are very likely to confuse learners at first. It will become important for dictionaries to collaborate with non-lexicographic resources like classroom teaching.

Lastly, I must also mention paralinguistic features like intonation because they can play crucial roles in the realisation of politeness (e.g. 11.1.3). It is evident that any dictionary in the present format, either book or electronic, cannot fully describe them in an easily accessible way. Nevertheless, I believe the development of technology can help lexicographers treat paralinguistic features more properly, and this is the basis of the fourth recommendation: Make the best use of the latest technologies. As discussed in 13.4, current technology has a great potential to improve the way paralinguistic features can be dealt with in the EFL context. I will return to this in 14.4.

In the next section, I will also consider the compatibility between pragmatics and lexicography, referring to the final recommendation: Pay attention to differences between pragmatic conventions in learners' native language and

English, with help from a team of Japanese and English-speaking lexicographers.

14.3 Users with specific linguistic and/or cultural backgrounds

One of the major findings from Part II was that there were many areas where Japanese and English differ strikingly in terms of pragmatics. Chapters IX and XII confirmed this, and the latter also suggested that if lexicographers were to improve the treatment of pragmatics, they would need to tailor their presentation of the pragmatic information to the needs of Japanese learners. As discussed in the previous sections, pragmatics and lexicography can be made compatible satisfactorily, but there is still more room for improvement in this respect. This is the basis of my final recommendation: Pay attention to differences between pragmatic conventions in learners' native language and English, with help from a team of Japanese and English-speaking lexicographers.

Since monolingual dictionaries are in principle expected to serve a broad readership, they basically cannot or should not focus on problems peculiar to Japanese learners alone. On the other hand, English-Japanese and Japanese-English dictionaries designed for Japanese learners can and should take into account such factors as differences between pragmatic conventions in Japanese and English. As discussed in 12.3.5, a serious problem in usage notes written by Japanese lexicographers for the four bilingual dictionaries was that they sometimes did not seem accurate enough. More importantly, this can potentially be the case with other information categories. I therefore recommended forming a team of Japanese and English-speaking lexicographers collaborating together to overcome that major disadvantage of bilingual dictionaries.

Apart from the final recommendation, I suggested as part of my first recommendation that bilingual dictionaries adopt explanations in Japanese rather than translation equivalents. This should not only reduce the possibility of causing some translation-related misunderstanding but also offset another major disadvantage of bilingual dictionaries: their inability to directly describe important functions of the use of language. This recommendation virtually buries major differences between bilingual and monolingual dictionaries, leaving the two languages used for them as the only difference between the two types of dictionaries, Japanese for bilinguals and English for monolinguals.

Now, it is also to be pointed out that ideologically there might be issues of colonialism, expansionism and anglocentrism in the five monolingual (or rather, monocultural) dictionaries serving a broad readership, as if the British publishers were compiling their dictionaries for imagined global learners of

English (see 3.3.5 for discussions of Anglo-Saxon standards of behaviour.). This may suggest that it is very difficult for monolingual dictionaries to change, but I may also need to point out here that there was an attempt by a monolingual dictionary trying to deal with problems for learners with particular linguistic backgrounds.[1] In addition, there were attempts to compile semi-bilingual and/ or bilingualised dictionaries dedicated to users with particular linguistic and cultural backgrounds in the past. LOEJD could also be considered to be an example of such attempts, though it did not draw upon the advantages. From the commercial viewpoint, it would not be practical to compile too many dictionaries tailored to the needs of a specific user, but as discussed in 9.2.2.2 there might be a Western and Eastern divide of politeness theory. It would be a useful idea to compile at least two monolingual dictionaries, one for the East and the other for the West.

The final recommendation is more concerned in an obvious way with bilingual dictionaries, but I should also like to add that, as seen in Chapter XI, monolingual dictionaries still have the potential to improve their treatment of politeness even without being adapted to the needs of particular markets. I will therefore offer to makers of both monolingual and bilingual dictionaries all the five recommendations for a better treatment of pragmatics. In the next section, I will close my discussions by identifying several remaining issues for the future of lexicography.

14.4 Closing remarks: Limitations of the study and implications for the future

Austin, father of pragmatics, is also the first to have pointed out the fact that every use of language can perform an act. This great finding has long affected pragmatic studies up to now, including the present book. It is possible to make pragmatics and lexicography compatible by focusing on important pragmatic functions such as speech acts. However, there are still remaining problems.

There are several issues I have not discussed fully. They would include pragmatic differences in varieties of English such as British and American. Even within the so-called English-speaking cultures, there may be fundamental differences in people's pragmatic preferences and conventions. Accordingly, it may be simply wrong to treat them collectively as pragmatics in English. In fact, popular English tests like TOEIC started introducing more varieties of English, including Canadian and Australian, together with the two major varieties, British and American. Although it is not really clear at the present time of writing how and to what extent they can/should be satisfactorily dealt with in lexicography, lexicographers should at least not ignore them.

In order to improve dictionaries' treatment of pragmatics, it is also necessary to consider the use of dictionaries in the EFL context. For instance, it would be necessary to consider such issues as the following: how pragmatic information in EFL dictionaries can be beneficial to learners when learning pragmatics in English; how dictionaries can more effectively be used in a classroom; and whether dictionaries' roles can be taken over in the future by other learning materials, such as applications for smartphones. It is also necessary to confirm how far pragmatically enhanced/improved entries, in relation to pragmatics (see 13.6 for the worked examples), can actually help learners in order to test the hypotheses of the present book that dictionaries can satisfactorily deal with pragmatics, and that pragmatic information in a dictionary can help learners with pragmatics.

In 2012, COBUILD6's successor, the seventh edition of *Collins COBUILD Advanced Dictionary of English* (hereafter COBUILD7), appeared. Although I cannot detect any major change between the contents of COBUILD6 and COBUILD7, the new edition offers a free mobile dictionary application for the smartphone platforms iPhone and Android. It proudly declares that even when learners do not have a proper dictionary with them, they can 'access concise definitions and examples, and hear pronunciations quickly' (back cover). Apart from this, we nowadays have access to free online dictionaries, including the nine dictionaries I examined. There are more options such as collaborative dictionaries, including the Simple English Wiktionary (https://simple.wiktionary.org/wiki/Main_Page). Their descriptions look too simple as a whole at this stage, and there is still much room for improvement in their treatment of pragmatics. However, it is clear that they have the potential to take over ordinary, conventional dictionaries.

Since one can easily record, watch and even send and share video clips with a smartphone, it is not very difficult to imagine that such technologies could also be incorporated into language teaching in the near future. As mentioned in 13.4, lexicographers have not utilised the latest technology very effectively for the proper treatment of pragmatics. Even the online versions of the nine dictionaries are no more than the same dictionaries that can be accessed using the internet. It is time for lexicographers to change; they need to think by all means what they can do to establish innovations in lexicography as well as language teaching. These are basically outside the purview of the current study, but I sincerely hope that surveys will be carried out in the future on the above-mentioned aspects of English teaching.

While in this study I have examined pragmatic behaviours of lexical items mainly from a lexicographic viewpoint, the findings will be of benefit to other fields in EFL industry. Therefore the topic for this book may better be considered lexical, rather than simply lexicographic, pragmatics. They will surely break new ground in the teaching of pragmatics as well as EFL lexicography.

Note
1 *Cambridge International Dictionary of English* (1995) contains sixteen lists of false friends, with each covering English words that may cause a trouble in relation to their differences from their equivalents in sixteen particular languages. Although this is rather restricted both in quantity and depth, this would suggest that monolingual works can treat users' linguistic backgrounds at least to some extent.

Appendices

Appendix I
Cover letter and instructions for EV

Obunsha Publishing Co., Ltd.
Foreign Language Dictionaries Group
55 Yokodera-machi, Shinjuku-ku
Tokyo 162–8680, JAPAN
Name deleted
E-mail address deleted
Fax: +81-3-3266-6333

Dear Informants,

The editorial committee is deeply grateful to you for having agreed to participate in our project for a dictionary aimed at Japanese intermediate learners of English. We are very sorry for the delay in starting the questionnaire; it took much longer than we expected to get into shape.

The aim of this questionnaire is to find out how English-speaking people actually use particular words and/or phrases in different situations. We carried out similar research some years ago and it was a great success. The emphasis at that time was on grammar, that is, whether a particular use of an expression is possible or acceptable out of context. This time we are focusing on how appropriate the use of a particular expression can be depending on the situation of utterance. Even a correct sentence may sound rude or polite in a particular context.

Because of the nature of this research some of the questions may be closely connected with your age, sex, the place where you live and/or your moral judgment on whether an utterance is appropriate or not. We would like to assure you that any piece of information which can be used to identify you will be kept strictly confidential; all the information collected will be used only for the above mentioned dictionary, and other educational and academic purposes. We would greatly appreciate it if you could try to give us as true a picture as possible of how you use and/or interpret a particular phrase in your daily life.

Whenever you answer the questions you must login to the questionnaire page. In order to get the login screen please type the URL in your browser and enter, so you will get the login screen. Then type your ID and Password carefully, and submit. In a few seconds, you will get a screen with two links: 'START from question no. 1' and 'TOPICS.' (The latter list is usually shown in the left of the screen as well.) To start click on 'START from question no. 1,' and you will get Question 1. From next time, if you should like to start with another question, go to TOPICS and click on the number of the question you want.

Below are some examples of how to answer the questions. There are ninety topics as a whole in this questionnaire with each numbered and titled:

56. Does 'rich' sound jealous?

Every topic is composed of one or several questions, and each topic begins with the advice given to a Japanese learner of English either in a class room or in a textbook. Although this part is followed by 'Do you agree?,' you do not have to answer. If you have something to say about this part, please leave your comments (see below for how to leave comments):

If you say somebody 'is rich', it will sound as if you are jealous of them. Do you agree?

Your judgment on the above advice is asked in (a) related question(s) which follow(s), usually numbered I, II and/or assigned a letter like (A), (B) and so forth. In the question(s) you are requested to pass your judgments on whether you would use a particular expression or how you would interpret it in a specified context. The context may be very specific or pretty general:

When talking about a wealthy person, would you say to another person 'He (She) is rich?'
Yes
No

Whenever you find alternatives like the above: Yes and No, please click on either. Depending on your choice you will then be guided to the next stage. For instance, if your choice is 'Yes', you will see:

Comments:

[   ]

[SUBMIT] [RESET]
Next Question (Skip)

Comments can be anything you would find worth mentioning. Although *we would highly appreciate your comments of any sort*, you can skip it if you find '(Skip)' below the blank space. To skip just click on 'Next Question (Skip)'; to leave your comments fill in the blank and then click. Please note: (1) You must click on SUBMIT to complete the question, or you cannot save the answer. (2) You can alter your answer(s) whenever necessary. To change or review the answer(s) go to TOPICS, and click on the number of the question you want. Do not forget to click on the SUBMIT button if you have made any alterations.

If your choice is '**No**', you will be guided to:

Reason(s):

What should be said instead?:

Comments:

SUBMIT RESET
Next Question (Skip)

Whenever you feel that you would not say a particular phrase or that it would be inappropriate, you are requested to give us your reason(s) and (an) alternative expression(s) you would use yourself or you would find appropriate in the specified context. These parts are compulsory; you can move on to the next section by clicking on 'Skip,' but the answer will remain incomplete. Remember you can check if you have properly put the reason with 'STATUSES' shown in the left side of the screen. To check just click on in it, and select the question you want.

An honorarium of 20,000 yen or its equivalent in US dollars or GB pounds will be paid by check at the end of March 2005. Please note: (1) You are basically required to finish all the questions in three weeks. (2) The honorarium will be paid only to those who have completed all the questions in a month (at the latest). If you cannot complete the questionnaire in a month for some reason please let us know before you start answering the questions. Also, if you would like the check to be delivered to the address other than that you gave us, please let us know.

Regards,
Name deleted
E-mail address deleted

Appendix II
Questions and the summaries of the results excluding statistically insignificant ones

The questions and the summaries of the results are given below. Whenever there are statistically significant differences between answers from British and American informants (See Section 4.2.1.7 for details), I give their results separately. Abbreviations used in the summaries are as follows: *E*, *Br*, *Am*, and *J* stands for English speakers, British, American and Japanese informants respectively.

1. Is it appropriate to use 'I see' to signal agreement?

'I see' is only used to indicate that the speaker has just understood something, and so 'I see' should not be used to just show that you are listening. Do you agree? Please answer the following question:

Mary and Laura are talking to each other.

Mary: I went to the movie with Robin yesterday. He's so nice....
Laura: I see.
Mary: We're meeting again tonight.

Would you find Laura's use of 'I see' appropriate?

| (E) Yes 35% / No 65% | (J) Yes 51% / No 49% |

3. When should we start using others' first names?

We should not ask others for permission to call them by their first names. Do you agree? Please answer the following questions:

I: Your friend, Peter, has just introduced a person to you by full name (given name and surname) at his house. If the person is of *almost the same age and your own sex*, would you say 'May I call you Y [his/her first name]?'

| (E) Yes 9% / No 91% | (J) Yes 58% / No 42% |

II: (In the same situation) If the person is of *almost the same age and the opposite sex*, would you say 'May I call you Y [his/her first name]?'

| (E) Yes 11% / No 89% | (J) Yes 53% / No 47% |

III: (In the same situation) if the person is of *almost the same age as your parents and of your own sex*, would you say 'May I call you Y [his/her first name]?'

| (E) Yes 38% / No 62% | (J) Yes 20% / No 80% |

IV: (In the same situation) If the person is of *almost the same age as your parents and the opposite sex*, would you say 'May I call you Y [his/her first name]?'

| (E) Yes 37% / No 63% | (J) Yes 21% / No 79% |

4. Should we thank others if they let us call them by their first names?
If someone asks us to call him/her by his/her first name we should not say 'Thank you' because it sounds overly grateful. Do you agree? Please answer the following questions:

I: Your friend, Peter, introduced a person to you by full name (given name and surname) at his house, and the person says 'Please call me X [his/her first name]' to you. If the person is of *almost the same age and your own sex*, would you say 'Thank you?'

| (E) Yes 8% / No 92% | (J) Yes 38% / No 62% |

II: (In the same situation) If the person is of *almost the same age and the opposite sex*, would you say 'Thank you?'

| (E) Yes 12% / No 88% | (J) Yes 38% / No 62% |

III: (In the same situation) If the person is of *almost the same age as your parents and of your own sex*, would you say 'Thank you?'

| (E) Yes 28% / No 72% | (J) Yes 60% / No 40% |

IV: (In the same situation) If the person is of *almost the same age as your parents and of the opposite sex*, would you say 'Thank you?'

| (E) Yes 27% / No 73% | (J) Yes 60% / No 40% |

6. Is it appropriate to say 'I don't like' a particular food?
'Like' should not be used when talking about one's own taste in food especially when you are not fond of a particular food. We should instead use 'care for' because it sounds indirect and more moderate. Do you agree? Please answer the following question:

You are invited to lunch by the Jackson family who recently moved to your neighborhood. Although you do not like fish, the Jacksons do not know that. Mrs. Jackson offers you some smoked salmon. Would you say 'Sorry, I don't like fish?'

| (E) Yes 31% / No 69% | (J) Yes 39% / No 61% | (Br) Yes 44% / No 56% | (Am) Yes 15% / No 85% |

7. Does it sound rude if we say 'Take good care of yourself?'
It is advisable to avoid saying something like 'Please take good care of yourself.' to someone because it sounds like we think they are very weak. Do you agree? Please answer the following questions:

I: One of your friends is going abroad to study, and you and your friends are saying 'Goog bye.' Would you also say 'Please take good care of yourself'?

| (E) Yes 55% / No 45% | (J) Yes 73% / No 27% |

II: Your teacher is going abroad to study, and you and some other students are saying 'Good bye.' Would you also say 'Please take good care of yourself?'

| (E) Yes 31% / No 69% | (J) Yes 71% / No 29% | (Br) Yes 19% / No 81% | (Am) Yes 46% / No 54% |

8. Is it 'bad' to be tired?
(1) If we say something to others such as 'You must be tired,' it might sound offensive because this is almost equivalent to 'You are old or weak.'
(2) 'I'm tired.' uttered in front of our boss will sound as if we are complaining to the boss because he/she forces us to work too hard.
(3) 'I'm tired.' will also sound as if we are revealing we are weak.

Do you agree? Please answer the following questions:

I: You go to the airport to meet one of your friends. After a while his/her flight arrives, and you finally see your friend. After exchanging greetings, would you say 'You must be tired?'

| (E) Yes 91% / No 9% | (J) Yes 54% / No 46% |

II: You go to the airport to meet your grandfather. After a while his flight arrives, and you finally see him. After exchanging greetings, would you say 'You must be tired?'

| (E) Yes 89% / No 11% | (J) Yes 66% / No 34% |

III: You are working overtime at your office because your boss asked you to. Although you like working, you begin to feel tired. If the boss is sitting near you, would you say 'I'm tired?'

| (E) Yes 24% / No 76% | (J) Yes 12% / No 88% |

IV: You are working overtime at your office because you have to finish a report by the next day. Although you like working, you begin to feel tired. If your colleagues are also working near you, would you say 'I'm tired?'

| (E) Yes 83% / No 17% | (J) Yes 77% / No 23% | (Br) Yes 91% / No 9% | (Am) Yes 74% / No 26% |

9. How should we use 'a certain ...?'

The pattern, certain + noun (e.g. *a certain person* and *certain persons*) can sound mysterious or even offensive because it gives the impression that the speaker is trying to hide something. Do you agree? Please answer the following question:

You are at the house of a friend. The friend introduces a university student to you: 'X [Your name], this is John McArthur. John is a student at a certain university in California.' Would you find this introduction appropriate?

| (E) Yes 20% / No 80% | (J) Yes 50% / No 50% | (Br) Yes 28% / No 72% | (Am) Yes 11% / No 89% |

11. Is it possible to invite others politely using 'Could you ...?'

You cannot properly invite a person to a party or similar event using 'Could you ...?' because it sounds like a request rather than an invitation. Do you agree? Please answer the following question:

Mr. and Mrs. Jones have recently moved to your neighborhood, and you are thinking of inviting them to your house for dinner. Do you find the following invitation appropriate: 'Mr. and Mrs. Jones, could you come to our house for dinner next Sunday?'

| (E) Yes 27% / No 73% | (J) Yes 59% / No 41% | (Br) Yes 17% / No 83% | (Am) Yes 42% / No 58% |

12. How should we use 'Of course?'

If we say 'Of course' in reply to a request or a question it will sound as if the answer to the question is obvious. Therefore, we should avoid the phrase. Do you agree? Please answer the following question:

You happen to see your homeroom teacher at the library, and the teacher says to you 'Have you finished your term paper?' If you have in fact finished it, would you say 'Of course?'

| (E) Yes 37% / No 63% | (J) Yes 67% / No 33% |

13. Is it appropriate to address the audience as 'everyone?'

When one gives a talk or a speech, 'everyone' or 'everybody' should never be used to address the audience because it is impolite. Do you agree? Please answer the following questions:

I: It is your birthday, and your friends hold a casual birthday party for you. You are asked to make a short speech. When giving the speech in this case, would you address your friends as 'everyone' or 'everybody?'

| (E) Yes 84% / No 16% | (J) Yes 58% / No 42% | (Br) Yes 91% / No 9% | (Am) Yes 76% / No 24% |

14. Does it sound rude if we say 'I know (what you mean)?'

'I know' or 'I know what you mean' will sound offensive when it is uttered in response to someone expressing their opinion, because it implies that you mean they are saying something which is too obvious to mention. Do you agree? Please answer the following questions:

You and your friend Carter are discussing opening a refreshment stand at the school festival. Carter says 'It's important to get a good place,' and you are indicating you agree with him.
(A) Would you say 'I know?'

| (E) Yes 63% / No 37% | (J) Yes 23% / No 77% |

(B) (In the same situation) How about 'I know what you mean?' Would you say that?

| (E) Yes 79% / No 21% | (J) Yes 39% / No 61% |

15. Should we avoid 'he' and/or 'she?'

'He' or 'she' should not be used to refer to a person when the person is in front of you or when the person is near you. Do you agree? Please answer the following questions:

I: You are waiting for your friend Mary outside a shop, when a male passerby asks you where he can find the museum. However, you are a stranger yourself in that neighborhood, so when Mary comes out of the shop you ask her if she knows the way. Would you say 'Mary, he's looking for the museum. Do you know where it is?'

| (E) Yes 48% / No 52% | (J) Yes 87% / No 13% | (Br) Yes 28% / No 72% | (Am) Yes 72% / No 28% |

II: You are waiting for your friend Mary outside a shop, when a female passer by asks you where she can find the museum. However, you are a stranger yourself in that neighborhood, so when Mary comes out of the shop you ask her if she knows the way. Would you say 'Mary, she's looking for the museum. Do you know where it is?'

| (E) Yes 48% / No 52% | (J) Yes 86% / No 14% | (Br) Yes 28% / No 72% | (Am) Yes 72% / No 28% |

16. Do you say 'Hey!' to attract others' attention?

One should not say 'Hey!' when they wish to attract the attention of others because it is rude. Do you agree? Please answer the following question:

I: You are in a cafe. You want to call a waiter or waitress, and one of them has just walked by you. Would you say 'Hey!' to attract their attention?

| (E) Yes 1% / No 99% | (J) Yes 18% / No 82% |

III: You are on board an airplane. You need to call a flight attendant, and one has just passed you. Would you say 'Hey!' to attract their attention?

| (E) Yes 1% / No 99% | (J) Yes 6% / No 94% |

IV: A gentleman passes by you and drops his handkerchief. Would you say 'Hey!' to attract his attention?

| (E) Yes 100% / No 0% | (J) Yes 32% / No 68% |

V: A lady passes by you and drops her handkerchief. Would you say 'Hey! to attract her attention?

| (E) Yes 100% / No 0% | (J) Yes 32% / No 68% |

17. Should we avoid 'eat?'

'Have' is more graceful or elegant than 'eat'. Do you agree? Please answer the following questions:

You are at home when the phone rings. Which do you think is better?
    a) Sorry, I can't talk now. I'm having dinner.

b) Sorry, I can't talk now. I'm eating dinner.
c) Neither of the above is acceptable

| (E) a) 75% / b) 17% / c) 8% | (J) a) 68% / b) 7% / 25% |

18. Do you say 'maybe' when you are not sure of your future plan?
If we use the word 'maybe' when talking about ourselves or our plans, we might sound insincere or evasive. Do you agree? Please answer the following questions:

II: You are asked by your friends whether another friend of yours, Geoffrey is free this coming weekend. You think he is free but you are not 100% sure. Would you say just 'Maybe'?

| (E) Yes 54% / No 46% | (J) Yes 36% / No 64% |

19. Is it better not to use 'wrong' when pointing out others' mistakes?
One should not say 'You're wrong.' even when you disagree with someone. Do you agree? Please answer the following questions:

II: During the lesson your teacher is scolding one of your friends, Charles for his failure to hand in a term paper on time, while, in fact you know that Charles submitted it on time. The teacher seems to be making a mistake, and you want to point out that mistake. Would you say 'You're wrong?'

| (E) Yes 8% / No 92% | (J) Yes 44% / No 56% |

20. Does it sound alienating when a Japanese person says 'We Japanese?'
One should avoid 'We American', 'We British' or 'We Japanese' because using these expressions has the effect of alienating people from other countries. Do you agree? Please answer the following questions:

II: Ken is a high school student in Japan, and he is giving a speech on his country in front of his classsmates. As there is an exchange student from the US present, he is giving his talk in English. In his speech, he says '<u>We Japanese</u> are generally kind.' Would you find the underlined part appropriate?

| (E) Yes 40% / No 60% | (J) Yes 59% / No 41% |

21. Does a male person usually not use the word cute?'
A male person does not usually use the word 'cute'. Do you agree? Please answer the following sentences:

(A) Would you say 'She is cute?' (About a baby)

(E) Yes 89% / No 11%	(J) Yes 89% / No 11%	(Br) Yes 80% / No 20%	(Am) Yes 100% / No 0%

(B) Would you say 'The dog is cute?' (About a nice dog)

(E) Yes 77% / No 23%	(J) Yes 70% / No 30%	(Br) Yes 69% / No 31%	(Am) Yes 87% / No 13%

(C) Would you say 'The bag is cute?' (About a nice bag)

(E) Yes 32% / No 68%	(J) Yes 52% / No 48%	(Br) Yes 20% / No 80%	(Am) Yes 46% / No 54%

22. What do you mean by 'my friend?'
One should avoid using 'my friend' when talking about one of our friends because it can be easily misinterpreted as meaning 'my only friend' and sounds unnatural. We should instead use 'a friend of mine' or 'one of my friends.' Do you agree? Please answer the following question:

One of your friends, John invites you to go to see a movie, but you are seeing another friend of yours. Would you refuse by saying 'Sounds nice, but I'm afraid I'm going to see my friend tonight?'

(E) Yes 21% / No 79%	(J) Yes 72% / No 28%

23. How do you reply to others saying 'Hi?'
When someone says 'Hi' to you, you should avoid just repeating 'Hi' and use another form of greeting. Do you agree? Please answer the following question:

You run into one of your friends Laura on the street, and she says 'Hi, X [Your first name].' Would you reply 'Hi, Laura?'

(E) Yes 86% / No 14%	(J) Yes 96% / No 4%

24. How do you answer the phone?
When answering the phone we should not say just 'Yes' instead of 'Hello.' Do you agree? Please answer the following question:

You make a phone call. The person who answers the phone just says 'yes.' Is this response appropriate?

(E) Yes 13% / No 87%	(J) Yes 51% / No 49%

25. Does 'Oh, good' sound cold?

The expression 'Oh, good' does not express your feelings, and so it is not appropriate to use this phrase when something good happens to someone around you. Do you agree? Please answer the following question:

One of your friends has just told you that he or she passed a very difficult examination. Would you say 'Oh, good?'

(E) Yes 40% / No 60%	(J) Yes 32% / No 68%	(Br) Yes 28% / No 72%	(Am) Yes 54% / No 46%

26. Is it polite to offer your help saying 'Would you like me to do …?'

When you are not sure if others wish you to help them, you may politely offer your help by saying 'Would you like me to do …?' Do you agree? Please answer the following questions:

I: You are standing in front of your apartment building. One of your neighbors who lives in the same building and whom you do not know very well comes up the street towards you. The neighbor is carrying two small bags, one in each hand, and so might find it difficult to open the door to the building. Would you say 'Would you like me to open the door?'

(E) Yes 75% / No 25%	(J) Yes 42% / No 58%

II: In an aircraft an elderly person sitting next to you seems to be having difficulty fastening his/her seatbelt. Would you say 'Would you like me help you fasten it?'

(E) Yes 73% / No 27%	(J) Yes 57% / No 43%	(Br) Yes 84% / No 16%	(Am) Yes 61% / No 39%

27. Should we avoid using 'with me' when we make an invitation?

We should not add 'with me' when we invite someone to go somewhere because they might find it difficult to refuse our invitation; if they refuse the invitation they will sound as if they do not wish to go somewhere *with you*. Do you agree? Please answer the following questions:

I: Mike is working on a term paper in a library. He is thinking of going out for a meal, when he notices that a friend of his James is leaving the library. Therefore Mike decides to ask him to come with him, and says 'James, would you like to go for a meal with me?' Would you find Mike's utterance appropriate?

(E) Yes 55% / No 45%	(J) Yes 41% / No 59%	(Br) Yes 44% / No 56%	(Am) Yes 68% / No 32%

APPENDICES

28. Is it rude to say 'Long time no see?'
It is advisable to avoid saying 'Long time no see' to our superiors like teachers because it sounds too informal. Do you agree? Please answer the following questions:

II: You see one of your former teachers after a long time. Would you say 'Long time no see?'

| (E) Yes 34% / No 66% | (J) Yes 50% / No 50% |

29. Can we sincerely apologize using 'regret?'
When someone uses 'I regret' they do not sound really sorry because 'regret' is normally used to avoid revealing a sense of responsibility, usually in a business setting, and so it sounds less personal. When we are really sorry we should use 'I'm sorry' or 'I apologize.' Do you agree? Please answer the following question:

Tom happens to drop his friend's laptop PC, and breaks it. So he decides to apologize and says 'I regret that I dropped your laptop.' Would you find Tom's apology appropriate?

| (E) Yes 5% / No 95% | (J) Yes 25% / No 75% |

31. Do 'Couldn't you do …?' and 'Don't you do …?' sound threatening?
Negative questions like 'Couldn't you do something?' and 'Don't you do something?' should not be used as a request or question because it might sound as if the speaker is blaming or threatening the hearer. Do you agree? Please answer the following questions:

I: You ask a passing stranger what time it is. Would you say 'Couldn't you tell me what time it is?'

| (E) Yes 1% / No 99% | (J) Yes 45% / No 55% |

II: You are chairperson of the organizing committee of the school festival and are about to close a meeting. As you seem to have discussed all the items on the agenda, you want to propose ending the meeting if there are no more comments. Would you make sure there are no more comments by saying 'Don't you have any more comments?'

| (E) Yes 0% / No 100% | (J) Yes 57% / No 43% |

32. Do you use 'Let's …' when confirming something that has been agreed upon?

'Let's do …' is used when proposing something and should not be used to confirm something which has already been agreed upon. Please answer the following question:

You are talking with one of your friends Tony over the phone.

Tony: 'What time shall we meet, then?'
You: 'It usually takes half an hour to go to the library. So how about 4 o'clock?'
Tony: 'Fine with me.'

You want to confirm what time you are meeting before hanging up the phone. Would you say 'Let's meet at 4 o'clock?'

(E) Yes 38% / No 62%	(J) Yes 68% / No 32%

33. Do you say 'What is your name?' when you ask others their names?

When asking someone's name we should avoid 'What is (What's) your name?' because it will sound rather rude, as if a police officer were questioning a suspect. Do you agree? Please answer the following questions:

II: You work part-time at a cleaner's. A customer comes to collect his/her coat. When asking the customer's name would you say 'What is (What's) your name?'

(E) Yes 77% / No 23%	(J) Yes 32% / No 68%

34. Do you praise someone with 'nice?'

When we praise something or someone it is advisable to avoid using the word, 'nice' because it may sound as if the thing or the person you are talking about is of normal or average quality. Do you agree? Please answer the following questions:

I: One of your friends asks you what you think about their new sweater. Would you say 'It's nice?'

(E) Yes 74% / No 26%	(J) Yes 87% / No 13%	(Br) Yes 65% / No 35%	(Am) Yes 85% / No 15%

II: Your father asks you about a new teacher, Mrs. Wilder. You are telling him that she is friendly and pleasant. Would you say 'Mrs. Wilder's very nice?'

| (E) Yes 95% / No 5% | (J) Yes 75% / No 25% |

35. Is it possible to use 'will' when talking of others' future plans?
We should usually not use 'will' when talking about others' future actions because it will sound as if we are in a position to decide their actions for them. We can use 'will' in this way only on such occasions as when we are representing an organization or we are talking about someone who is not able to decide their own actions, like children. Do you agree? Please answer the following question:

One of your friends William is having a barbecue party this weekend and is checking who is coming to the barbecue. William asks you whether you happen to know if another friend of yours, Geoffrey is coming. Although he is not with you at present, he told you last night that he was going to the barbecue. Would you say 'Geoffrey will come to the party?'

| (E) Yes 30% / No 70% | (J) Yes 54% / No 46% | (Br) Yes 19% / No 81% | (Am) Yes 43% / No 57% |

36. What is the difference between 'must' and 'have to?'
When refusing a request it is more polite to use 'have to' rather than 'must' because 'have to' implies you have no choice. Do you agree? Please answer the following question:

You are requested to work this weekend at the cafe where you work part-time, but you cannot because you want to prepare for your big examination. Would you say 'Sorry I must study?'

| (E) Yes 30% / No 70% | (J) Yes 76% / No 24% |

37. Does 'very' sound too strong when you recommend something?
You should avoid using 'very' when expressing your own judgment on something because it may sound as if you are trying to force the listener to accept your opinion. Do you agree? Please answer the following question:

Peter and his friend, John, are discussing where to eat lunch today. Peter asks John whether he has a particular restaurant in mind, and John mentions an Italian restaurant: he says 'It's very good.' Would you find John's utterance appropriate?

| (E) Yes 99% / No 1% | (J) Yes 74% / No 26% |

38. Is it rude to say 'sorry' when you request someone to do something?
When asking another person to do a particular thing we should avoid beginning our request with 'sorry' or it may sound as if we are taking it for granted that the person will agree with our request. Do you agree? Please answer the questions:

I: Arnold is asking a person standing near him how to get to the nearest train station. Would you find it appropriate, if he were to say 'Sorry, could you tell me how to get to the nearest train station?'

(E) Yes 64% / No 36%	(J) Yes 64% / No 36%	(Br) Yes 78% / No 22%	(Am) Yes 47% / No 53%

II: Arnold is asking one of his friends to lend him some money. Would you find it appropriate, if he were to say 'Sorry, could you lend me 100 dollars?'

(E) Yes 36% / No 64%	(J) Yes 67% / No 33%

III: You work part-time in a café. Your boss says to you 'I'm sorry, but another person has called in sick. Could you stay later tonight?' Would you find this utterance appropriate?

(E) Yes 94% / No 6%	(J) Yes 75% / No 25%

39. Does 'Yes, please' sound arrogant?
You should not say 'Yes, please' when accepting someone's kind offer of help except when they have good reason to do it (e.g. it is part of their job) because it might sound as if you are taking it for granted that they will serve you. Do you agree? Please answer the following questions:

II: You are reviewing your term paper on the lawn in front of the library. One of your friends sitting next to you says 'Would you like a cup of coffee?' If you want to have one, would you say 'Yes, please?'

(E) Yes 83% / No 17%	(J) Yes 67% / No 33%

40. Is it always appropriate to refuse something politely saying 'No, thank you?'
You should say 'No, thank you' when rejecting someone's kind offer to help because it is polite. Do you agree? Please answer the following questions:

(E) Yes 97% / No 3%	(J) Yes 96% / No 4%

II: You are reviewing your term paper on the lawn in front of the library. One of your friends sitting next to you says 'Would you like a cup of coffee?' If you do not wish to have one, would you refuse by saying 'No, thank you?'

(E) Yes 91% / No 9%	(J) Yes 77% / No 23%

41. Does 'yes' always mean you agree?

'Yes' should not be used just to signal that you are listening to others because it means that you agree with them. Do you agree? Please answer the following question:

Jim and Daniel are planning to go hiking near a lake. They have to use public transportation to reach the lake.

Jim: So I think we should take a bus instead. I know there's a direct bus service between this city and the lake.
Daniel: Yes, but buses are sometimes unreliable. They're often late especially on weekends. And they're a bit more expensive.

Would you find Daniel's use of 'yes' appropriate?

(E) Yes 90% / No 10%	(J) Yes 69% / No 31%	(Br) Yes 96% / No 4%	(Am) Yes 83% / No 17%

42. Do you refer to a baby or a pet as 'it'?

While 'it' can be used to refer to a baby or a pet, according to traditional English grammar, it is not a good idea to use it in this way because it can sound rather cold. Do you agree? Please answer the following questions:

I: Would you refer to a baby as 'it'?

(E) Yes 0% / No 100%	(J) Yes 11% / No 89%

II: Would you refer to a pet such as a dog or a cat as 'it'?

(E) Yes 0% / No 100%	(J) Yes 41% / No 59%

43. How do you tell the truth?

We should use such phrases as 'to tell you the truth' or 'as a matter of fact' only when we are revealing some important fact or emphasizing its accuracy. If we use them too often it will sound as if we are trying to hide something. Do you agree? Please answer the following questions:

Tess asks one of his friends David whether he is fine because he looks tired this morning. As David just sat up late with friends last night, he says 'To tell you the truth, I didn't sleep much last night.'

(A) Would you find David's utterance appropriate?

(E) Yes 93% / No 7%	(J) Yes 65% / No 35%

(B) If David says 'As a matter of fact, I didn't sleep much last night, would you find David's utterance appropriate?

(E) Yes 70% / No 30%	(J) Yes 50% / No 50%	(Br) Yes 59% / No 41%	(Am) Yes 84% / No 16%

44. Does it sound arrogant if we say 'I want' when we express our wishes?
We should avoid 'I want + (pro)noun' or 'I want to do' a particular thing because it might sound as if we are rude or selfish. We should instead use other expressions depending on the situation. Do you agree? Please answer the following questions:

I: You are at the house of a friend of yours, when you become thirsty. You ask the friend to give you something to drink. Would you say to the friend 'I want something to drink?'

(E) Yes 2% / No 98%	(J) Yes 46% / No 54%

II: You are having dinner in a casual restaurant, when you happen to drop a spoon. You ask the waiter to give you another one. Would you say to the waiter 'I want another spoon?'

(E) Yes 3% / No 97%	(J) Yes 45% / No 55%

45. What do you mean 'different?'
The meaning of the word 'different' may be sometimes ambiguous when it is used to describe people's appearances or the like. It can be taken either as approval or disapproval according to the situation. Do you agree? Please answer the following question:

When you are walking on the street more dressed up than usual, a friend of yours just passing by says to you 'You look different today.' How would you feel? Choose from a) - d) a reaction closest to yours.
    a) You feel glad.
    b) You feel sad.
    c) You want to know if your friend is complimenting you.

e) None of the above

| (E) a) 18% / b) 1% / c) 63% / d) 18% / e) 0% | (J) a) 61% / b) 2% / c) 21% / d) 16% / e) 0% |

46. Are you reserved or unsure?
When expressing one's opinion or even giving information to others some nationalities, like the Japanese, often use an expression which signals they are not really sure whether they are right or not, because this is considered polite or reserved in their cultures. Is this the same for English speaking people? Please answer the following questions:

You are asked by a passing stranger how to get to the station. After you have shown the stranger the way, the person also asks you if you happen to know how long it will take to get to their destination by train. You have been there once or twice, and you know it takes some forty minutes.

(A) Would you say 'I don't know exactly, but I think you can get there in 40 minutes or so?'

| (E) Yes 68% / No 32% | (J) Yes 86% / No 14% |

47. Does 'foreign' sound alienating?
The words 'foreigner' or 'foreign' should be avoided because they sound discriminatory. Do you agree? Please answer the following questions:

I: Would you say 'foreigner' when referring to a person from another country?

| (E) Yes 42% / No 58% | (J) Yes 74% / No 26% |

II: Would you say 'foreign student' when referring to a student from another country?

| (E) Yes 76% / No 24% | (J) Yes 58% / No 42% |

48. Is it cool to say 'gonna' or 'wanna?'
Such expressions as 'gonna' or 'wanna' should be avoided when we are in formal situations. Do you agree? Please answer the following questions:

You are having an interview for a university place, and wish to tell the interviewer that you are doing your best. Please answer the following questions:

(A) Would you say 'I'm gonna do my best?'

| (E) Yes 16% / No 84% | (J) Yes 55% / No 45% |

(B) Would you say 'I wanna do my best?'

| (E) Yes 11% / No 89% | (J) Yes 34% / No 66% |

49. Is it selfish to put 'I' first when listing subjects?
When listing several subjects in a sentence, we usually list them like 'You, he and I are close friends.' putting 'I' at the end. If the order is changed, it may affect the impression given and make us sound arrogant. The only exception is when you are to blame. In such cases, you should put 'I' first. Do you agree? Please answer the following questions:

I: Kevin's team won a soccer game; the score is 3 to 0. The scorers are Kevin, Tom and Richard. After the game Kevin says to Tom, 'I, you and Richard did a good job.' Would you find this utterance appropriate?

| (E) Yes 2% / No 98% | (J) Yes 22% / No 78% |

II: While playing soccer, Kevin, Tom, Richard broke a window of the school building. The teacher asks Tom who broke it, and he answers 'I, Kevin and Richard did.' Would you find this utterance appropriate?

| (E) Yes 12% / No 88% | (J) Yes 67% / No 33% |

50. How do you reply to 'How are you' when you are not just 'fine?'
We do not have to reply to 'How are you?' truthfully because it is just a greeting. Do you agree? Please answer the following questions:

I: When you have a slight cold, would you say 'I'm fine. Thank you.' in reply to a classmate saying 'How are you?'

| (E) Yes 66% / No 34% | (J) Yes 23% / No 77% | (Br) Yes 57% / No 43% | (Am) Yes 76% / No 24% |

II: When you have a bad cold, would you say 'I'm fine. Thank you.' in reply to a classmate saying 'How are you?'

| (E) Yes 26% / No 74% | (J) Yes 8% / No 92% |

III: When you feel very well, would you say 'I'm fine. Thank you.' in reply to a classmate saying 'How are you?'

| (E) Yes 82% / No 18% | (J) Yes 91% / No 9% |

51. How do you find it if someone repeats 'you know'?
If we use 'you know' too often it sounds as if we lack the ability to express our thoughts logically with using language. Do you agree? Please answer the following question:

You broke your leg while playing baseball a month ago. As you are anxious to play baseball again as soon as possible, you ask the doctor how much longer it will take to recover. Your doctor gives you the following explanation:
> 'I understand how frustrated you must be feeling, but, you know it's difficult to tell. Some injuries heal very quickly, but, you know, that's not the case with everyone. Try to be patient for a little longer.'

Would you find the doctror's use of 'you know' appropriate?

| (E) Yes 44% / No 56% | (J) Yes 75% / No 25% |

52. Do you call others 'liar?'
In English if you say 'You're a liar' to someone it might even sound as if you are trying to pick a fight. Do you agree? Please answer the following questions:

One of your classmates Henry often makes jokes and makes everybody laugh. One day when you are talking with Henry he very seriously says that he has seen a UFO.
(A) If you do not believe in UFOs, would you say to him '(You're a) liar?'

| (E) Yes 14% / No 86% | (J) Yes 34% / No 66% |

(B) (In the same situation) If another friend of yours were to call him a liar to his face, would you find this utterance appropriate?

| (E) Yes 25% / No 75% | (J) Yes 43% / No 57% |

53. Should we avoid 'OK?'
(1) We should not say 'OK' to our superiors or in a formal situation because it is an informal expression.
(2) It will sound too compelling if we request something by saying 'Is it OK if I do something?'
Do you agree? Please answer the following questions:

I: After class your teacher Mr. Cruise approaches you and asks you to help him carry the teaching materials to the teachers' room. If you are willing to help him, would you say 'OK?'

| (E) Yes 91% / No 9% | (J) Yes 57% / No 43% |

II: While you are trying to quickly finish your homework in the school cafeteria, you see one of your classmates Anthony. You notice that he is not doing anything, so you decide to ask him to get you a cold drink. Would you say 'Anthony, is it OK if I ask you to get me something cold to drink?'

| (E) Yes 39% / No 61% | (J) Yes 68% / No 32% | (Br) Yes 52% / No 48% | (Am) Yes 21% / No 79% |

55. In which situations do you say 'Pretty'
'Pretty' can be used when we do not really think that something is nice to look at, cute or attractive. Do you agree? Please answer the following question:

One of your classmates Mary shows you the new dress her parents bought for her, and asks you if you like it. However, you do not really find it cute or attractive. Would you say 'It's very pretty'?

| (E) Yes 47% / No 53% | (J) Yes 64% / No 36% |

57. Who can introduce themselves only by their surnames?
When we introduce ourselves we should give our full names (given name and surname) because only people with very high ranks such as nobles are allowed to give their family names alone. Therefore, if we announce only our family names, it will sound arrogant. Do you agree? Please answer the following question:

When introducing yourself, would you sometimes give your surname alone?

| (E) Yes 15% / No 85% | (J) Yes 2% / No 98% |

58. Should we avoid 'I think' when we have to mention something undesirable?
When we have to point out something undesirable we should avoid 'I think ....' Or it will sound as if we are enjoying pointing out bad things. Do you agree? Please answer the following questions:

I: You see your classmate Eric rushing out of the library. Soon after a vase is found to be broken. If your teacher asks you if you know who broke the vase and insists that you answer, would you say 'I think Eric did'?

| (E) Yes 57% / No 43% | (J) Yes 19% / No 81% |

II: Your younger brother Kevin is busy preparing to go camping tomorrow, but, according to the weather forecast that you you've just listened to in your room, it is very likely to rain tomorow. When Kevin says 'I hope it'll be fine tomorrow,' you feel you must tell him that it is going to rain. Would you say 'I think it will rain tomorrow'?

| (E) Yes 54% / No 46% | (J) Yes 31% / No 69% |

59. Does it sound arrogant if we use 'will' when talking about our personal plans?

'I will ...' (not 'I'll) in everyday conversation especially when talking about our schedules sounds arrogant because 'will' is usually used in public announcements. Do you agree? Please answer the following question:

You are going to see your cousin in Paris during the coming vacation. After school you are asked by a classmate about your plans for the vacation. Would you answer 'I will go to Paris to see my cousin?'

| (E) Yes 13% / No 87% | (J) Yes 80% / No 20% |

60. Does 'will' mean that we have just decided our future plans?

When you want to say you have a prior engagement (even if it is not true), it is advisable to avoid 'I will ...' because 'I will' can give the listener the impression that you have just decided to do something on the spot. Do you agree? Please answer the following question:

The manager of a restaurant where you work part-time asks you if you are free next Sunday. You know he wants you to work on that day. Although you are free next Sunday, you usually do not work on weekends and do not want to work. So you say that you have already promised to meet some friends next Sunday. Would you say 'I will see my friends next Sunday?'

| (E) Yes 6% / No 94% | (J) Yes 59% / No 41% |

61. How should we use the word 'homely?'

Especially when talking about a woman the word 'homely' can sometimes be ambiguous; and might even sound offensive. If this is the case it might be better to avoid the word altogether. Do you agree? Please answer the following question:

Roger, a close friend of yours introduces you to his elder sister Susan. She has a warm, comforting manner and looks like a woman who would enjoy being at home and running a family. If someone asks you what Susan is like, would you say 'She is a homely person?'

(E) Yes 20% / No 80%	(J) Yes 28% / No 72%	(Br) Yes 35% / No 65%	(Am) Yes 2% / No 98%

62. Should we use 'should' in our answers?

We ought to avoid using 'should' when answering even if the question contains 'should' (e.g. 'What should I do?') because the word 'should' is a very strong word and might sound too forceful. Do you agree? Please answer the following question:

You and Mike, a friend of yours are going for a drive tomorrow, and you want him to collect you at 9: 00. Before he leaves he asks you 'What time should I collect you?' Would you answer 'You should collect me at 9: 00?'

(E) Yes 25% / No 75%	(J) Yes 15% / No 85%	(Br) Yes 15% / No 85%	(Am) Yes 37% / No 63%

63. Can 'as you know' sound ironical?

If you say 'as you know' when it appears that the hearer does not know what you are talking about, it can sound ironical. Do you agree? Please answer the following question:

You are good with computers. Your friend Eric knows nothing about them. One day he asks you for help because he cannot make his new printer work. When you look at Eric's printer, you discover that he has not connected his printer to his computer. So you tell Eric that it is necessary to connect the printer to his PC before using it. Would you say 'As you know, it is necessary to connect the printer to your PC before using it?'

(E) Yes 10% / No 90%	(J) Yes 46% / No 54%

64. Should we sometimes avoid 'you' as a subject?

When we have to point out an undesirable fact or say something to others that is sensitive or difficult to say, it is a good idea not to use 'you' as a subject but rather use 'we' or something like 'These seats are occupied.' rather than 'you should not sit here.' In this way we can avoid responsibility. Do you agree? Please answer the following question:

You notice that someone is smoking though it is a non-smoking area. So you ask the person to stop smoking. Would you say 'You shouldn't smoke here?'

| (E) Yes 36% / No 64% | (J) Yes 63% / No 37% |

65. Do you say 'I like drinking' and/or 'I'm drunk?'

One should not say 'I like drinking' or 'I'm drunk' because it might give the listener the impression that you are an alcoholic or that you are blind drunk. Do you agree? Please answer the following questions:

I: You start a new part-time job, and your colleagues hold a welcoming party for you. One of them asks you if you are fond of alcoholic drinks, and in fact you are. Would you say 'I like drinking?'

| (E) Yes 24% / No 76% | (J) Yes 79% / No 21% |

II: During the welcoming party one of your colleagues asks you if you are OK. In fact, you might have had a bit too much beer but are not sick. Perhaps you are just slightly drunk. Would you say 'I'm just drunk?'

| (E) Yes 21% / No 79% | (J) Yes 63% / No 37% | (Br) Yes 30% / No 70% | (Am) Yes 11% / No 89% |

67. How do you reply to 'How do you do?'

One should not say 'How do you do?' in reply to another person's greeting 'How do you do?' because it will sound as if you are just repeating mechanically. Do you agree? Please answer the following question:

At the house of your friend you are introduced to a person of almost the same age as you named Harry Sharpe, and the person says 'How do you do, X [Your name]?' to you. When replying, would you say 'How do you do, Harry?'

| (E) Yes 30% / No 70% | (J) Yes 71% / No 29% |

68. Which do you think is preferable when mentioning something undesirable, 'I'm sorry' or 'I'm afraid?'

'I'm sorry I can't,' sounds like a complete refusal while 'I'm afraid I can't' is not. Therefore, 'I'm afraid' is preferable when one has to say something unpleasant. Do you agree? Please answer the following question:

You are late for an important examination; when you reach the hall, the examination has already started. You ask the person in charge if you can still take the test, but you are no longer allowed to join the test. In this situ-

ation, which of the following replies would give you the best impression?
   a) 'I'm sorry you're too late.'
   b) 'I'm afraid you're too late.'
   c) Neither of the above

| (E) a) 23% / b) 73% / c) 4% | (J) a) 41% / b) 57% / c) 2% |
| (Br) a) 13% / b) 85% / c) 2% | (Am) a) 35% / b) 59% / c) 6% |

69. Do you always begin your answer with 'Yes' or 'No' when answering a yes/no question?

When answering a yes/no question, you have to begin your answer with 'yes' or 'no' in order to signal your answer in advance. Do you agree? Please answer the following questions:

Paul Jones has gone to the station to meet his mother's friend whom he has never met. While he is waiting, a woman approaches him.

(A) If the person says 'Excuse me. Are you Paul?,' which of the following replies do you think Paul should use in this situation? Please choose the best reply from below. (*Paul is only supposed to answer the question, so please ignore any other utterances such as greetings.)
   a) 'Yes.'
   b) 'Yes, I am.'
   c) 'I am Paul.'
   d) None of the above are appropriate

| (E) a) 22% / b) 73% / c) 1% / d) 4% | (J) a) 15% / b) 72% / c) 10% / d) 3% |

(B) (In the same situation) If the person says 'Excuse me. Are you Mr. James?,' which of the following replies do you think Paul should use in this situation? Please choose the best reply from below. (*Paul is supposed to answer the question only, so please ignore other possible utterances.)
   a) 'No.'
   b) 'No, I'm not.'
   c) 'No. I'm Jones.'
   d) 'I'm Jones.'
   e) None of the above are appropriate

| (E) a) 8% / b) 55% / c) 22% / d) 0% / e) 15% | (J) a) 6% / b) 54% / c) 35% / d) 4% / e) 1% |

70. Should we say 'No' clearly when rejecting something?
When declining an invitation or when denying a request we should avoid saying 'no'. We should instead explain why we cannot accept the invitation

or agree to the request. Do you agree? Please answer the following questions:

I: You have been invited to a barbecue on the next Sunday by one of your classmates: he said 'We're having a barbecue next Sunday. Would you like to come?' However, you are taking a trip next weekend. Please choose the most appropriate reply from below:
    a) 'No, I wouldn't.'
    b) 'No, I wouldn't. I'm taking a trip next weekend.'
    c) 'Sounds nice, but I'm taking a trip next weekend.'
    d) None of the above is acceptable

(E) a) 0% / b) 1% / c) 92% / d) 7%	(J) a) 0% / b) 3% / c) 96% / d) 1%

II: Your teacher says to you 'I need to talk to you later. Are you free after school?' However, you are seeing your friends, and so you want to say that you are not free. Please choose the most appropriate reply from below:
    a) 'No, I'm not.'
    b) 'No, I'm not. I'm seeing my friends tonight.'
    c) 'I wish I was, but I'm seeing my friends tonight.'
    d) None of the above is acceptable

(E) a) 18% / b) 21% / c) 20% / d) 41%	(J) a) 9% / b) 31% / c) 50% / d) 10%

71. Do you say 'Your husband (wife, son, and daughter)?'
It is rather rude to refer to someone's spouse (or any family member) as your (his, her) husband, wife, son, daughter and so on, and we should call them by their first name. Do you agree? Please answer the following questions:

I: You are leaving your friend Mrs. Williams' home. Her husband is not in and so you want to ask her to say hello to him. However, you do not know his first name. How would you refer to him? Which of the following do you find most appropriate?
    a) 'Please say hello to your husband.'
    b) 'Please say hello to Mr. Williams.'
    c) Neither of the above is acceptable

(E) a) 65% / b) 27% / c) 8%	(J) a) 41% / b) 54% / c) 5%
(Br) a) 59% / b) 26% / c) 15%	(Am) a) 72% / b) 28% / c) 0%

II: You are leaving your friend Mr. Williams' home. His wife is not in and so you want to ask him to say hello to her. However, you do not know her first name. How would you refer to her? Which of the following do you most appropriate?

    a) 'Please say hello to your wife.'
    b) 'Please say hello to Mrs. Williams.'
    c) Neither of the above is acceptable

(E) a) 65% / b) 28% / c) 7%	(J) a) 46% / b) 50% / c) 4%
(Br) a) 61% / b) 26% / c) 13%	(Am) a) 70% / b) 30% / c) 0%

72. How should we use 'Could you ...?' and 'Could I ...?'
When we can make the same request with either of the following patterns: 'Could you ...?' and 'Could I ...?', the former does not sound polite because it sounds as if the speaker is trying to force the listener to serve him/her. For example, 'Could I have a glass of water?' is more polite than 'Could you bring me a glass of water?' Do you agree? Please answer the following question:

You work part-time at a watchmaker's. A customer seems interested in a watch displayed in the showcase. If the customer wanted to look at the watch, how would you prefer that they asked you?

    a) 'Could you show me the watch displayed in the showcase please?'
    b) 'Could I have a look at the watch displayed in the showcase please?'
    c) Both a) and b) are equally appropriate
    d) None of the above is acceptable

(E) a) 2% / b) 17% / c) 79% / d) 2%	(J) a) 53% / b) 26% / c) 19% / d) 2%

74. Do you praise someone with 'clever?'
It is advisable to avoid using 'clever' when talking of a person because it has both positive and negative connotations such as 'bright' and 'cunning.' Do you agree? Please answer the following questions:

I: You are requested to help your neighbor's son, Mike with his homework. Mike is an elementary school student, and you are surprised to find out what a quick learner he is. If you wanted to tell Mike's parents about him, which of the following would you find most appropriate?

    a) 'Mike is very clever.'
    b) 'Mike is very intelligent.'
    c) 'Mike is very bright.'
    d) None of the above is acceptable

(E) a) 14% / b) 20% / c) 65% / d) 1%	(J) a) 29% / b) 18% / c) 48% / d) 5%

II: While having dinner your father asks you about your new homeroom teacher Mr. Tom Smith. Mr. Smith is very intelligent, and you admire him. Which of the following answers would you find most appropriate?
    a) 'He is very clever.'
    b) 'He is very intelligent.'
    c) 'He is very bright.'
    d) None of the above is acceptable

(E) a) 16% / b) 73% / c) 5% / d) 6%	(J) a) 7% / b) 66% / c) 20% / d) 7%
(Br) a) 30% / b) 61% / c) 4% / d) 5%	(Am) a) 0% / b) 86% / c) 7% / d) 7%

75. Which do you prefer 'look at' or 'have a look at?'
'Have a look at' is preferable to 'look at' because it sounds lighter. Do you agree? Please answer the following question:

One of your friends, Peter seems to be having problems with his PC. As you are quite familiar with PCs, you are going to check if his PC is OK. Which would you prefer a) or b)?
    a) 'Don't worry. I'll look at your PC.'
    b) 'Don't worry. I'll have a look at your PC.'
    c) Neither of the above is acceptable

(E) a) 14% / b) 83% / c) 3%	(J) a) 30% / b) 64% / c) 6%
(Br) a) 7% / b) 87% / c) 6%	(Am) a) 22% / b) 78% / c) 0%

76. Which do you prefer 'help' or 'give somebody a hand?'
'Give somebody a hand' sounds lighter than 'help.' Do you agree? Please answer the following question:

You are looking for one of your contact lenses that you accidentally dropped, when a friend of yours Mary comes along. You want to ask her to help you find it. Which is better a) or b)?
    a) 'Mary, could you help me find my contact lens?'
    b) 'Mary could you give me a hand finding my contact lens?'
    c) Neither of the above

(E) a) 57% / b) 39% / c) 4%	(J) a) 71% / b) 26% / c) 3%
(Br) a) 41% / b) 52% / c) 7%	(Am) a) 76% / b) 24% / c) 0%

77. Do you say 'a thin person?'
It is advisable to avoid 'thin' when talking about a thin person especially a woman. We should instead use 'slim' or 'slender.' Do you agree? Please

answer the following questions:

I: (A) When praising the appearance of a male person for being thin which of the following would find you most appropriate?
    a) 'a thin man'
    b) 'a skinny man'
    c) 'a slim man'
    d) 'a slender man'
    e) None of the above is acceptable

(E) a) 12% / b) 2% / c) 46% / d) 31% / e) 9%	(J) a) 3% / b) 2% / c) 31% / d) 56% / e) 8%
(Br) a) 7% / b) 2% / c) 65% / d) 20% / e) 6%	(Am) a) 17% / b) 2% / c) 24% / d) 44% / e) 13%

I: (B) Which of the above do you believe we should not use? (You can select as many as necessary.)

(E) a) 26% / b) 44% / c) 9% / d) 21% / e) 0%	(J) a) 46% / b) 44% / c) 4% / d) 6% / e) 0%

II: (A) When praising the appearance of a female person for being thin which of the following would you find most appropriate?
    a) 'a thin woman'
    b) 'a skinny woman'
    c) 'a slim woman'
    d) 'a slender woman'
    e) None of the above is acceptable

(E) a) 12% / b) 2% / c) 48% / d) 37% / e) 1%	(J) a) 3% / b) 1% / c) 19% / d) 73% / e) 4%
(Br) a) 7% / b) 0% / c) 69% / d) 22% / e) 2%	(Am) a) 18% / b) 4% / c) 24% / d) 54% / e) 0%

II: (B) Which of the above do you believe we should not use? (You can select as many as necessary.)

(E) a) 30% / b) 56% / c) 7% / d) 7% / e) 0%	(J) a) 45% / b) 50% / c) 3% / d) 2% / e) 0%

78. Do you say someone is 'short?'
One should not use 'short' when talking about a person of below average height, but in the case of a woman or a child we can use 'petite.' Do you agree? Please answer the following questions:

I: (A) When referring to a male person of below average height which of the following would you find most appropriate?
    a) 'a short man'
    b) 'a small man'

c) 'a petite man'
d) 'a man of below average height'
e) None of the above is acceptable

| (E) a) 61% / b) 10% / c) 1% / d) 13% / e) 15% | (J) a) 35% / b) 30% / c) 4% / d) 17% / e) 14% |

(B) Which of the above do you believe we should not use? (You can select as many as necessary.)

| (E) a) 11% / b) 26% / c) 42% / d) 21% / e) 0% | (J) a) 30% / b) 25% / c) 25% / d) 20% / e) 0% |

II: (A) When referring to a female person of below average height which of the following would you find most appropriate?
   a) 'a short woman'
   b) 'a small woman'
   c) 'a petite woman'
   d) 'a woman of below average height'
   e) None of the above is acceptable

| (E) a) 24% / b) 9% / c) 61% / d) 5% / e) 1% | (J) a) 24% / b) 37% / c) 17% / d) 11% / e) 11% |

(B) Which of the above do you believe we should not use? (You can select as many as necessary.)

| (E) a) 28% / b) 20% / c) 9% / d) 43% / e) 0% | (J) a) 36% / b) 24% / c) 15% / d) 25% / e) 0% |

79. Do you use 'Ms.?'

We should use 'Miss' rather than 'Ms.' when we are not sure whether a woman is married or not as it sounds more polite. Even if they are actually married they will just correct the title and will not take offense. Do you agree? Please answer the following question:

Which of the following would you use to address a woman if you did not know whether she was married or not?
   a) 'Miss'
   b) 'Mrs.'
   c) 'Ms.'
   d) None of the above is acceptable

| (E) a) 32% / b) 1% / c) 61% / d) 6% / e) 0% | (J) a) 7% / b) 5% / c) 87% / d) 1% / e) 0% |

80. How should we make proper use of 'Excuse me' and 'I'm sorry?'

'I'm sorry.' is used to signal that you admit that you have caused others trouble while 'Excuse me.' is not. Do you agree? Please answer the following questions:

I: You bump a person accidentally in the train station.
(A) If it does not cause serious trouble and the person is just passing by which of the following would you say?
    a) 'Excuse me.'
    b) 'I'm sorry.'
    c) 'Sorry.'
    d) 'Pardon me.'
    e) None of the above is sufficient

(E) a) 22% / b) 20% / c) 45% / d) 12% / e) 1%	(J) a) 37% / b) 17% / c) 41% / d) 3% / e) 2%
(Br) a) 9% / b) 22% / c) 65% / d) 4% / e) 0%	(Am) a) 37% / b) 17% / c) 22% / d) 22% / e) 2%

(B) If the person falls down would you say any of the above?

(E) a) 1% / b) 56% / c) 3% / d) 0% / e) 40%	(J) a) 11% / b) 75% / c) 10% / d) 4% / e) 0%

II: When you sneeze which of the following do you say?
    a) 'Excuse me.'
    b) 'I'm sorry.'
    c) 'Sorry.'
    d) 'Pardon me.'
    e) None of the above is sufficient

(E) a) 75% / b) 1% / c) 0% / d) 17% / e) 7%	(J) a) 55% / b) 4% / c) 36% / d) 2% / e) 3%
(Br) a) 78% / b) 2% / c) 0% / d) 20% / e) 0%	(Am) a) 72% / b) 0% / c) 0% / d) 13% / e) 15%

III: You have arranged to meet a friend. You arrive just on time but your friend is already there waiting for you. Which of the following would you say?
    a) 'Excuse me.'
    b) 'I'm sorry.'
    c) 'Sorry.'
    d) 'Pardon me.'
    e) None of the above

(E) a) 0% / b) 28% / c) 24% / d) 0% / e) 48%	(J) a) 2% / b) 46% / c) 33% / d) 2% / e) 17%

81. Does the imperative sound rude?

The imperative or its equivalent can be very polite, if uttered to urge others to do something which would be beneficial to them, because it can help to throw off a possible sense of reserve which they might otherwise feel. Do you agree? Please answer the following questions:

I: You are receiving a guest on the front door step of your house. Which of the following would you say to welcome the guest?
    a) 'Could you come in?'
    b) 'Please come in.'
    c) 'Do come in.'
    d) 'Come in.'
    e) None of the above is acceptable

(E) a) 0% / b) 59% / c) 13% / d) 27% / e) 1%	(J) a) 4% / b) 86% / c) 0% / d) 10% / e) 0%
(Br) a) 0% / b) 43% / c) 22% / d) 33% / e) 2%	(Am) a) 0% / b) 78% / c) 2% / d) 20% / e) 0%

82. What is the difference between 'I'm glad to meet you' and 'I'm glad to see you?'

'I'm glad to meet you' and 'I'm glad to see you' are quite different in terms of their uses in actual situations. For example, the former should be used when you greet someone whom you have never met, while the latter is to be used to a person whom you have met before. Do you agree? Please answer the following questions:

I: When you meet someone for the first time, which of the following would you prefer to use?
    a) 'I'm glad to meet you'
    b) 'I'm glad to see you'
    c) Neither of the above

(E) a) 70% / b) 0% / c) 30%	(J) a) 65% / b) 31% / c) 4%
(Br) a) 56% / b) 0% / c) 44%	(Am) a) 87% / b) 0% / c) 13%

II: When you meet someone whom you have met before, which of the following would you prefer?
    a) 'I'm glad to meet you'
    b) 'I'm glad to see you'
    c) Neither of the above

(E) a) 1% / b) 64% / c) 35%	(J) a) 18% / b) 72% / c) 10%
(Br) a) 2% / b) 48% / c) 50%	(Am) a) 0% / b) 83% / c) 17%

83. Do Wh-questions sound rude?

It is advisable to use a yes/no question rather than a wh-question when we are trying to get to know somebody, say, at a party because a wh-question may sound as if we are questioning them. Do you agree? Please answer the following question:

You are going camping with Alan with whom you work part-time and his friends whom you do not know. After exchanging just brief greetings you want to find out more about them. Which of the following would you prefer?
    a) 'How do you know Alan?'
    b) 'Do you go to the same high school as Alan?'
    c) Neither of the above

(E) a) 87% / b) 10% / c) 3%	(J) a) 29% / b) 59% / c) 12%
(Br) a) 79% / b) 17% / c) 4%	(Am) a) 96% / b) 2% / c) 2%

84. Do you use 'interesting' when praising something?
'Interesting' cannot always be used when praising something because it is often taken to mean 'peculiar' or 'barely acceptable' especially when it is not followed by any positive remarks. Do you agree? Please answer the following questions:

I: You happen to see your teacher in the school library, and you ask her what she thought of the paper you submitted a few days earlier. The teacher says to you 'Ah, it was interesting.' How would you take the comments? Please choose the best answer from below:
    a) The teacher found it 'stimulating'
    b) The teacher found it good.
    c) The teacher found it just acceptable.
    d) The teacher found it poor.
    e) None of the above

(E) a) 26% / b) 11% / c) 9% / d) 6% / e) 48%	(J) a) 22% / b) 47% / c) 20% / d) 5% / e) 6%

II: After dinner, you ask your father how he liked the dishes you cooked that night. He says 'They had very interesting flavors.' How would you take his comments? Please choose the best answer from below:
    a) He had never had such delicious dishes before.
    b) He found them delicious.
    c) He found them eatable.
    d) He found them terrible.
    e) None of the above

(E) a) 6% / b) 11% / c) 27% / d) 8% / e) 48%	(J) a) 8% / b) 23% / c) 31% / d) 28% / e) 10%

85. How do you interpret 'difficult?'
In the Japanese language, the translation of 'difficult,' *muzukashii* can often be taken to mean 'impossible,' especially when you are refusing something

politely. Is this the same for 'difficult' in English? Please answer the following question:

You are taking a very important examination which is starting in 10 minutes. As it would take about 15 minutes to walk there, you decide to take a taxi. However, when you tell the driver that you have to get there in 10 minutes, the driver says 'It's difficult to get there in 10 minutes.' How would you take the driver's utterance? Which is closest to your interpretation?
    a) The driver thinks it impossible to get there in 10 minutes.
    b) The driver thinks that it is not easy to arrive there in 10 minutes.
    c) Neither of the above

(E) a) 6% / b) 91% / c) 3%	(J) a) 76% / b) 23% / c) 1%

86. Which is strongest among 'fairly', 'quite' and 'very?'
If we confuse such adverbs as 'very,' 'quite' and 'fairly,' it can cause a misunderstanding. For example, if we use 'fairly' while in fact meaning 'very,' we could inadvertently convey the wrong meaning. Do you agree? Please answer the following question:

One of your friends Mary lent you a CD of her favorite singer. It was really good, and you enjoyed it a lot. When returning the CD which of the following would you find most suitable for praising it?
    a) 'It's very good!'
    b) 'It's fairly good!'
    c) 'It's quite good!'
    d) None of the above is acceptable

(E) a) 90% / b) 0% / c) 6% / d) 4%	(J) a) 57% / b) 15% / c) 26% / d) 2%
(Br) a) 94% / b) 0% / c) 0% / d) 6%	(Am) a) 85% / b) 0% / c) 13% / d) 2%

87. Which do you prefer 'had better' or 'should' when giving advice to others?
We ought to avoid using 'had better' when giving advice to others because it might sound too forceful. Do you agree? Please answer the following question:

You come from London. As one of your friends David is planning to visit London, he asks you what particular places you recommend. You believe he must visit Big Ben and The London Eye. Which of the following would you find most appropriate?
    a) 'You had better visit Big Ben and the London Eye.'

b) 'You should visit Big Ben and the London Eye.'
c) Neither of the above is acceptable

| (E) a) 1% / b) 96% / c) 3% | (J) a) 28% / b) 67% / c) 5% |

88. Do you omit the subject of a sentence in order to sound casual?

While in English you usually do not omit a subject in a sentence except the imperative, you actually omit one in an informal situation or when you wish to sound casual like 'Need help?'. Do you agree? Please answer the following question:

You find an empty seat on a bus. Before sitting down, you say to the passenger in the next seat. Which of the following would you say?
  a) 'Mind if I sit here?'
  b) 'Do you mind if I sit here?'
  c) None of the above

| (E) a) 41% / b) 48% / c) 11% | (J) a) 13% / b) 74% / c) 13% |
| (Br) a) 30% / b) 57% / c) 13% | (Am) a) 54% / b) 37% / c) 9% |

89. Do you refer to your boyfriend or girlfriend as your 'lover?'

We should avoid using 'lover' when referring to one's regular companion with whom we have a romantic relationship because it might imply that one has a sexual relationship with the person referred to.

I: (A) Which of the following would you find most appropriate when referring to one's regular male companion with whom one has a romantic relationship?
  a) 'boyfriend'
  b) 'steady'
  c) 'lover'
  d) None of the above is acceptable

| (E) a) 92% / b) 1% / c) 0% / d) 7% | (J) a) 37% / b) 25% / c) 29% / d) 9% |

(B) Which of the above do you think we should avoid? (You can select as many as necessary.)

| (E) a) 2% / b) 48% / c) 50% / d) 0% | (J) a) 40% / b) 11% / c) 49% / d) 0% |

II: (A) Which of the following would you find most appropriate when referring to one's regular female companion with whom they have a romantic relationship?

a) 'girlfriend'
b) 'steady'
c) 'lover'
d) None of the above is acceptable

| (E) a) 94% / b) 0% / c) 0% / d) 6% | (J) a) 36% / b) 27% / c) 29% / d) 8% |

(B) Which of the above do you think we should avoid? (You can select as many as necessary.)

| (E) a) 2% / b) 49% / c) 49% / d) 0% | (J) a) 39% / b) 12% / c) 49% / d) 0% |

Appendix III
Text functions

Below is the framework of text functions and examples of each function.

I) *Evaluative*: expressing speaker's evaluation and attitude, such as negative and positive
Examples:
> (negative) *horrible; chicken; bitch; terrible; be always ~ing; bastard; prat; liar*
> (positive) *wonderful; terrific; a heart of gold; somebody*

II) *Situational*: relating to extralinguistic content; or responding to situation such as greetings/thanking/apologies.
Examples:
> (greeting) *hello; good morning; good afternoon; hi*
> (thanking) *thank you; you saved me; I can't thank you enough*
> (apologies) *(I'm) sorry; excuse me*
> (request) *I'd do appreciate it if you could...; Could you...?; I was just wondering...; Do you mind ~ing?*
> (inviting) *Would you like to...?; Are you happy with...?*
> (declining, rejecting or saying something unpleasant) *I wish I could... but...; I'm afraid...; (I'm) sorry, but...*
> (closing conversation) *It's been nice talking to you; I think I must go now*
> (pre-requesting) *Are you busy now?; May I ask you a favour?*
> (others) *that's it; never mind; Let's...; this is just to let you know...; here's...*

III) *Modalizing*:
a) *epistemic*: representing the speaker/writer's commitment to the truth value
Examples:
> (indicating likelihood and probability) *seem; certainly; as usual; never*
> (indicating futurity) NP *to come*
> (adding emphasis) *It is ~ that...*
> (adding emphasis by indicating certainty or drawing attention to veracity) *no doubt*
> (negating) *not; no; fail to do*
> (pre-empting) *needless to say*
> (denying) *the last person/thing etc; who knows/cares?*
> (casting doubts) *I'm not sure; not always; not 100%; not really; no*

way
(indicating ignorance) *good question*
(disclaiming knowledge) *don't ask me; that's news to me* (These examples overlap with *situational*, but I put these here as these are more concerned with the truth value.)
(deferring judgement) *time will tell; in due course; wait and see; no comment*
(indicating corrections or modifications) *in fact; I mean; at least*
(indicating criticisms) *jump to conclusions; find fault with; so-called*
(mitigating or downtoning by indicating vagueness and retreating from definite assertion) *in part; sort of; in a way; more or less; could; something like that*
(indicating inclusiveness or category membership through vagueness) *a; and so on*
(indicating degree) *to... extent/degree*
(signalling generalisations or approximations) *as a rule*
(signalling restatements) *in other words; that is to say*
(focusing or delimiting the truth value of the associated proposition) *in terms of...*

b) *deontic*:
Examples:
(expressing advice) *should*
(directing) *had better*
(conveying warnings, reprimands and exhortation) *and/or* following imperative
(conveying advisability) *if I were you...; I would...*
(conveying necessity) *necessary; important; desirable; ideal(ly)*

c) *conative*:
Examples:
(indicating ability and potential) *can; able; capable; afford*

d) *volitive*
Examples:
(indicating intention and preference) *would rather; feel like; willing; ready; right away*

e) optative (indicating hope):
Examples:
(expressing hope) *wish; hope; hopefully*

IV) *Organizational*:
a) controlling the continuity of text or propositional content
Examples:
> (indicating logical connections and relations by conveying purposes) *in order to do; lest ~ should...; with a view to ~ing*
> (indicating logical connections and relations by conveying reasons or circumstances) *because; since; for; as; due to; thanks to*
> (indicating logical connections and relations by conveying causes and effects) *lead to; result in; so that...*
> (indicating time or place by locating texts temporally and spatially) *so far; to date; at the (present) writing;* the use of past tense
> (distinguishing/ disambiguating/ identifying) *the;* the use of superlative
> (expressing connections and similarities) *similarly; in the same vein*
> (indicating relevance and pertinence) *in relation to; with respect to; to do with*
> (indicating exceptions) *apart/aside from*
> (functioning as concession) *after all; at any cost; in any way*
> (indicating contrast) *but; in spite of; while..., ...; (al)though..., ...*
> (indicating additional information) *and; as well as*
> (indicating temporal order) *and; and then; at first*
> (expressing deixis) *this; that*

b) organising and signalling discourse structure
Examples:
> (marking boundaries) *by the way; when it comes to*
> (marking the beginnings and ends of macro speech acts; establishing or concluding conversation) *so much for*
> (indicating sequencing of different kinds in text) *first(ly); second(ly); to begin with; in passing; as follows*
> (indicating sequencing of different kinds and signalling contrast) *on the one hand/on the other hand*
> (functioning as preface) *once upon a time*
> (signalling additional information) *moreover; in addition; also*
> (signalling clarification) *more precisely*
> (signalling suggestion) *I tell you what*
> (focusing or foregrounding the ensuing information or point) *above all; let alone; more to the point*
> (signalling counter-arguments, contrasts, denials and/or rebuttals) *on the contrary; however; nevertheless; in the light of; if you're more careful,...*

(signalling rebuttals) (signalling opinions or observations that contrast with previous perceptions) *with hindsight*
(signalling summaries) *in short; in a nutshell*
(signalling conclusions) *in conclusion*
(signalling quotation) *according to; as... puts it...*
(indicating attribution of source and opinions) *as far as... is concerned*
(indicating distance by attributing a remark to the community in general and signalling the need for inference or consideration) *It is said that...; they say...*
(maintaining or checking on comprehension) *if you see what I mean; Are you with me?*
(commenting the selection of lexis or manner) *frankly speaking; to put it ~ly etc*
(expressing discourse deixis) *as shown above; see... below*

Appendix IV
Research items

Below is the list of the 76 research items for my examination of the nine EFL dictionaries. When there is more than one item with a similar core function, they are grouped together. They are further arranged according to their accompanying functions and politeness values, if possible. Most of them have more than one sense or use, and only their most basic uses are considered here.

Formulae

(Apologising): (1) *I beg your pardon*; (2) *sorry*
(Asking someone to repeat what they have just said): (3) *excuse me*; (4) *I beg your pardon*; (5) *pardon*; (6) *sorry*
(Attracting someone's attention): (7) *excuse me*; (8) *hey*
(Disagreeing): (9) *I beg to differ/disagree*; (10) *please yourself*
(Reacting to someone's offer): (Accepting) (11) *please*; (12) *thank you*; (Declining) (13) *no thank you*
(Replying to thanks): (14) *don't mention it*; (15) *(it's) a pleasure*; (16) *not at all*; (17) *you're welcome*
(Showing indifference): (18) *what of it?*; (19) *who cares?*
(20) *after you*
(21) *excuse me* (Asking someone to move)
(22) *excuse me* (Telling someone you are leaving)
(23) *Goodness/God/Heaven/Christ knows*
(24) *Jesus (Christ)*
(25) *(I'm) pleased to meet you*
(26) *thank you* (Answering)
(27) *well done*

Speech act markers

(Getting permission): (28) *could I do sth?*; (29) *might I do sth?*; (30) *would you mind if I do sth?*
(Offering): (31) *would you care for sth/to do sth?*; (32) *would you like sth?*
(Prefacing): (33) *at the risk of doing sth*; (34) *pardon me doing sth*
(Requesting): (35) *could you do sth?*; (36) *I (woul)'d be obliged if S+V*; (37) *I don't suppose S could V*; (38) *I wonder (if/whether S+V)*; (39) *would you mind doing sth?*
(Suggesting): (40) *might at least do sth*; (41) *might like to do*
(42) *in God/heaven's name*
(43) *there(i)'s something in sth*

Politeness Markers

(Enhancers): (44) *kindly*; (45) *please*; (46) *with (all due) respect*
(Softeners): (47) *by any chance*; (48) *I'm afraid (that)* S+V; *(49) if you please*; (50) *maybe*;
(51) *perhaps*; (52) *would*

Others

a) Address forms: (53) *gentleman*; (54) *lady*; (55) *ladies and gentlemen*; (56) *madam*; (57) *my (darling/dear)*; (58) *sir*
b) Referring to a person: (59) *gentleman*; (60) *lady*
c) Referring to a sensitive issue: (Polite) (61) *so-and-so*; (62) *powder room*; (Impolite) (63) *dyke*; (64) *effing*; (65) *fag*; (66) *faggot*; (67) *half-caste*; (68) *scab*
d) Telling someone to leave: (69) *bugger off*; (70) *clear off*; (71) *fuck off*; (72) *piss off*
(73) *bloody* (Emphasising)
(74) *bloody* (Expressing anger)
(75) *motherfucker*
(76) *want*

Bibliography

(a) Dictionaries, glossaries and their abbreviations

Cambridge Advanced Learner's Dictionary, 3rd ed. (2008) Cambridge: Cambridge University Press [CALD3]

Cambridge International Dictionary of English (1995) Cambridge: Cambridge University Press

Cambridge Learner's Dictionary (semi-bilingual version) (2004) Tokyo: Shogakukan

Collins COBUILD Advanced Dictionary of English, 6th ed. (2009) Boston: Heinle Cengage Learning [COBUILD6]

Collins COBUILD Advanced Dictionary of English, 7th ed. (2012) Boston: National Geographic Learning [COBUILD7]

Collins COBUILD Advanced Dictionary (2009) Boston: Heinle Cengage Learning [COBUILD6]

Collins COBUILD Advanced Learner's English Dictionary (2003) Glasgow: HarperCollins [COBUILD4]

Collins COBUILD English Dictionary for Advanced Learners (2001) Glasgow: HarperCollins [COBUILD3]

Collins COBUILD English Dictionary, 2nd ed. (1995) London: HarperCollins [COBUILD2]

Collins COBUILD English Language Dictionary (1987) London: Collins

Core-Lex English-Japanese Dictionary (2005) Tokyo: Obunsha

Core-Lex English-Japanese Dictionary, 2nd ed. (2011) Tokyo: Obunsha

Dictionary of lexicography (1998) R.R.K. Hartmann and G. James eds., London & New York: Routledge

Dictionary of Linguistics and Phonetics, A, 5th ed. (2003) D. Crystal ed., Oxford: Blackwell

Grand Century English-Japanese Dictionary, The (2000) Tokyo: Sanseido

Kenkyusha Luminous English-Japanese Dictionary (2001) Tokyo: Kenkyusha

Kenkyusha Luminous English-Japanese Dictionary, 2nd ed. (2005) Tokyo: Kenkyusha [LEJ2]

Kenkyusha's Oyo Gengogaku Jiten [Kenkyush's Dictionary of Applied Linguistics] (2003) I. Koike ed., Tokyo: Kenkyusha

Key Concepts in Language and Linguistics (1999) R. L. Trask ed., London: Routledge

Kojien [Kojien unabridged Japanese Dictionary], 6th ed. (2008) Tokyo: Iwanamishoten

Longman Dictionary of Contemporary English, 2nd ed. (1987/1991) Harlow: Longman [LDOCE2]

Longman Dictionary of Contemporary English, 4th ed. (2003) Harlow: Pearson Edu-

cation [LDOCE4]
Longman Dictionary of Contemporary English, 5th ed. (2009) Harlow: Pearson Education [LDOCE5]
Longman English-Japanese Dictionary (2007) Harlow: Pearson Education [LOEJD]
Luminous English-Japanese Dictionary, 2nd ed. (2005) Tokyo: Kenkyusha [LEJD2]
Macmillan English Dictionary for Advanced Learners of American English (2002) Oxford: Macmillan
Macmillan English Dictionary for Advanced Learners (2002) Oxford: Macmillan
Macmillan English Dictionary for Advanced Learners, 2nd ed. (2007) Oxford: Macmillan Education [MED2]
Obunsha Lexis English-Japanese Dictionary (2003) Tokyo: Obunsha
O-Lex English-Japanese Dictionary (2008) Tokyo: Obunsha [OLXEJD]
O-Lex English-Japanese Dictionary, 2nd ed. (2013) Tokyo: Obunsha
Oxford Advanced Learner's Dictionary of Current English, 7th ed. (2005) Oxford: Oxford University Press [OALD7]
Oxford Advanced Learner's Dictionary of Current English, 8th ed. (2010) Oxford: Oxford University Press [OALD8]
Shogakukan Progressive English-Japanese Dictionary, 5th ed. (2012) Tokyo: Shogakukan
Taishukan's Genius English-Japanese Dictionary (1988) Tokyo: Taishukan Shoten
Taishukan's Genius English-Japanese Dictionary, 3rd ed. (2001) Tokyo: Taishukan Shoten
Taishukan's Genius English-Japanese Dictionary, 4th ed. (2006) Tokyo: Taishukan Shoten [GEJD4]
Taishukan's Unabridged Genius English-Japanese Dictionary (2006) Tokyo: Taishukan Shoten
Wisdom English-Japanese Dictionary, The, 2nd ed. (2007) Tokyo: Sanseido [WEJD2]

(b) Other references

Akasu, K. (1989) 'Goyoron kara mita *LDCE* (1987)' [An analysis of *LDCE* (1987) in terms of pragmatics] in: *Yoshizawa Norio Kyoju Tsuito Ronbunshu* [Papers to the Memory of Professor Norio Yoshizawa], Tokyo: Phonetics Laboratory, Tokyo University of Foreign Language, 291–98

Akmajian, A. et al. (2001) *Linguistics: An Introduction to Language and Communication*, 5th ed., Cambridge: MIT Press

Allwoods, J et al. (1977) *Logic in Linguistics*, New York: Cambridge University Press

Altenberg, B. (1998) 'On the phraseology of spoken English: the evidence of recurrent word-combinations' in: A. P. Cowie ed. *Phraseology: Theory, Analysis, and Applications*, Oxford: Oxford University Press, 101–22

Andersen, P. A., Heecht, M. L., Hoobler, G. D. and Smallwood, M. (2002) 'Nonverbal communication across cultures' in: W. B. Gudykunst and B. Mody eds.

Handbook of International and Intercultural Communication, 2nd ed., Thousand Oaks: Sage, 89–106

Anzai, T. (1982) *Hon'yaku Eibunpou* [English Grammar for Translation], Tokyo: Babell Press

Atkins, B. T. S. (1985) 'Monolingual and bilingual learners' dictionary: a comparison' in: R. F. Ilson ed. *Dictionaries, Lexicography and Language Learning*, Oxford: Pergamon, 15–24

Austin, J. L. (1962) *How to Do Things with Words*, Oxford: Oxford University Press

Azuma, S. (1994) *Teinei na Eigo • Shiturei na Eigo* [Rude Expressions in English • Polite Expressions in English], Tokyo: Kenkyusha

Beebe L. M. and M. C. Cummings (1996) 'Natural speech act data versus written questionnaire data: How data collection method affects speech act performance' in: S. M. Gass and J. Neu eds. *Speech Acts Across Cultures: Challenges to Communication in a Second Language*, Berlin: Mouton de Gruyter, 65–86

Béjoint, H. (1981) 'The foreign student's use of monolingual English dictionaries: a study of language needs and reference skills' in: *Applied Linguistics* 2/3, 207–22

Béjoint, H. (1994) *Modern Lexicography: An Introduction*, Oxford: Oxford University Press

Belson, A. (1981) *The Design and Understanding of Survey Questions*, Hants: Gower

Bergman, M. L. and G. Kasper (1993) 'Perception and performance in native and nonnative apology' in: G. Kasper and S. Blum-Kulka eds. *Interlanguage Pragmatics*, New York: Oxford University Press, 82–107

Blum-Kulka, S., House, J. and Kasper, G., eds. (1989) *Cross-Cultural Pragmatics: Requests and Apologies*, Norwood, NJ: Ablex

Bolinger, D. (1985) 'Defining the indefinable' in: R. F. Ilson ed. *Dictionaries, Lexicography and Language Learning*, Oxford: Pergamon, 69–73

Brown, J. (2001) *Using Surveys in Language Programs*, Cambridge: Cambridge University Press

Brown, P., and S. Levinson (1978) 'Universals in language usage' in: E. N. Goody ed. *Questions and Politeness*, Cambridge: Cambridge University Press, 56–289

Brown, P., and S. Levinson (1987) *Politeness: Some Universals in Language Usage*, Cambridge: Cambridge University Press

Cacchiani, S. (2004) 'Towards a model for investigating predicate-intensifier collocations' (Paper read at the 11th conference of EURALEX, Lorient: Université de Bretgnu Sud, 6–10 July 2004. Available at http://www.euralex.org/elx_proceedings/Euralex2004/106_2004_V3_Silvia%20CACCHIANI_Towards%20a%20model%20for%20investigating%20predicate_intensifier%20collocations.pdf)

Carter, R. (1988) *Vocabulary: Applied Linguistic Perspectives*, 2nd ed., London: Routledge

Channell, J. (1994) *Vague Language*, Oxford: Oxford University Press

Channell, J. (2002) 'Pragmatics' in: *Macmillan English Dictionary for Advance*

Learners, Oxford: Macmillan Education, LA12-3

Cowie, A. P. ed. (1998) *Phraseology: Theory, Analysis, and Applications*, Oxford: Oxford University Press

Cruse, A. (2004) *Meaning in Language*, 2nd ed., Oxford: Oxford University Press

Cruse, A. (2006) *A Glossary of Semantics and Pragmatics*, Edinburgh: Edinburgh University Press

De Cock, S. (2002) 'Pragmatic prefabs in learners' dictionaries' in: A. Braasch and C. Povslen eds. *Proceedings of the Tenth EURALEX International Congress, EURALEX 2002*, Copenhagen: Center for Sprogteknologi, II, 471-81

Doi, T. (1971) *Amae no Kozo* [The Structure of Reliance], Yokohama: Kobundo

Eelen, G. (2001) *A Critique of Politeness Theories*, Manchester: St. Jerome Publishing

Erjavec, T., Sangawa, K. H. and Erjavec, I. S. (2006) 'jaSlo, a Japanese-Slovene learners' dictionary: methods for dictionary enhancement' (Paper read at the 12th conference of EURALEX, Torino: Università degli studi di Torino, 6-9 September 2006. Available at http://www.euralex.org/elx_proceedings/Euralex2006/077_2006_V1_T.%20ERJAVEC,%20K.%20HMELJAK%20SANGAWA,%20I.%20SRDANOVIC%20ERJAVEC_JaSlo,%20a%20Japanese_Slovene.pdf

Fox, (1987) 'The case for examples' in: J. M. Sinclair ed. *Looking Up: An Account of the COBUILD Project in Lexical Computing*, London: HarperCollins, 137-49

Fraser, B. (1978) 'Acquiring Social competence in a second language' in: *RELC Journal* 9/2, 1-21

Fraser, B. (1990) 'Perspectives on politeness' in: *Journal of Pragmatics* 14/2, 219-36

French, J. R. P. and Raven, B. (1959) 'The bases of social power' in: D. Cartwright ed. *Studies in Social Power*, Ann Arbor: University of Michigan, 150-67

Fukuda, H. (2001) *Eigo no Saho: Yatteiikoto Waruikoto* [Etiquette in English], Tokyo: Kodansha International

Gardner, S. (2016) 'Sentence Combination with Jokes' in: J. Rucynski ed. *New Ways in Teaching with Humor*, Alexandria: TESOL Press

Gazdar, G. (1979) *Pragmatics: Implicature, Presupposition and Logical Form*, New York: Academic Press

Goffman, E. (1963) *Behavior in Public Places*, New York: Free Press

Goffman, E. (1967) *Interaction Ritual: Essays on Face-to-Face Behavior*, New Yorl: Anchor Books

Gramley, S. and K. Pätzold (2003) *A Survey of Modern English*, 2nd ed., London: Routledge

Grice, H. P. (1957) 'Meaning' reprinted in: H. P. Grice *Studies in the Way of Words* (1979) Cambridge, Mass.; Cambridge University Press, 213-23

Grice, H. P. (1969/1991) 'Utterer's meaning and intentions' in: P. Grice *Studies in the Ways of Words*, Cambridge: Harvard University Press, 86-116

Grice, H. P. (1975) 'Logic and conversation' in: Cole, P., Morgan, J. L. ed. *Syntax and Semantics 3: Speech Acts.*, New York: Academic Press, 41–58

Grice, H. P. (1975/1991a) 'Logic and conversation' in: P. Grice *Studies in the Ways of Words*, Cambridge: Harvard University Press, 22–40

Grice, H. P. (1975/1991b) 'Further notes on logic and conversation' in: P. Grice *Studies in the Ways of Words*, Cambridge: Harvard University Press, 41–57

Gu, Y. (1990) 'Politeness phenomena in modern Chinese' in: *Journal of Pragmatics* 14, 237–57

Halliday, M. A. K. (1978) *Language as Social Semiotic*, London: Edward Arnold

Hanks, P. (1979) 'To what extent does a dictionary definition define' in: R.R.K. Hartmann ed. *Dictionaries and their Users*, Exeter: University of Exeter

Hanks, P. (1987) 'Definitions and explanations' in: J. M. Sinclair ed. *Looking Up: An Account of the COBUILD Project in Lexical Computing*, London: HarperCollins, 116–36

Higashi, N. (1980) 'Jisho to Goyoron' [Dictionaries and Pragmatics] in: *Gengo* 9/12, 50–60

Higashi, N. (1981) 'Gogi no Hikaku' [A comparison between Japanese and English vocabularies] in: T. Kunihiro ed. *Nichieigo Hikaku Koza* [Comparative Studies Between Japanese and English], Tokyo: Taishukan Shoten, 101–62

House, J. and G. Kasper (1981) 'Politeness markers in English and German' in: F. Coulmas ed. *Conversational Routine*, The Hague: Mouton, 157–86

Huang, Y. (2014) *Pragmatics*, 2nd ed., Oxford: Oxford University Press

Hurley, D. S. (1992) 'Issues in teaching pragmatics, prosody, and non-verbal communication' in: *Applied Linguistics* 13/3, 259–81

Hymes, D. (1962) 'The ethnography of speaking' in: T. Gladwin and W. C. Sturtevant eds. *Anthropology and Human Behavior*, Washington D. C.: Anthropological Society of Washington

Hymes, D. (1971) 'Competence and performance in linguistic theory' in: R. Huxley and E. Ingram eds. *Language Acquisition: Models and Methods,* London: Academic Press, 3–28

Ide, R. (1998) '"Sorry for your kindness": Japanese interactional ritual in public discourse' in: *Journal of Pragmatics* 29/5, 509–29

Ide, S. (2006) *Wakimae no Goyoron*, Tokyo: Taishukan Shoten

Ide, S., M. Hori, A. Kawasaki, S. Ikuta and H. Haga (1986) 'Sex difference and politeness in Japanese' in: *International Journal of Sociology of Language* 58, 25–36

Ikegami, Y. (1996) 'Kotoba no Imi to Jisho' [Meanings of words and dictionaries] in Y. Ikegami ed. *Eigo no Imi* [Meanings in English], Tokyo: Taishukan Shoten

Imai, K. (2001) *Goyoron heno Shoutai* [An Introduction to Pragmatics], Tokyo: Taishukan Shoten

Imai, K. (2009) 'Maegaki' [Introduction] in: K. Imai ed. *Saishin Goyoron Nyumon 12 Shou* [An Introduction to Latest Theories of Pragmatics] (Translated and edited from three in-house textbooks at London University: *Pragmatic Theory* (D,

Wilson); *Issue in Pragmatics* (D. Wilson) and *Logic and Meaning* (T. Wharton)), Tokyo: Taishukan Shoten, iii-iv

Inoue, I. (2001) 'Teineisa' [Politeness] in T. Koizumi ed. *Nyumon Goyouron Kenkyu* [An Introduction to Pragmatics], Tokyo: Kenkyusha, 124–40

Iwasaki, H. (2002) *Eigo Jishoryoku o Kitaeru: Anata no Eigo o Kaeru Kaiteki Jisho Katuyojutsu* [How to Improve Dictionary Consulting Skills], Tokyo: DHC

Jackson, H. (1988) *Words and their Meaning*, Harlow: Longman

Kakehi, H. (1998) *Productive Shinkoukoueigo* [Productive New High School English], Tokyo: Daiichigakushusha

Kanazashi, T. (2001) *User's Guides in English-Japanese Dictionaries for Learners, with Particular Reference to Grammatical Information*, submitted to the University of Exeter as a thesis for the degree of Doctor of Philosophy in lexicography, September 2001

Kashino, K. (1996) 'Poraitonesu no ichi sokumen' [An aspect of politeness] in: *Eibei-Bunngakkaishi* 32, 15–25

Kasper, G. (2000) 'Data collection in pragmatic research' in: H. Spencer-Oatey ed., *Culturally Speaking: Culture, Communication and Politeness Theory*, 1st ed., London: Continuum International Publishing Group, 316–41

Kasper, G. (2008) 'Data collection in pragmatic research' in: H. Spencer-Oatey ed., *Culturally Speaking: Culture, Communication and Politeness Theory*, 2nd ed., London: Continuum International Publishing Group, 279–303

Katz, J. J. and J. A. Fodor (1964) 'The structure of a semantic theory' in: J. A., Fodor, and J. J. Katz eds. *The Structure of Language: Readings in the Philosophy of Language*, Englewood Cliffs: Prentice-Hall, 479–518

Kawamura, A. (2001) 'A critical study of *defining vocabulary*: hard words for Japanese users' in: *Random* 26, 49–69

Kawamura, A. (2002a) 'A Report on How Pragmatic Information is Presented in EFL Dictionaries Today' in: *Random* 27, 1–15

Kawamura, A. (2002b) 'A Plea for a Pragmatic Viewpoint in the EFL Context with Particular Reference to Lexicography' in: *Report* 22 (Foreign Language Center of Tokai University), 85–92

Kawamura, A. (2006a) *Nihonjin Eigo no Kanchigai: Neitibu 100 Nin no Ketsuron* [English Expressions Japanese Learners Often Misuse], Tokyo: Obunsha

Kawamura, A. (2006b) 'Problems in incorporating pragmatics into EFL lexicography' in: the JACET Society of English Lexicography ed., *English Lexicography in Japan*, Tokyo: Taishukan Shoten, 168–81

Kawamura, A. (2016) 'EFL jisho to goyoron—poraitonesu o chuushin ni' [EFL dictionaries and pragmatics with particular reference to politeness] in: K. Minamide, K. Akasu, N. Inoue, Y. Tono, and S. Yamada eds. *Eigo Jisho o Tsukuru—Henshu Chosa Kenkyu no Genba kara* [Making of English Dictionaries: From the Viewpoints of Editors and Researchers], Tokyo: Taishukan Shoten

Kepnes, J., (2016) 'Obama apologizes for Okinawa incident' Available at http://edition.cnn.com/2016/05/25/politics/obama-apologizes-for-okinawa-incident/index.html

Kess, J. F., and R. A. Hoppe, (1981) *Ambiguity in Psycholinguistics*, Amsterdam: John Benjamins

Koizumi, T. ed. (2001) *Nyumon Goyouron Kenkyu* [An Introduction to Pragmatics], Tokyo: Kenkyusha

Lakoff, R. T. (1973) 'The logic of politeness; or, minding your p's and q's' in: *Papers from the Ninth Regional Meeting of the Chicago Linguistic Society*, Chicago: Chicago Linguistic Society, 292–305

Landau, S. I. (2001) *Dictionaries: The Art and Craft of Lexicographers*, 2nd ed., Cambridge: Cambridge University Press

Leech, G. N. (1983) *Principles of Pragmatics*, London: Longman

Leech, G. N. (2005) 'Politeness: is there any an east-west divide?' in: *Journal of Foreign Language* 6 Available at http://www.lancaster.ac.uk/fass/doc_library/linguistics/leechg/leech_2007_politeness.pdf

Leech, G.N, and J. Thomas (1987/1991) 'Pragmatics and Dictionary' in: *Longman Dictionary of Contemporary English*, 2nd ed. (1991) Harlow: Longman, F12–3

Levinson, S.C. (1979) 'Activity types and language' in: *Linguistics* 17 (5/6), 365–99

Levinson, S.C. (1983) *Pragmatics*, Cambridge: Cambridge University Press

Lyons, J. (1977) *Semantics*, Vols. 1 and 2, Cambridge: Cambridge University Press

Maingay, S. and M. Rundell (1987) 'Anticipating Learners' Errors–Implications for Dictionary Writers' in: A. P. Cowie ed. *The Dictionary and the Language Learner*, Tübingen: M. Niemeyer, 128–35

Masuda H., Uchida, S., Hirayama, M., Kawamura, A., Takahashi, R. and Ishii, Y (2008) 'An analysis of *Collins COBUILD Advanced Dictionary of American English*' in: *Lexicon* 38, 46–155

Matsumoto, Y and I. Matsumoto (1987) *Eigo no Keigo Hyogen Handobukku* [A Handbook of Honorific Expressions in English], Tokyo: Hokuseido Shoten

Matsumoto, Y. (1988) 'Reexamination of the universality of face: politeness phenomena in Japanese' in: *Journal of Pragmatics* 12, 403–26

Matsumoto, Y. (1989) 'Politeness and conversational universals—observations from Japanese' in: *Multilingua* 8 (2/3), 207–21

Mey, J. L. (1993) *Pragmatics: An Introduction*, 1st ed., Oxford: Blackwell

Mey, J. L. (2001) *Pragmatics: An Introduction*, 2nd ed., Oxford: Blackwell

Miller, C. and Swift, K. (1979) *Words and Women*, Harmondworth: Penguin

Miller, G. A. (1974) 'Psychology, language and levels of communication' in: A. Silverstein ed. *Human Communication*, New York: John Wiley, 1–17

Miller, L. (2008) 'Negative assessments in Japanese-American workplace interaction' in H. Spencer-Oatey ed. *Culturally Speaking: Culture, Communication and Politeness Theory*, 2nd ed., London: Continuum International Publishing Group, 227–40

Minamide, K. (2003) 'Jisho ni iken o han'eisaseyo' [Putting your ideas into dictionary compilation] in: *Gengo* 32/5, Tokyo: Taishukan Shoten

Ministry of Education, Culture, Sports, Science and Technology (2002) '"Eigo ga tsukaeru nihonjin" no ikusei no tame no senryaku koso no sakutei ni tsuite' Available at http://www.mext.go.jp/b_menu/shingi/chousa/shotou/020/sesaku/020702.htm

Miyake, T. (2011) *Nihongo Kenkyu no Intafeisu* [The Interface of Japanese Studies], Tokyo: Kuroshio Shuppan

Moon, R. (1987) 'The analysis of meaning' in: J. M. Sinclair ed. *Looking Up: An Account of the COBUILD Project in Lexical Computing*, London: HarperCollins, 86–103

Moon, R. (1998a) 'On using spoken data in corpus lexicography' in: T. Fontenelle, P. Hiligsmann, A. Michiels, A. Moulin, and S. Theissen eds. *Actes EURALEX '98 Proceedings* vol. II, Liège: University of Liège, 347–55

Moon, R. (1998b) *Fixed Expressions and Idioms in English: A Corpus-Based Approach*, Oxford: Oxford University Press

Morris, C. (1938) *Foundations of the Theory of Signs* reprinted in: *Writings on the General Theory of Signs* (1971), The Hague: Mouton, 17–71

Murata, M. (1997) 'Jisho to goyoron: jisho ni miru hanashite to kikite no kankei' [Dictionaries and pragmatics] in: *Gengobunkaronso* 3, 39–58

Nakane, C. (1967) *Tateshakai no Ningen Kankei* [Human Relations in the Vertical Society], Tokyo: Kodansha

Naotsuka, R. (1998) *Obeijin ga Chinmokusuru Toki: Ibunka no Komyunikeshon* [When Western People Fall Silent: Cross-cultural Communication], Tokyo: Taishukan Shoten

Nattinger, J. R. and DeCarrico, J. S. (1992) *Lexical Phrases and Language Teaching*, Oxford: Oxford University Press

Nelson, G. L., W. E. Bakary and M. A. Batal (1996) 'Egyptian and American compliments: Focus on second language learners' in: S. M. Gass and J. Neu eds. *Speech Acts Across Cultures: Challenges to Communication in a Second Language*, Berlin: Mouton de Gruyter, 109–28

Nesi, H. (2002) 'An English spoken academic wordlist' (Paper read at the 10th conference of EURALEX, København: Københavns Universitet, 13–17 August 2002. Available at http://www.euralex.org/elx_proceedings/Euralex2002/036_2002_V1_Hilary%20Nesi_An%20English%20Spoken%20Academic%20Wordlist.pdf

Nomura, K. (2003) 'Komyunikeshon joho' [Communicative information] in: *Obunsha Lexis English-Japanese Dictionary*, Tokyo: Obunsha, xx

Norris, J. M. (2001) 'Use of address terms on the German Speaking Test' in: K. R. Rose and G. Kasper eds. *Pragmatics in Language Teaching*, Cambridge: Cambridge University Press, 248–82

Ohashi, J. (2013) *Thanking and Politeness in Japanese: Balancing Acts in Interaction*, Basingstoke: Palgrave Macmillan

Osugi, K. (1982) *Eigo no Keii Hyogen* [Polite expressions in English], Tokyo: Taishukan Shoten

Otani, M. 'A study of pragmatic information in English and Japanese bilingual dictionaries: from the perspective of apology and gratitude expressions' in: the JACET Society of English Lexicography ed., *English Lexicography in Japan*, Tokyo: Taishukan Shoten, 206–19

Pavlidou, T. (2008) 'Interactional work in Greek and German telephone conversations' in: H. Spencer-Oatey ed. *Culturally Speaking: Culture, Communication and Politeness Theory*, 2nd ed., London: Continuum International Publishing Group, 118–35

Quirk, R. , S. Greenbaum, G. N. Leech and J. Svartvik (1985) *Comprehensive Grammar of the English Language, A*, Harlow: Longman

Rose, K. R. and G. Kasper eds. (2002) *Pragmatics in Language Teaching*, Cambridge: Cambridge University Press

Rundell, M. (2006) 'More than one way to skin a cat: why full-sentence definitions have not been universally adopted' (Paper read at the 12th conference of EURALEX, Torino: Università degli studi di Torino, 6–9 September 2006. Available at http://www.euralex.org/elx_proceedings/Euralex2006/040_2006_V1_Michael%20 RUNDELL_More%20than%20one%20Way%20to%20Skin%20a%20Cat_Why%20Full_Sentence%20Definitions%20Have%20not%20been.pdf

Rundell, M. (2012) 'Stop the presses—the end of the printed dictionary' (A blog article posted on 5 November 2012) Available at http://www.macmillandictionary blog.com/bye-print-dictionary

Russo, I. (2008) 'Una bella esperienza, una buona prova: a corpus analysis of purely evaluative adjectives in Italian' (Paper read at the 13th conference of EURALEX, Barcelona: Universitat Pompeu Fabra, 15–19 July 2008. Available at http://www.euralex.org/elx_proceedings/Euralex2008/145_Euralex_2008_Irene%20Russo_Una%20bella%20esperienza,%20una%20buona%20prova_A%20corpus%20 analysis%20of%20purely%20evaluative%20adjectives%20in.pdf

Sakamoto, S. and S. Sakamoto (2004) *Polite Fiction in Collision: Why Japanese and American Seem Rude to Each Other*, Tokyo: Kinseido

Schmidt, R. and C. McCreary (1977) 'Standard and superstandard English: recognition and use of prescriptive rules by native and non-native speakers' in: *TESOL Quarterly* 11/4, 415–29

Scollon, R. and Scollon, S. W. (2001) *Intercultural Communication*, 2nd ed., Oxford: Blackwell

Searle, J. (1969) *Speech Acts: An Essay in the Philosophy of Language*, Cambridge: Cambridge University Press

Searle, J. (1975) 'Indirect speech acts' in: P. Cole and J. Morgan eds., *Syntax and Semantics 3: Speech Acts*, New York: Academic Press

Searle, J. R., F. Kiefer and M. Bierwisch eds. (1980) *Speech Act Theory and Pragmat-*

ics, Dordrecht: Reidel

Sharpe, P. (1989) 'Pragmatic considerations for an English-Japanese dictionary' in: *International Journal of Lexicography* 2/4, 315–23

Sinclair, J. M. (1984) 'Naturalness in language' in: J. Aarts and W. Meijs eds. *Corpus Linguistics*, Amsterdam: Rodopi

Spencer-Oatey, H. (2000) 'Rapport management: a framework for analysis' in H. Spencer-Oatey ed. *Culturally Speaking: Managing Rapport in Talk across Cultures*, 1st ed., London: Continuum, 11–46

Spencer-Oatey, H. (2008) 'Face, (im)politeness and rapport' in: H. Spencer-Oatey ed. *Culturally Speaking: Culture, Communication and Politeness Theory*, 2nd ed., London: Continuum, 11–47

Spencer-Oatey, H. and Žegarac, V. (2010) 'Pragmatics' in: N. Schmitt ed. *An Introduction to Applied Linguistics*, 2nd ed., London: Hodder and Stoughton

Sperber, D. and D. Wilson (1986) *Relevance: Communication and Cognition*, Oxford: Basil Blackwell

Stalnaker, R. C. (1972) 'Pragmatics' in: D. Davidson and G. Harman eds. *Semantics of Natural Language*, Dordrecht: Reidel, 380–97

Sugiyama Lebra, T. (1976) *Japanese Patterns of Behavior*, Honolulu: University of Hawaii Press

Summers, D. (1999) 'Coverage of spoken English in relation to learner's dictionaries, especially the Longman Dictionary of Contemporary English' in: T. Herbst and K. Popp eds. *The Perfect Learners' Dictionary (?)*, Tübingen: Niemeyer, 254–64

Svartvik, J. (1992) 'Lexis in Enlish language corpora' (Paper read at the 5th conference of EURALEX, Tampere: Tampereen yliopist, 4–9 August 1992. Availabe at http://www.euralex.org/elx_proceedings/Euralex1992_1/007_Jan%20Svartvik%20-Lexis%20in%20English%20language%20corpora.pdf

Swan, M. (2005) *Practical English Usage*, 3rd ed., Oxford: Oxford University Press

Takahashi, S (2003) 'Pragmatic transfer and pragmatic failure' in: I. Koike ed. *Kenkyusha Dictionary of Applied Linguistics*, Tokyo: Kenkyusha

Takiura, M. (2008) *Poraitonesu Nyumon* [An Introduction to Politeness], Tokyo: Kenkyusha

Tanaka, N., H. Spencer-Oatey and E. Cray (2008) 'Apologies in Japanese and English' in: H. Spencer-Oatey ed., *Culturally Speaking: Culture, Communication and Politeness Theory*, 2nd ed., London: Continuum International Publishing Group, 73–94

Thomas, J. (1983) 'Cross-cultural pragmatic failure' in: *Applied Linguistics* 4/2, 91–112

Thomas, J. (1995) *Meaning in Interaction: An Introduction to Pragmatics*, Harlow: Pearson Education

Tsuruta, Y. (1998) *Politeness, the Japanese Style: an Investigation into the Use of Honorific Forms and People's Attitudes towards Such Use*, submitted to University of Luton as a thesis for the degree of Doctor of Philosophy, September 2001

Tsuruta, Y., P. Rssiter, and T. Coulton (1988) *Eigo no Sosharu Sukiru* [Social Skills in English], Tokyo: Taishukan Shoten

Usami, M. (2002) *Discourse Politeness in Japanese Conversation: Some Implications for a Universal Theory of Politeness*, Tokyo: Hituzi Syobo

Van Dijk, T. A. (1976) 'Pragmatics and Poetics' in: T. A. Van Dijk ed., *Pragmatics of Language and Literature*, Amsterdam: North-Holland Publishing Company, 23–57

Vardaman, J. M. and T. Morimoto (1999) *Manaihan no Eikaiwa* [Bad manners in English Conversation], Tokyo: Kodansha International

Verschueren, J. (1999) *Understanding Pragmatics*, London: Arnold

Wakiyama, R. (1990) *Eigo Hyogen no Toreining: Polite English no Susume* [An Exhortation to Use Polite Expressions in English], Tokyo: Kodansha

Walters, J. (1979) 'Strategies for requesting in Spanish and English—structural similarities and pragmatic differences' in: *Language Learning* 9/2, 277–94

Wang, A. (2015) 'Pragmatic Information in Learner's Dictionaries: Redefined' in: L. Li, J. Mckeown and L. Liu eds., *Proceedings of ASIALEX 2015 Hong Kong: Words, Dictionaries and Corpora: Innovations in Reference Science*, Hong Kong: Hong Kong Polytechnic University, 204–12

White, R. (1997) 'Going round in circles: English as an international language, and cross-culturalcapability.' Available at http://host.uniroma3.it/docenti/boylan/text/white01.htm

Widdowson, H.G. (1979) *Exploration in Applied Linguistics*, Oxford: Oxford University Press

Wierzbicka, A. (1991) *Cross-Cultural Pragmatics: The Semantics of Human Interaction*, Berlin: Mouton de Gruyter

Wilkins, D. A. (1976) *Notional Syllabuses*, Oxford: Oxford University Press

Yagi, K. (2006) *Eiwajiten no Kenkyu: Eigo Ninshiki no Kaizen no Tame ni* [A Study of English-Japanese Dictionaries], Tokyo: Kaitakusha

Yamada, S. (1996) 'Instruction in the use of English monolingual learners' dictionaries for comprehension' in: M. Steven ed. *Proceedings of the 1995 Graduate Research Conference on Language and Linguistics*, Exeter: School of English and American Studies, 104–16

Yule, G. (1996) *Pragmatics*, Oxford: Oxford University Press

Index

A
absolute politeness   151
abstract meaning   16, 24
accompanying function   127
achieve one's goal   17
activity type   144
association rights   139
Austin, J.   4, 235
authority   36, 47, 67, 99, 213

B
Brown, P. and Levinson, S.   132, 134

C
cancellability of presupposition   17
Can you...?   122
command of linguistic resources   22
conative   277
conversational contract   133, 140
Cooperative Principle (CP)   20
core function   127, 142, 143

D
deference   137, 145, 150
deference and politeness   202
deixis   119
deontic   277
difference value   84 Note 1
distance   149

E
Eastern and Western divide in politeness; Western and Eastern divide of politeness theory   137, 138, 235
enhancer   123, 159, 281
entailment   16, 17
epistemic   126, 276, 277

equity rights   139
EV   51
evaluative   126, 276
explanation   111 Note 1

F
face theory   132, 134, 135
face-threatening act (FTA)   134
face-wants   132
FEIs [Fixed Expressions and Idioms]   111
fluency device   125
force   14, 16
formula; formulae   115, 227, 280
Fraser, B.   133

G
Good question! (Worked Example)   227
Grand Strategy of Politeness   152 Note 2
Grice, P.   20

H
hatarakikake   133
head act   142
hearer meaning   18
honorific   136, 137, 150

I
Ide, S.   133
identity face   138
I don't suppose   106, 139, 141, 215; (Worked Example)   226, 227
implicature   118, 119
intent   14, 17, 34
intention   14
interactional goal   139

issues of colonialism, expansionism and anglocentrism   234

J
jokes and humour   173
JV   51

L
Lakoff, R.   130
language resources   21
Leech, G.   20, 130
lexical phrases   125
lexical pragmatics, a definition   3
liar and *usotsuki*   42
linguistic politeness
 →politeness
linguistic resources   21

M
MC   55
MCYN   55
modalizing   126, 276, 277
Moon, R.   126
must vs. *have to*   43

N
Nattinger, J. and DeCarrico, J.   125
negative face   132
negative politeness (strategy)   134, 135

O
optative   277
organizational   126, 278, 279

P
polite and *teinei*   221
politeness   123, 129, 143, 144
politeness as an umbrella function   158, 231
politeness marker   123, 124, 281
Politeness Principle (PP)   130, 131

politeness value   159
positive face   132
positive politeness (strategy)   134, 135
power   149
pragmatically marked   18, 20
pragmatic failure   19, 29, 32, 33, 34, 35, 37, 85
pragmatics, a definition   22
pragmatic information, a definition   36, 37
presupposition   16, 17

Q
quality face   138

R
ranking of the imposition   149
rapport management   138, 139
realise one's intent   17
register   150, 151
regret   4, 5, 251
rights and obligations   149
rules of politeness   130

S
situational   126, 142, 276
social distance   149
sociality rights   139
speaker meaning   16
speech act marker   122, 142, 226, 280
speech act   121, 122
speech event   144
speech softener   124, 281
Spencer-Oatey, H.   138, 139
superstandard English   35

T
teinei   201, 202
text functions   126, 127
Thomas, J.   19

U

utterance   232
utterance meaning   16

V

values and/or outlook on the world   35, 48
volitive   277

W

wakimae   133, 137
Western and Eastern divide of politeness theory
→ Eastern and Western divide in politeness
Wilkins, D.   110

川村晶彦（かわむら　あきひこ）

略歴

成城大学社会イノベーション学部心理社会学科教授（異文化間コミュニケーション論および英語担当）。ロータリー財団国際親善奨学生として英国エクセター大学大学院留学（1999〜2000年、MA in Lexicography）。2014年、英国バーミンガム大学大学院博士課程修了（PhD in Applied Linguistics）。

Akihiko Kawamura is a Professor of Intercultural Communication and English in the Department of Psychological and Sociological Studies, Faculty of Social Innovation, Seijo University, Japan. He studied at the University of Exeter, UK, as a scholarship student of Rotary International (1999-2000), and gained an MA in Lexicography. In 2014, he obtained a PhD in Applied Linguistics from the University of Birmingham, UK.

主な著書・論文

- 'Problems in Incorporating Pragmatics into EFL Lexicography' in: the JACET Society of English Lexicography ed., *English Lexicography in Japan*, Taishukan Shoten (2006).
- 'Issues in Collecting Data for Better Treatment of Pragmatics in Language Teaching: A Case Study of the *Planet Board* Project in Lexical Pragmatics' in: *Random 33* (2011).

そのほか英国および日本の様々な出版社において『オーレックス英和辞典第2版』（旺文社、2013）などの辞書編纂に従事。

Hituzi Linguistics in English No.28

Lexical Pragmatics
Teaching English Communication and Pragmatic Skills to Japanese Learners

発行　2018年3月30日 初版1刷
定価　11000円＋税
著者　©川村晶彦
発行者　松本功
ブックデザイン　白井敬尚形成事務所
印刷所　株式会社 ディグ
製本所　株式会社 星共社
発行所　株式会社 ひつじ書房
〒112-0011 東京都文京区千石2-1-2 大和ビル2F
Tel: 03-5319-4916
Fax: 03-5319-4917
郵便振替 00120-8-142852
toiawase@hituzi.co.jp
http://www.hituzi.co.jp/
ISBN978-4-89476-903-8

造本には充分注意しておりますが、落丁・乱丁などがございましたら、小社かお買上げ書店にておとりかえいたします。ご意見、ご感想など、小社までお寄せ下されば幸いです。

刊行のご案内

Hituzi Language Studies

No.1 Relational Practice in Meeting Discourse in
New Zealand and Japan
村田和代 著　定価 6,000 円＋税

No.2 Style and Creativity
Towards a Theory of Creative Stylistics
斎藤兆史 著　定価 7,500 円＋税

No.3 Rhetorical Questions
A Relevance-Theoretic Approach to Interrogative Utterances in English
and Japanese
後藤リサ 著　定価 10,000 円＋税